Call of the Owl

By

Mary Bethel Hawkins

www.thekingstalent.com

© 2025 by Revolutionary Insights Publishing
www.thekingstalent.com
ISBN: Softcover 978-1-7357405-4-6
ISBN: E-Book 978-1-7357405-5-3

All rights reserved by the publisher. No part of this book may be reproduced or transmitted in any form or by any means, electronic or mechanical, including photocopying, recording, or by any information storage and retrieval system, without permission in writing from the copyright owner, except for brief quotations in critical reviews and articles.

Printed in the United States of America
Copy edited by Andrea V. Baugher
Cover Design: Sheena Pendley
Cover Art: Ethan Martin

To The Reader

Mom was adamant that the language of her family and neighbours be authentic, and so when she wrote this book, she wrote their language as she heard it. Since I was familiar with their language having heard them speak throughout my youth, I took the liberty to try to make their speech a little easier to read. However those unfamiliar with the Appalachian dialect may find it difficult. Therefore, I have translated a section of dialogue below to give a hint on how to read the dialect.

"What'cha gonna do 'ith stove wood?" I asked Mom.

"I'mma gonna bake a pie out'ta 'eeze here blackberries 'at I jist went up onna hill'n picked," she replied.

"Oh boy!" Woody yelled. "You hain't made us a pie fer a long time."

"I'm a gonna make 'his pie ta fetch ta y'ur new neighbors," Mom said.

Clarification

"What are you going to do with stove wood?" I asked Mom.

"I'm going to bake a pie out of these here blackberries that I just went up on the hill and picked," she replied.

"Oh boy!" Woody yelled. "You haven't made us a pie for a long time."

I'm going to make this pie to fetch (take) to your new neighbors," Mom said.

Table of Contents

Chapter I - In the Dark of Night 10

Chapter II - Mom, Dad, Poppy and Grandma 13

Chapter III - The Cottage 25

Chapter IV - Lesson of the Dolls 36

Chapter V - The Rooster's Tale 41

Chapter VI - The Little White Boots 45

Chapter VII - Special Delivery 49

Chapter VIII - Of Things to Come 54

Chapter IX - Ol' Bess 68

Chapter X - Neighbors 73

Chapter XI - A Precious Memory 87

Chapter XII - Dry Ridge 90

Chapter XIII - Our New Home 99

Chapter XIV - Inside the Outside World 107

Chapter XV - It Begins 117

Chapter XVI - A Child Such as I 125

Chapter XVII - The Outhouse 132

Chapter XVIII - Down to the Bars 136

Chapter XIX - Aunt Sissy and Uncle Clint 144

Chapter XX - The Picture Show 147

Chapter XXI - Our Thanksgiving 150

Chapter XXII - Grandma's Thoughtfulness 156

Chapter XXIII Sandy Closs 159

Chapter XXIV - Virgil Emmanuel Day 163

Chapter XXV - Remedies 172

Chapter XXVI - The Swimming Hole 175

Chapter XXVII - Sniggerfritz 183

Chapter XXVIII - Prepping for Winter 195

Chapter XXIX - Cold Fury 202

Chapter XXX - A Web of Smoke 205
Chapter XXXI - Yet Another Child Arrives 210
Chapter XXXII - Games to Be Made and Played 213
Chapter XXXIII - Poor Little Sister 222
Chapter XXXIV - Mealtime Adventures 227
Chapter XXXV - A Matter of a Dime 237
Chapter XXXVI - Terror in the Garden 243
Chapter XXXVII - Fighting Him Off 249
Chapter XXXVIII - Wartime 252
Chapter XXXIX - That Old-Time Religion 256
Chapter XL - A Scary Tactic 272
Chapter XLI - Brother Woody 275
Chapter XLII - Fighting Despair 280
Chapter XLIII - Pushing My Luck 284
Chapter XLIV - Mystery Meat 288
Chapter XLV - Laughter and Consequences 293
Chapter XLVI - Attending to Life 303
Chapter XLVII - Lurking Under the Cliff 306
Chapter XLVIII - The Ol' Scarecrow 313
Chapter XLIX - The Iron 316
Chapter L - Confound the Confound Luck 322
Chapter LI - Mom's Gas-Powered Washing Machine 325
Chapter LII - On the Rocks 327
Chapter LIII - Electricity 342
Chapter LIV - The Owl and the Knight 349
Chapter LV - No More School 358
Chapter LVI - The Wonders of Television 363
Chapter LVII - A Way Out 367
Chapter LVIII - A Whole New World 376
Chapter LIX - From Trouble to Hope 380
Chapter LX - Strength for the Battle 388
Chapter LXI - Like a Butterfly 395
Chapter LXII - A Penny Behind the Fuse 398
Chapter LXIII - The Handprints 407

Chapter LXIV - The Baptism 414
Chapter LXV - The Kiss 416
Chapter LXVI - In the Huckleberry Patch 419
Chapter LXVII - A Stake Through the Heart 430
Chapter LXVIII - The Sympathy Game 440
Chapter LXIX - The Ecstasy 447
Chapter LXX - And the Agony 456
Chapter LXXI - Making Matters Worse 463
Chapter LXXII - Uncle O's Little Market 472
Chapter LXXIII - The Little Salesgirl 484
Chapter LXXIV - The Picture 491
Chapter LXXV - The Assault 495
Chapter LXXVI - Shattered 502
Chapter LXXVII - Painfully Shy 510
Chapter LXXVIII - Fifty-Two Pick Up 523
Chapter LXXIX - Telling My Secret 527
Chapter LXXX - Secure 532
Chapter LXXXI - As Time Passed 537
Chapter LXXXII - Peace 541

Introduction

Let me tell you a little bit about mom and this book from the perspective of her youngest son. Sadly, mom passed away April 28, 2018, at the age of 82. As you will be able to tell while reading this book, mom was a very hard worker and she put that same effort into writing her story. Since she had a limited education, she taught herself how to write properly by reading books on grammar and asking advice from her granddaughter Heather, who had earned her PHD in English because as Heather says, "I had a grandmother who inspired me." Mom meticulously revised her book and worked hard to make sure she honored God with the story he had given her.

She tells about growing up in a poor family in rural Appalachia with a vividness that alone would make this book a charming and worthwhile read. However, by adding the tragic tale of how her father terrorized her, it adds a dimension of survival that makes her story intensely compelling.

Mom was a woman who put God, her husband, and children above herself. She was a great cook and made sure there was always plenty to eat. As dad would ask whenever company showed up and mom fixed supper, "Are you expecting an army to come marching down the road that needs to be fed?"

Mom and Dad had a loving relationship throughout their lives that is usually found only in fairy tales. Dad put mom on a pedestal, and he told us kids more than once, "If you ever lay a hand on your mother I'll kill you. That's not a threat, that's a promise." In our house we definitely knew that Mom was Dad's top priority. That didn't mean we didn't think Dad loved us, but he truly loved mom as he should. Dad never ceased to be mom's knight in shining armor, and mom never ceased to be the love of Dad's life.

Growing up Mom never told us about the horrific deeds of my Grandpa Lesher because she didn't want our relationship to be tainted. I knew him as an older man who loved to tell stories and laugh. He also loved the Cleveland Browns and Cincinnati Reds. I remember visiting at various times and he'd be watching the Browns on TV while listening to the Reds on the radio at the same time. It wasn't until after he passed away when I was 17 years old that I began learning of grandpa's actions toward my mom and others.

The relationship between my grandpa and grandma seemed to be good as I was growing up. I never heard them argue and every once in awhile I would see little displays of affection. Grandma seemed to spend her time cooking, catering to grandpa, and gossiping.

Dad lived to be 89 years old and passed away January 24, 2022. After mom passed, whenever we would talk about mom, tears would well into his eyes and a sadness would envelop him. I was alone with dad when he died, and I knew it would only be a matter of minutes until he took his last breath. I leaned down to tell him I loved him and whispered in his ear, "Dad, you're getting ready to see mom again, so tell her we love her, and we'll be right behind you."

Bill Hawkins, Jr.
May 10, 2025

I

In The Dark of Night

I was awakened suddenly with the uneasy feeling that I was in imminent danger. The room was dark around me, and my heart was palpitating as I groped for my bearings. To my left, the red luminous numbers on the face of the alarm clock were glowing like Christmas candles in a dark window on a cold, wintry night. As I listened to the deep, even breathing of my husband, who lay sleeping beside me, I wondered what had startled me awake.

Lying there in bed, I tried to convince myself that I had been awakened by a bad dream. Disturbing nightmares had interrupted my sleep for years; however, on this particular night, I sensed that a nightmare was not responsible for the anxiety building within me. Peering into the pitch-black night, I listened intently as a vaguely familiar sound drifted in through my bedroom window, but before I could identify it, the puzzling noise abruptly ended.

I lay quietly as I anticipated the next sound, becoming more agitated by the moment. The lonely yelping of a dog somewhere down the street and the shrill cadence of an annoying cricket nearby seemed only to heighten the foreboding feeling I was experiencing. I pulled myself upright in bed and onto my elbows—being careful not to disturb my still-sleeping husband—as the light from a passing car pierced the dark night and glided across my bedroom wall.

Concentrating on the soft, intermittent cries that had once again returned, I reluctantly allowed my mind to wander back in time as

I struggled to pinpoint the familiarity of the disturbing sound. My mind seemed to be spinning out of control. I felt hot tears begin to trickle down my cheeks and onto my pillow, as something inside me gnawed its way inexorably to the surface. I lay back onto the bed in terror and pulled the sheet up over my shoulders. "Oh, God!" I whispered. I had finally recognized the lonely, mournful cries of an owl that had wandered out of his natural habitat and into our tranquil suburban domain.

Trying desperately to regain my composure, I stared once again at the clock as it glared back at me. It was 2:32 in the wee hours of Saturday morning, and I was wide awake. It was apparent to me that I would be getting no more sleep for the rest of the night, so to avoid disturbing my husband, I quietly snuck out of bed and into the living room, slumped wearily onto the sofa, and began praying for strength.

Once again my soul was being wracked with a volley of emotions, even though I knew rationally that thirty-seven years had passed since I had been awakened in the middle of the night by the call of an owl—warning me that my father was sneaking quietly toward my bed.

Many times throughout my life, memories from my childhood had stirred different emotions within me. I was thankful that God had allowed bits of pleasant memories to be mingled with the mind-boggling episodes from those dark chapters of my life. Despite my best efforts to convince myself that I had overcome the trauma of those horrific experiences, and to never again allow the disturbing recollections to return to interrupt my life, I now realized that the hooting that had awakened me had once again overturned the simmering kettle of acid that had been, for most of my life, corroding ugly holes into my entire existence.

Having come far enough into my Christian life to know that Satan cannot do anything to a child of God unless God himself permits it, I pondered the dilemma I was in. Maybe the time had come for me to deal with the agonizing memories that I had for so many years been trying to suppress.

With this in mind, my thoughts were shifted for a brief moment to the fulfillment I was finding in being a wife, mother, and grandmother living in today's world. Shivering, I clung to that reality, thankful that I had my family and faith to sustain me and certain that if I were ever to fully enjoy all the blessings with which God had surrounded me, then my conscience would have to be purged of all the guilt and insecurities that had seemingly forever tormented me.

"Please, dear God," I pleaded softly, feeling myself being led toward a door I had tried to close on the cold, miserable truth. "Break these shackles and free my mind from its secret house of horrors." I relinquished myself to God's will, not realizing He would eventually lead me through the labyrinth of my youth in order to help me understand where my problems had begun. I truly believed He was there to rescue me from the personal hell that had been attempting to destroy me from the time I was a mere child, so at last, just two weeks past my fifty-fifth birthday, I started on the journey that I hoped would change my life.

II

Mom, Dad, Poppy, and Grandma

I was born the fourth child of thirteen children to a poor but proud family near the small town of Clendenin, located on the banks of the Elk River in Kanawha County, West Virginia. Like our preacher used to say, "Why, we were so poor that we had to fertilize our house in order to raise the windows."

During the years I spent at home with my family, we always had a baby in our house. Nine months and twenty-six days after my parents were married, my brother Woodrow was born. Two years and four months later, their second son, Marvin, was added to the family. Just thirteen months and eight days after Marvin's birth, their third son, Harley, was born. (He died three hours later, apparently from what now is known as SIDS). I was born eighteen days short of one year after Harley's death, and approximately every two years for the next seventeen years thereafter, a new baby was born until there were eleven boys and two girls in our family.

Dad and Mom housed, fed, and clothed my siblings and me, all the while instilling in us that we were to expect, and were entitled to, nothing more. We children were taught that any expression of love, physical or verbal, between family members was improper and carried with it a sexual connotation; therefore, our parents avoided any display of affection toward us or between each other while in our presence. On the surface, not one of us children seemed to despair from the lack of affection. As a matter of fact, our family seemed to be as normal as the other families living around our area, since as far as we knew the other parents treated their children in the same manner our parents treated us.

My siblings and I were taught to obey our parents and elders and never to question anything they might say or do. Dad was a very strict disciplinarian, and we could count on being punished for our misconduct and much of the time for our mistakes. Dad had absolutely no qualms about what he thought it took to enforce the rules he expected us to follow. Having privileges withdrawn was out of the question since we had no privileges. My siblings and I received no allowances and were unaware that most children no doubt received allowances from their parents. We had no rooms of our own to which we could be sent, and to our knowledge telephones and televisions did not exist in our area. We belonged to no clubs, nor did we take part in extracurricular activities, and we were not allowed to attend movies. Besides, Dad's idea of punishment was, in his words, "a good, hard beatin'." After all, that was how his parents had handled his siblings and him while they were children.

Dad's customary means of correction was to hit both the older and younger of us children repeatedly with his leather belt or with the wide leather strap with which he sharpened his straight razor. Worse yet, for the older children, he often went into the woods and cut a long, pliable branch, which he called a "withe," off a hickory sapling to use as his rod of correction. The severity of our punishment was determined by our father's anger at the moment rather than by the seriousness of our offense. Dad was determined to raise strong children, and since he believed that spankings were for sissies, he resorted to beating the fire out of any of us he deemed deserving of one of his "whuppins."

Mom often used a variety of disciplinary measures to her advantage when she found it necessary to punish a child while Dad was at work. She usually kept a supply of green willow switches on hand and when she deemed their use necessary would cut red welts across our legs and backsides by flailing us with the switches. Should the switches be out of reach, she would grab whatever was handy to use in their place. On at least one occasion, she literally brought one of my younger brothers to his knees by giving him a whack between his shoulder blades with an iron skillet.

My mother often used her own modes of correction to force the smaller children to obey. She sometimes threatened that an old man living in our area would come with a burlap sack and carry the misbehaving child away. At nighttime, she often declared that a bogeyman would appear out of the darkness to "get us" if we didn't go to sleep. For years, several of us children were afraid to go outside after dark or to enter a dark room because of our mother's scare tactics.

Many times, all Mom had to do was to say, "Just'u wait 'til y'ur daddy gits home an' I tell him on you!" She knew that the thought of getting one of Dad's beatings was usually all it took to reform the child for the rest of the day.

My siblings and I, our parents, and most of the people we knew who lived around us would habitually season our vocabulary with language that I would later learn was offensive and sinful. Except for attending school, we children did not mingle with the "outside world;" thus, fortunately for us, very few people knew about our colorful language. Although neither Dad nor Mom enlightened my siblings and me that using those "little dirty words" was wrong, they warned us very early in our lives that we were never to use God's name in vain. Dad more than once squinted his eyes and sternly said, "I'll beat'cha within an inch of y'ur lives if'n I ever hear a cuss word comin' from y'ur mouth!"

To emphasize Dad's warning, Mom acquainted each of us children with the consequences that my oldest brother had suffered when he had barely learned to talk. It seemed that about three years into their marriage, while Mom and Dad were still living with Mom's parents, the families were seated around the table enjoying their evening meal when Woodrow blurted out one of the forbidden swear words.

Grandma had made a big pot of vegetable soup for the families' meal from dried brown beans and a variety of fresh vegetables she had gathered from her garden. Woodrow was seated at the table along with the rest of the family, enjoying his bowl of soup with corn bread crumbled in it. Having eaten brown beans often but never tasted vegetable soup, Woodrow was carefully inspecting every spoonful of the unusual concoction, when suddenly he blurted out, "I be damn! 'Ere'sa bean!"

Both shocked and surprised, the adults gasped in disbelief at the young boy's choice of words. Shaking her head from side to side, my grandmother said, "Pawn my honor da God. Now where'd 'at young'un ever hear 'at kind'a talk at?"

Pushing his chair back from the table and jumping to his feet, Dad angrily yanked off his belt and walked around behind Woodrow's chair. Wide eyed already from the adults' response to his remark, little "Woody" slowly slid down in his chair. Dad reached down and grabbed the toddler by the hand and jerked him to his feet. While flailing the toddler with his belt, Dad yelled, "Don'chu ever talk like 'at a'gin er I'll beat'cha ta death!"

While Woody squalled as Dad slammed him back onto his chair, Grandma and Grandpa left the table without finishing their soup; Aunt Sissy sat at the table crying; Mom sat at the table but couldn't eat; and Dad returned to his chair and nonchalantly finished his bowl of soup. The story made an impression on all of us children. Thankfully, other than for our own foul language, most of us would hear very little of the vulgar and offensive language that repulses me today.

My father was from a large family of fourteen children. They had migrated to our small town from Clay County. His father, Henry Clay Lesher, had been shot and killed in a fight over another man's woman when Dad was a small boy. Dad's mother, Virginia Dare Carper Lesher, had remarried and eventually outlived three husbands.

Paralyzed from a stroke in her waning years, Grandma died in 1955. I was never acquainted with the majority of Dad's family since they and Dad seldom visited with each other.

According to Dad, none of his family had much schooling. Although my father had only a third-grade education, he was blessed with plenty of what he referred to as "common horse sense." Dad always accomplished whatever he set out to do but attempted to do very little that required a lot of planning. My father had lots of potential and more than likely could have done more with his life had he tried; however, his beliefs were the same as most adults in our community. They didn't believe in setting any goals for themselves; per their philosophy, it was better not to try at all than to fail while trying.

None of the adults seemed to expect much out of life. Most of them had the notion that their lives should be no better than the quality of life that their own parents had made for themselves. They believed that God had willed their lives to be such as they were—and they weren't about to question God's will. Dad actually taught us children to always keep our feet on the ground and never to expect too much out of life. He explained his opinion by saying, "Atta way, ya won't have so fer ta fall when y'ur wings gits clipped."

Unlike most fathers considered to be "country," Dad was determined to see his sons graduate from high school, yet like most fathers in our community, he expected his daughters to quit school by age sixteen. Any girl insisting on graduating from high school was looked upon as a worldly woman. A young lady's place in life was to marry while in her teens, have lots of babies, and stay home to raise them. A "country girl" was considered to be a spinster if she had reached her twentieth birthday and still not found herself a husband.

My father considered a good reputation as one of the most important accomplishments a person could attain in life. Around our community and the surrounding area, my father was indeed known as an honest, decent, and God-fearing man who worked very hard to support his family. He was determined to make his own way in life no matter how hard the times might have been. He never asked for and seldom received charity or relief from any source. He tried very hard to instill the same values in his own children. As I have pondered this fact, it has been difficult for me to understand how his ideals ran so amok during the time he was raising his family.

Dad was twenty years old, and Mom eighteen, when they married. Academically, Dad had only a third-grade education, while Mom had completed the eighth grade. While growing up at home, I never once saw Mom take time from her busy schedule to read the Bible or any other books. She impressed me as being intelligent, yet she seemingly had no desire to apply her abilities in any aspects of her life.

Mom's only sister, Mary, had received a sixth-grade education. When asked about her younger brother's limited education, Mom would facetiously say, "My brother Hubert was spoilt rotten. Just 'cause he wazzuh baby an' tha only boy, he wouldn't e'er cut loose of Mommy's apron strings, so he didn' git much schoolin." Mom enjoyed elaborating on the subject and would often continue even when no one seemed to be listening. "Hubert? Why, he wuz such a big baby an' was so spoilt an' lazy 'at when he cried an' begged Mommy not ta make 'im go back ta school, Mommy'd pet 'im an' say, 'Ya don't haf'ta go if ya don't want to.'"

According to Mom's version of events, even though she was twelve and her sister only nine years old at the time, they carried their little brother on their backs for miles to and from school, when he did attend. Fortunately for the sisters, their brother quit school after the first grade. I eventually learned that Mom's stories about Uncle Hubert's family were not always accurate. I remember him as a kind and loving man who worked hard to support his family. His entire family and I have always been very close.

Neither my mother nor her mother believed that women should bob their hair. Mom's long, straight, raven-black hair fell just below her hips. She either wore her hair in two braids, which she wrapped around her head, or she would pull the long tresses to the back of her head and form a twisted knot, which she fastened in place with long wire hairpins. She did not wear jewelry or makeup and frowned upon the women who did. She always looked clean in a print cotton dress when she went to town or attended church; however, she took no pride in how she looked in and around the home. She preferred loose, ragged dresses and no shoes, or shoes that looked as if they had been scavenged from the dump. "'Ese here are my comfor'ble clothes," she often said when being chided about her appearance. Other than for her sloppiness around the home, my mother was very sensitive about pleasing Dad. I eventually recognized that the desire to please her husband was motivated more by her fear of him than by her love for him.

My mother had high moral standards and agreed with the notion that a woman's place was in the home. Even though she didn't seem to find any fulfillment in her own work, she carried out her daily tasks tirelessly. She seemed only to exist from day to day, doing what she knew was expected of her and complaining very little. She also did whatever she thought was necessary to keep peace in our family. Unfortunately, her efforts often backfired, leaving her to suffer the consequences.

Mom taught us children to respect our elders and, when in the presence of others, to practice the manners she had taught us. She taught us children to appreciate and to care for our possessions and the possessions of others, regardless of how insignificant they seemed to be. She also insisted that we look and act our best when we were away from our own home or in the presence of strangers.

When Grandpa wasn't moseying around with the aid of his battered wooden cane, he could be seen sauntering slowly about, slightly stooped forward, with his left arm crossed behind his back, holding his right wrist with his left hand. Like his hats and shoes, he reserved a shellacked, newer cane to use for "special occasions."

Grandfather was never known as an ambitious man. He made it perfectly clear that he needed no help while tending to the only three "jobs" he was faithful to perform: producing his chewing tobacco, raising his chickens, and making his homebrew. Furthermore, he had no intentions of helping anybody else with their work. Mom often said of her father, "Poppy weren't nary bit afraid of work. Why, he'd lay down 'side any ol' job any time an' go sound ta sleep."

Although tobacco was not a crop normally grown in West Virginia, Grandpa reserved the edge of Grandma's vegetable garden for his small, personal crop of tobacco. From the moment the shoots peeped through the soil, he would inspect the plants several times each day until he was satisfied that they were ready for harvesting. When the tobacco crop was ready to cure, Grandpa would painstakingly bundle the wide leaves together into bunches and then carry them to the barn where he'd hang them from the rafters to dry. Once dried to his satisfaction, Grandpa would untie the bundles and carefully remove the stems before spreading out each leaf on the kitchen table. After he had sprinkled a small amount of sugar over each leaf,

Grandpa and Grandma Mullins.

he would stack the leaves into several small piles and then roll each pile into slender sticks of tobacco.

One by one, Grandpa would fold each stick in the middle, cross one pliable end of the slender roll over the other, and then twist the two ends until the folded stick was wound snugly into one neat twist of chewing tobacco. Then he would store the sweetened chewing tobacco to let it season for a while.

Grandpa always carried a small knife in his pocket. At the beginning of each day, he would get a twist and cut off a small chunk that he called a "plug." He would drop the plug into his pocket along with the knife. Throughout the day, each time he needed a fresh chew, he would snip a small amount from the plug, pop it into his mouth, and then return the plug to his pocket. Regardless of whether he was inside or outside the house, the strong, pungent smell of Grandpa's chewing tobacco permeated his clothes and the air around him.

While indoors, Grandpa always spat his ambeer inside the fireplace. Should his mouthful of ambeer accidentally land on the hearth instead of in the ashes in the fireplace, Grandma, upon hearing the loud splat, would scold him by yelling, "Jim!"

Grandfather wouldn't bother to look up but would sarcastically respond, "Hit's my 'backer. I'll spit whur I wanta spit."

Grandpa prided himself in his second project. Adamant about owning no breed of chicken other than the dominique strain, he was proud of the fact that he had his "dominecker" chickens eating from the palm of his hand. He would not permit anyone to feed the small flock as long as he remained physically able to do the job himself.

Grandpa had his own method of feeding the chickens. He would scavenge for broken plates and dishes, which he believed helped to keep his laying hens and lone rooster healthy. Each morning before letting the small flock out of the coop to run free for the day, Grandpa would sit on the large boulder near the coop and pulverize the broken dishes into tiny chips. Once he had added the proper amount of chips to the cans of chopped corn, he would allow the fat, revered chickens to eat from his hand before scattering the rest of the feed on the ground. I once asked Grandpa why he fed the "glass" to the chickens. He curtly replied, "Tain't glass! It's deesh. It's good fer 'im. It helps their craws d'gest their food bedder."

Our chickens and other country folk's chickens roosted in trees at night, but Grandpa wouldn't allow his flock to roost in trees. At the end of each day, he would dip a can of chop from the barrel, walk out onto the big boulder near the coop, and call the chickens into the pen by tapping the side of the can with the closed edge of his knife. Upon hearing the sound, the flock of pampered chickens would obediently come running from all directions to be fed and housed for the night.

During the summer months, fireworks often erupted when Grandma discovered that Grandpa's chickens had wandered into her tomato patch and pecked large holes into the ripe tomatoes. "If y'aint gonna help me raise a garden, leas' thang you can doo'za skeer 'em sh-t'n chickens outta my 'maydos'," she would angrily say to Grandpa.

Grandpa would shout at her, "Aw sh-t, Ceilly, a chicken's gotta eat!"

Mom often told the story about when she was a little girl, how her dad had kept a keg of "brew" fermenting in their loft. Although their family couldn't afford to buy fresh fruits to eat, somehow her father would always find a way to buy lemons, raisins, peaches, and other fruits for his own, and God only knows who else's, "homebrew."

On a few occasions during her father's absence, Mom and her sister would climb the homemade ladder that Grandpa had carelessly left resting against the wall below the attic window. Once they had entered the loft, they would steal pieces of the forbidden fruit from his barrel of brew. "No matter how skeered me'n Sissy was of Poppy, sooner or later tem'tation would gitta best of us'n we'd en' up gittin' inta hiz mash," Mom would say. Moving her opened hand in a downward motion and then pulling it upward with her fist closed, she would tell how they had run their hands down to the bottom of the wooden keg to retrieve the forbidden fruits. "We'd pull our han's outta 'at stuff'n lick tha juice off'n our arms, an' then we'd eat somma Poppy's fruit." Seemingly more amused than was her audience, Mom would continue, "Then we'd carf'ly put ever'thang back like it 'twas." They would then hasten back down the ladder and busy themselves at some task so their mother would not discover what they had been doing.

Later, upon discovering her daughters' secret, instead of punishing the sisters, their mother would lift the girls in and out of the scuttle hole in the ceiling so that they could continue helping themselves to Grandpa's fruit before it had fermented. Luckily for the girls and their mother, Grandpa never missed the stolen pieces of fruit.

Once the children were older and the family had started attending church, Grandpa no longer made his homebrew; however, he continued to enjoy his other two chores until the day he was confined to his sickbed, where he died in 1949.

My grandmother Celia Jane was a strong woman both physically and emotionally. The work involved in raising a family fell upon her shoulders. She was also the breadwinner of the family since my grandfather had failed to assume the role. Grandmother would walk more than three miles to town four to five times a week to clean houses for the city folk. On Fridays, Grandpa would walk out of the hollow to meet her while she was walking home from work. He would take his "weekly allowance" from her meager wages to spend in the way known only to Grandpa. Other than for the money he spent for the ingredients required for his homemade wine, none of the family would ever learn how, where, or when he spent the remainder of his part of Grandma's hard-earned income.

Grandma insisted that Grandpa would go to any extremes to avoid manual labor. She warned him one evening that if he didn't help her dig and store the winter's supply of potatoes that she would never again walk the three miles to town to her house-cleaning jobs—their only means of support. Grandpa picked up his hoe, walked over to the potato patch, and somehow managed to whack off the first joint of his thumb. Needless to say, Grandma dug the potatoes by herself. She could never believe that Grandpa had "accidentally" cut the end off of his thumb with a long-handled grubbing hoe.

Although Grandpa often verbally and physically abused my grandmother, she was a loyal and dedicated wife. Mom often told the story of how Grandpa, while waving a shotgun in the air, had threatened to kill her mother over some minor altercation. Screaming from fright, Mom said she had yelled at her father, "Poppy! Please don't keel my loodle white bunny wabbit!" She said she was surprised when her father suddenly looked over at her, laid down the gun, and walked away.

Grandma was a very thrifty woman who always taught her family "to waste not is to want not." She made all the clothing for herself and her children. Spending hours by lamplight, she also pieced and quilted covers for their beds. Her only "extravagance" seemed to be the few cents she spent on the snuff she habitually rubbed.

When I was in my teens, I was privileged to teach Grandma how to write. She was proud that at last she didn't have to sign her name with an X. Apart from her signature, however, her other writings were undecipherable to anyone but me. She often ran two words together and divided them wherever she pleased. Two words with seven letters each may have been written instead as four individual "words." Or she might write three "words" with three letters each and group the five remaining letters together to finish what should have been her second word. Much effort was required to read her letters; however, I was proud to know that she could at last pen her own thoughts onto paper, regardless of the errors.

III

The Cottage

Many episodes from my childhood have left themselves indelibly imprinted in my memory. I would learn throughout the next few weeks, while reliving my past, that those memories would invoke within me practically every emotion imaginable. While easing my way slowly through each of the occurrences, the memories of the particular clothing, odors, sounds, and even the weather at the time would cause me to feel as though I were once again experiencing events as they had taken place. I thanked God that, as I returned to one of my earliest recollections, not all my past was spent in fear of my father.

I was four years old, leafing through the pages of a book Woody had brought home from school, and I stopped to admire the picture of a white, vine-covered cottage nestled in an ocean of beautiful flowers. Dad had earlier in the evening announced that he would soon be moving us to a "new house" in the head of the hollow above where my grandparents lived. I imagined that the house would look like the quaint, well-cared-for home I was looking at in the book. Being so young, I couldn't remember any of their previous moves, but this would be Dad and Mom's sixth move in the nine years they had been married.

At the time, we were renting a house from its owner about eight miles south of Grandma's place. Since Dad had considered the distance he would have had to drive, through several creek crossings and over the rutted-out roads, in order to visit our maternal grandparents, our visits with them had been limited. Excitement was building within me when I learned that we would soon be living close enough to walk to their home.

A few days later we drove up the hollow toward the place Dad would be renting from a land company for $15.00 a year. With the picture of the white, vine-covered house in the book on my mind, I excitedly watched as Dad passed by my grandparents' home and drove on up the rough road to the very head of the hollow, where he stopped the car under a big sycamore tree. I looked across the creek, which weaved its way between the house and the big tree, at a small, ramshackle house. Bewildered, I blurted out, "Whur's our house?"

"Lookie over 'ere," Dad said, nodding across the creek toward the shack that slouched in the high grass. My heart sank as we stepped from the car. Even I could see that although the place where we were living presently had only a very small yard, it at least afforded us a bigger and nicer house than the one I was walking toward.

Stepping from one rock onto another, I watched as a wide brown leaf fell from the huge sycamore tree and floated leisurely downstream. The dried leaf, curled up around the edges, reminded me of a little boat. Excitedly I began making plans to turn over each rock in the shallow creek to look for "crawdabbers," and to launch more of the boats that had conveniently set sail just as we had arrived.

I leapt onto the bank and ran through the green grass to the front of the house. Carefully climbing the rickety steps, I peered through the door. Seeing nothing to interest me, I hurried back outside, knowing that the outdoors would make up for what the indoors lacked. The white, vine-covered cottage with its array of brilliant flowers no longer seemed important. I would now be able to enjoy my own ocean of wildflowers.

Later in the day when Dad returned with our household goods, he placed the few pieces of furniture against the walls, leaving the center of the floor as cleared as possible to accommodate Mom, the five of us children, and himself. I curiously watched as he and Mom maneuvered the heavy, cast-iron, wood-burning kitchen range into place, where he then hooked it to the rusty stovepipe running up through the kitchen ceiling and out the roof. While Mom assembled the beds, Dad drove away in the beat-up truck he had apparently borrowed to move our goods.

Sometime in the afternoon he returned driving our car. I watched as he parked beneath the big tree and stepped onto the ground with a crate in his hands. Setting the crate on the ground and opening it, he turned and opened the back door of the car. I curiously watched as our chickens, two dogs, and a cat were set free to acquaint themselves with their own little paradise.

I returned to chasing my brothers through the tall grass only to hear Dad yell for us to get inside. Once inside, we listened with much trepidation while Dad warned us about the deadly snakes that had no doubt infested the area. "Stay outta the tall weeds an' watch out when ya go in any of 'em buildin's, espeshly the torlet, and fer now, this house," he said.

The living room walls had been papered; however, most of the paper had been torn away, leaving wide cracks stuffed with rags and aged pages torn from catalogs. Directing our attention to the wide cracks in the floor, Dad said, "I'll haf'ta stop up theeze here open cracks in tha floors jis' like Ol' Man Carpenter done them there big cracks in'na walls so 'em snakes can't git inta our house." I was terrified of snakes, so at the mention of the slithery creatures, I jumped onto one of the beds that had been set up in the living room.

Dad walked outside, and I cautiously crawled off the bed and squatted on the floor. It was time for me to familiarize myself with my "new" home. After locating the widest crack in the floor, I quickly stretched out on my belly and cupped my hands around my eyes. Nervously, I peered down through one of the cracks, hoping that a big rattlesnake didn't peer back at me. Squinting my eyes, I curiously focused on movement beneath the house and was relieved when I recognized our own chickens clucking noisily as they scratched for worms.

Throughout the day our father continued to warn us children, "Now younguns, y'all wa'chout 'cause 'em 'ere snakes'll be comin' outta 'em high weeds an' down da crick fer wodder jist 'fore dark." I had begun to wonder if there was any place on our little farm where we could be safe from the threat of those snakes that my father seemed so concerned about.

Maynard and I on Birch Creek.

Running to the back I noted that the foundation was almost level with the ground, while both sides rested on flat rocks. A small stoop at the back door led to the entrance of the kitchen. Like all the other houses in which my parents had lived, the little dwelling had no electricity or plumbing.

Once it was dark outside, Dad, my brothers, and I went inside. Immediately, by the dim light from the kerosene lamp, Dad began the task of stuffing rags in the wide cracks between the warped, uneven boards in the living room floor. While Mom tore strips from an old sheet, she asked Dad whether he thought we could afford to buy some linoleum on payday to cover the living room and kitchen floors. Dad shrugged his shoulders and then said, "Hain't no need gettin' in a hurry fer no lernoleum; first thang I gotta do is build a room fer mine an' yourn's bed." He continued, "Hain't chu got 'nuff ol' rags ta stuff all tha cracks with?"

"Yell, we got plenty a rags, only thang is, we hafta wear most of 'em," Mom said, making sure to laugh at her own statement.

At bedtime my older brothers Woody and Marvin shared a single bed, while my younger brother Maynard curled up with me on the daybed in the only bedroom. Baby brother Arnold was already asleep in our parents' bed in the living room. I lay awake for a while wondering whether there were any snakes inside the house.

Throughout the summer, Dad worked strenuously as he attempted to build another bedroom onto the house. He was working a public job, so his spare daylight hours were limited once he'd worked all day and then drove the long distance to our home. He had agreed to allow Mom to cover the floors with new linoleum and to paper the walls with store-bought wallpaper, since he and Mom had killed two copperheads and one rattlesnake on the property.

Although our little shack was crowded and hardly fit for occupancy, neither Mom nor we children complained to Dad. With all the room on the outside, my brothers and I spent most of our time outdoors; in fact, the first time it rained after we had moved to the new location, Mom had to run us inside out of the rain. Once inside, she pointed out that the rain not only was coming down on the outside, but it was also pouring down on the inside.

Mom grabbed an armload of containers and passed them out to my brothers and me. We scurried throughout the rooms, placing bowls, pots, pans, and empty cans below the many leaks. Splashing into the numerous containers, the dripping water seemed to be playing a tune of its own. My brothers and I sat on the foreside of their bed and in unison began singing louder and louder as we imitated the noise. "Spa-lit spa-lat, pa-ing pa-ang, drr-ip drr-op," we sang.

Scurrying about the room, our frazzled mother didn't seem to be nearly as amused as were her three oldest children. Almost in tears, she fretted in disgust, "Looks ta me like y'ur daddy orta knowed 'at roof leaked worser than a sieve when he moved us inta 'his here place." With the volume of her voice rising, she continued, "Now ya younguns shet up an' help me catch this wodder 'fore it ruins ever'thang!"

When Dad came home from work later in the evening, Mom persuaded him to climb into the loft to check out the leaks. After pulling himself through the small opening, cut in the ceiling, he looked around and then hung his head down and asked for a bucket. Moments later he lowered the pail, now filled with water, to Mom as he swung himself down from the loft and reported that the attic was full of rusty pans and tin cans filled with rainwater.

"I set 'em cans back where they'd been, so I reckon we're ready fer tha next downpour," Dad said. "I guess ol' man Carpenter fergotta tell me 'bout tha rusty roof."

Dad bought a bucket of black tar on Saturday and crawled on top of the house, where he patched the rusty tin roof. He then continued with the construction of the extra bedroom, which he was building with green, unfinished, untreated lumber he had bought from a sawmill in town and scrap lumber he had hauled in from somewhere nearby. My brothers and I were kept busy carrying rocks from the creek for Dad to use in erecting a fireplace in the living room.

Fall was in full swing, and the steep hills were ablaze with each leaf on every tree appearing to have been carefully hand-painted a different hue from God's immense assortment of magnificent autumn colors. The huge sugar-maple tree in our front yard was adorned with beautiful shades of orange and gold. The Schumacher shrubs spilling over into the space reserved for our yard were now a bright crimson. Hundreds of beautiful fall wildflowers bowed their heads respectfully as the gentle breeze drifted throughout the valley. The air was filled with the songs of the many birds dancing cheerfully from branch to branch.

Everyone in the family had been working like beavers, and although I accomplished very little, I enjoyed the idea that I was helping with the work. Using a mowing scythe and a hand sickle, Mom had whacked down the tall grass and weeds. I and, I presumed, the rest of my family were beginning to enjoy the small, isolated farm that was slowly being whipped into shape.

With the new bedroom finished, I felt blessed to have my family and new home with its two small bedrooms, living room, and large kitchen. I wondered how, although Dad had built the new bedroom from the same type of lumber from which the house had been built, he had cleverly managed to leave out all the wide cracks.

The valley between the two ranges of mountains was not more than one hundred yards at the widest point. The house was located near a creek, called Birch Creek, that began there in the head of the hollow at the foot of the mountain-chain. It carved its trail deeper and wider as it wound its crooked path out of the hollow to eventually empty into the Elk River.

The former tenant had taken advantage of the shallow creek in an unusual way. He had built an outhouse and then erected it on two poles that he secured across the creek, allowing the human waste, along with pages from the Sears and Roebuck catalog, to drop through the toilet-hole to be washed away by the creek. It was obvious that Mr. Carpenter had created his own unique "automatic flush" toilet. Disgusted by the unsightly and unsanitary problem the outhouse was causing downstream, Dad quickly moved the rickety structure to a new site.

The water for doing the laundry had to be carried from above where the outhouse had emptied into the creek. Drinking water and water used for cooking the meals was carried from a hand-dug spring located around the side of the hill from the residence. Rainwater running off the roof, used for washing dishes and other needs, was caught in barrels and a large earthenware vessel kept below the eaves of the house.

Our family had acquired a milk-cow and an old mule, a necessity on the farm. The mule had been used to plow our garden, which was now depleted of its assortment of vegetables. The field of dried corn to feed the livestock had been cut and gathered into shocks.

Dad was busy preparing to dig the well he had been promising Mom. Mom, however, appeared to be skeptical when he informed her that he had contracted an old gent who lived on one of the ridges nearby to come to our place to locate a good vein of water. Mom reminded Dad that folks in our area referred to the man as a "Water Witch."

"He hain't no witch," Dad said. "He's a 'diviner.'"

Supposedly, the old gent was able to find underground veins of water by using a divining rod. "Hain't sure but what dat don't sound like witchcraft ta me," Mom reluctantly said.

"It hain't got nuthin' ta do with bein' a witch. He's jist got a gift a findin' wodder thatta way," Dad impatiently replied. Mom remained silent after Dad informed her that the man would be coming to our little farm to look for water—whether she liked it or not.

The man showed up early on a Saturday morning, and Dad, my siblings, and I ran outside to meet the "diviner/witch." I had been expecting the old man to be carrying some strange instrument that he would stick down into the ground to locate potable water; instead, I was surprised to see him arrive with what appeared to be a slender, forked branch he had apparently broken from a small bush. The stick was shaped like the letter Y.

With a prong of the stick in each hand and the straight piece of the branch sticking out in front of him, the diviner/witch walked to and fro across a small patch of ground at the back of our house, seemingly guided by the divining rod. Finally, the stick in his hands began to quiver, and the old man hesitated and then moved slowly from side to side. Suddenly, the stick began to shake violently while some unseen force pulled the end of the stick downward toward the ground. The diviner looked toward my father and yelled, "Thar's y'ur wodder vein, Mr. Lesher. You'll find plenty a good ol' col' wodder right cheer."

Dad yelled excitedly, "Whoopee!" He then walked over to where the man stood gripping the constantly shaking stick, still pointed toward the same spot on the ground. "Go fetch me a big rock!" he yelled to Woody.

Woody soon returned from the creek with the rock, and Dad placed it on the spot where the stick was still pointing. Teasingly, my father looked at the old gent. "We'll soon know jist how shore y'ur devinin' stick is," he said. "I'll be startin' on tha well tuhday." He shook hands with the diviner as he handed him what appeared to be a couple of one-dollar bills.

The "water witch" smiled and walked back across the creek to where he had tied his horse to the big sycamore tree. After slipping the tip of his divining rod beneath the saddle, he swung himself up onto the horse's back, guided the horse back to the road, and rode away.

Dad walked through the kitchen door and yelled to Mom, "Maw, y'ur gonna have a well fulla wodder 'fore ya know it."

"I'll believe it when I see it," Mom muttered.

Dad and my seven- and nine-year-old brothers began the work on the well immediately. The day wore on, and the work was slow and laborious as the hole was being dug deeper and deeper. Down inside the cavity, Dad was using a shovel and mattock to loosen the dirt, while periodically calling for the pickax to break up and remove large rocks he was encountering. Dad would throw shovels full of dirt and rocks to the surface, where Woody and Marvin hovered beside the deepening hole, waiting to scatter the debris before it could fall back inside the hole.

A few days after the work had begun, Mr. White, a neighbor who lived on one of the ridges nearby, dropped by to help with the work my brothers weren't capable of handling. The well was being dug about thirty to forty inches in diameter to enable Dad to maneuver around inside. Once the depth was too deep for the shovels of dirt to be thrown up and out of the hole, Mr. White hung a pulley from a tripod that he and Dad had rigged above the excavation; then he proceeded to lower a five-gallon bucket into the well by the rope that had been pulled through the pulley. Down inside the well, Dad filled the bucket with soil and rock he was removing from the well cavity. Mr.

White would then pull each bucket to the surface and empty it onto the heap of dirt for Woody and Marvin to scatter.

This process continued until finally, after hours of hard work, my father yelled to Mr. White that water had begun seeping through the dirt at the bottom of the well. While Dad continued to work down inside the well, I jubilantly ran to the house to fetch Mom to the site.

Mom left the meal she had been preparing for the hard-working men and accompanied me to where all the excitement was going on. "Daddy struck wodder, Mommy!" Woody excitedly yelled.

"Well, glory be da God!" Mom replied.

While the work on the well proceeded, I wandered away from the work area to chase the beautiful yellow-and-black-striped butterflies flying about the area. Having no luck at capturing any of the fragile beauties, I returned just in time to hear my father yelling from inside the spooky hole, "Okay, bring me up outta here."

Standing with one foot in the bucket, holding onto the rope with one hand, and guiding himself out of the hole with his other hand, my mud-splattered father was reeled up to the surface. Joyously stepping onto the ground, he threw his soiled hat into the air and shouted, "We hit pay dirt! Hal-lee-lu-yerda God!"

After lunch, Dad was lowered back inside the well, where he bailed out most of the water that had seeped inside. My two older brothers and I hurried to carry an assortment of flat stones, retrieved earlier from the creek bed, to the site. Mr. White loaded them into the big bucket and carefully lowered it by rope to the bottom of the well. At the bottom of the well, Dad proceeded to stack the rocks against and around the earthen walls from the bottom toward the surface. Our little crew continued the pace until Dad finally worked his way to the surface by climbing up the rock wall as it had progressed.

With the well completed and filling with water, Mr. White and Dad placed the well curb—a big wooden box they had built earlier—over the opening. Two leather strips cut from one of Dad's worn-out shoes had been attached to the wooden lid to serve as hinges. Dad hung a pulley from the pointed roof he had added to the curb and then pulled a new hemp rope through the pulley. One end of the rope he fastened to a brace on the curb, while he tied the remaining length to a pail that would be used to draw water from the new well.

We awoke the next morning to find the well filled with an ample supply of cool, mostly clear water that would supply all our water needs for as long as we lived on the property. In our area, water from wells was presumed to be as safe and pure, as the diviner had promised that ours would be, and, indeed, we found our water to be a big improvement over the sometimes-muddy spring water we had been forced to use since moving to the area. Whether the spirits had led the old gent to the correct spot to dig for water, or whether it was luck, the fact remained that the well was one of the best wells in the area. The two dollars, handshake, and expression of thanks from dad hardly seemed sufficient for the man credited with bringing water to our household.

IV

Lesson of the Dolls

Before I could reach the path I was anticipating in the psychological labyrinth of my past, my thoughts shifted to the realization that for years there had been a strain in my relationship with my mother. I would soon be reaching the strange course that had led me to mistrust my father, but I had never considered finding out why and when I'd lost faith in my mother. Somewhere in this maze there had to be some answers, and I was intent on sorting through my memories in order to understand where it had all begun. I had no idea at the time that each event I was to recall would eventually play an important part in my healing process.

Days had passed since I'd awakened in that haunted night, and I was finding a sort of therapy from opening the doors I had never allowed to swing wide. Life was resuming with my family unaware of what was going on inside me. I was glad to be traveling through the stage in which the memories I recalled were pleasant ones, and although I had no intention of rushing ahead of God, I was determined to see this journey end with good results. So, with Him holding my hand, I continued to return to my past.

I smiled as I remembered Betsy, the first of the only two dolls I can remember owning. Betsy seemed to have always been with me. I cannot recall her being new. I wondered whether Betsy could have been ragged and worn when she came to live with me. Although her little body had been riddled with holes, exposing the matted cotton she was stuffed with, I loved her very much. She had for a period of my life been my only friend and greatest treasure.

Betsy had been through more than a little girl's doll should be expected to go through in a lifetime. She had been used, abused, and I'm sure even drop-kicked a few times, since I had four brothers in my life. She was my only playmate since I seldom saw any children outside my own family.

Albert, Dad's youngest brother, was the only relative to occasionally pay us a visit. Uncle Albert was married and resided in another state. During this period in his life, he had no children of his own. He seemed to care very much for me and always referred to me as "my little girl." He never failed during these visits to bring a small gift for me.

Uncle Albert drove to West Virginia one weekend to visit with relatives. When he and Aunt Katie arrived at our house, my brothers and I slipped into the room, too shy to speak but listening to what they had to say. Peeking from behind a rocking chair, I timidly observed as Uncle Albert's eyes focused on me. With a twinkle in his eye and his broad smile exposing a mouthful of even, white teeth, he held up a big shopping bag and invited me to come take a peek inside.

After considerable prodding from my uncle, I was coaxed over to where he had lowered the bag and was holding it open. With my head tilted toward my raised right shoulder, I shyly looked down inside the grocery bag. My big brown eyes almost popped out of my head when they focused on a beautiful, shiny new doll. I thought to myself, "Surely this pretty doll isn't for me." Why, even my nice, generous uncle had never given me anything this extravagant before. I stood there in disbelief, afraid to touch the bag.

Uncle Albert finally reached inside the bag, pulled out the doll, and lovingly placed her in my arms. I felt as though my heart would explode. I pulled the doll close to my bosom, determined to lay claim to this gorgeous doll before my uncle could change his mind.

I lowered the doll and looked at her little body. I must have been beaming. She was beautiful! I gasped when I realized that Mom was calling my name. "Surely she's not going to make me give it back," I thought.

I must have looked relieved when it dawned on me that my mother was attempting only to remind me to acknowledge the gift. Why, I was so thrilled that I had forgotten all about any manners Mom had been trying to instill in me. "Thank ye, she's pur-dee," I shyly said, finally managing to pull my eyes away from the doll to look at my uncle.

"You're welcome," he said. "She hain't nurly as purdy as my loodle gurl is." My uncle stooped down and gave me a big hug while at the same time Aunt Katie kissed me softly on the cheek. Embarrassed, but with tears of joy filling my eyes, I ran out of the room and into the kitchen—clutching my special gift close to my heart.

Alone at last, I examined every inch of my brand-new doll. I gently touched the long dark eyelashes that shaded her big brown eyes, which closed when she was reclining and reopened when I picked her up. Her short curly brown hair and pearl-white teeth made her seem human. I felt as though I was the luckiest girl alive as I fingered the oodles of white lace adorning her petite, pale-green dress. I cuddled the dainty little feet that were outfitted in silky white socks and black patent shoes. "Gee whiz! She makes poor ol' Betsy look like she belongs in the trash dump," I thought.

For the next few days, I clung to my new friend, whom I had named Bonnie. To my dismay, the gloss was fast disappearing from her legs and arms. The rubber bands holding her arms in place had stretched, leaving Bonnie's arms dangling at her sides.

Sadly, a few days later my mother ordered me to "put Bonnie away," or my new doll would soon be in the same shape Betsy was in. Painfully, I accepted the fact that Bonnie was literally falling apart; therefore, I obeyed my mother and carried Bonnie into the bedroom, tenderly placing her crippled little body inside the big trunk. I quickly found my old, ragged Betsy doll and, hugging her close to my body, ran for my playhouse.

Days later I decided that I would sneak Bonnie outside to the playhouse so that Betsy could have a sister. Mom had evidently decided to allow me to play with my once-beautiful doll, since she pretended not to notice when I snuck past her. Later in the day I returned Bonnie to the trunk, where I thought she would be safe.

The next day, when I slipped into the bedroom to retrieve my doll, I was surprised to find her missing. I had for some time suspected that my brothers had been the culprits, intent on destroying my prize possession, and my suspicions were verified when I caught one of them using Bonnie for his punching bag. I angrily ran over, grabbed the fragile Bonnie out of his hands, and ran into the bedroom sobbing. Bonnie's arms and legs were cracked and barely hanging onto her broken, petite body. She was no longer the shiny, clean, gorgeous doll I had raved about just a few weeks earlier. I would have to get her some help immediately, or she was destined for the trash heap. Consequently, I decided I would carry her to Grandma the very next time I was allowed to go to her house. Why, even I knew that Granny could mend anything, no matter how far gone it might seem to be.

When I presented my doll to Grandma a few days later, she looked at Bonnie and then at me. "Bethel, Bonnie hain'ta kind a doll you can drag 'roun' an treat like you tre'ch yer other doll," she solemnly said. "She's mighty purdy on'na outside, but her innerds is made out'ta sawdust." She continued, "Now, loodle ol' Betsy hain't much ta look at, but her innerds is put together real good."

Devastated, I asked, "Cain't 'chu fix 'er 'ith somethin?"

Handing Bonnie back to me, Grandma replied, "Hain't nuthin' I can do fer her. She wuzzen made fer playin' with. She's jist ta set up on a shelf to look at."

Sadly, I realized that although my beautiful doll was practically brand new, if Granny couldn't fix her, then she was beyond being fixed. I returned home and handed her to Mom, knowing that she would probably toss Bonnie in the trash. I quickly found my ragged Betsy doll, whom I'd carelessly dumped for fancy Bonnie. Holding my old friend tenderly to my bosom, I began to appreciate her more than ever. I agreed with Granny. Old Betsy was not much to look at on the outside, yet she had something holding her together on the inside that kept her there for me no matter how rough life had treated her.

I had no way of knowing just how important the memory of my dolls, Bonnie and Betsy, would become. During a critical time in my life, I would recall how Granny had pointed out the contrast between Bonnie and Betsy; in spite of all the abuse I myself would suffer throughout the years, I would find myself bowing tearfully to ask God to help my life reflect that inner beauty and stability I'd learned from my Betsy doll. The lesson would continue to serve as a challenge to me throughout my Christian life; in addition, it would afford me an illustration to share with other ladies as I endeavoured to encourage and challenge them in their own Christian walk.

V

The Rooster's Tale

I had never realized the extent of what I had retained from my early years until I began to allow every memory to surface freely. I smiled while recalling the cute little dresses Mom used to sew for me on her treadle-operated sewing machine. Mom had learned from her mother that she could sew me a dress by using the fabric from one of the 100-pound sacks of feed purchased for our cow. Grandma also informed Mom that she could make herself a dress by matching three of the feed sacks; thus, Mom began to carefully choose each sack from the wide range of designs and colors that were available.

Once she had emptied the dairy feed from the sack, she would carefully unravel the stitches and then launder the fabric. Without using a printed pattern, Mom would then cut out the dresses and sew them on her manual sewing machine. During my early childhood years, all my dresses and most of my mother's dresses were made from the feed sacks.

Although Mom possessed few seamstress skills, I was proud of the cute little dresses she made from the sacks; however, I detested having to wear the undergarments she made from the unbleached sacks in which 100 pounds of chopped corn for the horse had been packed. She would cut out and sew a couple pairs of underwear from each sack, and since she could not afford elastic to encase the waistband and legs of the garments, she would substitute strips she had cut from discarded inner tubes. By day's end my waist and thighs would be oozing blood from the roughness of the fabric and the tightness of the crude "elastic."

Since complaining to Mom about the problem had brought me no relief, I was often forced to take matters into my own hands. She seemed to have a built-in warning signal, however, that never failed to alert her that I had once again shed my uncomfortable homemade undergarment. When that happened, she would come running toward me, shouting as she ran, "Git 'em son-za-bitchin' bloomers on 'fore I beat'a piss outta you!" Most of the time she would grab me by the arm and begin smacking my bare bottom, never once stopping to ask why it was so difficult for me to wear the "special" panties she had made just for me.

One sunny, warm morning I sneaked into the bedroom and grabbed my old faithful doll and ran quickly out the door. After I'd hurried down the front steps, I jumped into the yard, took a few quick steps, and stopped in my tracks. As usual, the homemade panties were rubbing my legs and cutting into my waistline. After looking around in all directions and seeing no one outside, I quickly yanked off my underwear and scurried back toward the house, where I cautiously tucked the garment beneath the bottom step. Realizing that my dress was too short to cover my backside, I clutched my doll close to my body and ran as fast as my skinny little legs would carry me, to the corncrib I had earlier made into a playhouse.

The small building's primary purpose was for storing the small harvest of corn raised on the tiny farm. The building's floor was about a foot above the ground, resting on posts. The hole cut out in the front wall and used for the doorway was several inches above the flooring of the building, making it impossible for me to enter the building "gracefully."

Standing on the ground, I reached up and slung my doll inside the doorway; then, jumping up and forward, I fell through the entrance like I had done numerous times before. To my surprise, I landed with my head and shoulders hanging inside the opening and my backside and legs dangling outside. Hanging there over the wall like a wet towel, I instantly realized that I was trapped in that position.

Frantically, I tried to pull my lower extremities inside the door, only to realize that it was impossible for me to get inside the building or down onto the ground. Scared out of my wits and with my bare bottom still draped over the entrance, I shrieked out in pain when I felt something or someone gouging my backside with a sharp object. Flailing my arms and kicking both feet, I had no choice but to scream for my mother.

Again and again I yelled, "Mommy! Help me!" It seemed that the louder I screamed the more violent the thrashing became. It was apparent to me that whatever was back there wasn't a bit timid about destroying my bare backside. Hysterical and in pain, my cries for help went unheeded while the mysterious enemy continued the attack.

"Help me, Mommy!" I screamed. "Somebody's tryin' ta keel me!"

Finally hearing my desperate cries, my mother came running out to see what was happening to me. "Shoo! Shoo, you son-za-bitch! Shoo!" she yelled as she ran to my rescue. Angrily, she yanked me out of the doorway, stood me on my feet, and unmercifully began bellowing in my face, "How many times haf I tol'jue da quit dat pullin' 'em bloomers off?" I rubbed my eyes with one hand and my rear with the other while Mom angrily shook her finger in my face and continued, "'At's jist whatch'ee git! It's good 'nuff fer ya!"

Not only did I not know what had been trying to destroy my backside, I stood there trembling from fear that my own mother was about to strangle me to death. I squinted my eyes tightly, anticipating that more damage was about to be done to my already stinging and bleeding bottom.

Finally realizing that I was apparently safe from further attacks, I wiped my teary eyes and looked up to see Mom returning to the house, and there, strutting majestically behind her, was our proud, monstrous rooster. Just as I breathed a sigh of relief, the big bird unexpectedly turned, lowered one wing tip to the ground, looked straight in my direction, and began prancing around in circles. Wide eyed, I stood there staring at his knife-like spurs. Suddenly, it became clear to me that this cocky old bird was the rascal that had been jumping up and repeatedly flogging my tender flesh with his six-inch-long spurs. Since I was too small to send him sailing across the yard with a good, swift kick, I did what I thought at the time was the next best thing. I stared at him menacingly while I shrieked, "You durdy sonza-bitch! Stay 'way from me, er I'll keel you!"

The rooster, seemingly ignoring me, stopped and began pecking at something he had discovered on the ground. I ran past my attacker and back to where I had hidden my underwear beneath the steps. With those dreadful underpants in hand and my back to the wall, I carefully stooped over and jerked them on with more speed than I had taken them off. I wondered whether maybe our big, bad rooster's intentions were meant to impress upon me that my bare bottom was too repulsive even for his evil eyes.

I vowed at that moment to take my mother's warning seriously, while promising myself that no matter how much pain I might have to endure, I would never again shed my crudely made underpants. The discomfort from the rubber waistband had been minor compared to the pain and humiliation I'd just received from that rooster and my mother; furthermore, I wasn't about to give the rooster the satisfaction of attacking me again. I had finally learned my lesson the hard way.

VI

The Little White Boots

Another cold winter had blasted our small, isolated farm. My brothers and I had been taking turns roasting our backsides in front of the fireplace while our forefronts continued to chill. It was Saturday morning, and Mom and Dad had just informed us children that the road leading out of the hollow was impassable by automobile; as a result, they would have no choice but to walk to town to buy the month's supply of groceries.

My family and other families living in the hollow did their shopping at the only market in town whose owners agreed to use their pickup truck to deliver the groceries to the mouth of the creek, to a spot known as "The Low Gap." The groceries were customarily dropped off and left at the spot, though no one might be there to receive them. The rightful owner of the truckload of groceries would later take his horse-drawn sled to the mouth of the hollow to claim the groceries—sometimes hours after they had been dropped off by the grocer.

Since my family was the only family living in the hollow at the time who owned an automobile, we seldom had to take advantage of the service; nevertheless, the condition of the road on this day would require Dad to take our horse and sled to pick up our groceries when he and Mom returned from town.

"You young'uns is gonna haf'ta stay with Granma 'til we git back," Mom said.

While Dad donned his heavy coat, cap, boots, and gloves, Mom buttoned up her coat and tied a scarf around her head before she bundled up my baby brother. My brothers jerked their jackets on, and I pulled on my coat as we walked out the door to walk the half mile to our grandparent's home.

"You help Granma watch'a boys, an I'll fetch'chu a new pair a shoes 'at'll keep yer feet good an' warm," Mom said to me while I shivered in the frigid air.

I was past five years old, and I knew that I'd have to stay and help Grandma whether or not I received new shoes; besides, although I needed new footwear, the thought of getting another pair of the ugly "clodhoppers" I'd always had to wear did not excite me one bit. I had seen pictures in the catalog of pretty shoes like the ones my doll had been wearing, so I no longer presumed that the brown, high-top shoes my brothers and I were forced to wear were the only type of footwear available. I had never asked for anything special since it was somehow understood by us children that our parents would make the decisions about what we would wear.

Finally, my parents returned from their shopping, and while Dad walked to our house to get the horse and sled to drive out of the icy hollow to retrieve our groceries, Mom stopped at Grandma's house to reclaim my brothers and me. We bade our grandparents goodbye and began trudging our way up the frozen dirt road to our home. Mom didn't mention the new shoes, and I didn't ask about them.

Piling in through the front door, we children immediately crowded around the fireplace while Mom stoked the smoldering coals. I had noticed that she had been carrying a gray bag like the bags from the shoe store where she had always bought the brown clodhoppers, and although I was curious, I hadn't asked if my new shoes were inside the bag.

While my brothers and I continued to huddle near the cold fireplace, trying desperately to capture a promise of heat before we froze to death, Mom set aside the poker and then sat down in a chair near the fireplace. I watched while she reached over and pulled a shoe box out of the gray bag. I curiously looked at the box and noticed that it was bigger than the shoe boxes she had in the past carried home. What I glimpsed when she opened the mysterious box and pulled out the shoes caused me to almost lose my breath. I couldn't believe what I was seeing! The new shoes weren't brown. Why, they were snow white!

Wide eyed, I ran over to my mother, screaming in delight. "'Em'za purdiest shoes in'na whole world!" I yelled. "Are they mine?"

"Yell, 'eeze are y'ern," Mom said, sounding pleased.

The little white boots were lined with soft, white fleece with their over-the-ankle tops turned inside out, forming a fluffy fur cuff. Jumping up and down, I was so thrilled and happy that I burst into tears. Scolding me, Mom yelled, "'Awl sh-t, young'un! Stan' still'n let me see if'n 'ese thangs'll fitch'ee." Ignoring my excitement, she yanked off my worn-out brown shoes and began shoving my foot into the soft white boot.

Immediately feeling the tightness of the boot on my skinny little foot, I shivered from fear. I curled my toes under as tightly as possible in hopes that Mom would not notice how cramped my foot was inside the precious, warm boot. She didn't bother to lace up the snow-white laces; instead, she stooped down while squeezing the toe of the boot and exclaimed, "Y'ur toes'r smack dab in'na end'a 'em boots! Hain't no way you c'n fool me!"

With tears of sadness, I began to plead, "Please, Mommy, please don't take 'em back."

"I'll jis' take'm back'n trade'm fer'tha same kind," Mom promised.

"But 'ey won't haf no more like 'eezuns," I whimpered.

"Jis'chu wait'n see," Mom said, closing the box lid on those darling, new boots.

Since I knew that my parents had always bought my shoes at least one size too big so that I wouldn't outgrow them before they were worn out, I realized that Mom would never relent and allow me to keep the adorable boots. My heart ached.

No matter how hard I tried for the next few days, I couldn't get those boots out of my mind. I slipped into Mom's bedroom a couple of times during the week and opened the box to take another look at what I coveted so much. I wondered whether I would ever own anything so beautiful as the little white boots.

The following Saturday, which seemed like an eternity to me, Mom again left us with Grandma while she returned the little boots. I was hoping for the best yet feared the worst. I suspected that she would return home carrying another pair of boys' shoes. Nervously and impatiently, I waited for my mother's return.

The moment she appeared at the door I jumped up and down yelling, "Jue gitt'm? Jue gitt'm fer me?"

"You'll see when we git home," Mom answered.

Finally, after an agonizing wait while Mom visited with her parents, she picked up the baby and the gray bag, and we began tramping our way home through the slushy snow. All I could think about was the little boots Mom might be carrying inside the bag.

After what seemed like an eternity, my brothers and I stood watching as Mom slowly reached down into what appeared to be the same bag she had returned to the store that morning. "Theez'n here's all 'ey had lef'," she said, pulling the shoes out of the bag. "Take'm 'n try'm on."

I gasped! It was indeed just as I'd feared. My cold-hearted mother had traded my pretty white boots for another pair of those ugly brown clodhoppers. I burst into tears. "Mommmy!" I bellowed.

Mom coldly snapped at me, "An' jist'chu be glad I fetched ye 'eez'ns."

I had no choice but to accept the brown shoes without further comment. Slowly and tearfully, I slipped my foot inside the awful shoe. The shoe was at least one size too big—exactly the way my mother preferred it to be.

VII

Special Delivery

While trying to stay warm inside the uninsulated living room, I sat near the fireplace watching Mom as she worked with several yards of white flannel she had bought days earlier. I watched as she cut the outing material into what I recognized was going to be diapers, baby gowns, and shirts. With my curiosity heightening, I scooted around the floor snatching up the snippets of material Mom had dropped. Without any conversation between the two of us, she raised the lid of the treadle sewing machine and began sewing the items.

I moved closer to the sewing machine, watching Mom's foot moving up and down to drive the machine. I wondered whom she could be sewing the tiny, soft clothes for, since my brother Arnold was almost two years old. I stood to my feet and inquisitively studied what appeared to be "belly bands." Why, even I knew that a belly band was used to wrap the belly of a newborn infant until after the umbilical cord had fallen off.

I listened to the tune Mom was humming and recognized it to be one of the hymns that had been sung on the few occasions I could remember attending church services. Mystified about the clothing and my mother's pleasant state of mind, I suddenly recalled a conversation I'd heard earlier between my mother and her mother.

"Marthy, are you in'na family way ag'in?" Grandma had asked.

"I thank so, Mommy," Mom had answered, sounding apologetic.

"Pawn my honor ta God! Hain'chu got more young'uns now'n you can take keer uv?" Grandma had asked, shaking her head in disgust.

At the time, I had wondered about the meaning behind the term "in the family way." I had concluded that it must have had something to do with us children from the way Grandma had responded to Mom's answer. Since children weren't supposed to inquire into adult conversations, I had walked away confused.

As I stood there looking at the baby items Mom was busily putting together, I thought to myself, "Why, Mommy is making clothes for a new baby that must be coming to our house." I had noticed that inches had been added to my hard-working mother's belly, and I wondered whether that could have anything to do with the mounting evidence that a new baby was on the way. I couldn't ask Mom about such a personal matter. I would just have to wait and see whether my mother would volunteer the information. I moved in a little closer, picked up one of the little gowns, and held it to my face. It smelled fresh and clean.

After Mom had finished sewing the last article of clothing, she rolled all the flannel pieces together and took them into the bedroom, where she stuck them inside the trunk where I had earlier kept my doll. She stepped back into the living room and looked at the small pieces of flannel that I had rolled up on the floor.

"Reach me 'em pieces," she said.

"Cain't I have 'em?" I asked.

"No, pick 'em up'n give 'em here," she ordered.

I handed her the scraps, and she walked over to the fireplace and threw them in the fire. She closed the lid on the sewing machine cabinet and pushed the cabinet against the wall, whistling the tune she had earlier been humming. I certainly was one curious little girl. It seemed to me that whatever was going on, Mom meant to keep it a big secret.

The next day, after my two older brothers had left for school and Dad was away at his job, Mom pulled out the gowns from the trunk.

I again watched with deep interest when she took her needle and a skein of pink embroidery thread and walked into the living room. She pulled a chair near the fireplace, sat down, and began making cross-stitches down the front of one of the kimonos.

Finally, I could stand the suspense no longer, so I bravely blurted out, "Mommy, what'chu doin'?"

Without looking up, she said softly, "I'ma fixin' some loodle clothes fer'tha new baby 'at's comin' to da house."

My eyes widened. "Why you makin' 'em pink?" I asked curiously, moving a little closer to Mom's chair.

She looked up from her sewing and smiled at me. "Cause pink's fer a girl," she said. "Jue wanna sister er a brother?"

"I drether have a baby sister, but how'd jue know it's a gonna be a gurl?" I asked, reaching over to touch the soft flannel gown that Mom was embroidering.

"Well, I went'n told'a stork ta fetch us a girl 'is time," Mom replied.

I had always been told that babies were delivered by a big bird called a stork, and here Mom was, telling me that a stork would bring the baby to our house; however, the things that I had observed and overheard were not coinciding with the story that storks deliver babies to homes. I was also finding it very difficult to believe that a stork could find our house, way up there in the head of the hollow so far from the rest of the world. Nevertheless, regardless of how it was going to be delivered, baby number seven would soon be coming to our house.

I was thrilled knowing that I would soon have a baby sister, since I was the only girl. I trusted my mother, and if she said she had ordered a little girl, then the new baby would be a girl. (At the time, there was no way to determine the sex of a child before birth.) Whether or not she was being delivered by a stork didn't seem important.

On a snowy morning in January not long after Mom had made the little clothes, I awoke to find my baby brother Arnold sleeping in my bed. Since he was the youngest child and had from birth slept with

Mom and Dad, I started for Mom's bedroom to find out what was going on.

"Come see what da stork fetched wha'l you wuz asleep," Mom said, upon my entrance to her bedroom. I was puzzled since there had been no baby when I had gone to bed the night before. Now, here I stood looking at Mom with a newborn baby sleeping beside her. I stood quietly for a moment while I silently asked myself, "Now if a stork did all the work, then why does Mommy have to stay in the bed?"

Mom called me over to the bed as she tucked the pink blanket around the new baby before carefully placing her in my arms. Sounding very pleased with herself, she said, "I ordered 'er fer you, jis' like I promised." She pointed out my sister's tiny hands and her pink, doll-like face. I nuzzled her soft cheek and could smell the baby powder on her body. Tenderly, I planted a kiss on her little cheek while hugging my baby sister close to my bosom and feeling the soft blanket against my face. My brand-new baby sister certainly was an armload. I was more convinced than ever that no stork had brought this seven-pound baby to our house.

After allowing me a few moments to caress my little sister, Mom took the baby out of my arms and placed her beneath the covers. "Her name'za gonna be Nina Jane," Mom said softly. I giggled with glee as I ran out of the room and into the kitchen. How the baby had arrived was still a mystery to me; nevertheless, I was thrilled to finally have a baby sister.

I poured milk over my own and my little brother's bowl of cold oatmeal and then grabbed one of the hard, dry biscuits that Dad had baked before leaving for work. I couldn't help but notice the mess he had created while preparing the meal. Drying dough was clinging to almost everything in the kitchen, including the oven door. I was glad that Grandma would soon be coming to our house to help me with the morning chores.

Nina's birth had left a lot of unanswered questions buzzing around in my head, and I wondered whether I would ever learn the facts. I felt certain that, should I ever learn the truth, it would have to come from someone other than my Mommy.

VIII

Of Things to Come

Dad drove his old Model "T" Ford into town five days a week and then commuted to and from work with one of his coworkers who owned a more dependable automobile. Mr. White also worked at the glass plant in Montgomery, and after walking from his home on the ridge, he also rode with the coworker.

Rarely was the evening meal not on the table when Dad arrived home from work. On this particular spring evening, in 1942, supper had been ready and waiting for over two hours, yet Dad was not home. Mom had finally given us children permission to go ahead with our meal without Dad, and with his food left warming on the stove, she apprehensively remarked, "I wonder whur'na worl' Daddy is 'his evenin'?"

In the meantime, Ol' Brownie, our cow, had broken through the fence and wandered into the heavy forest, making it necessary for Woody and Marvin to track down the rogue. After they brought the cow back to the barnyard, Mom, after milking the cow, returned to the house with the pail of milk. One of my brothers immediately informed her that Grandma was crossing the creek to our house. Mom, with panic in her voice, said, "Somethun's bound'a be wrong fer Mommy ta be comin' up here at 'is hour."

Mom hurried to the kitchen and set the pail of milk on the table and then hurried back to the front door. As soon as Grandma entered the yard, Mom impatiently yelled out to her, "Somethin's happen'ta Bud, hain't it?"

"Preston come'n tolt us 'at Romie an' Joe White was in a wreck, but he said 'at Romie hain't hurt as bad as Joe is," Grandma answered.

Mom's anxiety intensified as she began to cry.Mom's anxiety intensified as she began to cry. Burying her face in her hands, she asked, "Mommy, jue thank Bud is in enny danger a dyin'?"

"Now how in'na sh-t jue 'spect me ta know 'at?" Grandma curtly replied.

Mom was now sobbing, but instead of consoling her, Grandma stepped over closer to my mother and gruffly said, "Git holta yerself. Marthy. In'na mornin' I'll take care'a yer young'uns whilst you go ta Charleston."

"How'na worl' am I gonna git ta Charleston without no money?" Mom pitifully asked.

"I'll let'cha borry 'nuff money ta ride da bus," my grandmother said.

"'El, I'll be down 'ere soon as I git da milkin' done," Mom replied. "I jist got through with milkin' the cow, an' I gotta git in'na kitchen'n strain it." She walked into the kitchen with Grandma, my siblings and I following closely behind.

Each morning and evening after milking the cow, Mom would strain the milk by pouring it through a clean, white cloth to catch any hairs that might have fallen into the pail of milk. Seemingly in a trance, she picked up a big earthenware crock into which she began straining the evening's milk to use for the next morning. As was her custom, she retained a portion of the warm milk to strain into the churn to curdle for making butter.

Since we had no refrigeration, the cream would rise to the top of any milk left over from the morning's or previous evening's milking. During warm weather, the milk would begin the first stages of souring, known in our area as "blinking." This milk would also be poured into the churn and left to "clabber," or curdle. Once the churn of milk was clabbered, it was my job to churn the milk by vigorously moving the wooden dasher inside the churn up and down with the long handle. The churning was done about twice a week and kept our family supplied with plenty of fresh butter and buttermilk.

On this particular evening, however, instead of straining the milk into the churn, my mother stepped over to the stove and absentmindedly began straining the milk into the pot of pinto beans she had left warming on the wood-burning stove for Dad's supper.

I threw both hands over my mouth and stared at Grandma who was watching her oldest daughter fall apart. Granny yelled, "Marthy! Now jist look'it what you done!" Grandma walked over and spat a mouthful of ambeer out the kitchen door from the rub of snuff she was holding between her lower lip and teeth. Turning slowly and looking at Mom, she continued, "Throw 'em beans out an' git holda y'urself!"

Granny soon left for home, and Mom rounded up the family and ordered us to bed so we could go to Grandma's house the next morning. Granny had told Mom that she would prepare breakfast for us so that Mom could get an early start, especially since she would have to walk the three miles to town. I was apprehensive as I slipped into bed and hoped that nothing bad had happened to my daddy. I loved him very much and was sad to know he would not be spending the night at home with his family.

The next morning, after a big breakfast of Grandma's sourdough biscuits, fresh churned butter, and homemade apple butter, Mom walked out of the hollow and caught a Greyhound bus to Charleston. She returned in the early afternoon and informed her parents that the hospital had told her that Dad had several cuts and bruises and had been admitted for observation. Mr. White, however, had not been as fortunate; it seemed he was suffering from a concussion, a broken leg, and numerous cuts and contusions.

Once we were back home, Mom cheerfully told us children, "Daddy will probably git'ta come home tomarr'." I would never learn what caused the wreck nor what had happened to the coworker who had been driving the car.

The next day we kids heard the car coming up the road and knew it had to be our daddy coming home. "Ets run over an' welcome Daddy home," Mom said excitedly. Our enthusiasm upon seeing his safe return seemed to please my father very much. He kissed my mother on the lips and patted my brothers and me on our heads. I watched as he and Mom held hands while walking across the yard to our home.

For the next few days, Dad stayed home from work. On one of those evenings, I watched as he and Mom once again held hands while walking down the path toward the barnyard. Having never before witnessed any display of affection between my parents, I felt all warm inside and hoped that their "newly found love" would last forever. For the next few days, it became obvious even to a little girl like me that the wreck had drawn them closer.

However, to my chagrin, the honeymoon was soon over. Dad began arriving home from work in a bad mood almost every evening. If he was not angry when he got home, he seemingly would deliberately search for a cause to incite his anger. He had left the job in Montgomery shortly after the car accident and, since during the Great Depression employment was extremely scarce in our area, was blessed to be hired for a short while as a laborer for the Works Projects Administration (WPA). Fortunately, shortly before the WPA was disbanded in 1943, Dad was hired as a school bus driver for the Kanawha County Board of Education. Since this new job was providing better pay and benefits and was physically less demanding than any of his previous jobs, there seemed to be no apparent reason for his sudden change in attitude.

It was now fall, and Woody and Marvin had gone up on the hill near the house to drag shocks of fodder down to the barn. It was time for Dad to get home from work, and the boys had not yet returned. As usual, Mom was in the kitchen preparing the evening meal. I was in the front yard raking leaves into piles for my brothers to carry over to dump on the garden. With the chug-chug sound of Dad's Model T car getting louder and louder, I looked up to see him pulling into his customary parking area just across the creek from our home.

He stepped from the car, jumped the shallow creek, and stomped through the yard and past me without saying a word. To my surprise he headed toward the backside of the house instead of going inside through the living room door. I wondered what had brought on the break in his daily routine, so I cautiously sneaked around the side of the house and watched.

Earlier in the day my brothers had accidentally broken the twenty-gallon stone pot that Mom kept out back underneath the eaves to catch rainwater when it would run off the roof after a rain. Chills ran down my spine when Dad spied the broken container and angrily yelled, "Now who'na Sam Hill went'n broke 'at big jar?"

Mom stepped to the back door and said, "Bud, 'em boys wuz roundin' up rocks an' rollin' 'em close to the house fer you ta use in'na cellar, when one of the rocks hit 'hat 'ere jar an' busted it."

Dad's temper flared. He screamed, "Git ou'cheer, you boys, right dis minute!"

Mom nervously replied, "Em boys're on'na hill fetchin' fodder down to da barn."

Dad became even more infuriated. Swinging his arms back and forth and shaking his head from side to side, he stomped back and forth across the backyard before walking over and kicking what remained of the barrel, rolling it into the creek. "Confounda, confoun' luck! Hain't no use'n me workin' my ass off try'n ta haf' sumthin' 'round 'his son-za-bitch'n place," he bellowed. "Confounda, confoun' luck!"

Mom finally stepped outside onto the porch and said to Dad, "Now, Bud, what good'zit gonna do fer you ta act like 'at?"

Peeking around the corner of the house, I began to cry. I sensed that my mother would have been better off had she stayed in the kitchen. The thought had no more than entered my mind when Dad ran over and grabbed her by the shoulder. To my recollection, I had never before witnessed what was about to take place.

Violently, Dad began slapping Mom across the face as though she were one of us kids. I was terrified! I knew I was helpless in protecting my mother from Dad's abuse, but I had to do something to try to help her. Dad was out of control, and I was very concerned about what he might do to my Mommy; consequently, I ran back to the front of the house and frantically began yelling loudly for Woody and Marvin. Over and over I yelled. I had no idea what I expected them to do, but someone had to rescue our mother from the beating Dad was inflicting upon her.

After getting no response from either of my brothers, I quickly decided to go to where they could hear me. I ran as fast as I could through the yard and across the garden to the path that led up the hill to the cornfield. With all the vigor I could muster, I started the steep climb. The uncertainty of what was transpiring back at the house had wracked my small body with sobs.

Halfway up the hill I stopped to catch my breath. I again screamed, "Woody! Marvin!" Finally, after yelling four or five times, I was relieved to hear Woody's reply drifting through the tall trees. With the air passages in my nostrils tightening from crying, and not waiting for my brothers to get down the hill to me, I hurried up the hill to meet them.

At last I spied the welcome sight of my two oldest brothers slowly making their way over the mountain, pulling the large shocks of dried corn stalks and blades behind them. Woody immediately dropped the fodder shock he was pulling when he saw me frantically waving my arms to get his attention. He and Marvin ran to my side, Marvin still dragging his shock of fodder. Breathlessly, I fell at Woody's feet and blurted out, "Daddy's hittin' Mommy real bad! Hurry up'n help 'er!"

Marvin dropped his shock of fodder, and both of my brothers started running off the hill in front of me. I was finding that running down the hill was sure a lot easier than running up the hill had been.

With my spindly legs aching and both my sides burning, I struggled to keep my brothers in sight while they seemed to be sailing just above the ground.

Finally arriving at the foot of the hill, Woody stopped abruptly, and Marvin went crashing into him. I glanced again in their direction just in time to see them scampering to their feet. As I approached, Woody was breathlessly ordering Marvin to run and fetch Grandma. Marvin—looking as scared as I was feeling—quickly turned and started running down the dirt road toward Grandma's house.

Woody and I continued running toward the house. Scared, exhausted, and whimpering with each step, I again fell farther and farther behind. My imagination was running wild, and none of the thoughts were pleasant ones. The memory of one of Dad's earlier outbursts sent chills down my spine. Our horse had broken through the fence, and my father had grabbed the shotgun and shot the mare with shells he had previously loaded with salt. I feared that in his rage he might have turned the gun on my mother. I looked ahead to see my big brother standing in the backyard looking back at me. This new sense of urgency brought me quickly to his side.

"Whur'd jue las' see 'em?" Woody asked nervously.

It quickly dawned on me that Woody was unaware of where I had last seen my parents, so I whispered breathlessly, "They was at'ta back door."

Except for our heavy breathing, we moved slowly and silently to the corner of the house, hand in hand. Seemingly waiting for more strength, Woody stopped and gulped for air. Cautiously, we snuck around the side of the house and approached the kitchen door, only to be met with an eerie silence. We stopped for a moment and stood quietly, listening for any familiar sounds that the younger children should be making. Hearing nothing, we became even more alarmed. My big, strong brother looked nervously into my eyes and whispered, "Jue thank they're all dead?" I shuddered and then shrugged my shoulders, indicating silently that I didn't know.

Side by side and terrified of what we might find inside the house, my oldest brother and I walked through the door. My tears started flowing again when I looked over to see my father sitting calmly at the table, eating his supper. My two younger brothers were kneeling on their chairs cramming spoons full of pinto beans into their mouths. I stood gawking at Dad as he calmly pushed a mouthful of fried potatoes onto his fork with the hunk of cornbread he was holding in his left hand.

Woody looked at me in total disbelief. From the appearance of those sitting around the table, there was no indication that anything out of the ordinary had taken place. Mom was not at the table, but this was not unusual since she rarely sat at the table with the rest of the family. I brushed away my tears with the back of my hand and wiped my runny nose with the tail of my dress. I was grateful that at least my little brothers were okay. For a moment I wondered whether the whole thing had been a horrible nightmare.

Very calmly but cautiously, Woody and I made our way past Dad's chair and into the living room. Dad had not even looked around at us when we had entered the kitchen. It appeared as though he had forgotten about the whipping he had been so intent on giving my brothers. I was glad that my big brother did not know what had started the trouble in the first place.

As Woody and I entered the living room, we both looked down at our baby sister, who was crawling around on the linoleum floor, oblivious to what was going on around her. Woody reached down, picked her up, and, after looking around and seeing no sign of Mom, turned and started back to the kitchen.

I walked over and peeked through my parents' bedroom doorway and saw my mother sitting on the foreside of the bed drying her tears with a cloth diaper. She looked up at me, her face a deep red and her eyelids and nose puffy. As if pleading to be left alone, she motioned for me to leave the room. Obediently, I moved slowly toward the kitchen, my heart aching.

I walked over behind the chair where Dad was sitting at the table, and I leaned against the kitchen wall. Slowly, I slid down the wall to the floor. I did not know what to do, but one thing was certain: I was too exhausted and upset to join my family around the supper table.

In just a matter of minutes Woody appeared outside the kitchen door still holding my baby sister. Grandma walked past him and burst bravely into the room. She looked at Dad and asked patiently, "Whur's Marthy?

Dad looked at Grandma and then at Marvin who was standing beside her. Without responding to Grandma, Dad snapped at Marvin, "Why'd jue go fetch Celie up here?"

Marvin, wide eyed, shrugged his shoulders and grunted softly, "'Cause Woody tol' me to."

Dad scowled and, without saying a word, shook his head from side to side as he dropped his fork beside his plate. He pushed back his chair, stood to his feet, and stomped out of the room.

The stony expression on Grandma's face left no doubt that she was not leaving until she had gotten some answers from somebody. Mom's sister Mary, or "Sissy," as her nieces and nephews called her, walked into the room and stood beside her mother. Sissy was three years younger than Mom and at the time was unmarried and still living at home with Grandpa and Grandma.

Both women walked into the living room with Woody, Marvin, and me close behind. Looking around, Grandma asked impatiently, "Bethel, whur's y'ur mommy?"

"I'll fetch'r," I said, moving quickly toward the bedroom door.

Without entering the room, I softly informed my mother that Grandma and Sissy were in the living room asking for her.

"Don'tchu tell 'em he whupped me," Mom pitifully whispered.

"It's too late! They already know it, an' 'at's what they're 'ere fer," I said nervously.

Wearily pulling herself to her feet, Mom asked, "Whur's Bud at?"

"He wen' out'ta back door, an' I don't know whur 'e went," I answered.

Mom walked into the living room and dismally greeted her mother and sister. Grandma, shaking her head in disbelief, asked angrily, "Marthy, what's goin' on here?"

"Bud foun' my big jar uh'boys broke, an' he cut one a 'eez shins," Mom replied.

"Diddee hur'chu?" Grandma asked.

"Mommy, he hain't gonna hurt nobody. He jis' lost 'eez temper 'cause of 'at picklin' jar gittin' busted," Mom said, knowing that she was lying through her teeth.

Grandma looked over at me and stated, "He hit 'er! Didn' 'e?"

Mom looked at me and shook her head from side to side in an apparent attempt to signal that I deny Grandma's accusation. I tipped my head toward my right shoulder and timidly replied, "Yell, Grandma, he did. More'n once."

I could not believe that Mom was actually defending Dad's actions. I wondered whether everybody thought I was lying about what had happened; nevertheless, Mom's red, swollen face seemed to be sufficient evidence to convince Grandma that something unpleasant had taken place. She stepped over beside Mom and said, "I ain't shore't thangs're okay here, but I cain't stay here 'ith you an' 'ese young'uns."

"Hain't nuthin' ta worry 'bout," Mom said.

"Okay. He's yern ta put up with," Grandma remarked hopelessly as she walked slowly toward the kitchen door.

Mom didn't say a word to my brothers and me. She had to know how scared and worried we were, not knowing whether Dad had hurt her seriously. Dutifully, she picked up the milk pail and walked out the door. Woody and Marvin left to go bring the fodder the rest of the way to the barn.

I found myself alone in the house with my little sister and two younger brothers. My heart was heavy as I pondered the trouble and heartaches that the boys' accident had caused. I stared at the supper table. Somehow, although I had not eaten since breakfast, I could not bring myself to partake of the food. My stomach was empty, but food did not appeal to me after all that had taken place. I picked up my baby sister and began feeding her the fried potatoes I had spooned onto a plate.

A short time later I walked over to the door and looked outside in hopes of learning of Dad's whereabouts. I was surprised to see both my parents walking side by side up the path from the barn. I stepped back inside and began stacking the supper dishes, being careful to leave the food near my two older brothers' empty plates.

For the next few days, my parents seemed to be a little more civil toward each other than they had been for the past weeks; nevertheless, Mom seemed to be "walking on eggshells" when Dad was at home.

The episode also left its scars on my brothers and me. Every time Dad would lose his temper and start off on one of his rampages, we would run for cover. We were literally terrified of his temper tantrums and became more and more protective of our mother. Each of us learned rapidly that life was a lot simpler when we conspired with Mom to keep anything from Dad that might incite his wrath. Although she had never asked us to lie to Dad, Mom had become very experienced at "stretching the truth" (the term she preferred for the lies she often told when concealing episodes that would surely bring on Dad's fury).

Through it all, I loved my daddy very much and knew he was important to our family. I was concerned that one of the family members might make him angry enough to cause him to pack his few clothes and leave. I did my utmost to please my father. I never ceased hoping that one day he would pause to give his family just one morsel of kindness or warmth. Somewhere along the way, however, I acquired the notion that his actions were no different from those of any of the other fathers in the area.

Life went on, and no matter how hard the family tried to stay in Dad's good graces, it seemed that one or another of us children was always in trouble with him. One evening he came in from work in one of his rotten moods and immediately began looking for a reason to punish either my brothers or me. Woody and Marvin were usually the unlucky ones to get the "dirty end of the stick;" on this particular evening, however, they would, to my surprise, turn the stick and point it at me.

Keeping a supply of wood for the cook-stove and fireplace seemed to be a never-ending job. Like most fireplaces, ours burned loads of wood but put forth very little heat in return. The prior evening, Dad had given the boys strict orders to cut a supply of wood for the kitchen range and to add to the pile of wood they had been collecting for the fireplace. Woody and Marvin would saw the large, dry logs they had previously dragged in from the woods into proper lengths for the fireplace and chop the smaller branches into correct sizes to fit inside the firebox of the cook-stove. While Woody and Marvin pulled the crosscut saw back and forth across the log, my younger brother, Maynard, sat straddling the log to hold it in place so it would not roll while being cut.

On this memorable evening, I was stationed nearby watching the boys working feverishly cutting the firewood, when Dad walked over to the woodpile looking sullen, as usual. I watched uneasily as he cast his eyes on the handsaw lying on the ground, almost concealed in sawdust. He picked up the handsaw, shook off the sawdust, and began running his fingers along the teeth of the saw. Suddenly, he threw the saw to the ground and moved closer to my brothers. He yelled angrily, "Which one of ye loodle brats 'as been foolin' with my good han' saw?"

Seeing the terror in their eyes, compassion welled up within me for my hard-working brothers. I knew that both boys were in deep trouble. Not wanting to stay around to witness their beatings, I started to move slowly toward the house. While I was cautiously slipping past my brothers, Woody suddenly looked toward me, pointed his finger straight at me, and without blinking an eye, said, "She done it, Daddy! Not me nor Marvin done it. She done it!"

I was shocked to hear Woody placing the blame on me for dulling the saw. I had not touched the saw. I had been standing beside the corncrib, trying to tie a bow in a string that had been left tied to the door. I stopped in my tracks and looked at my brother in total disbelief.

Dad seemed to doubt Woody's statement. He looked at Woody, and then at me. Angrily, he asked me, "Wha'cha doin' with my good han' saw?"

Before I could speak, Woody answered Dad's question for me. "She picked it up'n pulled it 'cross 'is 'n here," he said, pointing toward the crosscut saw.

I yelled at Woody, "I did not. Yu're lyin' an' you know it!"

Marvin quickly chimed in, "Daddy, she'sa one 'at's lyin'. She dunnit jis' like Woody said she dunnit."

Dad had warned my siblings and me that if we were ever to backtalk him that our punishment would be doubled. I feared that my denying the accusation would be useless; therefore, I attempted to shrink in size by tightening every muscle in my small body while my father walked toward me swinging his belt and snapping it like a whip. He grabbed my hand and began whaling my legs and backside unmercifully. With my eyes squinted tightly, I sobbed loudly. I wondered how many licks my father would give me for something I had not done.

Five or six whacks later, Dad dropped my hand and stormed toward the house while working the belt through his belt loops. I moved as close as possible to my brothers, rubbing my welts and sobbing my heart out. Neither of them was moved enough to offer an apology for what they had done; instead, they beamed with relief that I had taken the punishment that rightly should have been theirs. I felt both sadness and anger. I was tempted to tell my two older brothers the same thing I had told the rooster when it had flogged me months earlier.

IX

Ol' Bess

My memories were flowing freely, and pieces of the puzzle were falling into place. I was gleaning titbits of information from each childhood memory that God was allowing me to recall. I could see why and when my family had begun to distrust each other. I realized that my search for the truth was just beginning. In order to understand the whole picture of how the wounds from my childhood had continued to fester throughout my adult life, I once again stopped and asked God to strengthen me while I continued moving through the labyrinth of my youth.

Except for the time he spent on his job, Dad spent very little time away from home. The only close friend he seemed to have was Joe White, the man he had been in the wreck with and who lived on the ridge behind my grandparents' place. Mr. White had become a regular visitor around our house. He and my father enjoyed listening to the prize boxing matches that occasionally aired at night over our battery-operated radio. On the night of the fight, the two men would load their cheeks with chewing tobacco and then place their chairs where they could spit their ambeer into the ashes of the fireplace while they listened to the broadcast.

While the match progressed, both men would become very animated and involved in the fight. When his favorite boxer would land a punch, Mr. White would jump out of his chair, yelling and swinging punches into the air. On the night champion Joe Louis was boxing, Dad would leap up out of his chair, yelling, "Hit 'em ag'in! Hit 'ta son-za-bitch ag'in!"

During other bouts, should the man for whom Dad was rooting lose the fight, Dad's excitement would turn to anger. On a couple of occasions, I witnessed my father pick up the portable radio and throw it against the wall, breaking it into smithereens. Mr. White's excitement would sometimes cause him to swallow his cud of chewing tobacco. I often wondered whether perhaps Mr. White wasn't enjoying watching my father's wild outbursts more than he was enjoying listening to the fights.

The two men soon broadened their Saturday night entertainment to include a few other men whom they had met. They did not frequent the bars; instead, they would ride their horses onto one of the ridges near our house and congregate on the natural-gas pipeline right-of-way. After having tied their horses' bridle reins to nearby trees, the men would each give the man supplying the booze his share of the cost of the liquor. The group would then settle themselves down on the ground to swap wild stories while drinking themselves into drunken stupors.

I was made aware that my wearied mother detested the use of alcohol when she broke down one day and shared her concerns with my siblings and me. She fretted that not only was Dad spending all his free time away from his family but that he was using money for whiskey that was needed for groceries and clothing. When she finally mustered enough courage to approach my father about his unacceptable interest, my father lashed out at her—in the presence of us children—by insisting that the decision of how he lived his life was his and his alone. "Hain't non'na y'ur bizness how I spen' my money," he yelled. "I'm the one 'at goes out'n works like a dog fer 't."

The Saturday night trysts continued throughout the spring, summer, and fall. Mom had apparently accepted the notion that it was futile to complain to my father about the problem; nevertheless, tensions remained high between them, causing him to quarrel with Mom about the most trivial matters.

One night in late fall, after one of the group's Saturday night excursions, Dad and the men mounted their horses and once again set out for their homes. Dad, realizing he was becoming too drunk to think clearly, untied Ol' Bess, the mare he'd traded our mule for, with the expectations that she would carry him safely home. While Ol' Bess made her way through the thick timber to the well-trodden path leading over the hill to our house, Dad teetered back and forth in the saddle. Finally, swaying side to side and too drunk to care, he went crashing to the ground. Fortunately, the obedient horse halted immediately and then stood waiting while my father made several unsuccessful attempts to climb back in the saddle. Unable to remount the horse or crawl to safety, my intoxicated father relinquished his will and curled up on the ground to await his fate.

Sometime later in the night, Dad sobered up enough to realize he was lying on the ground between the front and hind feet of his loyal horse. He scooted his body around to avoid his own vomit and then carefully made his way out from beneath the horse's belly. After staggering around repeatedly in circles, he finally was able to pull himself onto the horse's back. Having gained a new respect for the horse, which had been straddling him for hours, and less respect for himself, Dad and the mare slowly continued on their venture back home.

At last Ol' Bess and her inebriated rider exited the woods and entered the yard behind our house. When Dad recognized his surroundings, he kicked the spurs to the horse's ribs, causing her to gallop. Heading for the barnyard to bed down the horse, Dad bobbed up and down in the saddle until an unexpected violent whack across his throat sent him crashing to the hard ground. Quickly, he grabbed his neck with both hands and felt for blood. Relieved to find his head intact and no evidence of blood, he retrieved the horse's reins and began staggering toward the barn. Although he was still too drunk to walk straight, or to think clearly, he managed to lead the horse to the barnyard. His intentions were to remove the saddle, which he would throw inside the stall, and then to remove the bridle from the horse before turning her loose to run free inside the pasture field.

Assuring himself that he had safely taken care of the mare and her saddle, Dad began weaving his way across the garden to our front yard. Once he reached the house, he crawled up the steps, shoved open the door, and passed out on the living room floor. Forget about Mom, the kids, the horse, and the whole cruel world—Dad was too sick to care.

Later in the morning he awoke with a bad hangover and was feeling too ill to eat breakfast; nevertheless, he forced down a cup of black coffee before heading for the barn, apparently more troubled about Ol' Bess's welfare than that of his family. Once he reached the barnyard, he was puzzled to see the saddle lying outside in front of the barn. Opening the barn door, his eyes widened when he looked over to see Ol' Bess, bridled and standing inside the stall. To his dismay, it dawned on him that he had done the opposite of what he had intended to do the night before. He had put the horse in the stall without removing her bridle and had thrown the saddle outside onto the ground. My humbled father shamefully turned to my brother Woody, who had followed him to the barn, and said, "At dumbass horse's got more sense'n me!" He then ordered Woody to turn the horse outside and to carry the saddle into the barn, while Dad hurried to the back of the barn to upchuck the coffee and anything remaining of the whiskey he had consumed the night before.

With Woody walking closely by his side, Dad sauntered back toward the house. He glanced up at the clothesline as they walked past and said, "'Ere'sa dadblamed culprit 'at jerked me off'na horse's back las' night." Woody later revealed that he had muffled his giggles because he feared that laughing aloud at Dad's foolhardiness might have gotten his own head knocked off.

Dad returned to the house and began blurting out the chilling story of how he had fallen from the horse's back and lain on the ground with Ol' Bess straddling over him. "I 'member hearin'a dull thuds of 'er hooves stompin' at horseflies," he said, shaking his head from side to side. "I cain't believe as how she never stepped on me ner kicked out'ta few brains 'at I do got left."

Staring down at the floor as though too ashamed to look his family in the eyes, Dad continued with the story. "'At poor ol' thang. I put 'er in 'at barn without even givin' 'er a drank a wodder after her gettin' me back ta da house all in one piece." Again, shaking his head from side to side, he somberly looked over at Mom and remorsefully said, "I swear ta God, somebody orta horse whup me."

Neither Mom nor my siblings and I responded while we watched as Dad threw his hands over his eyes and began to weep. "I jist puked up some blood over 'ere at da barn," he finally said. "Looks ta me like God'sa try'na tell me sump'um or a tuther."

"What'cha thank He's a tryin' ta tell ya?" Mom asked.

"Well, I promised 'im if He'd spare my life, 'at I'd never take another drank a whiskey fer's long as I live."

Smiling broadly, Mom shouted, "Glory be ta God! Young'uns, yu'r daddy's fin'ly seen'n da light."

My brothers and I jumped with glee; however, our father did not respond to our jubilation. With his head bowed and his hands in his pockets, he walked through the kitchen and out the back door. I felt both happy and sad. I was happy that Dad's drinking would not make my Mommy cry any longer; still, I was sad because my daddy looked so forlorn. I secretly wished that I could give both of my parents a big hug.

X

Neighbors

When I was barely six years old, my mother quarantined me inside the bedroom that I shared with my brothers. After hanging a blanket over the window to darken the room, since none of the bedroom windows were covered with blinds, she said to me, "You've got a bad case a measles an' you'll hafta stay outta the light whilst you git well er you'll go plum' blind."

I was very concerned, so I spent the next few days and nights in the bedroom, hiding most of the time beneath the blanket on my bed. Mom would carry a bowl of oatmeal to me for my breakfast and then bring me a bowl of beans for my evening meal. At least twice a day, Mom would empty the bucket she had given me to use for a toilet.

Sometime during my confinement, my father came home from work one evening in one of his rages. Seeing my father coming home in a rage was in itself no surprise, since he came home most evenings exasperated. As a rule, the family would have no idea of what had brought on his unpleasantness; however, on this occasion, he seemed to have a good reason for his anger.

Dad had always warned my brothers never to start a fight with other boys, yet he had made it perfectly clear that he expected them to stand and fight when circumstances called for them to defend themselves or the family name. Listening from my bedroom, I was about to find out just how serious he had been when he had warned my brothers.

The family that lived about a quarter mile down the road from our house had a son and a daughter who were about the same ages as Woody and Marvin. On the way home from school that evening, the boy and Woody had exchanged words that had resulted in a fistfight between the two. Woody had arrived home from school with no bruises or other signs of the fight; therefore, none of the family, except for Marvin, was aware that the conflict had taken place.

The moment Dad walked through the door, however, he immediately started grilling my brothers about what had happened between them and the Boden boy. Ordinarily, Dad would have come home, yanked off his belt, and whipped my two brothers—and then asked questions. However, this time was different. He actually wanted to hear my brothers' side of the story. He snapped at Woody and Marvin, "Which one a y'all started 'at t'ere fight with Todd?"

With his voice shaking, Woody said, "He went'n starded da fight hisself."

Dad, seething with anger, asked Woody, "What fer'd he start it?"

Woody began cautiously explaining that for the past week Todd had been ridiculing him about his "big nose." "I got tard'a his big mouth an I tol' 'im I was gonna beat da sh-t outta him if he kep' it up," Woody said.

"Which one a you hit da firs' lick?" Dad asked.

"Well, 'is evenin' when we'uz walkin' from school, Todd went'n hit me in'na back with a rock," Woody replied.

"Yell, when ol' Todd seena 'far' in Woody's eyes, he starded runnin' fer home," Marvin said, giggling at the thought.

"So I guess you ketched'm," Dad stated proudly, looking over at Woody.

Without giving Woody a chance to respond, Marvin said, "Yell, Woody knocked 'im down onna groun' with 'is firs' punch."

Apparently intrigued about having an opportunity to explain for a change, Woody boastfully said, "Yell, 'at big coward wuz bawlin' like a loodle baby when 'e got up off'na groun' wipin' 'is bloody nose on 'is shirt sleeve."

"You mean ta tell me 'at'chu only hit'im one time?" Dad asked.

"Yell'n we know'd he'd try'n git us in trouble 'cause Todd yelled at us after we'd passed his house an' said, 'Y'ur both'n big trouble now! Y'ur gonna git it! Jist'chu waid'll y'ur daddy hears 'bout this, an' he'll beat'chur asses off'n y'all!'"

Dad quickly asked, "What'd he blame Marvin fer?"

"Fer not helpin' 'im out, I reckon," Woody replied.

To my surprise, Dad looked at my brother and said, "If 'at's what really happened, 'hen you better be glad jue whupped 'at no-good-fer-nuthin' brat, er I'd beat da piss outta you myself."

Apparently satisfied with my brothers' explanation, Dad proceeded to explain how he had learned about the incident. He told the family that when he was on his way home from work and had reached the section of road directly in front of the Bodens' home, he was forced to stop the car when he unexpectedly came upon a big boulder blocking the road. When he stepped from the car to roll the huge rock out of his way, he immediately realized that someone had deliberately rolled the rock off the hill and placed it on that particular spot.

The Bodens' house was located about fifty-five feet from the road that Dad had to travel to get to our home. The back of their house sat against one tall mountain, with the front of the house facing the road. Birch Creek, which began at the foot of the mountain behind our house and ran out of the hollow to empty into the Elk River, cut its way between the Bodens' yard and the road. On the upper side of the road, a heavily wooded strip of flat land about thirty feet wide joined the back of another rugged mountain. Dad knew that he was the only person regularly driving an automobile past the Bodens' home. Common sense had told him that the rock had been purposely placed in the road to block his passage.

Todd and his family knew that Dad had a reputation of giving my brothers some pretty hard beatings. Apparently, the family thought that if they could get Dad angry enough before he arrived home, that when he did get home he would immediately take his belt to both my brothers.

Dad told us that he stepped out of his car and was attempting to move the rock out of the road when he looked up to see Mr. Boden approaching with a shotgun pointed in his direction. Dad yelled to Mr. Boden, "What'na Sam Hill jue mean pointin' 'at gun in my d'rection?"

"'Cause y'ur mean-ass boys went'n starded a fight 'ith Todd," Mr. Boden answered, still pointing the gun at Dad.

Now my daddy did not tolerate threats from anybody—gun or no gun. He bravely said to Mr. Boden, "Ol' Man, you better put 'at 'ere gun down 'fore you git y'urself hurt!"

Mr. Boden defiantly said, "If'n you don't promise me 'at you'll give 'em boys a good beatin' jista soon as you git home, 'hen I'mma gonna shoot'chu ri'cheer 'n throw y'ur carcass in 'at 'ere crick."

Before Dad could reply, Todd yelled from the Boden's front yard, "Shoot 'im, Paw! Shoot da son-za-bitch!"

Seeing that Mr. Boden had been momentarily distracted, my "brave" father quickly jerked the shotgun from the angry man's hands and removed the live ammunition from the chamber. "The nex' time you pull a shotgun on me er enybody else, 'hen you better be ready ta shoot," Dad said to the perky old gent.

After dropping the live cartridge into his own pocket, Dad then handed the unloaded weapon back to Mr. Boden. "If'n my boys needs a whuppin, 'hen I'll take care of 'at, an' I shore don't need'a likes of you tellin' me when ta do it either."

Mr. Boden turned tail and headed for his home with Dad still warning him, "If'n eeny y'all ever blocks 'is 'ere road on me ag'in, 'en I'll park my car'n drag y'ur asses outta y'ur house'n beat da tar outta ever' one a y'all."

Woody and Marvin looked relieved. I scampered back to bed as Dad called for his supper. When Mom carried my bowl of beans into the bedroom, I said to her, "I shore do got a brave daddy, Mommy." Mom did not respond.

Todd and my brothers continued to walk the same road to and from school without any further clashes; however, as soon as school was out for the summer, the Boden family moved to some other area. With the house closest to our house now empty, I wondered what the next tenants would be like.

It wasn't long until a new family took up residence in the dilapidated log house that the Bodens had vacated. On the few occasions I had been with my parents when they drove past the new neighbors' house, I had noticed five towheaded boys and a chubby little girl playing in the yard. Their father had been walking in the yard with the aid of crutches, since his right leg was in a full-length cast. He had on each occasion greeted us by lifting his crutch into the air and nodding his head.

Mom had expressed on several occasions a desire to meet the family; however, Dad was not the least bit interested in finding out why, or from where, the strangers had moved to our creek. He let Mom know that he had no intentions of becoming acquainted with the family, so she finally stopped nagging him after he said to her, "Woman, you're jist plain nosy!"

Mom's curiosity about the family finally got the best of her. Early one morning she announced to my brothers and me that she had plans to visit the new family while Dad was at work. She warned us not to tell Dad about the visit since he had warned her to stay away from the strangers. "Go fetch me a arm full'a stove wood," Mom said to my brother, Marvin.

"What'cha gonna do 'ith stove wood?" I asked Mom.

"I'mma gonna bake a pie out'ta 'eeze here blackberries 'at I jist went up onna hill'n picked," she replied.

"Oh boy!" Woody yelled. "You hain't made us a pie fer a long time."

"I'm a gonna make 'his pie ta fetch ta y'ur new neighbors," Mom said.

My younger brother Maynard and I were hovering over the pail of juicy wild blackberries that Mom was inspecting for bugs and debris, when suddenly I snatched a handful of the ripe berries and crammed them into my mouth. Mom slapped at my hand and angrily ordered Maynard and me out of the kitchen. I left the room wondering why my mother was choosing to make a pie for the strangers when she rarely took time to bake a pie for her own family.

I returned to the kitchen and watched as Mom mixed some flour, salt, and lard into a stiff dough, which she dumped onto a paper flour sack that she had torn open and covered with a heavy layer of flour. After kneading the dough for a few seconds, she then dusted more flour on top of the dough. Mom separated the dough into two batches and then picked up a quart bottle of vinegar to use for a rolling pin. She rolled out the dough to fit inside the only pie pan she owned. With sides of the crust patted snugly against the side of the pan, Mom stepped over to the stove and carefully removed the small pot of simmering berries that she'd sweetened and thickened. She poured the berry filling into the unbaked crust. After rolling out another crust, she then placed it over the hot filling and trimmed the extra dough from the two crusts, flattening the edges of the crusts together with the tines of a fork. As she stuck the pie in the hot oven to bake, she looked at me and said, "Git in'na house an' make shore at Nina's got on'na clean dydie."

Later that morning, Mom placed the pan containing the piping hot pie on a folded towel and handed it to me. "You curry 'is hot pie'n' be curful'n don't drop it," she warned. The hot pie's aroma drifting throughout the room aroused my taste buds, causing my hunger pangs to peak; nevertheless, I spoke not a word as I obediently and cautiously held onto the pie and started down the steps. Mom swung my baby sister across her hip and took our toddler Arnold, by the hand. With my brothers and me in the lead, we started walking down the dusty road toward our neighbors' house. The tempting smell of the freshly baked crust wafting its way through the country air was more than I could bear. I held the pie with my left hand and balanced it against my belly. Slowly, I slipped my right hand over to the pie and pinched off a small chunk of the crust. Just as I pushed the crumbs into my mouth, my mother yelled to me, "Bethel! You quit dat stealin' 'at pie 'fore I kick y'ur hine en'." I heard the anger in her voice and almost choked on the piece of crust. Thoughts of taking a detour into the woods where I could snitch more of the pie were racing through my mind, when suddenly I stumbled and almost dropped the hot pie. I looked down and realized that our old mother cat must be craving the pie as much as I was craving it. Shoving the cat out of my way with my foot, I obediently continued down the road.

Just before we reached the neighbors' property, Mom seemed to be having second thoughts about the visit. She sternly warned my siblings and me again, "Now young'uns, don'ch'all tell Daddy 'bout me makin' 'is here pie." As for me, I wasn't about to tell Dad anything. I still remembered how scared I had been just a few weeks earlier when he had slapped her jaws over the broken earthenware barrel. Although I knew that Mom was going against Dad's wishes, I was excited about finally getting to meet the new family. I just hoped that it would be worth the risk we were taking.

As we approached the residence, the mother and father were sitting outside the crudely built house that had at one time been a barn. The man was small in stature and was sitting on the front stoop with his crutches lying in the grass beside his cast-bound, outstretched leg. The mother was an obese woman with straight brown hair, cut short like a man's haircut. I had never seen a woman with her hair cut above her ears. She was sitting on a wooden bench with her back leaning against the side of the house. The white-haired boys were running back and forth through the yard. The girl was nowhere in sight.

When we approached the creek in front of their house, the family scattered like scared rabbits. The boys ran to the back of the house while the mother jumped up and waddled inside. The man was the only person not to run from us. After crossing the creek and entering the yard, Mom looked up at the man and timidly said, "Hidee Neighbor, I'm Marthy Lesher'n I live on up in'na holler."

The puny, ugly man did not look at Mom when she spoke to him; instead, his eyes focused on the scrumptious blackberry pie I was holding. He did not reveal his name nor ask us inside his house. I could see that all he was interested in was the mouth-watering pie that I was begrudgingly holding out toward him.

"Howdy, Marthy," he finally said, reaching out for the warm pie.

Awkwardly, Mom again spoke, "I seed j'ur broke leg, so I figger't you'd like 'is here pie I jis' baked fer ya."

He turned his head to the side, and out squirted a mouthful of am-beer. Reluctantly, I stepped a little closer so that he could take the pie from my hands. Without taking time to look at the little girl who was attached to those long, skinny arms, he made a greedy smacking noise with his mouth before saying, "Mmmm, 'at shore does look like a mighty good pie." He took the pie from my hands and then looked over at Mom. "Yes, siree, Miss Marthy, 'his shore looks good," he said, while making a weird giggling sound.

Shifting the baby to her other hip, Mom stood there in the yard looking very uncomfortable. Neither she nor the man seemed to know what to say next. Finally, Mom turned to leave. "C'mon young'uns, we better git back 'cross 'at crick so y'ur neighbor can git in'na house an' eat 'is pie," she said. The man smiled broadly, exposing a mouthful of brown teeth rotted down to half their normal size. Slowly Mom started creeping back through the lush, green grass toward the creek, with my brothers and me trailing behind. The man's wife had stayed inside the house, and the boys we had seen running to the back of the house earlier had disappeared from sight. The only sounds I could hear were the sounds the bugs and birds were making, the thumping of the crutch as the stranger hobbled toward his door, and the clanging of a cowbell in the distance.

With Mom leading the way back across the foot log, I felt disappointed and a little angry. I stepped off the end of the log and looked up at Mom, who was standing in the road waiting for the last of her brood to cross the creek. "We los' a purfec'ly good pie an' we didn' even learn 'eir names," I remarked.

"Aw, shet up y'ur complainin'," Mom said to me. I felt a little better when she suggested that since we were already close to our grandparents' home, we would go on down the hollow to see Grandpa and Aunt Sissy. Grandma would be in town cleaning houses for the city folk; nevertheless, I was tickled to go anywhere except back home where the smell of blackberry pie would still be lingering throughout the house.

I skipped down the road through the dust, knowing I might as well forget about the "strange" family. They, no doubt, were devouring the blackberry pie that rightfully should have been ours in the first place; besides, if the rest of the family looked anything like the father, then I didn't care whether I ever met them.

Mom seemed to sense what I was thinking when she looked down at me and, breaking the silence, said, "If 'at 'ere woman's 'at 'ere stupid, 'hen I don't keer'f I ever meet 'er er not." I giggled and ran down the road toward Grandpa's house. Grandpa would probably have all of us angry at him before we left, but it would still be a treat for us to get to visit with him.

A few days later, everything was going along as usual, and no one had mentioned the new family. Mom had left me at the house to take care of the younger children while she and my older brothers went up the hill to pick blackberries for canning. Before leaving the house, Mom had filled a tub with warm, soapy water, which she had set outside on the ground, for me to wash the canning jars she would be needing. I dreaded washing the jars because no matter how careful I was, my mother would always find some of the jars not meeting her approval. I knew what she would say to me before she said it. She would shove the jar in my face and yell at me, "Git back out 'ere ta 'at tub 'n lick y'ur calf over!" (As a mother cow licks her calf, she must do it thoroughly. If she doesn't, then she'll need to lick her calf over.

Mom would always let me know when I hadn't done my job thoroughly.)

Back in the berry patch, Mom had sent Woody off the hill to ask the "strange" neighbors for the correct time. When he reached their house, there was no one in sight. He walked up to the door and could see the mother sitting inside. "Hey! Can ya gi'me a right time, please?" he yelled to her.

The woman walked over closer to the door and asked, "Yell, wha'chu say?"

"I need ta know what time it is," Woody said again.

The big woman walked back inside the room out of his sight. Momentarily she returned, holding her little finger on her right hand slightly left of being straight up, and her index finger on her left hand pointing down toward the floor. She then said to my astonished brother, "'At clock's big han's straight downards, 'n its loodle'ns nurly straight upperds."

When Mom and my brothers came off the hill, they were still laughing about how the woman had informed Woody that the hour had been half past eleven. Laughing and shaking her head from side to side, Mom said, "'At'ere woman's dumber'n ary bank mule."

My brothers began mocking what the ignorant woman had said. I giggled but found myself wondering why Mom had really sent Woody to their house. The thought crossed my mind that maybe Dad was right when he had accused Mom of being "just plain nosy."

After the event, every time one of us asked for the correct time, we were told, "The big han's straight downerds, anna loodle'ns almost straight upperds." My tender heart ached for the poor woman responsible for all the fun; indeed, she was stigmatized as being "stupid" for as long as she lived in the community.

The Cragle family lived on the opposite side of the creek from the new family. One Sunday, shortly after the new family had moved next door to them, Mrs. Cragle invited the new neighbors to visit Reamer Tabernacle, the small country church on the ridge that my family and our neighbors had begun attending. Mrs. Cragle had informed Mom that our neighbor's last name was Haskel.

On Sunday, when my Dad drove into the churchyard with our family of eight, we were surprised to see Mr. Haskel and his six children standing nearby. The mother was absent, as for some unknown reason she always stayed at home. Mom had told me it was because the man was ashamed of his wife's stupidity.

Without pausing to speak to the family, Mom walked toward the door of the church with us children filing behind. The new neighbor man suddenly stepped over and reached out to shake her hand. "Howdy ag'in, Miss Marthy. 'At dere pie ya gimme shore was good," he said. "I got'chur pie tin atta house, 'n you can stop by anytime you wanna git it."

Mom hurried inside without responding to our neighbor's remark. I sucked in a mouthful of air and quickly looked up at Dad. From his expression, I knew his mind was not going to be on the church services for the next few hours. I cringed as I hurried past Mr. Haskel. I was feeling as scared as my mother looked.

With Mom cradling Nina in her arms, she led the way to the center of the church where she rowed up the remaining five of us children on one of the crudely built wooden pews. Customarily, all the men of the church sat together, separate from their wives and children, during the church services. I watched as Dad entered the church and slowly stomped down the aisle past us. He sauntered over and sat down on the left front pew, where he routinely sat while "professing religion."

I looked across the aisle at the left side of the church where the six Haskel children were seated together on one pew. The oldest boy looked to be Marvin's age. He had buckteeth, and his short-cropped white hair stuck straight up like the bristles on a brush. The five boys and one chubby little girl looked frightened. I whispered to Woody, who was also gawking at them, "Ey shore are ugly, hain't 'ey?"

Mr. Haskel hobbled inside and sat down on the pew beside my father. I could see that Dad was already seething inside, and having to sit beside the man responsible for his agitation was not helping matters. I dreaded the ride back home and wondered whether maybe my mother was not thinking the same thing. Even I knew that she had defied my father after he had warned her to stay away from the new family. Not only had he been made aware of the forbidden visit, but, in fact, he now knew that a homemade pie had been delivered to the man who was now sharing a pew with him.

When my father would lose his temper in a place where he could not vent his anger, his countenance would change, and he would flex his jaw muscles as if gritting his teeth. I glanced across the aisle of the small church several times during the morning service and noticed that his jaw muscles seemed to be hard at work. I wondered whether Mom had noticed the same thing.

Once the service had ended, which seemed to be much quicker than usual, Dad hurried out of the church and immediately went straight to our car. Mom, my brothers, and I knew from previous experiences that we had better follow in close pursuit; therefore, I shoved the smaller children into the car before I quickly crowded myself onto the back seat. Dad had already begun cranking the old Model T Ford, and as the engine fired, he quickly jumped into the driver's seat and drove the car out of the churchyard. While we chugged along out the ridge road, I peeked over at Dad and noticed that his anger was no longer simmering; it now had reached the boiling point. I sat back nervously and waited for the fireworks to begin.

I had been led to believe that a wife was supposed to be under the control of her husband and was required to obey him in the same way his children were taught to obey. I knew that my mother had deliberately defied my father and would now have to pay for her actions. Concern and compassion welled up within me.

Once we were out of hearing range of the church, the inevitable uproar began. "So you tuck'im a pie, didgee?" Dad yelled, as he began grilling Mom about the visit with the Haskels. Mom ignored Dad's accusation and sat staring straight ahead. My heart seemed to jump into my throat when Dad reached over with his right hand and grabbed my mother by her left arm. With fire in his eyes, he yelled, "You deef er sump'n? Answer me, woman!"

"Now, Bud, all 'em young'uns wuz with me, an' 'ey know I didn' do nuthin' wrong." Taking a deep breath, Mom continued, "An' 'sides 'at, 'at ol' man's uglier'n a mud fence. Who in'na world'd want him?"

"Yell, ya not only give 'at ugly man a pie 'hind my back, but'cha kep' it a secret too," he yelled. "Confounda, confound luck! Y'aint got no time ta bake a son-za-bitchin' pie fer me an'na young'uns, but chee not only tuck anuff time ta bake 'im a pie—ya snuck off'n tuckit to 'im." And on and on Dad ranted.

My brothers and I sat quietly on the back seat, afraid to move. Mom turned her face to the side and stared out the window. I wondered whether being at church had done any of us any good. One thing was certain—we were hearing a longer and harder sermon on the way home than we had heard at church.

When we reached "the Low Gap," Dad maneuvered the car around and headed lickety-split up the hollow toward our home. Bouncing along through the creek crossings, over the humps, and across the rocks and ruts in the road, my brothers and I were finding it very difficult to sit upright on the seat. I pulled Arnold, our toddler, out of the floor and onto my lap, holding onto him with all my might. Four-year-old Maynard scooted down onto the floor and covered his ears with his hands as Dad continued to blast Mom with insults.

Finally, we reached the end of the road. Dad stopped the car under the big sycamore tree and, as he exited the car, gave Mom one final warning. "If'n ya know what's good fer ya, you'll stay 'way from 'at house down 'ere," he angrily shouted. He also had a warning for my brothers and me. "If'n she ever goes near 'at house ag'in, you loodle brats better tell me 'bout it er I'll beat'a piss outta all of y'all when I do find out," he said. I scooted out of the car, grabbed my two little brothers by their hands, and rushed toward the house. Having witnessed my father's angry reaction to our first visit to the Haskel's house, I softly whispered to my brother Maynard, "I wonder how Mommy 'spects ta git 'er pie pan back from 'at man."

Mom never again mentioned a desire to visit the family; in fact, she avoided speaking to Mr. Haskel, even while at church. Dad, on the other hand, held short conversations with Mr. Haskel every Sunday when they met at the church. The Haskels moved to another county near the end of summer, and I would always remember these facts from their brief time as our neighbors: my father did not trust my mother; my mother was prone to disobey my father; I was becoming more and more uncomfortable as our mother continued to ask us to keep the truth from our father; and Mrs. Haskel had been ostracized by my family because of what appeared to be her ignorance.

After learning that the two oldest boys were named Ferdinand and Luther, I decided, in my opinion, that their names were as ugly as the boys themselves. With memories like these, I was happy that the old log house was once again vacant. Recalling at the time our family's relationship with both families that had relocated after having lived near our home, I hoped the log house would remain empty for a very long time.

XI

A Precious Memory

Spring was just weeks away, and the earth was beginning to bustle with a new beginning. Here and there, brightly colored flowers had begun to poke their heads from beneath their winter blankets, adding splashes of great splendor to the landscape that was slowly coming to life.

Vivid, orange-breasted robins with their heads held erect could be seen throughout the valley as they searched for bugs and worms. Bluebirds were chattering cheerfully as they gathered materials to make nests for the new baby birds that would soon be welcomed into their families. Mom had already sown a bed of leaf lettuce and had planted onion sets in the garden that she had plowed just a few days earlier. Indeed, springtime in our hollow was being welcomed warmly by both man and beast.

One evening, an unexpected visitor appeared at our door. After having joined our family for a meal of fried potatoes, pinto beans, and cornbread, Mr. White retired to the living room to visit with my father. With no fights airing over the radio, he and Dad made themselves comfortable, while Woody and Marvin pulled out a checkerboard they had made from a piece of cardboard. Using shelled kernels of red corn and yellow corn for the checkers, both brothers stretched out on the floor with the checkerboard between them. Propped up on their elbows with their chins cupped in their hands, they began the competition. Dad had turned his wooden chair around backwards and sat straddling the chair, with his arms folded across the top of the chair back and his chin resting on his arms. Mr. White was seated upright in his chair, a big chew of tobacco wallowing in his mouth. From time to time, he would rear back on the hind legs of the chair, tip his head back, place his right index and middle fingers over his mouth, and then, while spreading the fingers apart and pressing them against the bottom and sides of his lips, suddenly rock himself forward and let go with a mouthful of ambeer into the ashes in the fireplace.

Mom was expecting her eighth child and had put the smaller children to bed, having then retired herself. With the sun having set and darkness moving in upon the land, a chill had engulfed the head of the sleepy hollow where we lived. Dad soon moved over to the fireplace and began building a small fire with wood that my brothers had carried inside earlier. I snuck over and sat on the floor near the warmth of the fire, listening to the two men's conversation and watching my brothers play checkers.

As the evening wore on, Mr. White suddenly asked my father if he would consider trading our little farm for his place on Dry Ridge. From listening to Mr. White's description of his property, it sounded to me as if he would be foolish to trade for our property, since his property was nothing less than a piece of paradise. He and Dad were in agreement that since they were both renting from the same land company, there should be no problem with the two men switching properties. Dad agreed to think about the deal.

When the men's conversation changed to tales about haunted houses, my brothers abandoned their game and began listening intently. Each man seemed to be trying to tell a spookier story than the other. Both men and my brothers were totally mesmerized by the stories. With the dim light from the kerosene lamp and the flickering flames from the fireplace casting spooky shadows across the floor near my feet—and with a ghost hiding behind every shadow—I moved over and crawled onto my daddy's lap, shivering from fright.

My father tenderly put his arm around me and pulled my face against his warm chest. The strong smell of the Prince Albert pipe tobacco he was smoking filled my nostrils and stung my eyes; nevertheless, my heart danced with joy while I reveled in this special moment of tenderness and warmth that I had always craved from my daddy. With one of his strong hands on my back and the other stroking my skinny little legs, I soon fell fast asleep.

Sometime later, I awoke to see Mr. White removing the carbide light from his hard hat. I watched sleepily as he unscrewed the top of the light and spat down onto the dry carbide inside the base of the light. After tightening the top onto the base, the gas from the wet carbide began forcing its way out through the center opening in the reflector of the light. He then flipped a small flint wheel, also located on the reflector, which ignited the gas. After opening a small water valve that allowed water to drip slowly down inside the base onto the carbide, Mr. White hooked the light back onto his hard hat and walked out the door, leaving the unpleasant odor of the carbide lingering throughout the small room.

With Dad's friend on his way home and my brothers ushered off to bed, my father carried me into the bedroom and laid me on the small daybed. Whimpering, I said to my daddy, "I'm skeered uv'a dark."

He tenderly stroked my face and whispered, "Go on back ta sleep. Daddy'll be right ou'cheer in'na room next ta y'urn, an' I hain't gonna let nuthin' hur'chu." He pulled the quilts up over my shoulders and then bent over and kissed me on the cheek. "G'night," my daddy whispered, while slipping out of the dark room.

I was seven years old and had never before been hugged or cuddled by either of my parents. I had no way of knowing at the time that the tender affection my father had just shown me would have to last me for a lifetime. Throughout all the heartaches and pain he would later cause in my life, I would never forget and would always be thankful for that one precious moment.

XII

Dry Ridge

Another dark cloud had settled down around my mother, and her only source of relief seemed to come from expressing her frustrations to my brothers and me. Having no one else with whom she could talk, she shared with us that she was convinced that swapping our place in the hollow for the property on Dry Ridge was a mistake.

Finally she attempted to reason with Dad. "Bud, 'at ridge is too windy'n cold in'na win'ertime an' too hot'n dry in'na summertime," she said.

"Now, Marthy. Hain't nothin' ta 'at excuse. You jis' wanna stay down here on Ol' Shit Crick close ta y'ur mommy," Dad sarcastically replied. "I knowed you'd ack like 'his, an' it hain't gonna do ya nary bitta good."

The rent on the property would remain $15.00 annually, the same amount Dad was paying for our little farm. Although the house was only one mile past where our family had lived on the ridge a few years earlier, Mom had never seen the house into which Dad was intent on moving us; however, she was confident that it would not compare with our property in the hollow that our family had worked so hard to improve.

She once again stressed to Dad her main concern, that once we moved to the ridge, we would experience water shortages during dry weather. "If'n 'at happens, 'hen I'll fetch wodder from the school bus garage. An' 'sides 'at, I done tol' Joe I'uz ready ta swap," Dad said.

Mom did not say another word but softly began to cry while Dad stormed out the door after yelling over his shoulder, "Gitta stuff ready 'cause we're movin' tamarr."

"How'd jue know 'hey hain't no wodder on the ridge?" I asked my mother.

"'Cause we lived out 'ere fer a few months," she said.

"In'na same house whur Daddy wants us ta move to?" I asked in astonishment.

"No, we didn't live 'at fer out'ta ridge. We lived in 'at big white house right 'fore you git ta the church," she said.

"'At'sa purty house! Why'd ju move 'way from 'ere?"

"'Cause 'at ol' man 'at owned 'at place worked us ta death'n tuck ever'thang we raised," she said. She explained to me that she and Dad had agreed to rent the house and instead of paying the owner in money (the property was not owned by the land company but was privately owned), they had agreed to give the owner one-half of all the produce that they were able to raise on the farm. When the time had come for them to divide the yield, however, the owner had insisted on taking more than his share.

"I cain't 'member us livin' out t'ere, " I said.

"You was borned out t'ere," Mom said. She wiped the tears from her eyes and went on to explain that she had been in the cornfield helping Dad cut and load corn stalks onto the sled when she went into labor.

"Whur was Woody'n Marvin at?" I asked.

"'Ey was with us in'na field," Mom said. She went on to explain how she'd had to be loaded onto the sled by Dad when she had gone into labor there in the cornfield. "Y'ur daddy jis' laid me on'na sled'n hauled me ta the house'n put me in'na bed while he went'n fetched the doctor." She explained that our family had moved off the ridge shortly after I was born.

On a beautiful Saturday morning in March 1943, to Mom's chagrin, my father loaded our big sled with a load of our crude furnishings and secured the load by wrapping a heavy rope over and around the furniture. While he tied the ends of the rope to the posts on the sides of the sled, he informed Mom that Mr. White would be using his own horse and sled to move his belongings. "'At orta cut our movin' time in half, 'cause we kin both haul each other's stuff on'na return trips," he said. He continued while Mom looked sadly on, "Jis'chu an'na young'uns foller the path up'pa holler 'hind y'ur momma's place an' on up'pa hill ta the house settin' 'cross a red-clay ridge road."

"Bud, it'sa gonna take us a spell walkin' 'at fer 'cause I cain't git'n a hurry," Mom answered.

Without responding to Mom's pitiful attempt at asking him to allow her to ride in our car, which he would later be driving to the ridge, Dad turned to Woody and said, "I'll fetcha chicken crate on'na ridge when I fetcha car." Transporting the chickens would be no problem, since we had already lost the majority of them to the foxes and opossums. "Woodrow, you'n Marvin fetch Ol' Brownie'n a cats'n dogs, an' be curful 'ith 'at cow," Dad yelled, as the horse pulled the load of furniture away from the house.

Mom obediently gathered her brood together and set out down the valley toward Grandma's house. She shoved my baby sister Nina in my direction and said, "Here, Bethel. You can take keeruv 'is here young'un."

I was seven years and five months old at the time, and Nina was two years and two months. I had planned to make the walk an exciting adventure, but, straddled with the care of my little sister, I felt cheated. "Cain't Woody'n Marvin take keera her?" I asked.

"You heared what I said!" Mom barked at me.

I squatted on the ground, my back to Nina, then grabbed her arms and pulled her up onto my back. Although she was small for her age, she was a heavy load for me to carry. Slowly, I stood to my feet and began following my mother, my brothers, and our animals down the road toward Grandma's house. My eyes were fixed on my mother as she waddled down the road. Because of her bulging belly, I had already begun to suspect that she was expecting baby number eight.

Grandpa and Grandma walked out onto their porch to greet us when we approached their house. My suspicion of Mom being with child was confirmed when Grandma said, "Marthy, y'know 'atchu could have 'at young'un any day now, an' you ortn't be walkin' up 'at steep hill. What'na shit's 'eeze young'uns gonna do'f you git down on us any 'ay?"

"Aw shucks, Mommy. If'n I git down, I'll have 'em young'uns load me on'na back'a the cow an' she can curry me a rest'a the way,"

Grandpa, squirting a mouthful of ambeer into the yard, shook his head in disgust and said, "'At man a yern's bound'a be crazy, movin' 'is fam'ly back on 'at God-fersook ridge!"

Woody and Marvin had been giving me breaks by carrying my sister for short distances. Much too soon to suit me, she had once again been deposited at my feet. Moaning and groaning, I managed to pull her up onto my hip and, holding onto her with both hands, continued to creep up the hollow behind my mother. I had no idea of where we were going or what we would find when we got there; still, although I was apprehensive, I was very excited. With Grandma's question to Mom still ringing in my ears, I uneasily looked back down the hollow we were about to leave. If Mom was going to give birth en route to our new destination, then I hoped she would let us know before we went farther into the wilderness. I stayed as close behind her as possible.

The month of March is known as the windy month in West Virginia, and although the wind was whistling through the trees lining the hills on either side of the footpath, the sun was cozy and warm. The boys stopped to allow the cow to drink from the creek that had long ago cut its path down the sleepy hollow. I knew I would miss the creeks and the soft, rushing sound the water made as it rippled over the countless rocks strewn throughout the creek bed.

After our little clan had made our way to about half a mile above our grandparents' place, I realized we had been traveling through Grandpa's pasture field when we approached the wooden bars in the fence at the end of the property that my grandparents had been renting from the land company since 1929. Mom pushed back three or four of the bars so we could exit through the barbed wire fence. After our family and the cow had crossed over to the other side, she replaced the bars and walked ahead to where the path crossed the creek for the final time.

"Come 'ere'n take 'is here young'un fer 'nuther piece so's y'ur sister can rest," Mom said wearily to Woody. Looking at the mountain looming before us and realizing how difficult it had been for me to carry Nina on level ground, I doubted that I would be able to tote her to the top of the steep, rugged mountain.

I watched as my mother placed her feet on the slippery rocks and clumsily maneuvered her way to the other side of the shallow creek that ran alongside the base of the pristine mountain. One by one, we children followed, the older children helping their younger siblings to the other side of the creek. Up the hill, over the rocks, through mud and wet leaves we trudged, often sliding back a step for each two steps we had taken. I knew we were on the right path when I looked down at the sled tracks that had cut deep grooves in the wet earth. Knowing Dad would soon be coming back off the hill with a load of Mr. White's furniture, Mom ushered the family up the mountain.

A short time later we reached the first plateau on the side of the mountain. I stopped on the soft, green moss and took Nina from my brother's back. Apparently frightened from being perched on the side of the mountain, my baby sister threw her arms around my neck and held on tightly. Slowly, I labored up the hill with my heavy load, but within minutes I was forced to stop and rest. After sitting the toddler on the cool, damp ground, I turned to look back to see how far we had traveled. Large beech trees lined the bank of the meandering creek. Maple, white oak, hickory, and elm were among the many trees towering toward the heavens. Here and there, majestic, blue-green cedars stood out among the budding redbud and dogwood trees that were breaking forth with new life. The odor of rotting wood filled the air from the many dead tree trunks that had fallen to the ground to decay.

Birds of all sizes and descriptions noisily chattered and fluttered throughout the forest, warning each other that humans were invading their tranquil domain. Down over the side of the hill, I watched as two chipmunks frolicked in the leaves. Although I was not sure where we were going, I was certainly enjoying the new adventure. The hills were both beautiful and peaceful. I reached down and picked a leaf off the mountain teaberry plant and put it into my mouth. Feeling all bubbly inside, I began to realize that Grandpa had been wrong. God had not forsaken this land. Why, His handiwork was on display for as far as the eye could behold.

Interrupting my thoughts, Mom yelled to me to keep pace with the rest of the family. "I hafta rest," I replied. "I cain't hardly curry Nina."

"Woody, wh'on't chu lead'a cow an' let Marvin fetch'a baby?" Mom pleaded.

Marvin walked back, picked up our sister, and took off up the side of the mountain. I breathed a mouthful of fresh air and continued the climb. I was thankful that Mom had slowed to a snail's pace, and as I approached my weary, haggard mother, I listened to her assuring the smaller, whining children that we were almost to the top of the mountain.

A short time later, I looked up to see Marvin, still holding my baby sister, standing on an uprooted, rotting tree trunk and gazing back at us. Trying to assure myself that he was not waiting for me to give him a break from toting our baby sister, I called out to my mother and said, "Mommy, wh'on't chu rest fer a loodle bit?"

"Yell," Marvin said. "You rest too, an' 'en you can curry Nina rest'a the way."

"I cain't curry Nina any futher," I said breathlessly, realizing what a mistake I had made by suggesting the break.

With the heavy forest blocking our view from seeing where the mountain would level out, Mom and I seated ourselves on a big boulder that had dislodged from the road bank and rolled to the edge of the path after one of the hard winter freezes had thawed. Woody stopped and tied the cow to a tree. Marvin jumped off the log and stood Nina at my feet, where she immediately grabbed onto my aching legs. While my two oldest brothers began grabbing handfuls of rocks and throwing them over the side of the mountain, aimed at a spot on a large sycamore tree trunk, my younger brothers stood in the path, whining.

Our little family rested for a few minutes, and then, even though she was exhausted, Mom insisted that we move on when she heard Dad coming down the hill with a load of Mr. White's furniture. She pulled herself off the rock and stubbornly but cautiously continued with the laborious climb. Although I could hear Dad yelling at the horse, I could see nothing ahead but more mountains. I wondered how much farther from civilization we would need to travel. Once again, I pulled my sister up the side of my body and scooted her onto my hip. I sure hoped Mom had been right when she had said we were almost to the top of the mountain.

Up the hill we trudged, until finally we could see Dad going down a less-steep haul road, the sled loaded with Mr. White's furniture. I asked Mom why we weren't traveling the haul road and was told that Dad had assured her that the steeper road was much shorter.

Although at the time I had no idea how strenuous climbing the mountain must be on my pregnant mother, I was struck by her apparent tenacity and pioneer spirit. "Git on up'pa hill 'cause I can see the top now!" she yelled. I sighed with relief.

When we finally emerged from the heavy forest, Woody, yanking on the rope tied to the cow's halter, crowded himself and the cow past Mom as they entered into the edge of a field of stubbly weeds and small shrubs. Finding new strength, my siblings and I hastened through the small white pines lining the footpath through the field.

The dogs began yelping excitedly when they jumped a rabbit from its hiding place in the pines and chased it across the path just ahead of us.

At last, Mom, my brothers, and I stopped and gawked at the little shack we would soon be calling our home. Knowing we were now close enough for her to walk the rest of the way, I quickly dropped Nina to the ground, grabbed her by the hand, and half-dragged her toward the house. Just in front of me, Woody yanked at the rope and tried to force the milk-cow to move out a little faster. Having been left behind to saunter the rest of the way alone, Mom yelled to Woody, "Stop 'at runnin' 'at cow 'fore she bruises 'er bag!"

My brothers and I, yelling with delight, crossed the red-clay road and entered the driveway that ran right up to the house's front porch. None of us had thought to stop to see whether the house was still occupied by Mrs. White and her children, when, suddenly, Mr. White appeared from the backside of the house, leading his mare that was pulling a sled-load of household goods that looked worse than ours. He stopped in the front yard and waited for Mom to approach. "The woman an'na kids done went off'n the hill out on'na point," he said to my mother. "The house's all yern."

Dad on Dry Ridge.

Back out the driveway to the roadway I ran. Looking down at the deep ruts in the road, I took note that the narrow sections between the ruts were wide enough to accommodate the wheels of a car, so I figured that if anybody could drive on the road, it would be my daddy. He had always assured the family that he was one of the best drivers around. Quickly, I swung back by the house just in time for Mom to grab me and put me to work.

Later in the day, as I pondered the difference between our new ridge property and the home we had just vacated, I wondered whether the move onto the ridge would bring my father out of his doldrums. I asked myself why, if he had liked our property in the hollow, had he referred to it as "Ol' Shit Crick"?

For the next few days, I did all I could to help Mom make the old shack a more comfortable place to live. I, for one, was certainly excited and happy with our new residence. I was also encouraged as I noticed that Dad's attitude seemed to be changing, that he had been taking an active part in sprucing up the dilapidated shack and the grounds around it. There was nothing to indicate that in the very near future, my own father would cause my small world to come crashing down around me.

XIII

Our New Home

Summertime had arrived, and things seemed to be going very well around our new place. I now had a three-month-old baby brother named Thomas. My father seemed to be more at ease, and Mom, since Dad's public job consumed most of his daylight hours, had been working hard doing both her and Dad's share of the work.

School was out for the summer, and I would be starting first grade in the fall. Since I wanted to enjoy the summer and our new surroundings on the ridge, I tried to push the thought of school to the back of my mind. I knew that, upon my father's request, the elementary school principal had deferred my attending school the previous year because of the distance I would be required to walk to and from school. I tried not to think about having to leave the security of my home to attend school.

Our property had burst forth with its own share of rugged beauty. The spacious, level land that had been cleared to accommodate our ridge property had been cut out in the middle of a heavily wooded area. The red-clay road, which I would learn later became at times a sea of red mud, was now dry and firm enough for the car to pass over.

Although I did not realize it at the time, our frame dwelling was merely another isolated shack located about four miles from town. The house had been built years earlier from green, untreated lumber. Like most of the houses in our area, the outside walls had never been painted. Its warped boards had faded to a silver-gray from the years of exposure to the sun and elements. The ends of the boards near the ground had been eaten away by decay.

The insides of the boards used to build the outside walls of the house served also as the inside walls, affording no insulation. The cracks between the boards in the walls of the bedroom that my five siblings and I shared allowed the sunshine to peek through during summer and, we would later learn, snow to blow inside during the winter.

The colorful wallpaper on the living room walls had been papered over so many times that it appeared to be at least an inch thick. In some places, especially in the corners, the paste had failed to hold the paper to the walls. The loose, sagging wallpaper had been haphazardly nailed to the walls with roofing nails.

I had watched Mom hang wallpaper when we lived in our house in the hollow. To adhere the paper to the walls, she had made a paste by mixing together powdered starch and a small amount of water and then slowly stirring the mixture into a pot of simmering water until it had reached the desired consistency. After cooling the mixture, Mom had dipped a rag into the sticky goo, smeared the paste onto the backs of the previously cut lengths of wallpaper, and then hung the sticky strips onto the wall boards, smoothing out the wrinkles with a clean cloth. As I stood looking at the tattered wallpaper on the walls of our new residence, I wondered when my mother would find time to replace it.

The top surface on the wall-to-wall linoleum that covered the rough, uneven boards on the living room and kitchen floors had been worn through in the heavily trafficked areas to expose the black undercoating. Both the linoleum and the wallpaper in the kitchen and living room were designed with large red roses on a gray background.

The dwelling had been divided into four rooms. Needless to say, the 12' by 15' living room was crowded when our growing family of nine gathered inside. My family had always referred to the living room as "the house." For example, should Mom be in the kitchen and need a chair brought in from the living room, she would say to one of us children, "Go in'na house an' fetch me a cheer." The words *living room* were among many others that my parents verbalized as being too sophisticated for our family's vocabulary.

The fireplace in the small living room had been built from flat stones carried in from the fields. The firewalls, hearth, and chimney had been chinked with red-clay mud. Between several of the rocks, the chinking had dried and cracked, leaving gaping spaces. In numerous places, small bees were busily at work boring tiny holes into the dried mud. The open hole for the stovepipe in the living room ceiling was evidence that the crudely made fireplace had not provided sufficient heat during the blustery winters. For now, however, winter was months away, and how they would heat the house seemed to be the furthest thing from my parents' mind.

My siblings and I shared the 9'x21' bedroom on the backside of the house. Woody and Marvin's full-sized bed, with rusty coil springs that supported a cotton-filled mattress, had recently been passed down from my parents' bed after they had bought a new mattress and was placed in the back of the room against the outside wall. My brother Maynard slept alone in a small cot placed against the opposite side of the room.

At the time, I was sharing the second full-sized bed with my little sister and our brother Arnold; however, every two years after the birth of a new baby, the toddler at the time would be added to my bed. I had no store-bought mattress on my bed; instead, Mom had sewn several feed sacks together to make a tick, which she had filled with straw gathered from the fields. Once she had placed my homemade mattress onto the coil bedsprings, the entire bedroom would smell like freshly cut hay.

After sleeping on the ticking for a few nights, I would often leave the room with scratches on my legs and backside, caused by the sticks, briars, and thorns that had been crammed carelessly inside the ticking along with the straw. I would also soon learn, to my dismay, that after a few nights of bed-wetting by my siblings, that they and I would often crawl out of bed smelling more like ammonia than new-mown hay. By the grace of God, however, I didn't complain and, having no choice, soon learned to accept what I could not change.

The small bedroom, shared by my parents and the baby, was barely large enough to accommodate their full-sized bed and was squeezed in between the kitchen and a small stoop at the back entrance. The front porch, about five feet deep and running the width of the house, was in bad need of repair. On the day we moved to the ridge, Mom had walked out on the porch and, after looking around, said to me, "Good God Uhmighty! The win' cain't be vury strong up 'ere, or 'is here rotten thang'd be scaddered all o'er the hillside."

None of the windows or doors had screens. The threat of the house becoming infested with flies had prompted Mom to buy "fly strips" to hang from the ceiling. With no screens on the doors, keeping the dogs and cats out of the house had also become a problem. One of my father's hunting dogs was especially obnoxious. Once he had been run out the front door, he would rush around to the back of the house and come inside through the back door. The dogs never seemed to accept the fact that they were not welcome inside our living quarters. On a few occasions, when one or the other of my parents had entered the kitchen to find one of the canines searching for food, the poor dog had immediately been kicked across the floor and upended into the yard. Not until years later did I realize the cruelty of the act.

Our home on the ridge had no electricity, gas, running water, or any of the other conveniences that most city folk thought were essential. There was no mail route, school bus, or telephone service. I did not realize at the time how isolated our family was from the rest of civilization.

One Saturday morning, because the house was in dire need of new linoleum, curtains, and wallpaper, Mom informed me that Dad had given her permission to refurbish the rooms by charging the goods at the small department store in town. "Git sumpin' 'at's purty, Mommy," I said.

"I hafta git what I can 'ford ta git," she said.

I stayed home to babysit my siblings and worked very hard doing all the chores. Finally, when Mom returned, I ran outside to see the new goods she had purchased. "The 'livery truck's brangin' the stuff all the way ta the house when 'hey brang 'his month's supply a groceries," Mom said.

While my siblings and I hovered around our mother's feet, my little brother Arnold asked, "Jue brang us any blubber gum, Mommy?" Without answering Arnold, Mom reached into the car and picked up a small paper bag from off the seat. While the smaller children yelled in delight, she handed each of us a piece of penny bubble gum. Having a piece of bubble gum to chew was a rarity for us children, so when we were fortunate enough to receive the gum, we would chew on it for days. When we went to bed at night—because Mom had on a few occasions had to cut gum out of our hair—we would stick our wad of gum in a safe place. The next morning after we had eaten our breakfast, we would retrieve the gum and chew it for the rest of the day.

When the delivery truck dropped off our groceries and dry goods, I ran over to see what Mom had bought. "'At'sa same kind'a rug an' paper 'at's in'na house already," I said to my mother.

"Daddy tol' me 'at I had ta git da cheapest thang I could git," Mom replied. Although Mom had chosen the same bright colors and wild patterns the previous tenants had used, I could hardly wait to see the newly covered walls and floors.

Almost all the furnishings in the house were homemade, secondhand, or patched-together pieces from what at one time had been an assortment of other articles of furniture. To my knowledge we had never owned anything any better than what we had at the time, and although my mother must have desired more and better furniture, I had never once heard her complain about what she did or did not have.

The only furniture in the living room was a small table, Mom's treadle sewing machine, an old steamer trunk, a porch rocking chair, and four ladder-back chairs that were used in the kitchen at mealtime. Dad had replaced the broken wicker bottoms in the chairs and rocking chair with strips he had cut from more of the discarded inner tubes. For additional heating, a potbellied stove that would burn coal or wood would later be erected in the center of the living room, with the stovepipe extending through a hole in the ceiling and roof.

The six-foot-long homemade table in the kitchen had been placed close to the wall near the doorway leading into the living room. Mom had covered the table with two and a half yards of new oilcloth. Dad had built a bench the same length of the table and placed it between the table and the wall. During mealtime, the bench would be filled with several hungry little boys and my sister, Nina.

The same wood-burning kitchen range we had used while living in the hollow was equipped with an upper compartment we called the "warmin' closet." We children were given only two meals a day, so on the rare occasions I was blessed to find a few hard morsels of cornbread that had been overlooked in the "warmin' closet," I would grab the precious nuggets and hurriedly devour them before my older brothers could discover what I was eating.

Dad was proud of the farm's twenty-five acres of level or sloping land, a rare commodity in our vicinity. He wasted no time in expressing his big plans for the ridge property. Since he was working year round at a public job, it came as no surprise to hear that he was expecting Woody and Marvin to carry out the work. My younger brother Maynard was now old enough to handle some of the lighter work, and, of course, there was Mom. Dad seemed to think she was as strong as an ox, and he had already proven that he had no qualms about expecting her to work like one.

Dad had found a way to use even the steepest part of the property behind our house. A short distance over the side of the hill, he and my brothers had dug a large rectangular opening backed into the hill, which would function as a cellar, and then built several wooden shelves against the three clay walls. The front section and door of the cellar were built with slabs that Dad had salvaged from a sawmill. Before adding an A-shaped tin roof to the newly built cellar, a few inches of dirt had been shoveled onto the outside top of the ceiling boards to serve as insulation. The much-needed cellar would eventually prove to be a success when the inside temperature remained approximately the same all year long.

The ten-foot-deep, hand-dug well was located no more than ten feet to the left of the front porch. During periods of dry weather, the water level in the well was either extremely low or nonexistent. It was not uncommon early in the dry season to find tiny creatures, which Mom called "wiggle tails," swimming about in the bottom of the half-empty pail. On the occasions this occurred, Mom would say to my brothers or me, "Throw 'em 'wiggle tails' out'n go draw me another bucket'a wodder." The purity of the water had never been in question, although during summer, the water level receded to such a shallow depth that it prevented the bucket from sinking to be filled.

Once the well was dry, my brothers were required to carry water from a nearby shallow spring to supplement the fifty-five gallon drums of water that Dad was hauling from the school bus garage. During these difficult periods of water shortages, Mom sometimes said to me, "I knowed 'his is how it'd be 'fore we move't out 'ere on 'his daggone ridge."

She had no choice however, but to wait patiently for a heavy rain to once again fill the shallow well with what no doubt was surface water. Occasionally, after a heavy downpour, we had to wait for at least a couple of days for the muddy water in the well to become clear enough for human consumption.

The garden was separated from our front lawn by a wire mesh fence that served as a trellis for a beautiful, pink climbing rosebush, to which I would soon be painfully introduced. The scarcity of grass on most of the lawn was blamed on the lack of fertile topsoil; however, a contributing factor was no doubt the result of what soon would be ten active children constantly running to and fro.

Each spring the garden's outer boundaries became a breathtaking scene of pink blooms on the peach trees and white blossoms on the apple trees trembling in the spring wind. Although my brothers had told Dad about pesticides and pruning, Dad could never understand why the fruit trees produced only a spattering of puny, diseased fruits, when in early spring the branches had been loaded with an abundance of promising blooms. He failed to accept the fact that he may indeed increase the quantity and quality of the much-needed fruit by pruning and spraying the trees.

For the first few months after moving to the ridge, my family appeared to have adapted well to the change. The younger children were enjoying playing in the red-clay dust or mud just as much as they had enjoyed frolicking in the creek in the hollow. The older family members were kept too busy to notice how good or bad life had become there in the West Virginia backwoods. From all appearances, none of us were concerned that our house was nothing more than a dilapidated shack; after all, our family members were together, and that was what mattered most. At the time, the words "poverty stricken" and "under-privileged" were not part of country folks' vocabularies; besides, our neighbors' homes and ways of life were no better than our own. I was happy and content with the only lifestyle I had ever known, totally unaware of the impending nightmare that would begin before the end of my first school year.

XIV

Inside the Outside World

The school year 1943–1944 had almost arrived, and, after having seen the schoolbooks that Woody and Marvin had brought home the previous years to study, I could hardly wait to learn to read. I was also excited about having my own paper and pencils; yet, with the first day of school drawing near, the happy anticipation I thought I would have had given way to fear. I had already seen the outside of the school when Dad had driven our family past it while we were living in the hollow. In my opinion, the school building was gigantic, and I was concerned that I would never find my way out again once I had gone inside. I wondered how I would survive in a world seemingly so foreign to my own small world.

Kindergarten was not a requirement when I was a child. Since the principal had the previous year postponed my first year of school, I would be one year older than my first-grade peers, and I was becoming even more apprehensive about joining them.

When I reflect on the cultural shock that I experienced when I left the security of my home to attend school, it is difficult to comprehend how the faculty of the school could have expected children like me to immediately adjust to a world whose customs and lifestyles were so different from our own. Realizing how naïve and ignorant I was at the time, I can now understand why my introduction into society was such a mind-boggling experience.

My small world began to change on the day after Labor Day in 1943. All decked out in brand-new clothes and with my sack lunch in hand—consisting of a biscuit spread with peanut butter—I bid my mother, little brothers, and sister farewell as I walked out the door with my older brothers on our way to school. We walked over the hill and down the hollow behind my grandparents' home, where we continued down the dirt road toward town. When I'd begin to lag behind, Woody would yell at me that I was going to make him late for school; in order to keep pace with my brothers, I sometimes had to run during our three-and-a-half mile trek.

Finally, my brothers and I arrived, on time, at the front of the only elementary school in the area. After learning which room I belonged in, Woody confidently escorted me into my classroom. No one had prepared me for what I was about to face, and while I timidly looked around at the other students who were already seated, I felt very alone. Tears welled up in my eyes when my brother turned and left the room.

Finally, after what felt like several minutes, the teacher walked over and asked for my name. "Mary Bethel Lesher," I said softly, fighting to hold back tears.

"I'm your teacher, and my name is Mrs. Shaffer," she said, pointing out a desk in the middle of the room and telling me to be seated. "You can set your lunch on your desk until later when I assign you a locker."

I walked over and sat down at the desk, holding onto my sack lunch tightly. "What in the world is a locker?" I wondered.

During morning recess, I was learning that doing something as simple as getting a drink of water could be very complicated. Having never been in a house with indoor plumbing, I did not know that such contraptions as commodes or drinking fountains even existed. I was baffled when I was expected to know how to use the strange apparatuses. The "outside world" was indeed proving to be as peculiar as I had feared.

Since Mom and Dad had always been too busy to take the time to answer any questions from us children, I had learned already how to do a lot of things by quietly studying how other people accomplished their tasks. When my teacher lined up the class in the hallway after instructing us to get a drink of water, I was glad to be toward the back of the line, since I seemed to be the only child in the class of thirty who had no idea of what to do.

I watched pensively as my peers, one by one, stepped up to the water fountain mounted against the wall. I marveled as they each sucked at the stream of sparkling, clear water gushing forth into an arch and then splashing back inside the bowl. When I alertly observed that they each had been turning the shiny handle on the side of the fountain, I assured myself that by the time it was my turn to step up to the fountain, I would have mastered the new experience.

Although I was a year older than most of my classmates, I was no taller than they were in stature. I stepped onto the small platform beneath the spigot and stood on my tiptoes. Holding onto the fountain with my left hand, I confidently leaned over, turned my head to the side like my peers had done, twisted the handle with my right hand…and squirted my nose full of water. Gasping for breath, I tried a second time, gulping at the stream of water as fast as I could. I had barely wet my tongue when my impatient teacher ordered me to move on so the other students could take their turns. Disappointed, I stepped down off the platform and slowly walked to the back of the line, hoping no one had noticed my blunder. Drinking water like the city folk was certainly not as easy as it had appeared to be.

The teacher soon moved the class away from the drinking fountain and informed us that we needed to use the bathrooms. The boys were taken out of the line and sent to the opposite end of the hallway. The girls were turned and marched to the entrance of the girls' restroom. This time, however, my teacher instructed six of us girls at the back of the line to take turns in the bathroom first.

I had never heard of an "inside toilet," so when I walked into the immaculate room, I was one puzzled little girl. I stood staring at six brown metal stalls with legs about ten inches tall. The glossy black-and-white ceramic tiles on the floor and walls of the restroom glistened beneath the bright lights. I had never seen anything so clean. Why, even the fresh smell of antiseptic was a new experience for me.

I waited and watched as each girl disappeared inside the stalls and closed the door. Realizing that I was expected to do the same, I walked over to the sixth cubicle and found that it was locked from the inside. Bending down, I looked underneath to see whether the locked enclosure was occupied. It was empty. I turned and could see the feet of the other five girls dangling from the white stools on which they were sitting. Nervously, I stood and waited for one of my classmates to vacate her stall, still not knowing how to do what I believed I was expected to do once I was inside the cramped quarters.

Before the girls opened the door and stepped back outside, I listened as they each did something that made a swishing sound like splashing water. When the girls walked over to what I had concluded were wash basins, I watched closely when they each turned on the spigot and began washing their hands. When one of them reached up and pulled a tan sheet of folded paper from the box on the wall, I was awe stricken. I gawked as she unfolded the paper and used it to dry her hands. Knowing it must be the first day of school for these girls too, I wondered how they could know all about these strange fixtures when I was being overwhelmed by the whole experience.

When the first girl exited her "inside toilet," I timidly stepped inside and looked down at the bowl of crystal-clear water. I was shocked to think that anyone was expected to urinate in a white bowl filled with water that looked much cleaner than our drinking water at home. I became even more frightened when I realized that I might have the wrong idea of what we were supposed to be doing inside those stalls. Wide eyed, I decided I had better not take a chance on messing up what appeared to be a perfectly clean bowl of water.

Quickly, I unlatched the door and walked outside with the rest of the girls, secretly praying I would be able to make it through the day until I could get back up the hollow far enough to do what I would surely need to do by the time school was dismissed.

Before morning recess was over, however, my need to relieve myself was becoming urgent; therefore, pushing my fears aside, I crept around the side of the building looking for a privy. When I failed to spy what I would recognize as an outhouse, I began to panic. I knew there was no way I would take a chance on messing up the clean bowl of water in the bathroom. In my situation, I wondered what the school expected me to do.

Finally, I had no choice but to sneak back inside the bathroom to look once again for something I might have overlooked earlier. The stalls were empty, and the bowls appeared to be as clean as they had been earlier in the morning. I looked at the roll of toilet tissue hanging on the wall beside the commode. There had to be some explanation, and I figured it had to be nearby. Feeling very anxious and becoming more desperate by the minute, I looked once more at the "clean" water before glancing at the handle behind the toilet. "What would happen if I were to pull down on this little handle?" I asked myself, unaware that it had been put there for that very purpose. I recalled the swishing sound I had heard earlier, so I carefully but nervously put my hand on the handle. At the moment I started to trip the handle to see what would happen, I froze! The question had just entered my mind that if pulling down on the handle would cause water to run into the bowl, then how was I supposed to stop the flow of water? More confused than before, I jerked my hand off the handle as if it had suddenly burned me. There was no way I was going to pull that handle until I had found out how to shut off the water.

Standing there all alone, staring down at the clean water in the commode, I realized that it didn't look any different than it had no doubt looked before my peers had gone inside earlier in the morning. Realizing I was wasting precious time, and that I had to use the toilet before someone entered the room and found me dallying around inside, I turned around and stepped outside the stall.

Becoming more desperate by the moment, I hurried over to the locked stall, bent down quickly, and crawled under the door. Looking into the dry bowl that for some unknown reason was filled with what I thought were dried leaves, I dropped my drawers and hurriedly did what I needed to do. Grabbing a piece of the soft toilet tissue from the holder, I thought to myself, "No wonder Daddy keeps the toilet paper for his own use." After dropping the piece of toilet tissue, which I had never before been privileged to use, inside the bowl of "dry leaves," I crawled back underneath the stall and bolted for the outside door.

Returning outside to the playground where the rest of my classmates were playing, I prayed that I would not have to go back inside that restroom with the urge to do more than what I had just done. I was also deeply troubled that someone would discover my secret.

Recess was too soon over, and my classmates and I returned to our room. But with all the anxieties and unanswered questions running through my mind, I could not concentrate on anything the teacher was saying. I wondered whether I would ever fit into this strange world into which I had been thrown.

Finally, the morning hours passed, and it was time for the noon recess. I pulled out my lunch bag and looked around the room to see what the other children had brought in their lunches. From what I could see, there was no one with sandwiches made with anything other than store-bought, sliced bread. All kinds of interesting goodies were being pulled out of the sacks. I thought to myself, "I'll eat my peanut butter biscuit and act like I haven't seen the apples, oranges, lunch cakes, and candy bars on all the other desks around me."

When I pulled the thick homemade biscuit out of the sack, one of the boys giggled and poked the boy sitting in front of him. "Look what she brung in her lunch," he said, snickering. Before I knew what was happening, the whole class was laughing and pointing at my lunch. I felt like crying, yet I kept my composure. I hid behind my lunch sack, wondering why the teacher was ignoring what was happening, and slowly choked down the delicious peanut butter biscuit. I had never tasted anything so good. I was glad that Mom had bought the jar of peanut butter especially for our school lunches. I could not understand what was so funny about eating it on a homemade biscuit. I wished only that I had a drink of water.

I rolled up the brown lunch bag and stuck it inside my desk, recalling the instructions that my mother had given my brothers and me earlier. "You young'uns be shore'n fetch 'em 'pokes' [paper bags] back so I can pack y'ur lunches in 'em tamarr," she had said. I did not know at the time that my rumpled sack would be just one more reason for my classmates to ridicule me.

After the lunch break, our teacher marched my classmates and me outside to the playground. The troubled feeling I had been experiencing because of my peers poking fun at me was pushed to the back of my mind. While the other children ran and played on the playground, I stood against the brick wall of the school and watched. I wanted very much to be a part of the fun but was totally ignorant on how to go about including myself in their games.

I made it through the rest of the day and, at the school day's end, stood outside by the doorway until my brothers came to escort me home. My brothers did not ask me how the day had gone, and I did not volunteer any information. When we arrived home, the only thing my mother said to my brothers and me was to change our clothes so that we could wear them to school the following day.

The next day, I returned to school wondering what I would face on that particular day. During the morning hours, my thoughts were more on my problems than on my schoolwork. I had never known that life outside the country could be so complicated. I was still concerned about the restroom situation, but I was determined to act as though I knew as much as the other girls seemed to know.

Just before the noon hour, a student from one of the higher grades came into our room with a note from the principal. The school had no intercom system; therefore, messages from the principal's office had to be hand delivered. The teacher took the note from the student and looked it over quickly. After the delivery boy had left the room and closed the door, our teacher looked up and revealed the contents of the note. "I don't believe any of you are responsible for what's going on here; however, the principal has asked me to make this announcement," she said. Looking around the room, she continued, "It seems that some of the students have been going over the riverbank at the back of the school to do what they should have done in the restroom, and we want you to know that the commodes in the bathrooms are for that purpose." Then, to my surprise and relief, she added, "All you have to do is to pull down on the handle behind the commode and the water will automatically flush away the waste and any toilet paper that you have used."

"What a relief," I thought to myself, squirming in my seat. Not only had I learned how to use the commodes, but I had learned that other pupils had been as uninformed as I had been. Having overcome this hurdle, I felt confident that I would be able to face any problems that might arise in the future.

I later learned that the first floor of the two-story building housed two rooms each for the first- through third-grade classrooms, a large kitchen and cafeteria, the principal's office, the teachers' lounge, and the boys' and girls' bathrooms. Two rooms each on the second floor were required for fourth through sixth graders, with bathrooms at each end of the hallway. I did not venture away from my classroom or locker for fear that I would be hopelessly lost inside that big, complicated building.

I made it through the first three months feeling confident that I was excelling in my studies. The first- through third-grade students had been chosen to perform in the school's Christmas Play, and I had been selected to play the part of Mary, Christ's mother. The part required me to sing a lullaby to Baby Jesus. I was very pleased to be included in the play, although my family would fail to attend.

After the Christmas break, I returned to the school and was terrified when I realized that I could not recall where my classroom was located. Feeling alone amidst the crowd of students in the oversized building, and after peeking through a couple of the classroom doorways and not being able to recognize either of them as my room, I leaned up against the wall in the hallway and began crying softly. I was very frightened and had no idea what I should do.

Finally, a couple of the sixth-grade girls stopped alongside me after I overheard one of them say, "Look at that little girl. She's crying." I timidly peeked up through my long bangs when the same girl asked, "What are you crying about, little girl?" I was too shy to tell her that I was lost.

The other girl moved over closer to me and placed her hand on my shoulder and asked, "What did Santy Claus bring you for Christmas?" I hugged the wall even closer, still too scared to say anything. She began to tell me what she had received from Santa Claus. Her long list included a beautiful doll, books, crayons, a watch, and some clothing. She once again asked what Santa had brought me for Christmas.

Although I had received an orange, a few pieces of candy, a pair of new socks, and a dime paper-doll cut-out book, I said to the girls, "I diden see no Sanny Claus."

"Aw, come on. Tell us what you got," one of the girls pleaded.

"Nothin'," I replied. "I didn' git nothin'."

The two girls started pitying me and telling me they understood why I was sad. "We'd be sad too, if Santa Claus had forgotten to stop at our house," one of them said. Up until then, I had never expected much from Santa. I had never received more than one inexpensive toy at Christmas time; in fact, I had no idea that other children had apparently been receiving expensive toys and clothing—just because it was Christmas Day.

The two girls did not seem to know what to do to help me, so they walked away and left me cowering in the hallway. Although I had been crying because I was lost, I was now also sad because I knew that

I was probably the only girl at school who had not received a doll from Santa. Suddenly, it dawned on me. The reason my classmates had been treating me differently was because they thought that I was poor.

Finally, the school janitor walked over to me and asked me whose room I was supposed to be in. Mr. Birdwell was a small wrinkled man who always wore khaki pants and a long-sleeved khaki shirt. He walked through the halls chewing on a round, wooden toothpick. The key ring that dangled from one of his belt loops must have contained twenty or more keys. I trusted Mr. Birdwell and found it easy to answer his question—maybe because he reminded me of my father. Anyway, I gave him my teacher's name, and he took me by the hand and led me to my classroom. When my teacher hugged me before directing me to my seat, my heart skipped with joy. Happy to be back in my classroom and to see my teacher once again, I soon forgot about Santa Claus overlooking me at Christmas time.

The books, paper, and pencils were furnished by the school, affording me a more equal opportunity—one I found to be more rewarding and joyous than anything I had ever before experienced. I soon became the best reader in my class. When my teacher would compliment me on my good grades, my heart would almost burst with joy and pride, although neither of my parents recognized nor acknowledged my achievements in any way or at any time.

XV

It Begins

With my traumatic return to school after the Christmas break behind me and having proven to myself and my parents that I could walk the three miles to and from school in the cold weather, I thought my life was almost perfect. I was no longer concerned that "Santa" had apparently forgotten me on Christmas morning; instead, I believed in my heart that my parents had given my siblings and me the best Christmas they could afford. My classmates were still excluding me from their games on the playground, yet I went about my day with no outward appearance that I was disturbed by their thoughtlessness. I was actually waiting for the chance to prove to them that, although they might have thought they were richer than I was, I was just as intelligent as most of them.

One wintry evening shortly after Christmas, I stood watching as my father, for the first time that I could remember, began playing with my two little brothers and two-year-old sister, Nina. Dad had gotten down on the floor on his hands and knees, pretending to be a horse. I watched as my two younger brothers took turns hopping onto his back for rides around the room. Dad would slowly move back and forth across the room on his hands and knees and then rear his torso up in the air like a bucking bronco. The child riding on his back at the time would giggle excitedly and yell, "Giddy-up, horsey! Giddy-up!" My father would drop again to his hands and knees and return to the mounting place, where he would buck the rider off his back and then remain motionless while the next cowboy climbed aboard.

My little sister soon began yelling, "Me, Daddy! Me ride horsey!" When Dad stopped to allow Nina to mount, I picked her up and sat her atop my father's back, her little legs barely dangling over each side. I watched while he took her for a short ride and then brought her back over to where I was sitting on the edge of my chair. As I lifted my sister off my father's back, I debated whether I was "too old" to try riding the "funny old horse" myself. I was eight years old and had only once or twice seen my daddy do anything indicating that he was enjoying having his children around him, so I desperately needed to be included in the rare episode of fun.

As the boys took a few more turns, each screaming in delight, I continued watching the horse whinnying and galloping around the small room. After a few minutes, I decided that if I wanted to go for a ride on the pretend horse that I had better jump on his back in a hurry. The bucking bronco was beginning to look as if he had just about given his last ride; thus, throwing caution to the wind, I slid off my chair, ran over to the hitching post and jumped on Dad's back. Tapping him lightly on the shoulder, I yelled, "Giddy-up horsey!" My "horse" took a few steps forward and then stopped abruptly. He did not buck me off his back like he had done my little brothers; instead, he started moving across the floor very lazily while he slowly slid me off his back and round in front of him. I shivered from fright when his hand touched me in a way that I recognized instantly as wrong.

Although I knew nothing about "the birds and the bees," somehow I knew that what my father had just done was not right. I looked into his eyes, and his expression troubled me. My brothers had begun playing at something else, evidently realizing that Dad had lost interest in playing rodeo with them. I was confused, disappointed, and very scared as I found myself alone, except for the younger children, in the room with my father.

Quickly tearing myself from Dad's clutches, I ran out of the room and into the unheated bedroom that I shared with all the other children. I fell across the bed and began sobbing. With my tears soaking into the straw-stuffed mattress, I found myself wondering what I had done to cause my daddy to touch me on the private parts of my body.

My mind wandered back to the night when we were living in the hollow and I had been in a position that could have—yet had not—brought on my father's unexpected actions. I recalled how he had taken me onto his lap because I was scared by the ghost stories that he and Mr. White had been telling, and how he had tenderly tucked me into bed, assuring me that I had no reason to be afraid. Now, here I was, just one year older, filled with fear and trying to determine how I might avoid my father, whom I loved very deeply.

For the next few days, as I thought about the sad situation I had gotten myself into, I wondered what I should do. I wanted to talk to my mom about what Dad had done, but I was too confused and scared; besides, should my mother believe what had happened, I felt certain she would tell me it was all my fault for having climbed onto his back. I finally told myself that the act had probably been an isolated incident that would never happen again; nevertheless, I promised myself that I would never be alone with my daddy again.

Days later, however, although Dad was ignoring my siblings and me as he always did (except for when he was angry with us, I could not get the incident out of my mind. I wanted to believe that, because I had spurned his advances and had run away from him, he had realized I wanted no part of his sick behavior. I couldn't help, however, but to blame myself for having climbed onto his back wearing the short dress I had outgrown yet had to wear.

Staying out of a person's reach when there are nine people living in a two-bedroom shack is next to impossible. With the sole source of heat and light being in the living room, it was extremely difficult to stay in the bedroom, and I had begun to experience just how impossible it could be during the bitter cold evenings. It seemed to be a regular occurrence for my father to reach out and grab me when it became necessary for me to go near him. He would pull me over against his legs and try to touch me in the way he had done previously, while at the same time making repulsive remarks to me and laughing as though it were all a big joke. I had no idea what some of the expressions meant. I had, however, determined that they were suggestive and inappropriate.

Each time he grabbed me and tried to hold onto me I would scream and fight like a wild animal caught in a trap; nevertheless, he would hold onto me until my mother walked into the room. Although Mom failed to say a word, he would loosen his grip and shove me away as if I were the one who had instigated the ordeal. I had no doubt that my mother was aware of what was going on. I could not understand why she remained silent and was allowing Dad's actions to continue. I was absolutely devastated.

I tried to stay close to my mother's side while Dad was around, thinking that somehow I would be safe if I stayed in her sight. There were times, however, when it seemed she would deliberately leave me alone with my father. I wondered whether she was denying what she had at times witnessed or whether, for some reason, she wanted Dad to have his way with me.

Over the next few weeks Dad's actions grew even more aggressive. It no longer seemed to bother him when other members of the family were present. "Daddy, leave me alone!" I would scream. When he persisted, I would scream even more forcefully. "Mommy, help me! Please, make him quit!" Sometimes he would hold my small body down on the floor and kiss me on the mouth while I tearfully sputtered and spat like a dog with rabies.

Only on a few occasions did Mom scold Dad for his behavior towards me. "Bud, y'orta be 'shamed'a y'urself," she would manage to say, using the same tone of voice and showing about as much concern as when she was scolding one of the little boys for bedwetting. Most of the time, however, she would not even bother to enter the room where the attack was occurring. I had begun to feel completely helpless, having no idea to whom or where I could turn for help.

I felt that I could not hate my father and mother for what was happening; as a matter of fact, I loved my parents dearly. The fact that I loved them made the ordeal even more traumatic. I had accepted the fact that, no matter how much I loved my parents, I would never be able to express my love to either of them. At this stage, if I were to show my dad any attention, I was scared he would view it as encouragement to continue what he was trying to do to me; in addition, I imagined that if I showed my mother any attention, she might misinterpret it as my overlooking her failure to protect me from my father's abuse. I realized that I was in a dilemma. Although I felt very strongly opposed to the actions of both of them, I had no choice but to remain silent and to hope that God Himself would intervene.

I coveted the right kind of attention from my parents, and as I pondered the situation I was in, my mind wandered back in time to an event when I had tried to solicit attention from my mother. Shortly after we had moved to the hollow, although I was only five years old, I had been doing all I could to help Mom with the housework and caring for my two younger brothers. She seemed never to stop work from before dawn until after dark, taking short breaks only when the baby needed to nurse. Although my help was not acknowledged, I enjoyed doing anything I could to help my mommy. At that particular time of year, the garden had been harvested, and Mom had canned gallons of vegetables, fruits, and wild berries, and although her days were long and her work hard, she continued to keep up the pace, day after day.

On one particular evening, I decided to surprise Mom and have the dishes done when she returned from milking Brownie, our cow. I had helped with the dishes often but had never attempted to do them alone. I thought that maybe she would give me some special attention if I had cleared the table, washed and dried the dishes, and swept the kitchen floor before she arrived back at the house. I was anxious to see her reaction when she walked into the kitchen.

Our cast-iron, wood-burning cooking stove was equipped with a warming tank on one side, which Mom kept filled with rainwater that ran off the roof just outside the kitchen door. While the meals were being cooked, the water in the tank would heat. I had watched Mom dip the warm water out of the reservoir and fill the dishpan many times, so I was confident that I could manage the chore. Since I was too short to reach the center of the big table or to reach the dishpan, which I had placed on the lukewarm stove, I pushed one chair in front of the table, one in front of the warming tank, and one in front of the stove, in order to solve my height problem.

Back and forth I hastily scampered, dipping the warm water from the tank and transferring it to the dishpan. Finally, after I was satisfied that I had filled the pan with ample water, I dropped the big bar of homemade lye soap, which Mom used for the dishes, the laundry, and every other purpose for which she needed soap, into the pan of warm water.

Up and down I hopped, from the chair in front of the stove, over to the table, and back again. I washed the dishes and piled them inside our largest baking pan, since we owned only one enamel dishpan. I could barely master the big rag that Mom used for a dishcloth; even so, I was very careful not to drip water onto the kitchen floor while I hastily did my work.

Once I had washed the last pan, I stood on the chair and was hurriedly wiping off the oilcloth table covering when Mom walked into the kitchen carrying a pail of foamy warm milk. Her eyes sparkled when she looked at me wiping off the tablecloth with the big dishcloth in my small hand. She glanced at the chairs in front of the stove and table and smiled at me as she asked, "Jue do all 'em deeshes all by y'urself?" I thought my heart would burst with pride while I proudly took all the credit.

Mom didn't say anything else to me or even attempt to give me the hug that I thought I deserved. She continued to strain the pail of milk into a large stone crock through a strainer she had recently acquired. I finished the job I had started, realizing sadly that the pleased look on my mother's face would be all the recognition that I would receive. I was disappointed; nevertheless, I felt good in knowing that—hug or no hug—I had made my mommy's load a bit lighter.

I soon realized, however, that I had started what would be expected of me from that day forward. It was no longer by choice that I would push a chair up to the stove to begin washing the dishes while Mom was busy at some other job. If I failed to start the job right after the meal, one or the other of my parents would say, "Bethel, git starded on 'em deeshes!" Being told to do the dishes before I had had a chance to start the job on my own took all the enjoyment out of the chore. Although I did not mind helping with the work, I did wish that I could hear a word of praise or see some sign of appreciation once in a while.

Recognizing the fact that none of my siblings were receiving any special attention either, I had, at the tender age of five years old, concluded that it must be wrong for me to expect any form of affection or validation from my parents. Sometime and somewhere along the way, I honestly began to feel guilty for having the desires to be hugged and commended by Mom and Dad. I decided that they both probably loved my brothers and me and that I should not be so selfish as to expect them to demonstrate that love toward us. I worked harder and harder, however, still hoping that someday, somehow, I would be able to extract even one morsel of praise from either of my parents.

Now here I was, just a few years later, scared out of my wits because my father was forcing his "affections" upon me. I didn't at the time realize the power of prayer, since I had never heard either of my parents pray or even mention prayer. Although I had attended church a few times, I had never attended Sunday School, so the only thing I knew about Jesus was what my mother had told me. She had often told all of us children that if we were to do anything bad, Jesus would not like us. I wondered at the time whether Jesus was angry with me for having climbed onto my father's back. The thought made me very sad and remorseful.

I kept hoping that things would get better and that Dad would stop groping me; yet as time went on and his behavior continued, my hopes began to dwindle. The bubbling joy that had once filled my heart was now being emptied and replaced with a torment that I could hardly bear.

XVI

A Child Such as I

Mother Earth had awakened from her long winter's nap and was busy arousing new life in the animals, birds, trees, grass, and the beautiful wildflowers that had always captivated me. I was glad that I lived in the country, where God's creation was spread in such splendor. I awakened each new day to the sounds of the rooster crowing and to the chirping of the birds as they rushed to build new nests in anticipation of hatching their babies.

On my walk to school one morning, I thought about my classmates, whose days must have been very dull with their bus rides to school or their walks along the paved streets with colorless, concrete sidewalks staring them in the face. I imagined how many of them would peer out their bedroom windows only to be greeted by the side of their neighbor's house blocking their view of even more houses and streets.

I had made it through the frigid winter without missing much school, and I was confident that I would be able to finish out the rest of the term. The distance that my brothers and I were walking to and from school each day didn't seem nearly as far now that spring had arrived. I enjoyed school and tried not to think about the ordeal that I had been going through at home. Unlike in today's world, there was in the 1940s and '50s no help for abused children like me, and although my world had changed, I was still functioning in a way that no one outside my family had become aware of my problem.

I was still very timid and was finding it difficult to make friends with any of the girls, although I had tried on several occasions. The girls fortunate enough to have their own jumping ropes would pick the girls they wanted on their teams, which not once included me. On several occasions when I walked over to where they seemed to be having so much fun and asked whether I could join them, they shoved me away, saying, "Get your own rope to play with."

During the noon hour, some of the girls usually huddled together on the stoop that led into the cafeteria to play "jacks." They also excluded me from their games. When I tried to join in with the group that was running around playing tag, some of the other girls would push me to the side and tell me to get out of their way. I had gone through the first months of school standing around, watching the rest of my classmates having fun. I could not understand why the teacher on playground duty was ignoring the way the other kids shoved me away. I wanted very much to be treated like one of the crowd.

One evening, as I was making my way home from school, I was thinking about how much I wanted to jump rope with the girls in my class, when suddenly it dawned on me that maybe I could have my own team of girls to play "jump-rope." I knew that my parents didn't have the money to buy a new jump rope, so I hadn't asked for one; however, there had to be some way for me to acquire my own rope and my own friends.

After returning home from school, I went directly to the barn, where I found a piece of worn, heavy rope that had been used as a plow-line (one of two ropes tied to the horse's reins and held onto by the farmer as a means of guiding the horse). Although it was now too short to be used for a plow-line, I knew that if I were to ask Dad for the length of rope, he would no doubt answer me in his usual way by saying, "No! I might need 'at someday."

I retrieved the rope, took it to the house, and hid it under my bed. Dad would never miss the rotten section of rope, so that was the least of my worries. I was concerned, however, that the kids in school would probably make fun of my country jump rope; nevertheless, the next morning I found a big grocery bag and crammed the unsightly rope inside. Now that I had my rope, I would need to find some girls brave enough to join me in playing our own game of jump rope.

Once I was back at school, I dreaded pulling the rope out of the crumpled paper bag; even so, when the recess bell rang, I bravely picked up the large sack from my locker floor, took out the rope, and sauntered onto the playground. But when the girls on the playground already playing with their ropes looked up to see the rope in my hand...the jeers began. The boys came running over to see what all the ruckus was about and immediately joined in the finger pointing and laughter. When some of the boys recognized the rope as a plowline, they began ridiculing me for bringing the cumbersome rope to school. "So 'hat's whure 'at smell of horse manure's been comin' from," one of the boys yelled, laughing menacingly.

I felt like running off the playground and never looking at my peers again; instead, I held the old rope against my chest and stared at the ground. There was no way I was going to give my cruel classmates the opportunity to see the tears I was choking back.

Finally, everybody returned to their games, and I timidly walked around the playground with the frayed rope in my hands. I approached one of the girls whom I had noticed had also been shunned by our peers. "Would jue play 'ith me?" I asked. "I got my own rope."

"Who'll we git'ta turn the other end?" she asked, smiling.

"I figured we might git a girl over 'ere 'at ain't got no rope either," I said. By the time we had finally gotten two more girls for our team, the bell had rung, calling us back to our classrooms. The four of us made plans to meet there on the playground at noon. I returned to my classroom feeling embarrassed about my big clumsy rope but proud that I had stood up to the kids who had excluded me from their playground activities.

The sneers finally faded as the boys and girls became accustomed to seeing a small group of shy girls skipping and jumping rope alongside them. We had proven to them that we could jump as well or better with our rope as any of them with their fancy, store-bought ropes. Within days, a small group of girls had joined us.

This incident would remain in my memory as my first lesson in taking a situation in hand and not allowing the circumstances to determine the outcome. I had no idea at the time that this small act of strength would be part of a reservoir that would encourage me to persevere, when later I would despair of life itself.

Near the end of the first grade it had become evident to my teacher that I was academically advanced beyond the other children in my class. I had learned to read and was taking advantage of the achievement by checking books out of our small class library. The "library" consisted of one small bookshelf stocked with more books than I had thought existed.

When we read aloud in school, I realized that I was able to read much better than my peers; still, I hadn't thought much about it until one day when the teacher unexpectedly asked me to do her a favor.

One Monday morning, Mrs. Shaffer instructed the class to read silently while she went out of the room to the office. "If you come to a word that you don't know, you can raise your hand and ask Mary to help you," she said to the class. She then turned to me and requested that I walk up and stand near her desk. "You're in charge," she said. "If they need help with their reading, you tell them the words." My teacher then walked out of the room.

I was dumbfounded. Here I was, "The Little Country Bumpkin," helping the "City Slickers" with their reading assignment. My self-confidence soared. When my classmates asked for help, I would timidly walk from desk to desk pronouncing words for them. Some of the students were still reading from the book *Ted and Sally*, which I had already completed. I knew every word in the book and was almost through the book entitled *Dick and Jane*. Though I felt good about the honor the teacher had given me, I was very embarrassed to have been singled out.

After a short time, the teacher returned to the room and sat down at her desk. I returned to my seat, happy that my frightening job was over. Mrs. Shaffer called me up to her desk. "Mary, I have talked it over with the principal, and we believe that you are ready for the second grade," she said. I was shocked!

Mrs. Shaffer instructed me to collect my belongings from my desk and to follow her. "We're going to meet your second-grade teacher," she said. While silently doing as she had requested, tears welled up in my eyes. Seemingly surprised to see the tears, Mrs. Shaffer bent down and placed her arm around me. "Why are you crying?" she asked. She looked into my eyes and wiped away the tears with a soft handkerchief that smelled like a fresh-cut rose. "You should be happy knowing that you are going to a higher grade before the year is out," she said softly.

"But I don't wanna leave y'ur room," I whimpered. She assured me that my second-grade teacher would be just as nice to me as I felt she had been. Seeing the determination in her eyes, I knew that I had no choice. As I pondered the fact that I had barely come to know my classmates and first-grade teacher, I trembled as Mrs. Shaffer began leading me across the hall toward the second-grade class. I once again felt afraid and very alone.

When I returned home from school later in the day and told my mother about my promotion, she remarked, seemingly unimpressed, "I bet'cha doln't git sent on up'ta the third grade when school's out."

"Bet'cha I do," I said. I believed I had achieved a lot, especially with all the pressures brought on by the changes from my backwoods lifestyle and the worries I had about my father's behavior toward me.

I soon settled in with the rest of the class and realized that I could do the second-grade work, despite there being only a few weeks left in the school year. I liked my second-grade teacher, but not as much as I had liked Mrs. Shaffer. One of the things that especially impressed me about Mrs. Younger was the fact that she smelled as fresh and pretty as Grandma's lilac bush.

The bookshelf in the second-grade classroom was bigger than the one in the first-grade classroom. I regularly signed out and read the books, digesting the simple stories with much interest. Having never owned a book of my own, I was enjoying looking at the brightly colored pictures and learning all of the new words that I had never before heard. I wasn't afforded much time to read at home since my chores kept me busy until bedtime; however, I did not allow the lack of time to discourage me. I read when I walked along the dirt road from school, and I even carried a book with me when I went to the toilet. Although the stories had little depth, my imagination often carried me into a fantasy world that made my heart dance with delight.

A couple of weeks or so before school was dismissed for the summer, the source of my greatest joy was suddenly snatched away. I had returned a book to my teacher that I had signed out just the day before. Mrs. Younger thumbed through the pages as she normally did whenever one of her students returned a library book. My heart quickened when she held the book out in front of her and sternly said, "Class, continue with your work while I take this book to the office." I squirmed nervously in my seat, wondering what the book I had just returned had to do with Mrs. Younger's trip to the principal's office.

In a matter of minutes, Mrs. Younger returned to our classroom without the book. She ordered me to approach her desk. "You will not be allowed to take any more books home with you," she sternly said, shaking her finger in my face.

I could feel my whole body trembling as I choked back tears. With no compassion in her voice, Mrs. Younger then loudly announced for the class to hear, "That book you just returned is filthy!" I did not respond to her remark but slowly returned to my seat.

I was aware that my baby brother had gotten hold of the book and had slightly soiled a few of the pages, but I had wiped the spots away with a wet cloth. I didn't think the book was filthy. Apparently, my definition of "filthy" was different from my teacher's definition of the word.

I felt as though the whole class was laughing at me. Having my teacher embarrass me in front of the class was bad enough, but thinking that I would never again be permitted to check out books from the school…that was far worse.

After school, crying softly, I walked along the muddy road up the hollow to Grandma's house. I had had a whole new world offered to me only to have it suddenly jerked away. "How am I expected to survive in this new world of thoughtless city folk?" I asked myself.

I wiped the tears from my eyes and continued walking. Soon, I would be arriving at Grandma's house, where I could get a cold biscuit to eat while I walked the rest of the way home. I began to feel better, and just as I jumped to the other side of a narrow drainage ditch that spanned the width of the road, I glanced over to the shoulder of the road at a spot of color that had caught my eye. I stopped for a moment to investigate. There, right before my eyes, was the prettiest Jack-in-the-pulpit I had ever seen. I bent down and gently lifted the hood-like covering on the flower, being extra careful not to damage the flower's delicate insides. My heart danced with joy at the beauty and flawlessness of God's tenderness in forming such a unique masterpiece. I looked up through the underbrush at several other species of wildflowers that seemed to greet me as I walked along the road I had traveled so many times. Suddenly, I realized that I was smiling, when just moments before I had been crying. Feeling comforted by my encounter with such beauty, I reminded myself, "I'd better hurry up the road, or I'll get a whipping for arriving home late."

I would later remember my pleasant encounter with the gorgeous Jack-in-the-pulpit and would glean from the simplicity of the experience the fact that behind every cloud there is a ray of sunshine. I reminded myself that if God could care for the delicate little flower growing there against the rugged hillside, then He could take care of a child such as I.

XVII

The Outhouse

The sound of laughter was seldom heard around our home when I was growing up. On the few occasions when my father would hear my siblings or me laughing, he would scold us and then say, "If you young'uns hain't got nothin' ta do, 'hen I'll find plenty fer you ta do." There was one occasion, however, when the urge to laugh became too much for the whole family.

Since the land behind our house was the steepest part of the property, and since no one lived within miles of the backside of the small farm, Mr. White had cleared the hillside and built his outhouse over the side of the hill, without digging a container hole to hold the human waste.

Dad, on the other hand, believed that the proper way to install an outhouse was to first dig a pit about four feet deep, with the length and width of the open pit slightly smaller than the base of the outhouse. After the privy had been constructed, it would then be placed over the pit, with the holes in the seats resting directly above the pit. Once the container hole was almost filled to capacity with human waste, usually years later, the structure would then be moved to a new location, and the vacated pit filled to the top with large rocks and dirt. Dad had made plans when we moved onto the property to build this new and improved outhouse, but, having given other jobs priority over the new toilet, we were still using the privy that Mr. White had built.

One Saturday morning our family had just finished eating our breakfast, when Dad grabbed the roll of toilet tissue, which was reserved for his use only, and walked briskly toward the outhouse. Mom had left for the barnyard to do the morning milking, and I was in the kitchen preparing to wash dishes. I had just raked a few table scraps into my hand and walked outside to feed them to the dogs, when I heard a loud racket coming from the direction of the outhouse. Looking toward the barn, I was surprised to see Mom jump to her feet from the stool she had been sitting on while milking the cow. With bucket in hand, she and my two older brothers began running in the direction of the noise.

Puzzled, I ran down to where Mom and my brothers had stopped to look down over the side of the hill toward the outhouse. I gasped when I looked over the hill. Dad was standing almost on the same spot where the outhouse was supposed to be, with his trousers down around his ankles and the flap on his winter underwear drooping limply below his buttocks.

"Daddy!" Woody yelled. "What happened?"

Sheepishly looking up the hill and realizing that an audience had gathered, Dad quickly jerked up his trousers. "Now what'na tarnation 'uz it look like happened?" he yelled. "I had'da jump when 'at dad-blamed torlet went'n rolled in the holler."

"Jue yell Ger-ron-ni-mo 'fore ye jumped?" Woody asked.

My mouth dropped open and my eyes widened when I heard my oldest brother's question. I didn't know whether to regard him as brave or stupid. I doubted seriously that the situation Dad had found himself in seemed as funny to him as it did to his observers. He remained silent for a moment, then, staring toward the hollow, said, "I don't reckon she wuz as sturdy as I thought she was."

I wanted to laugh, but I was afraid that it wouldn't be the wise thing to do at the moment. From past experiences, I knew that what had seemed at times hilarious to my siblings and me had been to my father no laughing matter. Mom and my brothers also stifled their laughter as we all stood staring over the hill at the comical sight.

"Come on, boys," Mom said to my brothers. "Et's git down 'ere an' git dat cow milked 'fore she starts holdin' up her milk." While Mom, Woody, and Marvin hurried back to the barnyard, I scurried back to the kitchen, hoping that Dad would stay outside until after Mom had returned to the house.

Just as I finished washing the dishes, Dad, looking dejected and downcast, stepped through the door and moseyed into the living room. Mom walked into the kitchen behind him and said to me, "We'll hafta go easy on 'at milk 'cause Ol' Brownie wouldn' let down her milk after Daddy's accident."

My brothers returned to the house, and they, Mom, and I walked over to where Dad was sitting with a sheepish grin on his face. Mom looked down at Dad and asked, "Bud, what 'na worl' happened ta 'at torlet?"

While waiting for Dad's reply, I recalled how he had looked standing there in his underwear, staring over the hill at the toilet he had suddenly and prematurely had to vacate. When I glanced over at my brothers, I noticed that I wasn't the only one about to burst out laughing.

With his family waiting anxiously for him to either explain or explode, Dad grinned and finally said, "I'z settin' there readin'a funny papers when I heared a creakin' noise." He paused and then continued, "Yell, I figured it'uz jista torlet settlin' down a loodle more, when all uva sudden, she starded a turnin' over."

"Y'u're jist lucky 'at you didn' end up over 'at hill inside 'at torlet," Mom said.

"Yell, I jis' barely had 'nuff time ta jump up'n jump out'ta door holdin' on ta the short piece'a torlet paper I'd tore off'na roll when I'd first set down," Dad said. He explained that he'd not had time to grab the roll of toilet paper before the old, rotten privy had begun rolling over the steep hillside and down into the hollow below, where it crashed into smithereens.

Woody bent over with laughter. "Yell, 'ere Daddy stood 'ith 'is britchers down 'roun'iz lags," he said. "He 'uz lookin' back 'cross 'iz shoulder like Ol' Bess does 'hen she's lookin' back at me hookin' 'er ta the plow."

The rest of the family broke forth with laughter only to have Dad look up at us and say, "Shet'jer mouths an' pay attention ta me." We all hushed quickly and looked at Dad. "All y'all go down over a hill when you need'a go to the torlet until I can git another'n built," he said.

"When's 'at gonna be?" Mom asked.

"I'll hafta start it taday," he answered. Then he looked at my little brother Maynard and said, "You git over 'at hill'n fetch my torlet paper back ta da house." Maynard jumped immediately and began running to recover the roll of toilet paper from the wrecked outhouse.

In a few days we had a brand-new, twin-hole toilet. Dad had wisely built the second toilet over a pit, no doubt realizing it was more sanitary and much safer.

XVIII

Down to the Bars

School was soon out for the summer, and I had been promoted to the third grade. Dad had gone to work with some of the other school bus drivers, repairing or replacing roofs on school buildings in and around the county. The labor was difficult, so I was relieved when he came home each evening too exhausted to notice any of his family, especially me. I was still staying as far out of his reach as possible, which was a lot easier now that warm weather had arrived.

The well was now dry, and the rain barrels had been empty for weeks. Even the barrels of water that Dad had been hauling from the bus garage had been rationed. Along with having to wear our clothes longer between laundries, the family was now required to take sponge baths, since the Saturday night baths in a galvanized washtub had become extinct. By mid-summer, we older children had learned that we could help to conserve water by taking along a bar of soap when we made our bi-weekly trips to the quickly diminishing swimming hole in the hollow at the rear of our property.

When the drought extended into weeks and Dad was no longer allowed to haul water from the bus garage, my brothers were forced to carry water, bucket by bucket, from a pool that had been created by crystal-clear water that was seeping out of an underground coal mine deep in the hollow behind our house.

With the water crisis increasing daily, and the already enormous pile of laundry mounting, washday had become even more of a problem than the baths. Knowing that she had a toddler and an infant both in need of clean diapers (disposable diapers were unheard of at the time), Mom had realized that the mound of soiled laundry would have to be carried to the creek to be scrubbed on the washboard (this was also before laundromats existed).

At the base of the hill, between our grandparents' home and ours, the small pool in the creek seemed to always contain an ample amount of water for doing the huge loads of laundry. Realizing that she could wait for rain no longer, Mom finally accepted the fact that the back-breaking task was inevitable.

Monday through Friday, Mom began her day at 4 a.m. by fixing breakfast and seeing Dad off to work about an hour later. On the day she planned to do the laundry, she would put a pot of pinto beans on the stove to cook while preparing to spend the day down by the creek. At the break of dawn, Mom would leave for the barn to milk the cow. I would get all the children out of bed and see that they each ate their part of the same breakfast, except for the eggs, that Mom had prepared for Dad.

Once Mom had returned with the pail of milk and had strained part of it into a jar, she would place the jar of milk inside the bucket used for drawing water from the well, then lower the bucket down into the well in order to keep the milk cold.

Woody and Marvin would harness the mare and lead her to the front of the house. After Mom had sorted the laundry into two huge piles, she would place each pile in the center of a bed sheet, tie the corners of each sheet to form a bundle, and then tie the two bundles together and swing them onto the horse's back behind the saddle. With one bundle of soiled laundry hanging over the old mare's right side and the other bundle hanging over her left side, it was then time for my mother to load me, my little sister, and my youngest brother onto the horse's back.

Wash day standing L to R: Woody, Marvin, Mom holding Arnold, Me, and Maynard in saddle on mule.

Once everything was ready for the trip to begin, I would look the "ten feet" down to the ground from my perch on what felt like the back of a giant giraffe. Holding onto the babies with one hand, I would pick up the bridle reins with the other; then, with my heart in my mouth, I would begin the descent over "Pike's Peak."

The dented, sooty washtub in which Mom would heat the water was always entrusted to Woody or Marvin to carry down to the creek. More often than not, the boys would end up with more soot on themselves than was left on the tub. Another brother would carry the galvanized tub Mom used for the washing, placed upside-down over his head, as he too, began the journey over the hill. Another child would tote the washboard used for scrubbing the clothes. Mom had earlier tied a large bar of lye soap and a box of bluing inside one of the bundles of laundry she had slung over the mare's back. A ten-quart pail and two quart-size pails were hung on the saddle horn for my brothers to dip and carry water from the creek. Mom would walk in back of the troop carrying a jar of drinking water and a glass bottle of "Magic" (bleach).

Once she was on the way to the creek, the gentle, aged workhorse would choose her own pace, which was, thank God, very slow. She must have remembered our route from instinct because she certainly didn't get any directions from me. It took all of my ability to keep myself and the babies on the horse's back.

Once we had begun our descent down the steepest part of the mountain, I would wrap the bridle reins around the saddle horn so that I could use one hand to hold onto the saddle. With the mare sometimes stumbling over rocks or slipping on the hardened clay, I was terrified that she would spill me and the babies, head first, off her back and down the steep mountain.

By God's grace we always arrived safely at the water hole, and never once did I have to command Ol' Bess to stop. It seemed that she was just as pleased as I was to finally reach our destination. The horse would stand near the entrance to the pasture and wait for my brothers to drop the bars [poles] that Grandpa had used for a gate in the fence in order to get to the hole of water on the other side. (Mom would innocently refer to the trip we took on wash day as "going down to the bars.") Once through the bars and inside the pasture-field, the old mare's load was pulled off her back, and she was turned loose to graze on the lush, green grass growing in abundance alongside the creek.

Mom would sit the baby and toddler in the middle of a quilt she had spread on the grassy ground and then expect me to care for them and the other children younger than I. The job left no free time for me to run and play with my older brothers.

Mom would immediately begin the work by arranging two piles of flat rocks about 16 inches apart and a foot high. She would then start a fire between the stacked rocks with dry wood that had been collected from the nearby forest. She would carefully place the sooty tub, which the boys had begun to fill with water, on the piles of rocks. With the fire lapping up around the sides of the tub, my brothers would rush back and forth carrying water from the creek and pouring it into the washtub.

The tub for washing was placed on a large tree stump that had previously been flattened on the top and rolled near the creek. Once again, my brothers would carry enough cold water from the creek and hot water from the sooty tub to partially fill the tub. Once she was satisfied with the amount of water in the tub, Mom would then lean the washboard in the tub of warm water, grab the bar of lye soap, and, bending forward over the washboard, begin the backbreaking job of scrubbing the laundry.

The boys would again fill the hot tub with water from the creek. After they had gathered additional wood and stoked the fire, they were then set free to begin playing "Cowboys and Indians." Woody would let out a war whoop and lunge toward Marvin. Marvin and Maynard would jump on their imaginary horses and, while slapping themselves on the rear, race across the field ahead of the savage Indian.

Mom always insisted on scrubbing the light-colored clothing and white linens until they were spotlessly clean. No matter how weary she may have been, after she had scrubbed the enormous pile of whites and linens and had squeezed out the excess water, she would then carry the wet articles over to the tub of steaming water to which she had added the proper amount of bluing. Using a long stick, she would then poke each article below the surface of the water and allow the tub of bluing water to simmer for a few minutes. The bluing process was an important aid in accomplishing Mom's expectations of returning to the house with a load of sparkling white laundry.

As she walked toward the heaping pile of grimy dungarees waiting to be washed, she would reach up with her right hand, crook her index finger, and wipe the perspiration from her forehead. Having had nothing to eat since before dawn—yet taking no breaks except to nurse the baby or to take a drink of water now and then—she would breathe a sigh of relief once she had finally scrubbed the last pair of denims. Seeing the wearied look on her face and admiring her determination, I could hardly wait until I would be old enough to help my mother with her heavier tasks.

With the hardest part of her work now behind her, Mom would dump the tub of dirty water onto the ground and then call in her cowboy and Indian to refill the tub with clean rinse water. Once again, my brothers would hastily transfer water from the creek to the tub before remounting their imaginary horses for a few more rides across the green pasture.

While continuing her laborious pace, Mom would remove the laundry from the bluing water with the long stick and carry each piece to the tub of cold rinse water. As weary as she must have been, once the linens and all the clothing had been rinsed and wrung out by hand, she would bundle the wet laundry together to be loaded onto the horse's back.

Each of us would repeat the same steps we had taken earlier in the day. Mom would drape the quilt, on which the babies had been camped out, across the horse's back to protect the clean bundles of laundry, and then she and my brothers would shove the bundles up onto the mare's hindquarters. The smaller children would collect the articles they had carried "down to the bars" earlier.

Woody and Marvin would extinguish the fire by dumping the last tub of water over the live coals. They would once again drop the bars in the fence for the horse and her heavy load to pass through. Back up the hill the family would scurry, rushing to get home so that Mom could prepare supper before Dad's return from work.

Going up the hill took much more effort for all of us than coming down had taken. There was no doubt that Mom was hungry as well as exhausted. She apparently realized that she could wait for supper just like we children had to do, since the only time we had anything to eat in the middle of the day was when Dad was home. I didn't know how my siblings were feeling, but although I had become accustomed to feeling hunger pangs, the desire for beans and "taters" seemed more intense on the days we spent down at the bars.

Since the laundry was now soaking wet, Ol' Bess's load was much heavier than before, which forced her to choose each step carefully as she struggled up the rutted mountainside. Perched precariously on her back, I watched as she seemed to struggle to stay on her feet. I could imagine the results should the aged mare flip over backwards from the weight of the heavy load slung over her hindquarters. I had no doubt that both the babies and I would be crushed under the weight of the oversized horse. I always looked forward to arriving at our front porch, where Mom would help me off the horse's back and set my feet on the hard-baked red-clay earth.

Once the baby and I were freed from our harrowing experience, Mom would lead Ol' Bess to the backyard, where a long piece of heavy wire had been tied between two locust trees to use for a clothesline. She would slide the bundles of laundry off the horse's back and into the washtubs the boys had placed beneath the clothesline. My mother was just as particular about how the clothes were hung on the makeshift clothesline as she was about the whiteness of her linens. If she didn't have time to sort and hang the clothes before time to prepare supper, she would wait until after the family was busy devouring the meal before she would return to the clothesline.

Mom would first painstakingly sort the pieces of laundry before handing each article on the clothesline by their groupings and lengths. Knowing the enormity of Mom's responsibilities, I always wondered why she was so particular about how the clothes were hung on the line, knowing that, since we lived miles inside the boondocks, only our own family members would have a view of the clotheslines.

While I realized that this particular responsibility seemed to be the only job my mother took pride in doing, I often watched as she hung the last article of laundry on the line and then stepped back proudly to watch the sparkling clean clothes blowing gently in the fresh, country breeze.

Although my mother had fretted to my father about moving onto the ridge, no matter how much extra work she and we children were required to do, throughout the drought and for years to come, I never again heard her complain to my father. She, my siblings, and I did the best we could do and expected very little in exchange; besides, having to endure daily hardships was a part of our normal way of life. With the exception of my having to ride the horse, "going down to the bars" was simply a family excursion for my siblings and me.

XIX

Aunt Sissy and Uncle Clint

Shortly before school was to begin in the fall, Mom's sister (Sissy) and her husband, Clint, moved onto the ridge. When they were first married, they had moved into the log house in the hollow that had been vacated by the Haskels. The small cottage they were now occupying was located around the point, back toward the town-side of our property.

An agreement they and my parents had for some reason made was allowing me the privilege of spending Friday nights at their home. I was overjoyed. "Sissy" and Uncle Clint treated me like I was special, and I loved both of them with all my heart. I appreciated the fact that they also showered affection on each other, especially since I was not accustomed to seeing any type of affection between Mom and Dad.

My aunt and uncle were as poor as the rest of the families in the area. Their little cabin had only two rooms. Their small living room also served as their bedroom. The kitchen was about half as big as the living room and was furnished with a cast-iron stove that burned wood, a small table with four chairs, and a white hutch. Uncle Clint had built a small wooden shelf against the wall in one of the corners to accommodate two wash basins and the bucket that held their drinking water, which they carried from a spring on the property.

I enjoyed the softness of the feather mattress and the fluffy soft pillows that were covered with starched pillowcases that Sissy had hand embroidered. I had never slept in a bed as comfortable and fresh smelling. Having a top sheet to sleep under was also a new experience for me.

My dear aunt and uncle seemed to delight in ending my day with laughter. Every night after we had settled ourselves in bed, they would tell funny stories that made me laugh. On one particular night, I laughed so strenuously that it caused me to start coughing. While trying to laugh and cough at the same time, I sounded like a barking dog. The bed literally shook from all the laughter. I seldom saw adults laughing and enjoying themselves, so it was refreshing to be included in the fun without being made to feel guilty.

Uncle Clint and Aunt Sissy.

The only unpleasantness I experienced while visiting with Sissy and Uncle Clint was the following day as I waited painfully for my brothers to arrive to escort me home. I would stand in front of the living room window, feeling very sad and crying softly. Once my brothers would pop over the knoll, which was about fifty yards in front of Sissy's house, I would run over and hug Sissy tightly. I would then walk out the door to return to a life that was continuing to lose its luster.

One Saturday morning, after only four or five overnight visits, I was told by my parents that, for no apparent reason, my special privilege was being revoked. I didn't know the reasoning behind my parents' decisions, yet I knew better than to try to change their minds.

The next time I saw my relatives and told them that I wouldn't be staying overnight with them again, Uncle Clint made a comment that at the time I didn't understand. Without looking up from the work he was doing, he mumbled to Sissy and me, "One thang fer shore, they know if loodle Betty [his nickname for me] hain't 'ere ta keep 'er shoulder t'da wheel, the whole shebang 'ud fall apart."

Although my Friday night visits had ended abruptly, I continued to take every opportunity to visit with my special relatives. Their lives had enriched my life, and even to this day, I know that their love for each other and for me was real. I am grateful that no one can take away the memories of the time I spent with the two people who showed me more affection and stability than any adult during my childhood years.

XX

The Picture Show

The family had worked hard all summer. The crops were harvested, the canning was done, and the beginning of a new school year was just over the horizon. I was still avoiding being alone with my father since his behavior toward me had not improved; however, I was trying very hard to live my life to its fullest. "What will the third grade hold in store for me?" I wondered aloud.

Mom returned from town with two new pairs of pants and two shirts each for Woody, Marvin, and my younger brother Maynard, who would be entering the first grade. She handed two new dresses to me before she emptied the contents of a big paper bag onto the floor. While shoving two pairs of socks and a pair of brown clodhoppers toward each of my brothers and me, she said, "Y'all better take good keer'uv 'is here stuff. Ye know it hasta last ye fer tha whole year long."

A couple of months into the school year, my teacher announced that the following day the high school would be showing a movie for the students in our elementary school. She told the class that we would each need to bring twenty-five cents to school the next morning to pay for the movie.

My brothers and I had never been privileged to attend any of the extracurricular activities that charged an admission; nevertheless, when we arrived home from school, I asked Mom whether she would give my siblings and me a quarter each for school the next day.

"Now what'na shit's 'at fer?" she asked.

"Fer a movie at'ta high school," I said.

"You young'uns know 'at Daddy ain't gonna let y'all 'tend a show," she said. "An' 'sides 'at, I ain't got no money." She looked into my eyes and pitifully continued, "If I did haf any money, I could fin' a better way ta spend it than givin' it ta y'all ta go to a picture show."

Early the next afternoon, my teacher lined up the class, except for me, to join with the other classes who were boarding the school buses to be taken to the high school. Once my classmates had exited the room, Ms. Irwin informed me that I was the only student in the entire grammar school not attending the movie. I wondered how my brothers had gotten the money to attend the event. At the time, television hadn't been introduced to our area, so with the exception of my father, none of our family had ever before seen a movie. As I sat silently, I contemplated the questions I would have for my brothers while we walked home from school in the afternoon.

My teacher soon informed me that since I was the only child unable to go on the trip, she was required to stay at school with me. She then dryly said to me, "Mary, you step back to the bookshelf and get a book to read while I grade some papers."

I walked to the back of the room, but before I had had a chance to select a book, Ms. Irwin called out to me, "Mary, would you like to go to the movie as my guest?"

I felt the blood rush to my face. Mom had always warned my siblings and me that we were never to ask anyone for money or for favors of any kind. "No, ma'am," I answered quickly. My heart began to pound rapidly when the thought entered my mind that to go as the teacher's guest might mean I would get in for free, simply by being with the teacher. I wanted to go to the movie with all my heart, but I was too timid and embarrassed to ask Ms. Irwin whether "going as her guest" meant she would have to pay my way. I was concerned that, should the term not mean I would get in free simply by being alone with my teacher, she might feel that I was asking her to buy my ticket.

I decided to keep my mouth shut and just read a book; therefore, my teacher and I sat there in the empty classroom the entire afternoon.

Later, on the way home from school, my brothers shared with me their excitement upon seeing their first moving picture. "You orta seen President Lincoln's bed movin' 'round the room," Woody said excitedly. None of us realized at the time that what Woody had seen was not the bed moving at all; instead, he had been viewing the president's bed being filmed from different angles as the cameraman moved around the room.

Listening to my brothers excitedly describing the scenes from the movie, and watching their expressions of disbelief, I was even more disappointed to have missed what they had experienced. When Marvin told me that the movie had been about Abraham Lincoln's life, I felt even worse. I loved reading or hearing stories about President Lincoln, and I feared that I would never again have the opportunity to see a movie about him moving from one place to another. Neither my brothers nor I realized the man was not Lincoln at all; instead, the character had been an actor merely portraying our former president.

Walking along the country road, I reflected on what I had missed. I was even more disturbed when I realized I had been the cause of the teacher missing the historical movie. "Woody," I asked, "What'd my teacher mean when she asted [asked] me if I'd like ta go to the movie as her guest?"

"She was jist sayin' you could set by her if you was too skeered to set by y'urself," my oldest brother said.

"What a relief!" I said. "She orta knowed 'at I didn' have any money, so I'm glad I didn' go with her 'cause she wouldn' think I'uz 'spectin' her ta pay my way."

When I asked my three brothers how they had managed to go to the movies without any money, they each gave me the same answer. It seemed that they too were the only students in their classrooms without the quarter needed to pay for the event, so their teachers simply told them that they could go for free.

XXI

Our Thanksgiving

Thanksgiving Day was not celebrated by my family, nor by other families in the area where I was raised, in the same, traditional way others celebrated the day. While the more fortunate families were getting together to visit and to feast on a meal of turkey, dressing, and all the trimmings, my family and Mr. White were gathering together to butcher the hog we had fattened for the kill.

In early spring, my father would buy a pig to raise for butchering on Thanksgiving Day. This particular day of the year was chosen because the men were off work for the holiday, and the weather was cold enough by the end of November to keep the meat from spoiling, since we had no source of refrigeration. Early on, the pig was fed a diet of potato peelings, the few table scraps left over from the meals, and dishwater. When a new calf was born, for the first four milkings, the hog was given any milk left over after the calf had sucked its fill from the cow. Once a day an armload of purslane (weeds) was pulled by one of the younger brothers and thrown into the wire-fenced pen for the hog to eat.

Six weeks before Thanksgiving, the hog was taken from the open pen and confined in a small pen with a wooden floor, while he was being fattened for slaughtering. Since Dad always wanted the hog to be as fat as possible so the renderings would make more and better lard, the animal's diet was changed from the slop to fresh pails of water and an ample amount of corn we had raised.

By the time he was fourteen years old, my brother Woody had been given the job of shooting the hog. No one seemed to think about the gruesome act they were asking the young boy to perform; however, he didn't seem to mind what he had to do. It was merely another of the jobs that went along with farm life in and around our territory.

Early on Thanksgiving Day, the old, soot-covered washtub was filled with water and placed over an open fire near the hog pen. While the water was heating, the men would prepare the area where the hog was to be slaughtered, scraped, cut up, and prepared for curing.

Once the water was scalding hot and the area readied, my siblings would gather around to watch the slaughter. I, on the other hand, always got as far away from the site as possible. Having witnessed the event for the first time at age eight, I had seen enough of the blood and gore.

After Woody had shot the hog between the eyes, Dad would immediately jump into the pen, grab the hog by the front legs, and roll the huge swine over onto its back so that a sharpened knife blade could be rammed into the dying hog's neck to cut the jugular vein. This was done in order to bleed the hog. Dad called the act "stobbin' the hog."

Once the bleeding had slowed, the hog was then grabbed by the hind legs, dragged out of the pen, and laid on the sled near the scalding area. The hog's hair was loosened by placing burlap sacks over the hog and then pouring buckets of boiling water over the sacks. After allowing the heat from the hot water to penetrate the hog's skin, the sacks were removed. Dad and Mr. White would begin scraping the hair from the hog's hide, using large knives or sharpened machetes. After the hair was scraped off one side of the hog, the carcass was turned over and the procedure repeated on the other side.

The hind legs were then split near the hocks, exposing the hamstrings. Each end of a thick dried branch about sixteen to eighteen inches long was then inserted between the exposed tendons of the legs. A rope was lowered from a pulley attached to a tripod that had been constructed previously for the occasion. Grabbing the center of the brace between the hog's legs with a hook tied to the end of the rope, the slaughtered and scraped hog was hoisted upward—the hind parts lifted first and the head hanging downward. Once the tripod was safely supporting the weight of the animal, the neck was cut around the base of the head, and the head was removed.

Next, using care not to puncture the intestines, the sharp blade of a butcher knife was inserted at the point of the hog's anus and pulled downward, splitting open the animal's belly to the point where the head had been removed. The large intestine was cut free and the anus tied off. The membrane holding the intestine was cut, allowing the steaming entrails to fall into a tub.

The organs were removed, rinsed, and set aside for later distribution among our friends and relatives. Unfortunately, the liver was one part of the hog that we could be assured Dad would keep for our own family. Since we had no source of refrigeration, the liver would be carried to the house immediately to be cooked. Mom would place the big, repulsive hunk of fresh liver inside a big pot of water and allow it to simmer until it had the same consistency as a chunk of wet sawdust. The only thing worse than having to eat the disgusting liver was the fact that we children had to act as though we were enjoying eating it. Years later, when I realized liver could be prepared in different ways to make it look and taste more appetizing, it became one of my favorite foods.

After rinsing the inside of the body cavity with pails of cold water, the carcass was then lowered back onto the sled that had been scrubbed clean by one of my brothers. Dad would then cut the meat into sections to cure for the family, or into serving portions to give to our relatives. Using an axe to chop alongside both sides of the backbone, Dad would remove the bone, allowing both sides of the hog to fall free. The tenderloin, which was located along either side of the backbone's cavity, was removed and saved to divide between Mr.

White and our relatives, and a small portion reserved for our own family.

The shoulders and hams were removed and one each laid aside to be preserved with curing salt, while the other two were sliced and placed in the giveaway pile. The mid-line (called the "midlens" by the folks in our area), which was the belly area, was dissected from the rib cages and divided to be sliced later for bacon. Our family's portion of the bacon was left intact and cured. The backbone and ribs were cut into several slabs.

After Mr. White had received his portion of the fresh pork, the remaining meat was carefully sorted to be distributed among our family and Dad's and Mom's relatives. Taking special care to divide the meat evenly, Dad would often say, "We gotta be curful that none of 'em gets their feelin's hurt or 'ey'll be miffed at us 'til nex'cheer."

Very little of the meat was wasted. Mom was happy to give the feet to Dad's sister. Uncle Abner always asked for the "lights" (lungs) of the animal and the parts he called "mount'n oysters" (testicles). He also liked the tail and ears. While we pleased him by giving him the "special parts" of the hog, which he alone had asked for, he pleased us by taking the undesirable parts off our hands. Of course, choice pieces of the fresh meat were also included with the "special parts."

Culling pieces of the pork, and meat cut from the head, were ground with a hand-turned grinder and made into sausage and souse. Because much of the sausage would be given away, our family usually had only one or two messes of the tasty patties that Mom would prepare with ground sage. Should extra sausage remain after all portions had been claimed, Mom would brown the small patties on both sides, place them inside heated canning jars, and fill the jar with hot, sizzling grease. During the winter months, she would set one of the sealed jars of sausage on the fireplace hearth to heat overnight so we could each have a sausage biscuit for breakfast. The sausage biscuit was a rare and special treat for my siblings and me.

The bones from the shoulder and ham were kept to season the beans Mom cooked each day, and the smaller bones were given to our grateful dogs. Excess fat cut from the different pieces of pork was placed in a deep pan and rendered inside a hot oven. The hot, liquified grease was then poured into heated glass jars, sealed, and set aside to cook before it was carried to the cellar for my mother to use for lard.

The hog's skin was made into tasty pork rinds by baking the squares of skin in a hot oven or by deep frying a few of them at a time. Once they were cooled, my siblings and I would quickly devour them and wish for more.

After rubbing the ham, shoulder, and slabs of bacon with brown curing salt, Dad would run a piece of heavy wire through each piece of the meat and suspend it from a rafter in one of the out-buildings. Hanging the meat prevented mice and other pests from eating or contaminating the meat.

By the time all the relatives and neighbors had received "their share" of the meat, we were left with very little of the butchered hog. I could never understand why my family would go to all the work and expense of raising a hog just to give the best parts of the pork to relatives who could have raised and butchered their own hogs.

Every year I would remind myself that the hog had been raised for one reason—to be butchered on Thanksgiving Day for meat for the family. After Thanksgiving, however, each time I passed by the pigpen, I felt a sense of loss. I always knew that, come the following spring, the pen would be filled with life once again and the whole ordeal would be repeated.

Ordinarily, the first thing Dad did after the meat had been readied for Mom's handling was to dispose of the hog's head. Mom had always warned Dad that if the head were left out in sight, she would not go near the pile of meat. Dad was perfectly aware that she was absolutely terrified of the hog's head.

While he and my brothers were cleaning up the mess left over from the butchering, Dad was wearing a hard hat that he had worn while working in the coalmines. Mom was in the kitchen canning quarts of lard, and I was seated nearby churning milk.

Everything was going along very well, when, suddenly, Mom screamed as the outside door was shoved partially open. She rushed over and quickly slammed the door shut. I could hear my father laughing loudly outside on the porch. Having the door slammed shut in his face certainly wasn't something that he would laugh about, so I wondered what was causing him to laugh while Mom continued to scream.

I stepped closer and watched as Dad began shoving on the door, trying to get inside the kitchen. Mom was on the inside, pushing against the door to keep Dad outside. "Bud, go away! Don't chu do 'his!" she yelled.

Finally, Dad forced the door slightly ajar and pushed his head inside. Mom let out another blood-curdling scream. I moved over to where I could see around my mother and could hardly believe what I was witnessing. My father had cut a strip off the top of the hog's head, with the ears attached, and had somehow fastened it to the top of his hard hat.

Frantically, Mom yelled, "Oh my God, Bud! You're gonna mark my baby!" Dad suddenly stopped in his tracks and let go of the door. Removing the disgusting hat from his head, he slowly walked off the porch and into the yard, apparently no longer in a jovial mood. He had just heard for the first time that baby number nine was on the way—and he wasn't laughing any longer. For once in her life, my mother had gotten the last laugh.

XXII

Grandma's Thoughtfulness

Walking to and from school during the winter months could be very difficult had my siblings and I not found ways to make the walk more enjoyable. My brothers and I could choose one of three ways to get to and from our school. When the weather was nice, I thoroughly enjoyed the excursions, no matter which road we traveled. Trudging through the red-clay mud took a little more intuitiveness to make the walk interesting. Although it was about a mile shorter than the road over the hill and down the hollow, we avoided walking the ridge road as much as possible when it was wet and muddy. On a few occasions, however, despite the road being extremely wet and muddy, Woody insisted that we walk the ridge road.

The red clay was very sticky and clung to our shoes like paste. Sometimes my brothers and I would play games to see who could get the most mud to stick to the bottoms of our shoes. At the end of the ridge road, the build-up on our shoe soles was usually thick enough that we appeared at least four inches taller than our actual heights. It was not difficult to get the mud to cling to our shoes; the hard part came when we had to use sticks to scrape the mud off our shoes once we had left the ridge road.

When my brothers and I reached the end of the ridge road and had cleaned our shoes, we would walk over another hill onto the railroad tracks. We would then walk the railroad ties for a short distance to the street that would take us to our school, located about a half mile down the street.

Our trek would carry us past the school bus garage, where Dad always parked our car while he was at work. He would leave home too early in the morning for us to ride to school with him, and in the afternoons we were not allowed to wait for him to drive us back from school because we had to hurry home to do our chores. Our parents had warned us that we should never stop to talk to anyone on our way home from school lest we arrive at home late.

On most of our trips home from school, my brothers and I would take the route that led us past Grandma's house. We could walk up the hollow and climb the hill to our house in about the same amount of time it took us to walk the ridge road; however, convenience was not the only reason we often chose the road that passed by Grandma's house.

My mother's mom seemed to be sensitive to each of my sibling's and my needs. One of the things Granny did for us was the highlight of our school years. Every morning she would bake enough biscuits or cornbread to give each of us an afternoon snack to eat as we continued our journey home. She would split open the biscuits or hunks of cornbread and spread pinto beans, which she had mashed, between them. Occasionally, she would surprise us by spreading the bread with mustard and adding slices of onion. We would never have asked for our special treats; nevertheless, Granny was always standing by her door, waiting for us to arrive. Since we were not allowed to stop to chat, she would hand the food to my brothers and me as we passed by her front door. With our biscuits in hand, our little gang would hurry up the hollow, munching on our scrumptious treat as we readied for the steep climb up the mountain.

My older brothers and I had stopped carrying sack lunches to school to avoid the heckling from our peers. If our classmates didn't tease us because we had brought biscuits instead of sliced bread in our lunches, they would point out the rumpled lunch sacks that we were required to carry until they were worn out.

We had grown accustomed to hunger pangs long before school age. Snacks between meals were non-existent in our family. We were lucky to get two full meals a day, so Grandma's biscuits were appreciated more than she could realize. Even while our little group continued to grow in number, she thoughtfully added the needed biscuits to her already generous handouts.

Grandma no doubt sacrificed deeply in order to give, in the only way she knew how to give to us children. Years later, she would receive a token of our appreciation when my brother Woody returned to assure her that he might not have graduated from high school had it not been for those biscuits filled with the thin layers of beans—and the thick layers of Grandma's thoughtfulness.

XXIII

Sandy Closs

Christmas was the most exciting time of year around our house. Mom and Dad did their best to see that each of us children had at least one orange, a few pieces of candy, and, when possible, a ten- or fifteen-cent toy on Christmas Eve.

Grandpa Mullins, Mom's father, enjoyed playing Santa for the children in our family. Grandma would prepare Grandpa's disguise and inform Mom in advance that Grandpa had "agreed" once again to "thrill" our family with his attempt at pretending to be the jolly old elf. Any gifts or treats that Mom had bought for us children had been left with my grandparents earlier so that Santa could load them into his sack.

Dad had reluctantly agreed to allow "Santa" to visit our home to hand out the children's gifts. Since I'd been attending school, I had shared much information about Santa Claus with my younger siblings. Even our Grandpa, who had scoffed at the idea that Santa's sleigh was pulled by reindeer, had changed his mind and was anxious to give Santa a helping hand.

I had been given advance notice by Grandma that we could expect Santa's visit at dusk on Christmas Eve. Dad had emptied an extra shovel full of coal into the potbellied stove and had moved his chair to one side of the room, pausing long enough to ask whether I wanted to sit on his lap. I ignored his question and immediately moved to the other side of the room.

Mom had begun to encourage the children to listen for Santa's reindeer to land on the roof. Her excitement had quickly become contagious, and I had joined with my older brothers in preparing the children for the unexpected visit from the man in the red suit.

As prearranged, Grandpa had donned his disguise and walked up the hill, across the narrow field, and out the driveway to our front porch. With his walking cane in his right hand and his left hand grasping a burlap sack filled with crumpled papers and our treats, he stepped onto the porch and stomped his feet loudly.

"Listen young'uns!" Mom yelled. "Who's 'at on the roof?"

"Whoa, reindeer, 'et's see if we got somethin' fer the young'uns 'at lives here," Santa yelled.

The little children ran over and held onto my legs. I bent down and tried to assure them that Santa would be dressed in a red suit and would be very kind to them. "He's gonna brang you somethin' purty," I said. I had shown them pictures in a book that I had brought home from school one evening and wondered whether they were visualizing how Santa and his reindeer would get off our roof and inside our house to give them gifts.

Finally, after several thumps on the outside wall and with Grandpa yelling for his reindeer to stop, Mom opened the door, and an old man dressed in a long, black woolen overcoat walked into the room. While my parents and older brothers tried to act surprised, all my younger siblings broke forth in a chorus of loud squeals, easily recognized as squeals of sheer terror rather than squeals of delight. From the expressions on their faces, they were scared silly from the sight of the strange old gent with a burlap sack thrown over his shoulder.

I looked closely at Grandpa while the children held onto me tightly. "Santa" had a paper bag pulled down over his head with holes cut out for his eyes, and a long white beard made from cotton glued onto the bag. A moth-eaten black stocking cap was pulled down over the top of the bag he had covering his face.

Determined not to retreat, "Ol' Sandy Closs," as Grandpa preferred to call himself, moved closer to the little ones while assuring them that he had just dropped in from the sky. He declared that he had parked his sleigh and reindeer outside on the roof and had shinnied down the outside of the chimney. His audience, however, didn't appear to be buying his story, as they screamed even louder.

"Ho, ho, ho!" Santa Claus exclaimed. "Come here, young'uns, an' see what Ol' Sandy Closs brung you fer Christmas."

Grandpa always delighted in teasing small children and never seemed to be happy unless he had one or two of us angry with him when he was around. Chuckling, he nudged the crying children with his cane and goaded them about their fears.

The children younger than I, except for Maynard, refused to go near Santa. Maynard bravely walked over and accepted an orange, a couple pieces of hard candy, and a small bag of marbles that brought a grin to his face.

Santa tried again to coax the children over to the opened bag. With no response except for more crying, he reached over with his cane and hooked my three-year-old sister, Nina, around her neck and began pulling her toward him. Nina continued to whimper until Grandpa reached inside the bag and handed her an orange, two pieces of candy, and a nickel coloring book. My little sister held on to her gifts and scampered back against the wall behind the potbellied stove.

Woody and Marvin were each given their treats along with one red and one blue sponge ball. In addition to the orange and two pieces of hard candy, I received a small box of crayons. Since my two smaller brothers were too frightened to approach Santa, he stepped alongside them and, after punching each of them with his cane, dumped the few articles that remained inside his sack onto the floor before wadding up his sack and pushing it underneath his arm.

Even on Christmas Eve, in addition to having the children scared out of their skin, Grandpa had already managed to irritate the older kids and to upset my father. Although I enjoyed Grandpa's attempt at playing "Ol' Sandy Closs," I believed that he was giving Santa a bad name; after all, I was in school and had seen the real Santa when he had come to our classroom and handed out candy to each of us. He was a rotund, jolly old man in a red suit who made children happy rather than frightened and angry. I was also wise enough to know that Santa didn't look like Grandpa and that Grandpa most certainly didn't look like Santa.

While the children were either jumping with glee or screaming from fright, Santa exited the room in the same manner he had entered. Stomping across the porch, he yelled, "Gitty up, you lazy reindeers! It's time ta git home an' git'ta bed." And then, into the night he disappeared, leaving behind several squalling or angry children and two frustrated adults who were thankful that Christmas came only once a year.

We older children were careful not to reveal the fact that our counterfeit Santa was none other than our grandfather. I suspected that the reason Mom and Dad had consented to Grandpa's playing Santa in the first place was not merely to entertain our family but to put some joy into our grandparents' Christmas as well.

XXIV

Virgil Emmanuel Day

Japan bombed the U.S. fleet at Pearl Harbor, Hawaii, in a surprise attack on December 7, 1941, and four days later our country was at war with Japan, Italy, and Germany. Dad and Mom had become more aware of world events since the war had begun, since each evening they listened to reports broadcast over the radio. My brothers believed that Tojo was responsible for the sneak attack, and when they were angry with each other one brother would sarcastically call the other "Old Tojo" or "a dirty Jap," and then their own war would ensue between the two of them. I knew very little about the war; yet, I was afraid that the Japanese would be attacking our area at any moment.

Dad came home from work one evening and unnerved the entire family when he informed us that he had heard that an air-raid blackout had been ordered to go into effect at dusk. Although our small, isolated clapboard house was miles from town, with our only source of light being a single kerosene lamp, Dad insisted that blankets be hung over the windows to prevent our dwelling from being detected from the air. "You young'uns stay 'way from 'em 'ere winders an' git'ta bed early," he warned, before tuning in for any bulletins on the battery radio. I was very concerned when I went to bed, afraid that before the night was over, our home would be bombed, wiping out our entire family. I wondered how many of us would go to be with Jesus and whether any of us would go to be with Satan.

The economy was weak, having not recovered fully from the Great Depression; consequently, some foods and other necessities were in short supply, requiring ration stamps to be spent sparingly. Sugar and lard seemed to be the two food items Mom and our relatives missed most, since the lard rendered from one hog was not adequate to last our family until the next butchering. I once overheard Aunt Becky telling Mom to substitute mineral oil for lard when greasing her bread pans.

On a Saturday morning in April 1945, I watched as Mom and Dad were leaving for town to buy groceries, leaving my brothers and me home to care for our siblings. "Brang us some 'blubber' gum, Mommy," the smaller children begged. Mom did not respond to their requests, and I knew that neither bubble gum nor candy was on her shopping list since sugar was being rationed.

Later, when my parents returned home, I was surprised to see Mom in tears. She was almost due to deliver baby number nine, so I wondered whether there was a problem with her pregnancy that she had just learned about. "What'sa matter?" I asked as she approached the house.

"Pres'dent Rose'velt's dead," she replied.

"What'cha cryin' 'bout 'at fer?" I asked. "Cain't 'ey jist git 'nuther pres'dent?"

"He's been our pres'dent for 'bout twelve years an' the best'un we've ever had er ever will have," Mom said sadly. "Hard'a tell what'll happen 'ith 'his war goin' on an' thangs so tight."

Feeling her pain, my heart ached for my distraught mother.

The next month, on a stormy night in May, our family was aroused out of our sleep in preparation for the arrival of the new baby. Mom had warned us earlier in the evening that if the baby was coming, it would be on a stormy night like the one we were experiencing. I realized the truth of her statement when Dad ordered my three oldest brothers to go stay the rest of the night with Grandma.

The mud caused from the heavy rains had made the ridge road impassable, so Dad had been forced to leave the car down at my grandparents' house the night before. He told Mom that he would walk down to Grandma's house with the boys and would send his sister Becky, whose house he would pass after my grandparents, back to help with the birthing.

Arriving at Grandma's house and realizing that the creeks were out of their banks, Dad woke Grandma and asked her to take in my brothers for the rest of the night. After informing Grandma that he would send his sister back to our house on his way to get the doctor, Grandma quickly agreed that my brothers could stay with Grandpa and that she would accompany Aunt Becky to help with the birthing.

I was in bed with the smaller children, hoping that they would sleep through what I knew was about to take place. I listened as the women arrived and began heating pots of water on the stove in which they had hastily built a fire. Mom's intermittent soft moans sent chills down my spine. Being ignorant concerning childbirth, I was terrified that my mother would die before Dad could arrive with the doctor.

After what seemed like an eternity, Dad and the doctor burst through the door, soaking wet from head to foot. I listened while Dad explained that the doctor had driven his own car and had parked it at the foot of the hill behind our property. They had then walked the mile up the hill through the wet forest.

With Mom's moans and grunts intensifying, Dad excitedly exclaimed, "Marthy, Doc tol' me 'atta Germans surrendered!"

"Glory be ta God!" Mom said through her pain.

"Yes, indeed," the doctor said, "Today, May the eighth, will always be known as V.E. Day."

"What'cha mean by V.E. Day?" Mom asked.

"Victory in Europe, of course," the doctor said.

Between her moans, Mom replied, "If 'is'n here's a boy, 'hen I'm gonna name him for V.E. Day."

A few minutes later, the doctor said to Mom, "You didn't get your girl you've been trying for, Mrs. Lesher. It's another big boy."

"An' I'mma gonna call him Virgil Emmanuel so he can always 'member 'at he wuz born on Victory in Europe Day," Mom said, sounding exhausted.

The date May 8, 1945, had been good to our family. There were still only two girls among the ever-mounting number of brothers; still, brother number seven had arrived on a very important day in our nation's history. I waited patiently for the doctor to leave so that I could go into the living room, where Mom's bed had been moved a few days prior to give the doctor more space to work. I had heard the women commenting about what a plump little boy Mom had just delivered. I now knew for sure that no storks had been dropping all those babies at our door, but I still had a lot of questions that needed to be answered.

Dad finally left to walk the doctor back to his car, and the women left for their own homes. I wandered into the room to see my brother and was shocked when, as I examined his soft little body, I noticed an abnormality on his pudgy, pink cheek, slightly in front of his earlobe. I held him over to where my mother could see the spot I was pointing out, and asked, "Jue think that's where you marked him 'ith 'em hog's ears 'at Daddy skeered you with?"

Mom rubbed her fingers over the area in question and said, "Bethel, look it 'at. Hit looks jis' like a tiny loodle pig's ear."

"Yell, I thank so too," I said.

"Wait'll daddy sees 'at," Mom said, placing Virgil beside her and pulling the blanket over his head to help keep him warm.

When Dad returned, Mom showed him the baby's cheek and reminded him of the scare he had given her on Thanksgiving Day. Dad looked at baby Virgil and then walked away without speaking.

Sissy came out to our house later in the morning and helped Woody milk the cow before he left for school. I had to miss school to care for the family. Although I was doing my best at the age of nine and a half, Mom realized I needed help with the housework. With three weeks of school remaining before the summer break, I was glad when Dad came home from work and announced that he had made arrangements for one of the girls whose family lived farther out the ridge to come to our house to stay for the nine days Mom would be confined to bed.

After supper, as he walked toward his car to bring the young woman to our house, Dad yelled back across his shoulder, "Bethel, you take keer'a thangs whilst I go fetch us a hired girl."

About half an hour later, my siblings and I almost ran over each other as we scampered out the door to meet our hired girl. Dad pulled the car in front of the house, opened the car door, stepped onto the ground with a big grin plastered across his face, and said, "Come on in, Reetie, an' don't let all 'ese here young'uns skeer ya ta death." Rita walked over and met with Dad at the front of the car. I noticed that she was carrying a large paper bag that apparently contained her clothing. I had been wondering how the teenage neighbor would look, and, having seen her mother on a few occasions, I imagined that she too would be a tall, skinny woman with rotten teeth and stringy, shoulder-length hair. I was stunned, however, when I peeked around my brothers and saw Rita strutting toward our front door—looking nothing at all like her homely mother.

I thought to myself, "No wonder Daddy's grinning like a fox in the hen house." The hired girl was actually a fully developed, grown woman who appeared to be about eighteen years old and was very pretty. Her red-painted lips, sparkling like ripe cherries in the noonday sun, accentuated her curly blond hair and pearly white teeth. I gawked at her bosom that seemed to be straining to burst free of the tight dress she was wearing.

Rita wriggled her way between the seven of us children and pranced over to Mom's bed. "Hiye do, Marthy, let me see 'at new baby," she said, laughing loudly with a pitch at the end that sounded like a chicken strangling on water. Mom pulled the blanket back, and

Rita stooped down and looked at my new baby brother. "He's really cute—looks jis' like his daddy," she said, giggling and looking teasingly at my father.

"Yell, I reckon he does," Mom said.

Rita, finding plenty of chores to do, went straight to work. While I was doing what I could to help, the two of us conversed only when necessary. I was glad that she was there to help me, and while I watched her doing Mom's work, I was convinced that she would carry out all of Mom's duties very efficiently.

On Rita's second evening at our home, I no doubt gave her the scare of her life. I had helped her prepare the evening meal and had carried Mom's food to her bedside. Once Rita and the family had been fed, she and I then washed the dishes before she left for the barnyard to milk the cow. The older children went along to take advantage of the nice weather. Ordinarily, when Dad was home, he would keep us children busy doing the chores in order to "keep us out of mischief." On this particular evening, however, he seemed to be content to sit inside while we children went outside to play.

While Rita was milking the cow that Dad had traded Brownie for, the boys and I decided to play with the farm wagon. The wagon was approximately forty inches wide by six feet long, with two long poles that connected to the front of the wagon and hooked to the harness traces when being pulled by our horse. My big brother Woody situated Marvin, Maynard, and me around the wagon so we could help shove in order to roll the wagon as fast as possible. Marvin and Maynard were stationed at the back of the wagon to push, while Woody got in front to pull with the long poles. Woody positioned me between the front and rear oversized spoke-wheels on the left side of the wagon.

After a few grunts and hard shoves, the wagon started to roll. "Faster! Faster!" Woody yelled. I soon realized my brothers were doing all the pushing and pulling while I was straining every muscle in my body just to hold onto the wagon and stay on my feet. Running as fast as my spindly legs could carry me, I began yelling for my brothers to stop the wagon.

"Stop! Stop!" I frantically yelled.

"Faster! Faster!" Woody yelled.

"Help! I'mma gonna fall!" I screamed. With the wagon picking up speed, I realized I had nowhere to go but down, so down I went—flat onto my belly. The boys either didn't know or didn't care that I had dropped to the ground beneath the wagon. I had no time to roll from beneath the wheels nor to alert my brothers that I was about to die, when suddenly, the rear wheel of the wagon rolled directly over my body.

I let out a blood-curdling yell that could have raised the dead, convinced that the big wagon wheel had left its tracks from my toes to my head. Lying there in the dirt, screaming and fearing that I had been wounded for life, I was too terror stricken to look for blood or even to feel any pain.

Hearing my screams, Rita jumped up off the milk stool to see which of us children was lying on the path and flat as a pancake. Startled, Ol' Jersey, the cow, kicked over the milk pail, spilling all the milk onto the ground.

Having finally realized one of the crew had fallen by the wayside and was lying in the middle of the road and likely bleeding to death, my brothers ran the wagon into the side of the corn crib and ran over to see whether I was still breathing.

Rita ran over, picked me up off the ground, dusted off my clothing, and attempted to assure me that all my parts were still intact. Whimpering with fear from the dreadful ordeal I had just endured, I waited for some expression of sympathy from my brothers. Marvin looked me over and then sarcastically said, "You big sissy, you!" I nervously glanced back up the path and was surprised to see my younger brother Maynard still standing back at the start line.

Rita looked at Woody and Marvin and said, "You boys are lucky! Her guardian angel must'a been lookin' over 'er. Y'all could'a kilt y'ur loodle sister!"

"If she could'n keep up, 'hen she orta stayed in'na house," Woody said.

Rita shook her head from side to side and then half dragged me to the "milk gap" (the place outside the barn where the cow is fed while being milked). She retrieved the empty milk pail and tried to coax Ol' Jersey to give a little more milk. By this time, however, Ol' Jersey had decided that she was keeping any milk she had left.

Rita picked up the empty pail and called for the boys to shut Jersey in the barn for the night. Then, with the empty pail in one hand and the nape of my neck in the other, our hired girl sternly ordered me to the house.

"What happened to the milk?" Dad asked as we walked through the door with the empty ten-quart bucket. Rita said only that the cow had kicked over the pail and spilled the milk just as she had finished milking. She didn't mention why the cow had overturned the bucket, and for that I was eternally grateful. I suspected that had Dad known what had really happened, he would have grabbed his hickory withe, and Woody and Marvin would have been in worse shape than I.

Dad seemed satisfied with Rita's answer and did not comment one way or the other about why the cow had kicked over the pail. I thought to myself, "If that had been Mommy instead of Rita, Daddy probably would've kicked her rear and then yelled at her for the rest of the evening." Since we had no source of refrigeration, each night's milking was our supply of milk for the next morning. Needless to say, the next morning we had to eat our oats and drink our coffee without milk, since it was too early for Ol' Jersey to be milked.

Our family was getting along exceptionally well with our hired help. Dad, especially, seemed to be enjoying her company. On several occasions, in my presence, my father gave Rita affectionate pats or playful pinches on her backside. To my surprise, instead of resisting his saucy behavior, Rita turned and smiled at him and then began with her loud, silly giggles.

Mom was out of bed and ready to resume her role in the household on the tenth day after Virgil's birth. As Dad handed Rita her wages and prepared to take her home, Woody and Marvin asked for permission to accompany them. "No! Hain't no need'n y'all taggin' along," Dad unequivocally answered.

I was sorry Rita had to leave. Everything had gone along exceptionally well while she was with us. I had even had no "run-ins" with Dad. I was hopeful that he would continue to act like a "normal" father once Rita was gone. I should have known, however, that I was expecting too much.

XXV

Remedies

Since Virgil was the seventh son, some of the people in our area believed he would be able to cure thrush inside a baby's mouth, once he was old enough to blow his breath into the child's infected mouth. Whenever the mothers carried their babies to our home seeking his curing power, Virgil would run and hide, compelling Mom to drag him back outside and then insist that he blow into the baby's mouth. Reluctantly, he would quickly puff one big breath into the child's mouth while the mother held the baby's mouth open. He'd then scamper away and hide until the mother and her baby had gone.

This practice was only one of many beliefs and home remedies used by families in our area to "cure" the sick. My father believed that a healthy dose of Black-Draught would cure most ailments we children might have experienced. Black-Draught was the cheapest and no doubt the foulest-tasting laxative on the market. At least once each month Dad would line us up and then measure one teaspoonful of the dry granules for each child. We knew he expected us to place the spoonful of the laxative on our tongue and then wash it down with a large gulp of water. Without uttering a word, each of us would shiver, cough, and gag as we swallowed the remedy, realizing that if we protested, Dad would yank off his belt and give us a healthy dose of his own medicine. With nine or ten children receiving the strong laxative at the same time, a major problem arose, since we had only one outhouse to share amongst us.

Should a child come down with an earache, either Dad would blow smoke from his pipe into the ear or Mom would expose her breast and fill the ear with warm breast milk before plugging the child's ear with a piece of cotton. A stomachache was treated by giving the child a teaspoonful of sugar to which a few drops of turpentine had been added. A severe cut was treated either by pouring kerosene over the gash or by making a poultice from a chew of tobacco and plastering it against the cut. A boil on the skin was covered with wet slivers of soap and bound loosely in hopes of bringing the pus-filled swelling to a head. The boil was then opened with a needle and squeezed to remove the pus. A severe cold or flu was treated by making a tea from a weed the country folk called "old field blossom." A poultice made from mustard and slices of onion was applied to the chest of a child with croup. A colicky infant was given a warm tea made from the catnip plant, which was gathered and then simmered in sweetened water.

Medical and dental care was almost non-existent. None of the families were covered with health or life insurance. A child was taken to a doctor only when his life was threatened with a serious illness or injury. When the elderly became ill, hospitalization was not a consideration. The family accepted the fact that their loved one would either get better or die. When a person died, the cause of death was considered to have been "consumption." The mattress on which the person had died was burned immediately.

Preventive dental care was not an option. The dentist was visited only when a decayed tooth needed to be extracted once the pain had become unbearable. Neither my siblings nor I owned a toothbrush since Mom believed she could not afford to buy toothbrushes and toothpaste. When I entered the first grade and learned that I should be brushing my teeth at least twice daily, I was embarrassed to let the teacher know that I had never owned a toothbrush. Apparently detecting my concern, she informed me that I could brush my teeth by chewing the end of a willow twig and then using the frayed end to scrub my teeth. I began the practice the very next day, and although the twig tasted extremely bitter, I continued to brush with the green twigs until I learned that I could dust a damp cloth with baking soda to clean my teeth. Still having never brushed my teeth with a proper brush, I would, at the age of fifteen, buy my first toothbrush with my very first paycheck.

Shampoo was another luxury our family couldn't afford to buy. We had no choice but to wash our hair with the same bar of soap that we used to wash our hands. My hair was long and difficult to wash. One afternoon, when school was being dismissed for the day, my teacher informed the class that the following morning she would be checking our hair for lice, since a student had been infested with head lice. When Mom learned about the problem, she said to my brothers and me, "Young'uns, you be curful an' don't fetch 'em lice home. Keep y'ur head away from 'em tabby-headed young'uns."

Mom had recently begun buying a laundry detergent called "Duz." Since the slogan, "Duz does everything," was written on each box, Mom ordered me to fill the wash basin and to use a handful of the powder in the water to wash my hair.

The next morning, when my teacher began checking the class for head lice, she inspected my hair thoroughly, no doubt because I was the only girl in class with long hair. When she finished pulling my hair up, down, and sideways, she announced for the whole class to hear, "You don't have lice, but you have dandruff."

When I returned home in the afternoon and informed Mom that the teacher had advised me that I had dandruff, Mom immediately began examining my scalp. "'At teacher don't know what she's talkin' 'bout," she exclaimed angrily as she shoved me aside. "'At 'ere is Duz in y'ur hair 'at you didn' get rinched out. You hain't got no dander!"

XXVI

The Swimming Hole

One of the ladies whose house Grandma cleaned on a weekly basis volunteered to save her Sunday paper for my family to read. We children walked past Mrs. Snyder's home each evening on our way home from school, just before we left the street to begin walking the railroad tracks. When Grandma informed the lady that my brothers would be thrilled to get the day-old paper, it became a weekly ritual for Mrs. Snyder to roll the Sunday newspaper into a bundle, tie it with a string, and leave it on her front porch for Woody to retrieve after school.

When we arrived home from school, Woody would untie the papers, and he and Marvin would go straight for the comics. Mom often had to threaten my brothers to make them leave the paper long enough to do their chores. None of the paper was read except for the comics, so little did the nice lady know that after the boys had read the funnies, the paper would then be used for building kites, to help start fires in the stove, and, of course, substituted for toilet tissue since Dad reserved the "real thing" for his own use.

Throughout the years the paper brought a lot of pleasure to my brothers when they weren't hard at work. Besides raising a big garden, they were required to plant two big fields of corn, which was used to feed the work horse, milk cow, hog, and chickens. We had no tractor or any of the farming implements that would make the job easier, so everything had to be done the hard way—by hand.

The fields were planted, cultivated twice, and harvested manually by Woody, Marvin, my mother, and Maynard, once he was old enough to help with the work. Dad helped only with harvesting the crops.

Dad set high standards that my brothers and mother had to meet when working in the fields. When my father came home from work in the evenings, he would go to the cornfields to inspect the work they had done, and if their work did not meet his expectations, he would send the three of them back to the fields to redo their work.

Prior to Woody taking over the jobs, Mom had plowed the garden and fields with Ol' Maude, the work horse that replaced Ol' Bess. Woody and Marvin were eventually required to prepare all the fields for planting, although they were hardly able to handle the heavy plow pulled behind the horse.

After the fields had been plowed, the large clods of earth were then pulverized by pulling a "hary" (harrow) in the same manner the plowing had been done. Dad had made the triangular harrow by bolting three 1-inch by 6-inch by 8-feet boards together and then inserting discarded railroad spikes, which my brothers had retrieved from alongside the railroad tracks, through holes he had bored in the boards with a hand-cranked auger. The crudely built harrow was then hooked to the "singletree" (swingle tree), which was attached to the traces on the horse's harness.

The soil was then pulverized even more by replacing the harrow with a heavy "drag" that Dad and the boys had made by bolting together poles they had cut in the forest. They had then piled heavy rocks onto the top crossbars of the frame for added weight. With the drag hooked to the harness traces, the field was repeatedly crisscrossed, crushing any clods of dirt that the harrow had missed. The field was ready for the corn to be planted once the soil had been prepared, inspected by Dad, and had furrows made in it by pulling a lightweight plow with the horse.

Dad was one of the few farmers in the area who owned a corn planter. The planter held both seed corn and fertilizer in the metal pockets on its sides. Woody and Mom would take turns walking through the furrows and jabbing the metal tips of the planter into the ground about a pace apart. By pushing the handles together and then pulling them apart, the planter would then release the proper amount of corn and fertilizer into the soil. The entire field of corn was planted in the same manner. Marvin and Maynard would walk behind Woody or Mom, each carrying a hoe to pull loose soil over the hills of corn that had just been planted.

When the corn was a few inches tall, approximately five plants were left to grow in each hill, any extra plants being pulled by hand and discarded. The corn was cultivated by breaking up the dirt around each hill with a hoe and pulling the loose soil around the plants. Dad was especially particular that the weeds be cut and the soil overturned in the bulks between the rows. This was usually the stage of work that caused Dad to angrily send his "careless farmhands" back to the field to repeat their work; consequently, I was always frightened and could also see the fear on Mom's and my brothers' faces during these ordeals. These reprimands always brought back the memories of my father striking my mother.

After the field was hoed for the first time, the corn was allowed to grow for a few more weeks, and then the entire process was repeated. Finally, after every hill of corn had been hoed and the fields had met with Dad's approval, he considered the cornfield to be "laid by." Knowing that the hard work was behind them, Mom and my brothers were ready to celebrate. While Mom moved on to a less back-breaking job, my brothers would head for the large pool of water located about a mile over the hill in the hollow behind our property. While my father was at work, I spent each day doing the same things I had before the abuse had started; however, once he was home from work, I became more reticent, conscious of my surroundings and cautious with my every move. I was grateful that, although I did not work in the fields, I was usually permitted to go to the swimming hole with my brothers because I had carried out Mom's chores inside the house, which enabled her to work in the fields.

Because my brothers were not allowed to wear shorts or swim trunks, before leaving for the swimming hole they would cut off the legs of their worn-out jeans and then wear their trousers over the cut-offs.

As a rule, I was not allowed to wear a swimsuit, shorts, or pants; however, when I was allowed to go swimming with my brothers, I would wear a pair of my brother's baggy trousers underneath my dress. To tighten the waistband, I would run a string through the loops and tie it snugly.

My brothers and I would walk off the heavily wooded mountainside to the creek in the hollow below. After reaching the large, deep hole of crystal-clear water, which flowed over a solid rock bottom and pooled in the soft creek-bed before lazily continuing out of the hollow, my brothers would remove their dungarees and jump in the water, wearing only the cutoff jeans. I would usually climb about on the huge boulders before testing the invigorating and inviting water.

Usually, my brothers and I would have the big hole of water all to ourselves; yet on rare occasions, a few of the young boys living in the hollow would appear unexpectedly. I was extremely shy and self-conscious, so when the "uninvited" boys arrived, I would sneak out of the water and sit silently behind one of the boulders.

Woody, Marvin, and Maynard had learned to swim and would frolic freely in the deep hole of water; however, I could not swim. Although they wanted to teach me to swim, I wanted no part of their generosity, simply because I was afraid they would playfully push my head under the water, causing me to drown before they realized what was happening.

One day, when I was approximately ten years old, my brothers were taking turns paddling back and forth on an old log they had thrown into the pool. While one brother straddled the log, the other brother would shove the log out into the middle of the deep pool of water. The other brother would then stretch out on the log, reach over the sides with both hands, and paddle continuously until he had reached the outer edge of the swimming hole. He would then roll off the rotten log, and the other brother would climb aboard and paddle back to the opposite side of the pool.

I was splashing around in the shallow water and minding my own business, when Woody got the bright idea that I should take my turn riding the log. I faltered for a moment, wondering whether I could trust my brothers not to push me off the log into the deep water. After some assurances from both Woody and Marvin, I decided to move over to where they stood holding onto the log to keep it stationary while beckoning me to crawl aboard.

Slowly, I ventured out into the deeper water and pulled myself onto the wet log. While lying tensely on the log, holding on with all my might, my brothers gave me a gentle shove toward the deepest part of the pool. Then, while I watched nervously, they scampered over and stood on the big boulder at the back edge of the water hole. I didn't want my jovial brothers to know I didn't trust them and that I was wondering why they were being so nice to me. If they didn't have in mind to do me harm, I certainly didn't want to give them the idea.

With the log floating lazily in the deep, cold water, I began paddling myself to the other side. Abruptly, Woody lunged forward and dove into the water. My heart leapt into my throat! I watched to see where he would surface, when almost immediately I felt the back end of the log moving. Screaming frantically, I turned my head quickly but could not see Woody. Suddenly the log flipped, and before I knew what was happening, I went tumbling into the "bottomless" pool of water.

Realizing I was in the deepest end of the pool, I fought the water with both hands, struggling frantically to stay afloat. Swallowing mouthfuls of the ocean of water, in which I was slowly drowning, I grabbed for the log. Marvin appeared from out of nowhere and quickly shoved the log out of my reach. "Help! I'mma gonna drowned!" I yelled.

Woody, apparently undaunted by my pleas, yelled back to me, "Swim, you loodle coward, er we'll let'cha drowned!" I began kicking with both feet and paddling with both hands. As I thrashed around and realized that neither of the boys had any intention of helping me, I paddled even faster.

"Jist relax and paddle like a dog," Woody yelled.

"I'mma tryin' to," I yelled back, while at the same time looking around to see whether my brothers were making any attempt to rescue me. I feared that I was going to sink to the bottom and die, when I caught a glimpse of both of my big brothers, standing calmly on the huge boulder, laughing and enjoying the pitiful sight of their little sister fighting for her life.

"Kick 'em feet!" Marvin yelled.

Finally, it dawned on me. I was moving forward and had reached shallow water! I stood to my feet and struggled toward the creek bank. Looking straight at my thoughtless brothers, I tearfully screamed, "I'mma gonna tell Daddy on both a you son-za-bitches! Jist chu wait and see!"

Woody jumped off the boulder and splashed into the water. As he swam toward me, Marvin yelled, "Git 'er, Woody! Push 'er head under a wodder!"

Woody swam across the water hole to where I was frantically trying to crawl out of the water. With anger in his voice, he warned me that he was going to hold my head under the water if I didn't promise him that I would not tell Dad what he and Marvin had done.

"I promise! I promise!" I yelled. "I jist wanna go home."

"You're gonna get back in 'his wodder an' show us how good you can swim!" Woody yelled. At that particular moment I had no desire of going back into any water for as long as I lived. However, I knew better than to try to run away from my brothers, so I slid back into the cold water, trying desperately to act as bravely as possible. Still worried that Woody and Marvin were intent on holding my head under the water, I hoped they were satisfied in having tortured me enough for one day.

Squatting in the shallow water, afraid to move, I was puzzled when it dawned on me that my brothers were frolicking in the water, noticeably ignoring me. Within a few minutes, Woody looked over at me and asked, "What's wrong? You skeered'a the wodder?" I didn't want him to know that it wasn't the water I was afraid of; instead, it was my two big brothers who were scaring me silly.

Trying to appear as calm and relaxed as possible, I was relieved when the boys began competing against each other. "Hey Bett, you count fer us an' see which'n can hol' 'is head under da wodder longest," Marvin said. Glad to oblige them, I began counting while both brothers dunked their heads below the water's surface. After a few dousings, they started begging me to see how long I could keep my head submerged. Naturally, I declined.

Woody agreed to count if Marvin and I would compete with each other. Being naturally competitive, I nervously crouched down and lowered my head under the water. After holding my breath and staying under the water for as long as I could, I popped my head out of the water only to realize that I had been betrayed. I looked around in a panic at the deserted pool. "Oh, my God!" I screamed. "I've been left down here'n 'is spooky holler all by myself!"

I yelled for my brothers, but they didn't answer. I was terrified to walk home alone, yet it looked as though I would have no choice in the matter. I pulled myself out of the water and made my way nervously through the deep weeds and into the dark, shadowy forest.

Cautiously, I hurried up the hill, wondering whether I would be eaten by a big black bear or by one of the bogeymen that Mom insisted lived in the deep, dark forest. There were also those venomous diamond-back rattlesnakes and deadly copperheads that were no doubt making their way through the weeds to strike at my ankles as I passed by.

I peered nervously up the side of the mountain through the wild grapevines and sagging tree branches that hung over my path like a vampire hovering over his victim. The thought entered my mind that, for once in my young life, I would be delighted to see my brothers jump out from behind one of the big trees where they had been waiting to scare me even more than I was already scared.

A surprisingly short time later, I found myself arriving home with all my body parts intact. Woody and Marvin were already calmly going about their business when I ran into the house, huffing and puffing from the fast climb up the hill and the fury boiling within me. I ran over to Mom, knowing better than to look for any sympathy but hoping to persuade her that my brothers needed to be punished for having left me alone with my head submerged in the water.

But before I had an opportunity to begin the performance I'd been rehearsing since exiting the spooky forest, Mom angrily looked over at me and yelled, "Young lady, I orta bea'chur ass off'n you. Why ain't you git outta 'at wodder when 'em boys told ye to?"

"Ey're tellin' a durdy lie," I sobbed. "Ey run off'n lef' me 'ith my head stuck under a wodder, not knowin' if I wuz alive er dead."

"You hain't goin'ith 'em boys no more if att'sa way you're gonna act. Jist'chu 'member that!" Mom yelled.

I could see that Mom's mind was set, especially since I believed that she had been waiting for an excuse to deny me swimming privileges. She preferred that I stay home to help her with the work and to care for the younger children, so I imagined that she was elated to have found an excuse to keep me home. I wasn't about to appeal my case before Dad. Oh, he would probably side with me, but he would be expecting something from me in return.

Although I didn't like what had happened, I had to abide by Mom's ruling and keep my mouth shut. I was happy that I had at least learned to swim well enough to perhaps prevent myself from drowning. Although I might have learned the hard way, at least I'd learned before having been restricted from the water.

XXVII

Sniggerfritz

It had been a beautiful and bountiful summer. The summer flowers had bidden farewell, and the fields and forest were now refurbished with a brand-new decor. Fall had always been my favorite season, and, as was my custom, I was looking forward to picking colorful bouquets of Black-Eyed Susan's and Goldenrods to arrange in quart-sized canning jars to display throughout our humble dwelling.

Every fall my siblings and I took to the forest to help ourselves to our share from Mother Nature's cupboards. After gathering hazelnuts and black walnuts from the forest, we would hull the tasty hazelnuts and then crack them by biting down hard on them with our molars. Since the hazelnuts were the easiest to hull and crack, we children would sometimes come to blows over who was entitled to the biggest share of the tasty nuts.

Hulling the black walnuts was a very messy job. Once we had stripped them of their outer hulls, we would spread the walnuts outside in a dry area and leave them to dry. The black, oily substance between the outer hull and the hard-shelled nut would stain my siblings and my hands and was almost impossible to remove. We were persistent, however, and did not allow the certainty of stained hands to deter us. We knew it would wear off by the time school was to begin.

Later in the fall, my older siblings and I would spend many precious but frustrating hours trying to crack the walnuts by placing one at a time on a rock, and then pounding it with another rock. We were often disappointed once we had reached the kernels to find that they had either dried out and shrunk to a non-edible morsel, or that the blow from the rock had smashed the tasty kernels into a powdery mass of crumbs. Sometimes we would walk off in total defeat and leave the walnuts for the squirrels to carry back into the forest for their own winter's supply.

Equally frustrating, it seemed as if Mother Nature had intended for the birds to feed on the small pods of sour fox grapes we sometimes were fortunate enough to find; in fact, it never ceased to amaze me that the abundance of the grapes were always resting in the tops of the tallest trees, which were set among thick patches of thorny briar vines. Only my three oldest brothers were brave enough to work their way to the coveted finds, and although their limbs and lives were at risk, they insisted on retrieving the small pods of the tiny tart and bitter grapes, which they would share with the rest of us children.

The 'possums often beat us to the persimmon trees, always staking their claims on the sparsely scattered trees even before the fruit was ripe enough for humans to sample. Although the grapes and few persimmons we managed to pick were not at all pleasing to the palate, the change in our standard diet of beans and "arsh tater" (Irish potato) was delightful.

One Friday evening, after one of my brothers' excursions to the woods to find the fruit and nuts, Dad came in from work in one of his rare good moods. After grabbing a fistful of the sour grapes, he informed Mom that he'd heard that the young couple living back out the ridge about two miles—in the house in which I was born—were moving away and that they were selling all their furniture and household goods. Dad's announcement brought no response from my mother.

Dad seemed almost embarrassed as he stood staring at the floor. "They hain't askin' very much fer 'at stuff an' it looks real good," he said.

My siblings and I moved a little closer to where Dad had, for a change, sat down at the table after washing his hands and hanging the towel on the sixteen-penny nail that Mom had driven into the wall for that purpose. After he had filled his plate with beans and fried potatoes, Dad looked around for the usual uncut slab of cornbread. "Whur's y'ur bread at?" he asked impatiently.

Mom hurriedly brought the pan of bread from the kitchen and flopped it onto the platter she had shoved near Dad's plate. Then, bowing his head and speaking softly, Dad pitifully said, "Thur only askin' a hundred dollars fer the stuff, an' I know't 'at dere's an awful lotta money fer a man ta come up with 'ese here days."

Mom stepped toward the doorway leading into the living room, apparently ignoring what Dad was saying. Looking angrily in Mom's direction, Dad yelled, "Marthy, hain't chu heared a word I was sayin'?"

Mom stopped and looked back at my father as though she were bored with the whole idea. "What're you thankin' 'bout doin' anyway?" she asked, stepping into the other room.

"Ah nuthin', I don't reckon," Dad answered hopelessly as he reached over and broke off a hunk of the bread.

All the kids and I crowded around the big table. Mom returned to the kitchen and picked up the milking pail. Without saying a word, she walked outside. Failing to ask the blessing on the food, Dad seemed to be in deep thought as he picked at the fried potatoes and pinto beans on his plate. I crumbled a small piece of cornbread into my plate of beans, and when I lifted a spoonful of the food to my lips, Dad looked over at me and asked, "What'chu thankin' 'bout?"

"Jis' wonderin' what all 'at stuff you tol' Mommy 'bout looks like," I said.

Once the food had been eaten and my older siblings had begun leaving the room, I began to feel uneasy, so I quickly stood to my feet and started stacking the dishes, hoping that Dad would also leave the area. Finally, he pushed his chair back from the table and walked out the kitchen door onto the front porch.

After I had poured some water into the dishpan, I looked out the window and was relieved to see my mother returning to the house. I could see Dad through the opened door, sitting flat on the floor of the porch with his legs outstretched and his back leaning against the support post. Mom walked into the kitchen and took care of the milk, handing the pail to me to be washed. She picked up a rag and began wiping the dishes I had washed. Almost immediately Dad yelled impatiently, "Marthy, get'chur ass ou' cheer!"

"What'cha want me fer?" Mom asked, looking very apprehensive as she walked toward the porch and stopped in the doorway.

"I've been a thankin' 'bout 'is here stuff 'at Burl an' Sybil's a sellin'," Dad said. "I thank I'll go in town tamar'n git money atta bank ta buy it with."

"Now Bud, how'na worl' can we pay 'at money back?" Mom asked.

"'Em payments had'n orta be 'at much," Dad answered.

"We're still payin' on all 'em young'uns school shoes an' clothes 'at I hadda buy on credit," Mom replied.

"Now don't chu start 'at ol' stuff 'ith me. I've made up my min'," Dad said sternly.

Mom didn't say another word but walked into the kitchen and grabbed the rag she was using for a dishtowel. Dad walked into the living room and turned on the battery radio.

The next morning Dad drove to town and borrowed the money from the local bank. With his good credit reputation, he was always able to borrow money or charge whatever he needed, although he seldom borrowed money. A short time later he returned and yelled for Marvin and Woody to harness the horse and hook her to the sled. "You boys git ready ta go with me ta fetch 'at stuff back," he said.

It wasn't long before Dad and my brothers arrived back at the house with a load of the nicest furniture I'd ever seen. While they were carrying the furniture inside, Dad was mumbling to himself about whether he had made a wise decision in borrowing the money to buy the furniture, which looked brand new. Once all the furniture was unloaded, Dad and the boys left to bring the last load of goods to our house.

When the last article had been carried into the living room and the sled returned to the barnyard, without asking Mom's opinion Dad started ordering the boys to place each item where he had decided to put it. "We're leavin' 'at dresser an' chest in'na "house" [living room] 'cause hit'sa purdy. I want 'at stuff left'n here whur't can be looked at," Dad said to whomever was listening.

To my knowledge, none of the families living around us owned sofas or other pieces considered to be living room furniture, so none was included with the goods that Dad had bought from the family. In addition to the bedroom suite, a white-painted kitchen buffet cabinet, which was similar in design to a china cabinet, was placed in one of the corners in the kitchen. The flour bin, located inside the cabinet beside the storage shelves, could store a twenty-five-pound sack of flour. By turning a little crank located on the bottom of the flour bin, Mom could easily sift the flour she would need for making bread. The flour bin and sifter would prove to be an appreciated aid for my mother, relieving her of having to wrestle with the twenty-five-pound sack of flour each time she prepared a meal. Mom and I placed all the dishes in the new cupboard and then stood back and admired the attractive pieces of furniture we now owned.

Looking at the empty orange crates in which we had been storing our dishes, Mom looked at me and said, "Now we can give 'em boys 'em wooden orange crates 'at 'hey been wantin' fer buildin' go-carts." She then pulled out three pairs of thin plastic drapes included with the purchase. Having no curtain rods to hang them, my mother cleverly secured a safety pin to one end of a strip of cloth, which she had torn from a ragged sheet, and then pulled the narrow strip through the plastic drapes where the rod was supposed to go. She then picked up a hammer and scavenged a few rusty nails before climbing onto a chair, where she proceeded to drive a long nail into the upper corner of each of the window facings. After I handed her a pair of the drapes, she tied one end of the strip of cloth onto one nail and, pulling the cloth taut, wound the other end around the nail at the opposite corner of the facing before tying the end securely. She proceeded to hang the other pair of kitchen curtains in the same way and then stepped off the chair and away from the window. "Now, hain't 'em purdy?" she declared. "I hain't never seen 'his ol' kitchen lookin' so good."

"No, me neither, Mommy," I said approvingly.

I was delighted when Mom and Dad took the new bed and passed their bed down to my older brothers, knowing that I would be given my brothers' old bed and could throw out the straw mattress I would no longer be needing. My brothers' mattress was worn out and falling apart, but it was a giant step up for me and the three younger siblings sharing my bed.

Since none of us had more than one or two changes of clothing each, most of the family's clothing fit in the chest of drawers, which Dad had insisted belonged in the living room. None of us owned pajamas or any kind of night clothing. We had never considered sleeping in anything other than our daytime clothing.

My joy over the new furniture was short lived, when just three or four days later I found myself alone inside the house with my father. It had been a couple of weeks since he had last made any unsavory remarks to me; still, I had remained cautious. Since Mom had again insisted that I stay in the kitchen to wash dishes while she was at the barn milking the cow, I wondered whether maybe she wasn't thinking that, somehow, Dad had seen the futility of his actions and would no longer be a threat to me. No matter what she might have been thinking, I couldn't understand how she could justify leaving me alone with my father. It seemed plausible to me that my well-being wasn't of utmost importance to my mother.

I was proud of the furniture, but my father was trying to make me feel obligated to him because he had bought the stuff. "I done went'n bought 'is here stuff 'cause I figgered it'd make you happy," Dad said in the same sick voice I had heard too often before.

"I don't want 'at ol' stuff," I bellowed. "I jist wan'chu to leave me alone!" I pulled my wet hands out of the dishpan and ran out the door and down to where Mom was milking the cow.

She looked up at me and asked, "Now, whats'a matter 'ith you?"

"Mommy, he's talkin' durdy to me ag'in!" I yelled at her as I wiped at the tears blurring my vision.

"Bethel, he hain't gonna hur'chu!" she scolded.

"Hain't 'ere somethin' you can do so he'll quit botherin' me?" I asked.

"No! Now git back ta the house'n git them deeshee done," she said. "You can see I'mma strip'n 'his cow [squeezing the remaining milk from the cow's teats], an' 'en I'll be back ta house. Besides, he won't do nuthin' ta you."

The thought entered my mind that caring for the cow was more important to Mom than taking care of my problem. Feeling ashamed to even think such a thought, I stalled until she finally stood to her feet and called for Woody to tend to the cow.

When we entered the kitchen, I could see Dad sitting in the living room whetting his pocketknife on the strap he normally used to sharpen his straight razor, and sometimes for whipping us kids. He did not look up. Mom went about her task of straining the evening milk and storing it for the night. I returned to the pan of unwashed dishes, feeling in my heart that Mom had no intention of approaching my father about his actions toward me. "It'll soon be bedtime, and maybe then I'll be safe," I thought to myself. I had no way of knowing that eventually nighttime would become even more threatening than the daylight hours.

The family soon gathered in the living room, where Mom had carried our kerosene lamp and set it on the new dresser. The little children were playing on the linoleum-covered floor, while Woody and the older boys hovered around the radio listening to a program called "Inner Sanctum." Mom had seated herself near the oil lamp and had begun patching a pair of ragged jeans. My sister was hovering over her pretend doll, which was a couple of diapers rolled together and wrapped inside a worn receiving blanket. I was hiding nervously in the shadows, wishing that I, too, could lead a normal life without having to stay alert.

Dad had moved from off the straight-back chair he had been straddling and onto the stool that was included with the dresser. I watched as he leaned forward and placed his elbows on the dresser, his chin resting in his hands. By the light from the kerosene lamp, he sat silently, gazing at his own image in the big, round mirror that was attached to the back of the dresser. Finally, looking bewildered, he said aloud for the family to hear, "Set here, you son-za-bitch, an' watch y'urself starve ta death try'na pay fer 'is here stuff." None of the family responded. I felt both pity and disdain for my father as I wondered whether he was now worrying because he had bought the new furniture.

Our family usually retired for the night shortly after dark, and sometimes I lay in bed wondering what I would do should one of my family members die during the night. Usually, I would begin crying before I could get the question out of my mind. Knowing that I had been thinking unpleasant thoughts about my father during the day, I would feel very ashamed and sad. I was beginning to question whether God was hearing my prayers at night or whether, because I had thought bad thoughts during the day, He was angry with me.

One night, after the family had gone to bed earlier than usual, my siblings and I were lying in bed wide awake, the sky outside barely dusk. For one reason or another, several of us children had begun giggling about something we had found to be very funny. The longer we giggled, the louder we became. And the louder we became, the more we giggled. Hearing the laughter was in itself comical to me since I seldom laughed or giggled and rarely heard any of the other family members laughing.

Finally, after we had been giggling for a few minutes, Dad yelled from his and Mom's bedroom and said, "Now you Sniggerfritz 'ad better quit dat sniggerin' in 'ere, er I'mma gonna come in 'ere an' give y'all somethin' to snigger 'bout."

Dad's choice of words to reprimand us children, who couldn't quit laughing in the first place, proved to be unwise. My siblings and I had never heard such a silly word as "sniggerfritz," so we began giggling even louder than before. Finally, we had to stifle our laughter by holding the bed covers against our mouths as Dad yelled out that he'd warned us for the last time. After we had made ourselves tired from the giggling and our efforts to keep Dad from hearing us, we fell asleep.

During the night I was awakened by my little brother Thomas, begging for a drink of water. I lay quietly, pretending not to hear because I didn't want to get up and go into the dark kitchen to get the water from the water bucket. I thought that if I just ignored the plea, my brother would fall asleep and forget about his thirst.

After Tom had pleaded for some time with no response from me, I heard my brother Arnold say, "Oh, shet up, Tom, an' swoller y'ur spit like I'mma doin'." I decided I might as well get out of bed and get both of the boys a drink of water.

The kitchen window had been raised to allow the gentle breeze to blow into the crowded bedroom. Mom had made a curtain from a feed sack and hung it over the lower half of the window to discourage any animals or bugs from coming inside through the open window. After taking a few matches from the matchbox, which I kept beside my bed to use in place of a flashlight, I struck one on the side of the box to light my way across the floor to the kitchen. Slowly and carefully, I crept out of the bedroom, across the living room floor, and into the kitchen. As I proceeded across the kitchen floor toward the bucket, which was sitting on a small table, I suddenly caught a glimpse of movement in the center of the room. With my heart already pounding, I shivered as I realized immediately that the animal was much too big to be one of our dogs. Jumping backwards away from the big black form, I stumbled over a twenty-five-pound sack of cornmeal that had been left leaning against the kitchen wall. I dropped the match as I landed on the hard floor and let out a hysterical scream.

I finally managed to strike one of the matches I was still clutching, and, realizing that no one was coming to my rescue, I screamed even louder as the unwelcome visitor grunted and then exited clumsily through the opened kitchen window. Quickly pulling myself up onto my feet, I immediately jumped for the living room doorway just in time to see a dim light suddenly enveloping the room. I was greatly relieved when I turned to see my father staggering slowly toward me, holding the kerosene lamp in one hand and his forehead with his other hand. I gasped when I noticed the trail of blood trickling down his cheek below his left eye.

Sounding more angry than concerned, he yelled, "What in'na Sam Hill's a matter 'ith you?"

"I seen a big black sumthin' in the kitchen, an' it went outta wender!" I cried out in one breath.

"Well, wha'dit look like?" Dad asked angrily.

"I don't know. My match went out when I fell over 'at sack'a meal." I said tearfully.

"You didn' see nuthin'! Ya jist got skeered when ya fell an' y'ur match went out," Dad yelled.

"Huh uh. I seen sump'm big'n black go out dat wender," I insisted.

"Git y'ur ass back in 'at bed 'fore I kick it clear up 'tween y'ur shoulders!" Dad yelled as he turned toward his bedroom and I walked toward mine, thankful to be alive and hoping that after all the excitement my brothers had forgotten about their thirst.

The next morning, after Dad had gone to work and the rest of the family were seated around the breakfast table, Woody questioned me about the hair-raising event. As I explained what had taken place, he walked over and began inspecting the opened window. The opening was about twenty-six inches above the floor and wide enough for a large animal to crawl through. After he had examined the window frame closely, Woody announced that he had found red clay smears on the curtain and window facing, and several black hairs clinging to splinters on the window ledge.

"Somethin' did crawl through 'his wender, and it wasn' a dog," my brother stated.

Marvin stepped over to the window and said, skeptically, "Woody, you're as bigger a coward as Bethel is."

Woody looked at Marvin angrily. "Speakin' of cowards, you're the one 'at pulled da sheet so hard ta cover your head up 'at it went in 'hind a bed against the wall!"

Marvin yelled back at Woody, "That was jist 'cause you wuz yankin' so hard on it tryin' ta cover up y'ur own head."

Both my brave brothers finally explained that when they had heard my screams, Woody, who was sleeping on the forefront of the bed, grabbed the corner of the top sheet and started yanking it up over his head. With Woody already pulling on the sheet, Marvin, who no doubt was just as scared as Woody, jerked the sheet even harder to cover his own head. To their chagrin, the sheet had gone sailing across both boys and landed at the backside of the bed.

"A lotta help y'all was," I interrupted the boys. "Both'a y'all was so skeered 'at all you done was ta cover up y'ur heads while I was in'na kitchen 'bout to be et up by a bear."

Woody and I were convinced that a bear had indeed been in the kitchen. We figured that the burning match and my screams had frightened the bear enough to send him exiting the room in the same way he had entered. Although the rest of the family viewed my unnerving ordeal with skepticism, Mom insisted on closing the window at night from that day forward.

As for my father, well, he was so angry with me that he refused to comment. Mom finally told me what had happened to his face. She said that when I had screamed, Dad had awakened from a deep sleep, jumped out of bed suddenly, and fallen against the bed railing, cutting a small gash in his forehead. I felt ashamed of myself as I realized that I was laughing at Dad's mishap.

A short time later, apparently realizing that it was dangerous for me to carry a lighted match to find my way through the dark rooms, Dad brought home a new flashlight and, without saying a word, handed it to me to keep beside my bed.

XXVIII

Prepping for Winter

There was no shortage of work to be done around the little run-down farm. The fruits and vegetables had been harvested, and Mom had canned all she could gather from the fields to help get us through the long, cold winter ahead.

After its last hoeing, the field corn had been left standing in the fields to dry on the stalks and be husked by hand. During early fall, Dad always helped my brothers with husking the corn and hauling the feed into the barn to winter the livestock. The "shuckin' pag" the family owned was a very important tool to have on hand at harvest time; however, Dad always reserved the husker for his own use. He would buckle the leather strap around the palm of his hand in order to rip the dry husks from the ears of corn with the small, pointed metal tip of the husker, while my three oldest brothers were required to use only their bare hands to shuck the corn. Throughout the years, they often came in from the fields with blood oozing from their hands after having worked in the corn for hours without the aid of a shucking peg.

A corn-cutter or machete was used to cut down the dried corn stalks once the ears of corn had been removed. The stalks, with their blades intact, were bunched together into shocks and bound with straps made from tender, pliable hickory branches or strips of bark peeled from hickory trees. To prevent the wind from blowing the shocks over onto the ground, my brothers would bunch the stalks together around hills of corn that had been left rooted in the ground in several places throughout the field. These dried fodder shocks were stored in the barn or hauled in by sled-loads throughout the winter as needed for feeding the horse and cow.

One large field was always sowed in soybeans or lespedeza for forage. The fields of forage and volunteer hay were cut with a cradle scythe. This farm implement was a rarity in our community; consequently, once he had his own fields harvested, Dad would loan the cradle scythe to the neighbors to do their own harvesting.

My oldest brother and sometimes my mother were responsible for cutting the hay and lespedeza. To cut the ripe feed, the cradle scythe was swung through the grass from right to left in a sweeping motion, allowing the sharp blade to cut the grass, which then fell into the cradle. The cradle scythe was then tipped upward onto its side, allowing the cradle of harvested hay to fall to the ground in straight rows across the field. The cut forage was then left on the ground to dry. The work was backbreaking and very tiring, yet the job was always finished without any complaints.

The following day, my brothers would overturn the rows of forage with pitchforks and then leave the hay to dry in the sun for yet another day. The hay was then piled into heaps, loaded onto the sled, and hauled to the barn. When the hay crop yielded more forage than could be packed into the barn, the excess was stacked into a huge haystack and left in the field until it was needed. The haystacks were formed by packing the loose hay around a vertical pole protruding from the base of a platform that had been built previously from poles cut from the heavy growth of timber on the property. The hay in the haystack was packed tightly, with the base wider than the top of the stack to enable it to repel water. In addition to the corn and forage raised on the farm, it often became necessary for sacks of grain and baled hay to be purchased at the feed store in town to supplement the animals' feed through the winter.

With all the work and expense required to winter one cow and one horse, a person might question whether the animals' output justified the expense of their upkeep. The men in our area evidently believed it was justified, since it seemed that a man's success was determined by the qualities of his milk-cow and workhorse. In some households, a man's horse and cow often got more respect than his wife and children. When the men gathered to talk, they could usually be heard boasting about their horses, cows, and hunting dogs, while at the same time their families were never mentioned and were being kept in the background.

The manner in which the gardens and fields were planted remained the same, year after year. After Woody had learned about crop rotation in school, he informed Dad that he had read in a book that the corn and vegetable yields could be increased by rotating the crops. Dad was not impressed by what Woody had learned. "Jist what does 'em people 'at wrote 'em 'ere books know 'bout raisin' crops?" Dad asked, laughing and shaking his head. "Why, I bet'cha 'ey don't even know one seed from anuther un."

"Why don't chu try it one year an' see if it helps?" Woody asked.

"I've seen corn an' stuff raised my way all a my life, an' I hain't about to change thangs now jist 'cause you read somethin' in a book," Dad said as he kicked the cat half way across the porch because she was purring and rubbing against his trouser legs. "A cornfield's made to raise corn in it ever' year an' not somethin' else," he said, walking away. He continued to insist that the fields be planted his way, year after year, and in spite of his "profound knowledge and expertise," God continued to bless our family with crop yields that never failed to help carry us through the frigid winters.

Once the hay had been harvested, the field of potatoes was hand dug and stored for winter. When the bin in the cellar was full, the extra potatoes were packed inside a "tater hill." To make the potato hill, loose soil was piled up about a foot high in the garden and the center scooped down enough to make a "nest" in the soil. Loose straw or rags were then placed in the nest and the potatoes piled in on top of the straw/rags. Additional straw was piled around and on top of the potatoes to prevent them from freezing during the winter months. Dirt was then shoveled onto the nest until the heap was cone shaped and about three-feet-high. The soil was then patted down tightly with the back of the shovel, which allowed the potato hill to repel water. The potatoes could be removed during winter, as needed, by carefully scooping out a small hole in the side of the hill, painstakingly reaching in through the straw, and transferring the cold potatoes into a bucket. Once a bucket of potatoes was removed, the straw and dirt were replaced, leaving the remaining potatoes stored until needed. Potatoes stored in this manner were sweeter and retained more water than potatoes stored inside the cellar.

During the summer months, the forest looked as if it were covered with heavy green blankets; yet, once fall arrived, the green blankets were replaced with an assortment of colorful patchwork quilts. Now that winter was beginning to bring on her wrath, the leafless tree-covered hills were beginning to look like an expansive battlefield of Confederate soldiers shouldering their weapons and ready for battle.

One late Saturday afternoon, Dad, Mom, and my three oldest brothers had walked over to one of the corn fields to gather fallen tree limbs, which they would burn in a huge bonfire. I was left at the house to do the dishes and to care for the younger children. I looked out the door and noticed my younger brother Arnold standing in the front yard holding a baby diaper against his nose. Since he had periodically been experiencing severe bouts of nosebleeds for weeks, and since the diaper in his hand was saturated with blood, I immediately went outside to check on his condition.

Once I'd brought my brother inside the living room, I was alarmed when I discovered that his nose continued to bleed profusely. I quickly applied cold wet cloths to the back of his neck—with no results. I then tried sitting him in a chair with his head tipped back, but I still could not control the blood flow. Realizing that both he and I were needing help, I warned him to stay seated in a chair until I could call my parents in from the field.

I ran out in the backyard where I began yelling loudly for my parents. I knew that they should be able to hear me since the field was no more than 150 yards from where I was standing. After failing to get a response, I decided to run over to the field to tell my mother how seriously Arnold's nose was bleeding.

When I got to the edge of the field, I saw my mother sitting on a large log that was lying farther out into the corn field. Dad was standing a short distance from my mother beside the brush pile he was burning. I ran over and jumped up on the opposite end of the long log from where Mom was sitting, and I began babbling frantically about how I had tried unsuccessfully to stop Arnold's nosebleed. While I talked, I began bouncing up and down on the end of the unsteady log. Suddenly, a blacksnake about five feet long slithered out from underneath the log. I let out a bloodcurdling yell as the snake abruptly stopped, licked out his tongue, and looked straight at my mother. Not seeing the snake and not knowing why I was so alarmed, Mom turned and began scolding me for bouncing on the log on which she was still seated.

I began jabbing my finger back and forth in the direction of the frightened snake. Mom's angry expression immediately changed when she looked in the direction I was pointing and saw the five-foot-long snake looking straight in her direction. Without hesitation, she frantically jumped up and yelled, "Oh my God, Bud! I bet'cha I marked my baby 'ith 'his big snake!"

Having heard throughout the years the many unusual ways my mother had unexpectedly announced that a new baby was on the way, my father, brothers, and I accepted the news without responding. Woody, Marvin, and Maynard dropped the branches they had been carrying to throw on the fire and ran over toward the log. Dad looked startled but didn't say a word as he walked over and picked up a hoe that was leaning against the log that Mom had suddenly vacated. I gasped as he took a step toward Mom, raised the hoe above his head, jumped forward quickly, and whacked off the snake's head.

Without exchanging a word about the snake, the baby, or my brother Arnold—who was certainly bleeding to death back at the house—Mom and Dad began walking slowly toward the house. My brothers stayed to guard the brush fire, and I started running as fast as I could to get back to Arnold's side.

As soon as he walked through the living room door, Dad immediately began packing Arnold's nose with gauze the doctor had given him when Arnold's severe nosebleeds had finally prompted Dad to take him to the doctor. Arnold's head was once again tipped back to try to stop the blood that had begun running out of his mouth. As the bleeding slowly subsided, I stayed by my brother's side, terrified that he might die.

Before my parents walked out the door on their way back to the field, I looked over at my father, who appeared worried. I wondered whether his concern was for my brother or whether he was merely worried because he had just learned that baby number ten was on the way.

The reason for my brother's nosebleeds was never determined. The bouts, which lasted throughout his early childhood, would appear suddenly and for no apparent reason and then stop as rapidly as they had begun. Sometimes the loss of blood would leave Arnold's body in such a weakened state that he had to be carried from his chair to the bed. On those occasions, when the bleeding could not be stopped, Dad and Mom would take Arnold to town to see the same doctor who had delivered Mom's babies. The doctor treated Arnold by clinically examining him, packing both nostrils with gauze, and then releasing him back into my parents' care.

According to Mom's recollection, the doctor never once mentioned that my brother should receive blood transfusions to replace the volumes of blood that he had lost. Right or wrong, no one ever mentioned taking him to a different doctor, and although the nosebleeds eventually ceased, he remained in poor health until, at the age of fifty-one, he died from complications after having suffered a debilitating and paralyzing stroke.

XXIX

Cold Fury

"Next time, pay 'tenchun to what'chur doin'!" Dad yelled, yanking me abruptly out of bed and beating me with his belt in the dark bedroom at 5 a.m. I was tempted to tell my father that he was the one who needed to pay attention, but from the fierceness of the thrashing, I knew I had better take the beating and wait for my mother to explain why I had been chosen, before sunrise, to bear the brunt of Dad's fury.

After giving me five or six whacks with his new plastic belt, Dad yelled out an expletive as the belt broke in half. Seething with rage, he then threw me back onto the bed before stomping out of the room. I was eleven years old and had no idea what I had done to deserve this whipping; in fact, I was convinced that my father had whipped the daylights out of the wrong child, just like he had done years earlier when he had punished me unjustly for dulling the hand-saw.

Once I heard his old car pull away from in front of our house, I jumped out of bed and ran to the kitchen to ask Mom why Dad had whipped me at such an early hour. "Y'ur daddy wen' out dere ta put oil in'na car like 'e has to every mornin'," Mom said. "When 'e bent down ta git da can a oil, the can 'uz settin' on'na porch upside down an' had run down through the cracks in'na porch."

"Well, why'd he haf'ta whup me fer?" I pleaded. "I wad'na one 'at spilt it."

Mom explained that Dad had returned to the kitchen and asked her who had overturned the can of oil. "I told 'im it must'a been you," she said. "You know y'ur daddy. He 'uz so mad 'at he had ta whup somebody."

"Well, you didn' haf'ta blame it on me," I whined.

"Young lady, you shet y'ur sassy mouth, er you'll git another whuppin'," she said firmly. "You swep' off da porch yesterday an' should'a seed 'at can 'uz open."

"They wad'n no can a oil settin' on 'at porch yesterday," I declared, the tone of my voice softening.

"You better not tell y'ur daddy 'at," Mom warned. "Now git back in 'at bed an' quit 'at bawlin'."

I knew I might as well forget about the whipping, so I returned to my bed to wait until it was time to get dressed for school. Welts from the disciplinary hands of a parent weren't considered child abuse when I was a child; furthermore, I knew better than to tell anyone how I had received the "unjust" welts on my thighs and backside the width of my father's wide belt.

I felt a guilty sense of pleasure when I later learned that, since Dad had been outside in the frigid weather for several minutes on that frosty morning, his new plastic belt had become so cold and brittle that it had snapped before he could inflict more harm to my backside than the rooster had a few years earlier.

A few days later, Mom called my school-age siblings and me to get out of bed to get ready for school. "'Ere's a big snow on, but Daddy hain't back from the garage, so I guess 'ere's gonna be school," she said.

I ran over and looked out the window. There must have been four inches of snow on the ground, with big flakes still falling from the gray, overcast sky. "Hit's gonna be cold but fun walkin' ta school 'is mornin'," I said.

After breakfast, my four brothers and I ran outside into the winter wonderland and began our journey to school. I looked at the fuzzy blanket of brilliant white snow and at the drooping tree branches that seemed to be enjoying their share of showing off Mother Nature's latest style. Recalling the pictures of bridal gowns I had seen in the catalogs we had received in our mail, I envisioned the wintry scene spread before me as a world of brides dressed in white gowns with long, flowing trains, walking down an aisle covered with goose down as they slowly made their way to the arms of their grooms waiting patiently out of sight.

My hands were freezing cold although I had them buried inside my coat pockets. Without gloves or boots to help protect us from the biting chill, my siblings and I walked briskly in an effort to generate a little heat. Since both the senior high and junior high school were housed in the same building, which was about a half-mile beyond the elementary school, my oldest brothers no longer walked to and from school with us younger children since they had farther to walk. Knowing that I was now responsible for my little brothers' safety and welfare, I was constantly attempting to hurry Maynard and Arnold along; however, with my toes feeling like wooden spokes on a wheel and my chilled jaws almost frozen shut, neither my body nor my voice were very capable of giving them the added instruction.

I was reminded of the few times when I had arrived at school too cold to function. Unable to speak because of the freezing condition I was in, I couldn't voice my thanks to the principal when he had instructed my teacher to allow me to stand in front of one of the hot air vents in the school's hallway so that my hands would thaw enough to enable me to open my locker door. I thought about the tingling sensation and the pain I had felt as my body had begun to thaw. The thought of the warm school and the beauty of the undisturbed snow blanketing the earth made my heart toasty warm within me. I thanked God for the strength He always seemed to give me, which enabled me to do what was required of me, while also giving me the insight to enjoy the beauty that He alone had created.

XXX

A Web of Smoke

The following year, sometime in early spring, I committed a sin that slipped right past my father. Dad had ordered an interesting machine called a "Roll Your Own Cigarettes Machine." Almost every evening, he would fill one of the compartments of the machine with Prince Albert pipe tobacco, insert several cigarette wrappers in another section, fill its small water tank with water to moisten the glue on the cigarette papers, and then crank the handle on the side of the machine to roll almost perfectly formed cigarettes that he would pack inside an empty tobacco can.

After he had paid off the debt at the bank for the used furniture, Dad was clearing enough money to allow him to switch to Camel cigarettes sold by the carton. Curious as to why my father smoked a pack of the cigarettes almost daily, and knowing where he stored the opened carton, I decided to steal one of the smelly cigarettes and to sneak off and experience for myself what the attraction may be.

I had found myself alone in the house with only my younger siblings, so I walked over to the chest of drawers and removed a pack of Camels from the carton stored in the top drawer. After returning the carton to its exact original spot, I ripped the top off the pack, nervously removed a cigarette, and stuck it inside my pocket. I then hurriedly strutted across the floor, where I spied Dad's heavy overcoat hanging on a nail in the adjoining bedroom. "Good," I thought to myself. "I'll hide the cigarettes in that coat pocket, and I'll have time to smoke the rest of them before Daddy needs his coat for winter."

With my cigarette in hand, I then slipped into the kitchen to get a match. Suddenly feeling guilty, I snuck out the door and around the house to the chimney. The "chemley corner" was my siblings' and my den of sin. When my siblings and I wanted privacy, we would sneak around the corner of the house and huddle beside the chimney, where we could feel hidden from the family and the rest of the world.

The smell of musty, dried mud mixed with an overpowering odor of "ammonia" gave the chimney corner its own personality. Standing there in the malodorous corner with my face turned to the wall, I put the cigarette in my mouth and lit it. After a few quick puffs, I realized that it didn't taste nearly as good as I had anticipated.

Concentrating fully on puffing on the Camel, I forgot about the match still burning in my right hand. Suddenly, I felt the sting of the flame on my fingertips. I flung the match to the ground and rammed my burning fingers into my mouth. Realizing that it was going to take more than saliva to make my fingers feel better, I removed them from my mouth and took a few more drags off the cigarette. Inhaling the smoke, I made several attempts at blowing the smoke through my nostrils like I'd seen my father do on numerous occasions.

Before I knew what was happening, my head began to spin as though it were on a swivel. With the smoke burning my eyes, the rancid taste of the tobacco biting my tongue, and my stomach crying foul, I peeked around the chimney to assure myself that I was still alone. Satisfied that no one was watching, I threw the cigarette to the ground and, since I was barefoot, squatted down and picked up a small stone to extinguish the burning tip. I then hurriedly crammed the cigarette butt into a hole that a bee had bored in the dried mud in the side of the chimney.

With my head swimming and my stomach turning flip-flops, I staggered back to the kitchen, where I gulped down a swig of brine from the jar of pickles sitting on the table. One way or another, I had to get that awful taste out of my mouth. I shook my head and coughed and sputtered as I found the washbasin and slapped a handful of the water across my face. With my head spinning, I needed to get back to normal before Mom or my older brothers appeared and discovered what I'd been doing.

Finally, after I'd begun to feel relatively stable again, Mom and my brothers returned from the field. I tried to act as innocently as possible, while at the same time keeping a safe distance so they would not detect any smell of the cigarette still lingering on my clothing.

The very next day, Dad started grilling the boys about which of them had stolen a package of his cigarettes. Naturally, the boys denied knowing anything about the matter. Mom piped up and asked Dad whether he could be mistaken about the number of packs he'd already smoked. Angrily, Dad turned to Mom and said, "You shore you hain'ta one 'at's been stealin' 'em y'urself?"

Mom walked inside, ignoring Dad's sarcastic remark. I slithered off like a snake, hoping that the stolen pack of cigarettes wouldn't be discovered before I could come up with a plan to return them. After all, I couldn't think of throwing them away. "Why, that would be even worse than stealing them," I thought.

A few weeks later, I had the answer to my dilemma when I discovered a cigarette inside a pack that Dad had discarded inside the toilet. Granted, I didn't know how the one cigarette was going to help me get out of the trap I'd found myself in, yet I knew there had to be some way I could use the single cigarette to my advantage.

I took the cigarette back to the house, sneaked back to where I had earlier hidden the pack, and carefully inserted the cigarette into the pack to replace the one I had smoked a few weeks earlier. I had no idea how I would be able to return the opened pack to the carton, so I decided to be patient and watch for the opportune time.

On Sunday afternoon my ears perked up when Dad, sitting on the front porch talking to Mr. White—who had stopped in uninvited—asked Marvin to go inside and fetch him a package of Camels.

Quickly, and being careful not to arouse Dad's suspicion, I volunteered to go for the cigarettes. Walking cautiously into the bedroom, I took the opened package from the coat pocket instead of from the carton in the drawer. I slowly and bravely walked back outside to the porch and handed the already opened pack of Camels to my father.

Dad looked at the pack of cigarettes and then at me, "Now, why'ja go an' tear the top offen 'his package fer?" he scolded.

I had never realized that when Dad opened a package of cigarettes, he removed only a portion of the top. Since I had torn off the entire top of the pack, I lied and said, "I'z only tryin' to be helpful." I didn't dare tell him the truth.

Dad took a cigarette out of the pack, lit it, and took a few puffs. "'His here thang shore tastes awful stale," he said. Holding out the pack, he looked straight at me and asked, "You shore 'ese thangs wadn't already open?"

Thinking fast, I answered, "No, they jist had a loodle puncture on the top." I knew that I had just told another falsehood, and I was becoming unnerved.

Dad examined the pack and, apparently seeing that it was missing only the one cigarette that he had just lit, removed the cigarette from between his lips and threw it onto the ground. After lighting up another Camel and then throwing it onto the ground, he told me to fetch him a new pack. "An' 'is time I'll open 'em fer myself," he said angrily. He then ordered me to throw the first pack that I had given him down the toilet hole. I did as he ordered, thankful that Dad was unaware of my finagling things for weeks in order to work my way out of the web I'd woven around myself.

Later, I mused about the fact that Dad had immediately realized it when one package had been missing from the carton but had never mentioned the extra pack of cigarettes mysteriously appearing. I didn't know whether he had noticed it or not, but I wasn't about to bring it to his attention. I was thankful the ordeal was over, and I had already decided that I would never put another cigarette to my lips for as long as I lived. I also promised myself that I wouldn't do anything this dishonest and foolish again. My experimenting had proven to me that sucking on a pickle was much more enjoyable and a lot less dangerous than sucking on a cigarette.

XXXI

Yet Another Child Arrives

One cold, rainy night toward the end of May, I was awakened as Dad summoned me to get my siblings, except for Nina and my two youngest brothers, out of bed so they could ride to my grandparents' house when he drove there to bring Grandma to our house. "The baby'sa comin'," Dad said sleepily.

Mom had delivered all her babies at home. Some of them had been delivered by the doctor who had come to our house, while the others had been delivered by a midwife. Tonight, she had decided it would take too long for Dad to drive to town to bring the doctor, so she elected to have the midwife deliver baby number ten.

The midwife was a "strange," elderly lady who lived about two miles out the ridge past our residence. I didn't know how accurate the stories were, but the rumors had it that she had been known to cast spells on those whom she disliked. I didn't know any better at the time than to believe all the stories. One thing was certain: I was terribly afraid of her.

Mrs. Taylor was a very wrinkled old lady who wore her gray hair in a neat little chignon at the back of her head. Her teeth were stained a chestnut brown from the tobacco she chewed.

Whether she was working in her garden or on her once-a-month trip into town to buy groceries, she always dressed in her starched sun bonnet and an ankle-length cotton dress with a white butcher's apron worn over it. Her shoes were black high-top button shoes like her ancestors had worn. I always wondered where she managed to find the ancient-looking clothing.

There were no telephones in the area, so once he had dropped off Grandma to stay with Mom, Dad sped off to get the midwife. I was lying nervously in bed with my little sister and brothers Tom and Virgil, wondering whether the reason I was being allowed to stay home for this birthing was because Mom must be thinking that the time had come to educate me about the matter. Though I was almost twelve years old, I did not feel ready to learn about birthings, and if I hadn't thought that Dad would have beaten me within an inch of my life, then I would have braved the dark night and traveled alone to join my brothers who were finishing out the night at Grandma's house.

A few days earlier, Mom had moved her bed into the corner of the living room and was presently occupying the bed, moaning and groaning and making all the sounds that I would later discover women usually make when giving birth. I was getting more nervous by the minute and was hoping that Grandma would not need me to help prepare for the birthing.

I had no way of knowing the truth about having a baby. The few girls I was acquainted with were just as ignorant as I was about such hush-hush matters, so the only thing I knew about pregnancy and childbirth was what I'd figured out for myself. I didn't know it at the time, but my ideas were far from accurate.

I was greatly relieved when, within minutes of the midwife's arrival, Mom's moans and groans were replaced by the cries of a newborn baby. After Mom's bed was cleaned and everything was back to normal, I was called into the room to hold baby number ten. When the midwife lay my eleven-pound baby brother Romie Dale in my arms, I immediately started examining him to see whether Mom's scare from the blacksnake had marked him in any way. I was delighted when I found that he was perfectly formed. I had hoped for a sister, but I was happy to settle for another little brother, especially after I had considered that a girl might have to endure the same abuse from our father that I was fighting against.

My thoughts once again were directed away from the disturbing thought, and I stopped and thanked God that He loved me enough to not allow the horrific memories I was living with to overcome me; instead, He had never once failed to gently pull me back from the edge of despair and to direct my thoughts to memories that brought a more calming effect to my soul.

XXXII

Games to be Made and Played

Although we might not have received toys for Christmas or any other time of the year, my siblings and I always had interesting ways to entertain ourselves. Little time was left for play after our responsibilities had been carried out around the farm; however, there was never a time when any of us could say that we were bored. During any free time the boys had, if they weren't playing with the things they had already made, they were making new things with which to play. Sometimes they would share their creations with the younger kids; more often than not, however, the younger children were merely their spectators.

There's no doubt in my mind that my brothers were daredevils. It amazes me to this day that none of them were seriously injured from their daring escapades, although most of them still carry minor war wounds and battle scars from their childhood years. But age didn't matter; battle scars could appear at any stages of their lives.

My brother Tom no doubt carries a scar on his scalp today and probably has no memory of how it got there. Mom and Dad had returned from the grocery store one Saturday with a horse-drawn wagonload of groceries. After emptying the boxes and storing our month's supply of food, Mom set a couple of the cardboard boxes in the living room, knowing that the little boys would find hours of pleasure pushing each other across the linoleum-covered floor in their pretend cars.

Shortly after dark, Dad and my brothers were seated around the crowded living room visiting with Mr. White. Tom, a toddler at the time, was crawling around the floor, pushing one of the empty boxes. When Tom suddenly sat down near Woody's feet, Woody playfully picked up the cardboard box that Tom had been playing with and turned it upside-down over the toddler, completely concealing his little body.

At the time, Arnold, who was around six years old, was wandering around the room, carrying Dad's claw hammer. Turning around and seeing the overturned cardboard box near Woody's feet, Arnold pulled the claw hammer back over his head and brought it forcefully down, claws first, on the overturned box. Immediately, to Arnold's surprise and to Woody's horror, the box let out an ear-piercing scream.

Quickly grabbing the box and pulling it off the child, Dad frantically shouted, "My God, Marthy, Arnold jis' knocked Tom in'na head 'itha claw hammer!"

The blood was pouring down over little Tom's face and dripping onto the floor. Mom ran into the room and grabbed the injured, screaming child out of Dad's lap and yelled for a towel. Scared as much as the rest of the family, I ran to the kitchen, grabbed the soiled towel the family had been using to dry our hands, and ran back to Mom's side. Mom grabbed the towel out of my hands and slapped it over the cut on my little brother's head. While the adults were all frantically discussing ways to stop the blood that was flowing freely, I looked around to see where Arnold had gone, after I'd realized that he must be scared out of his skin. With little Arnold nowhere in sight, I decided to worry about him later and to stick around to see whether Tom would live or die.

Dad kept reminding Mom to hold the towel tightly against the wound, since every few seconds she seemed intent on pulling the towel back to see whether the blood had stopped flowing. Finally in desperation, after realizing that the blood was flowing faster and harder than before, Mr. White suggested that Mom press a handful of flour into the gash as he had done to stop the blood when his son had been hit by a piece of tin that had been picked up by the wind and blown off their roof. Without questioning the idea, Mom handed Tom to Dad and started toward the kitchen to get the flour.

My father quickly overruled Mr. White's home remedy. "Marthy, fetch me a big, clean white rag!" he yelled, as Mom stepped back into the room carrying a handful of flour. "I ain't puttin' no flair in 'at cut!" Dad emphatically said.

Mom immediately ran into the bedroom and came out with a white cloth, which she hastily reached to my father. Dad threw the bloody towel to the floor and began pressing the clean cloth over the deep cut in the crown of Tom's scalp. Thanks to the first-aid class that all the bus drivers were required to attend, Dad had at last taken charge of the situation.

Although one could see the fright in his eyes, my pitiful little brother was no longer crying, and after several minutes, the blood began to coagulate. Dad then shaved the hair from the area and cleaned around the wound. "Don'tchu let him go to sleep," he warned Mom, as he quickly left to drive to the school bus garage to get first-aid supplies from the kit he carried in his bus.

Dad returned in short order and bandaged Tom's head. Once Tom was turned free, he toddled over and began shoving the damaged box across the floor, blowing air through his lips as though it were the noise from his pretend car's motor.

Arnold eventually returned to the living room, scared and no doubt surprised that Dad hadn't given him a whipping immediately after the incident had occurred. I must admit that I, too, was surprised. One thing was certain: none of us were going to remind Dad that Arnold and Woody were both responsible for the wound. Eventually, Tom's head wound healed, his hair grew back, and he was left with nothing worse than a couple half-inch scars on his scalp.

It was not unusual for the boys to suffer repercussions from their sources of entertainment. When the games they were playing didn't offer sufficient excitement or challenge to meet their expectation, my brothers often used their skills to add their own touches of endangerment to the sports.

Dad returned from his job earlier than usual one late afternoon to catch Woody and Marvin in the middle of one of their daring events. The boys had made slingshots by cutting two forked branches from a maple tree and then tying strips of rubber, which had been cut from a discarded innertube, to the prongs. Each brother then helped the other brother tie a leather tongue he had cut from a worn-out shoe between the two dangling ends of the rubber bands on each slingshot. (Marvin once received a hard whipping from Dad, when on one occasion, not being able to find a worn-out shoe, he had cut the tongue out of the shoe he was wearing at the time in order to finish making his slingshot.) With their homemade slingshots finished, the boys gathered a pocketful of small stones and set out to practice their aim.

Woody and Marvin had a lot of fun playing with their slingshots until the day Dad popped around the curve at the top of the hill to catch them in the middle of their dangerous game. Dad stopped the car and watched, unbeknown to my brothers and a neighbor boy, Bob Palmer, as two of the boys pretended to be rabbits while the one with the slingshot was the hunter. The "rabbits," hiding behind stumps or tree trunks, would suddenly expose their heads as they attempted to dart to a safer hiding place. The hunter, with his slingshot loaded and ready to shoot, immediately fired a pebble at the rabbit. Fortunately for the rabbits, the hunter missed his target.

Once Dad had quietly watched the boys for a few minutes and was satisfied that they had indeed been shooting at each other with the slingshots, he quickly approached the boys, kicked their backsides, and then took away their slingshots. "You dumb heads could'a got chur eyes knocked out 'ith 'em rocks," he yelled.

One of the less daring sports my brothers participated in was running up and down the road rolling a hoop with a hook. They had made the hook from a long metal rod they had picked up from the abandoned debris left near one of the oil rigs located on the ridge. The hoop was a discarded, rusty band that had come off a wagon wheel.

One of my brothers would stand the hoop on the ground, hook the crooked rod around the hoop, and then run up and down the road pushing the wheel in front of him. Back and forth he would run, rolling the hoop with the rod. Taking turns, the boys would usually compete against each other to see which of them could roll the hoop the longest without the hoop falling over onto the ground.

As my brothers matured and were doing more work in less time, and with other brothers now able to help out with the work, they were finding more free time to pursue their adventures. They were delighted when the grocers packed our groceries in wooden crates that had been used to ship citrus to the grocery store. The crates were sometimes given to Woody and Marvin to use for the bodies of go-carts and wagons. My talented brothers would make wooden wheels for their vehicles from four round blocks they had sawed from a dry log. An auger was used to bore holes in the center of the wheels to accommodate the axles. The axles were made from long steel bolts that had also been retrieved from the oil well debris. With a little work and a lot of imagination, the boys soon transformed the fruit crates into go-carts or wagons that had only to be pushed or pulled up a steep incline and ridden speedily back down the side of the hill.

Mom kept a few of the crates, which she turned on their ends and stacked in the kitchen corner to store supplies and groceries. The crates also made handy shelves for the living room, when nailed in the corners. Mom would embroider doilies and place them on the shelves, and then set the few trinkets or pictures she owned on the doilies.

My brothers knew they had arrived at the age at which Dad "trusted" them when he allowed them to carry a sharp knife in their pockets. Eventually, both Woody and Marvin became very proficient with their knives, making whistles from twigs while walking home after school. They delighted the family when they sometimes passed the whistles down to their younger siblings. When the children blew on their whistles, they were thrilled at the sounds they heard. The store-bought whistles may have been prettier, but the homemade whistles sounded as good as, or better than, the whistles my brothers could not afford to buy.

Living on an isolated ridge in the country was the ideal place to fly kites. The absence of overhead wires was only one of the many advantages. Whenever my brothers wanted a kite, Woody and Marvin would build the kites from Mrs. Snyder's passed-down newspapers. They'd make a paste from flour and water and use it to glue the edges of the paper over the dried reeds that were the cross pieces of the kite's body. The kite's tail was made by tying scraps of material a couple of inches apart onto a twine attached to the body. Somehow, Grandma always seemed to have a nice ball of twine on hand that she would give my brothers for flying their kites. The crudely constructed kite would fly just as high and as gracefully as any of the store-bought kites that we children had seen flying high above the ground while we walked home from school.

Since Dad didn't believe in any of us doing any unnecessary work on Sundays, Sunday afternoons were the only days my brothers took time to fly their kites. The open sky and gentle breeze were an open invitation for them to soar their kites into the heavens.

The crude rendition of the bows and arrows my brothers made were a delight for the boys. After the boys had cut the appropriate hickory branch and had bent it into the desired shape, they would then tie the arch with a heavy string and set it aside to season. The arrows were made from long, slender dried twigs. My brothers spent most of their time target practicing rather than hunting for anything to kill. Remnants from the hickory saplings the boys had split to make their bows were sometimes used across their backsides when Dad discovered that they had scored direct hits on a few unfortunate birds.

At least one swing always hung from one of the trees in the yard. The swing was made by hanging a discarded tire from a tree branch with cable the boys had salvaged from the abandoned rigs. My older brothers left the swing for the younger children to enjoy, while they found more excitement in going into the woods to swing from grapevines or to ride over slender trees.

When one of us was given a ball, we took special care not to lose the precious gift. Aunt Gracie made the balls by unraveling worn-out socks and then winding the long fibers tightly into balls. She would then sell them to Grandma for a few cents each. Grandma would sometimes give one or two of the yarn balls to us children for Christmas.

We spent part of any free time we had on Sundays, and in late fall after harvest, playing a sport we called "Handy Over." Our family was blessed with enough kids in the family to form two teams. While the game was being played, all the players on each team would line up under the eaves of the roof on one or the other side of the house.

One member of the first team would yell, "Handy over!" As he yelled, he would throw the ball with enough force to cause it to roll over the crest of the tin roof and down the other side. A person on the rival team was supposed to catch the ball and quickly slip around the side of the house, where he would tag a member of the first team with the ball. Both players would then run back to the other side of the house and join the members of the tagger's team. The tagged player would then become an extra player on the team that had tagged him. If the ball wasn't caught when it rolled off the roof, it was thrown back over the house to the first team in the same manner it had been thrown to the second team. The game would continue until one team had tagged all the other team's players, claiming them for his own team.

One afternoon, my father brought home a big bus tire, which Woody and Marvin soon claimed. One brother would roll the tire to the highest part of the red-clay road in front of our property and turn it loose over the hill to see how far it would roll. The other brother would be waiting at the foot of the hill to retrieve the tire and return it to the top of the hill, where he would turn it loose to roll down the hill to the other brother.

The boys soon found, however, that the simple act of rolling a tire was not much of a challenge; therefore, one of the boys would curl up inside the part of the tire designed to fit on a rim, and the other would then roll the tire over humps and bumps until the brother curled up inside the tire fell out onto the ground. Once the brother inside the tire had fallen out, they would trade places and begin the challenge again.

One day I was watching Woody roll the tire with Marvin curled up inside, when to my surprise and horror, Woody turned the tire loose over the steep hill behind our house with Marvin still curled up inside it. When the tire hit the barbed wire fence at the bottom of the hill, out popped Marvin onto the ground. Although, except for a few scratches, Marvin was not injured, I had a feeling that he intended to give Woody a few fresh wounds in return.

Sure enough, when Marvin had finally regained his balance, he was on the warpath—and heading straight for Woody. Woody's laughter shifted to concern when he saw the fire in Marvin's eyes. After a few choice words and some promised threats from Marvin, Woody walked off, probably thinking to himself that he had asked for the scolding Marvin had given him. Neither of them dared to get back inside the tire again. Their trust of each other had gone over the steep mountain with the tire.

My younger brothers could be found almost every day playing beside the isolated ridge road. Since they had nothing to do but to look after each other as they played together, they occupied themselves by carving out small, narrow ridges in the red-clay banks beside the roadway. Tiny tunnels, garages, and intersections defaced the otherwise undisturbed earth. With only small blocks of wood to use for cars, my darling little brothers spent many pleasurable hours driving their own "toy automobiles."

Most of the time my siblings got along well together. Their free time was too precious to waste fighting with each other. With no neighbor kids with whom they could play, when fights did break out amongst them, their rifts didn't last long.

XXXIII

Poor Little Sister

School was out for the summer, and with all the summer work Dad had lined up for the family, there was hardly time left for us children to relax. My family didn't know the meaning of "vacation." Everyone big enough to work had their responsibilities year round. Everyone, that is, except my only sister, Nina.

Mom was in the fields every day helping the boys since Dad continued to work for the Kanawha County Board of Education during the summer. I had my hands completely full with responsibilities, yet I miraculously managed to carry out what was expected of me. I didn't mind the work I had to do; I did mind, however, that my sister refused to contribute her fair share of helping with the chores. I knew that when I was even younger than she, I had already been assigned my share of the work. I had tried repeatedly, with no results, to persuade Mom to insist that my sister help me with the work that she was capable of doing.

Since I had started to school, my grammar—and thus my speech—had been slowly improving, causing my mother to question my loyalty. One day when I asked her to order Nina to help me with the dishes, she scolded me by saying, "You thank y'ur sumpin', tryin' ta ack like 'em city slickers."

"What are you talkin' about?" I asked. "I haven't done anything wrong."

"Don'chu try'n git above y'ur raisin's, young lady," she said. "I been list'nin' ta how you been tryin' ta talk so prissy."

I'll admit that I felt very uncomfortable knowing that I had begun to act, think, and talk differently than I had been taught at home. I immediately decided that I would have to talk one way when I was at home and another way when I was at school. I also knew that if I were to get any help from Nina, it wouldn't be because my mother had ordered her to do so.

One morning, while Mom and my three oldest brothers were getting ready to leave for the fields, knowing that I was being left in charge of the younger children and to do all the housework, I screamed at my sister, "Why don't chu get y'ur lazy tail in here'n help me 'ith 'ese deeshes, or at least watch the baby while I do 'em by myself?"

"Why don't chu make me if you thank y'ur big enough," she yelled back to me.

"Mommy, make 'at lazy whelp git in here'n help me, er I'mma gonna knock 'er block off," I yelled to my mother.

"You orta be 'shamed a y'urself, treatin' y'ur only loodle sister that a way," Mom said to me. I knew that my mother was trying to make me feel guilty; instead, her remarks had only fueled my anger.

Finally, Mom and my brothers headed out for the cornfield, and I quickly developed a plan to do something about Nina's laziness and bad attitude. I decided I would mop the floor with my "only loodle sister."

I yelled to Nina and told her to come into the kitchen if she wanted to see something funny. Naturally, she came running into the room. I immediately ambushed her. I was standing near the outside door, and when she stepped near me, I quickly upended her onto the kitchen floor. But before I could proceed with my plans, Mom popped unexpectedly through the door at the same moment that Nina screamed out that I had already half killed her. "She started it!" I yelled quickly.

"I hain't da one 'at starded it! I'z jist playin'. She grabbed me an' throwed me onna floor," my sister yelled to Mom.

Without saying a word, my mother reached over to the cupboard and grabbed a willow switch that she had used earlier in the morning on one of my younger brothers for fighting with another brother. With her lips pursed and without batting an eye, she headed straight for me. For the first time in my life, I decided that I would run from my mother in order to avoid being whipped with the switch.

Mom yelled as I turned and broke for the door, "You git'chur hine en' back here, young lady, er I'mma gonna beat a life outta you."

I was barefoot and wearing a dress that was at least two sizes too small and four inches above my knees. I knew that my mother would leave welts on me from my backside to my ankles, so I quickly jumped off the porch and ran into the front yard, with Mom, her switch in hand, right behind me.

I turned to my left in an attempt to run behind the house, but before I could change gears, Mom yelled for backup. To my surprise, Woody ran from the back of the house and started toward me. I swirled around and ran right past my mother to the other side of the house. "Marvin!" Woody screamed, "Gitter! She's headin' y'ur way!"

"Mary Bethel!" Mom shrieked. "You'd bedder stop 'is, 'cause y'ur gonna git twice the whuppin' fer runnin' from me."

My brother Maynard jumped off the porch and joined in the pursuit. With my brothers closing in on me and Mom still threatening to kill me, I zigzagged from one direction to the other until I finally realized that the only place I could go was toward the garden. Determined to flee my mother's wrath, I glanced at the wire fence that divided our yard from the garden. Without breaking stride, I darted past Mom and her army and headed for the wire fence.

Without hesitation I quickly glanced at the thorny rambler rosebush entwined in the fence and in a split second decided that I would rather face the danger that lay in front of me rather than the danger that lay behind me. So, with my heart thumping and my mind starting to shut down, I clenched my fists, jumped into the air, and hurdled over the three-foot-high fence.

"Ouch! Ouch! Ow-ee!" I screamed upon landing, both from pain and terror. "My foot! My foot is cut plumb off'n me!"

Looking down at the ground and assuring myself that my foot was still attached to my leg, I cautiously felt around for the object I had apparently landed on. When I saw the lower, broken half of a glass, I realized that I had just located Mom's favorite water glass that had mysteriously disappeared. Knowing that one of my siblings had no doubt broken the glass and hidden it in the rosebush, I left the evidence where it had been hidden. "I jist about cut my foot off on a piece of glass," I sobbed.

Ignoring my pitiful but exaggerated cries and the blood gushing from my right foot, which was caused by the glass and the monstrous thorns on the rosebush, my angry mother slowly dragged me through the thorny bush and up and over the fence. I screamed out with all the vigor I could muster, wondering whether my injury might warm my mother's cold heart and move her to forgive my transgression.

Mom stood me on the ground, briefly looked down at the wound, and then ordered me to sit on the porch. I hobbled over and sat down on the floor of the porch, whimpering softly as I contemplated my mother's next possible move. She walked over and sat next to me and pulled my bleeding foot up to where she could examine it. "Yell, it's good 'nuff fer ye," she said. "I tol'gee not ta run from me." As my mother released the grip on my foot and shoved it off her lap, she continued, "Maybe you'll listen nex' time."

"Nina, fetch me 'at ol' sheet dat's in'na dresser drawer," she said. "An' Woody, you git me the lamp so I can pour some lamp oil in 'his cut."

While my siblings stood and watched, my mother yanked my foot onto her lap and began to apply pressure to the deep cut. "Ouch!" I screamed. "You hain't gonna pour lamp oil in 'at cut are ye?"

"Shet up an' hol' still," Mom said.

Woody unscrewed the burner from the lamp and poured the kerosene across the cut on my foot while Mom held my foot so I couldn't jerk it away. I had seen the younger children screaming, in what I had thought was pain, when Mom had treated their cuts with the kerosene. Squinting my eyes tightly, I gritted my teeth but uttered not a sound.

After Mom had turned me loose, she looked at me menacingly and said, "If'n you ever run from me ag'in, 'hen I'll beat chu to death an' 'hen turn you over ta y'ur daddy so he can whup ye too." I wondered silently why my father would need to whip me if she had already beaten me to death.

I sensed that the injury to my foot was minor compared to the switching that I would have received should my angry mother have caught me. I had never run from a whipping before, and I had no intention of running from one again.

As everyone returned to their jobs, I hobbled back to the kitchen to finish the dishes. The only thing I had accomplished was to severely cut my foot, leaving me with a scar that I still carry to this day. The worst part of the whole ordeal, however, was knowing that I wouldn't get to finish what I'd started to do to my "poor loodle sister."

XXXIV

Mealtime Adventures

Dad had been coming home each evening in a bad mood, and Mom's attempt at humoring him had failed to help. When he arrived home from work, he didn't ask about the big bloody bandage on my foot. Knowing that, if the food was not prepared to his expectations, he would sometimes take out his frustration on my mother, I hobbled nearby and watched as he washed his hands and sat down at the table.

If Mom had made a bad batch of bread, Dad wouldn't bother to ask her whether she was out of some of the ingredients she had needed; instead, he would periodically pick up one end of the table and, with the meal and dishes still on it, upend everything onto the middle of the floor.

On this particular evening, after Mom had turned out a big pan of cornbread onto a platter, broken off a hearty chunk of the bread, and placed it in Dad's plate, Dad asked the blessing and then picked up the piece of bread, looked at it, and threw it across the room. My three oldest brothers and I immediately jumped up and moved away from the table. Dad jumped to his feet, stepped to the side of the table, and with one motion of his hand, swiped the dishes and food onto the floor. Without hesitation, he then overturned the table on top of the spilled food and broken dishes.

It had become a regular event for Dad to go into one of his rages at the table. I often wondered, during the times when I was cleaning up the spilled food and broken dishes, if Mom wasn't spending more money on replacing the dishes than she was on buying food and clothing for the family. The only family member to profit from Dad's actions was my grandfather, who would climb the hill to our house regularly and tell Mom, "I come up'ere ta curry y'ur busted deeshes off'na hill ta feed ta my chickens."

Every time Dad overturned the table, the older boys would run like scared rabbits, and as the traumatic episodes continued, my younger siblings and I began following close behind. The smaller children were usually too scared to cry. They would huddle around me for what they must have felt was protection and comfort. I was comforted in knowing that they trusted me to protect them.

Sometimes Mom would come into the room and start crying at the sight of the entire meal and broken dishes scattered across the floor. More times than I care to remember, she would walk away calmly into the kitchen, pick up the bucket she used when milking the cow, order me to clean up Dad's mess, and then leave for the barnyard. Woody and Marvin would join her at the milk gap, well aware that it was best to stay out of Dad's sight until he had calmed down.

Whenever Dad destroyed our evening meals, we children went to bed hungry; unfortunately, the cold biscuit and bowl of oats that we each had eaten for breakfast would have to last us until the next morning. There was not much any of us could do except to stay out of his way while his temper was out of control.

On several occasions, I witnessed him slapping my mother and whichever child was closest to him at the time; however, he would usually rant and rave for a while, and then, like a hurricane when it hits land, his fury would peter out. I was thankful that he usually took out most of his destructive actions on objects rather than on Mom and us children. I didn't know at the time what had constrained him, but I now believe that God's angels must have been very busy protecting our family from serious harm during those violent outbursts.

I usually closed those sad days by thanking God that none of us had been seriously harmed.

Needless to say, none of our table settings matched. Occasionally, we children had to eat from tin bucket lids when all the saucers and plates had been broken. We didn't mind having to eat our food out of the tin pans since it was much easier to scoop up a spoonful of beans from a lid with a rim than to chase them around a flat plate.

Since our family owned only four forks, my siblings and I used spoons to eat our meals. Actually, I was in the seventh grade before I even attempted to eat with a fork, and even then, it took a little practice before I could pick up a mouthful of beans with the tines of a fork.

With our family continuing to increase in number, seldom did we have anything to drink with the evening meal. However, my siblings and I were thrilled when we each were blessed with a cupful of fresh milk, although it had to be served in tin cans since water glasses didn't last long around our house. On a few occasions, we children ignored the beans and potatoes Mom had cooked, opting instead to crumble our cornbread into the cans of milk and scoop up the mixture with our spoons.

Mom continued to avoid eating at the table when Dad was present until, eventually, Dad decided to eat his supper alone in the living room. After Mom had carried his food into the room and handed it to him, she would return to the kitchen and sit in Dad's empty chair to eat her meal alongside us children.

One evening my mother and I were surprised when Dad came home from work and walked into the kitchen carrying a big box. "What's in 'at box 'ere?" Mom asked.

"I got 'his set a unbreakable deeshes from a man 'at come by the bus garage sellin' 'em," he said.

Mom began opening the carton while we children gathered around to watch. She looked puzzled when she reached inside the box and pulled out a cup and saucer like we had never seen before. "Hit's a whole set uv 'em here deeshes 'ey're makin' now outta 'at plastic stuff," Dad said.

"Will 'ey break?" Mom asked.

"'Ey hain't s'posed to," Dad said. "You keep my ol' plate'n cup'n bowl 'cause 'em plates're too flat to hold many beans."

I wondered whether Dad had finally realized how much it had been costing him to replace all the dishes he had been breaking. It was a miracle that his favorite plate, bowl, and cup had survived the many trips on which he had sent them crashing to the floor, along with the rest of the dishes.

Realizing that it was always my responsibility to clear the floor of the spilled food and broken dishes, I appreciated the eight-place setting of unbreakable melamine dishes. Although I wouldn't have to contend with any more broken dishes, I suspected that I would be picking up spilled food for as long as I lived at home.

During the weekdays, Mom would arise at 4 a.m. to prepare Dad a full breakfast. She would build a fire in the kitchen stove so the oven would be hot by the time she had a batch of eighteen to twenty biscuits ready for baking. Once the bread was almost baked, she would then call Dad out of bed so that he could eat and be ready to leave for work by five o'clock.

Mom would never perk coffee; instead, she would pour the proper amount of ground coffee into the bottom of her large enamel coffeepot and then fill the pot with water. Once the pot had begun to boil on the hottest cap of the stove, she would then move the pot onto a cooler cap, farthest from the heat source, and allow the coffee to brew until it was very strong.

One morning, when Mom filled the coffeepot with grounds and water, she noticed that the old coffeepot had sprung a leak. The small hole in the bottom of the pot was allowing water to leak slowly onto the hot stove cap. She quickly emptied the pot and found a small piece of fabric to stuff into the tiny hole from inside the pot. She then poured the coffee grounds and water back into the pot and continued using it until she could go into town the following payday to buy a new, aluminum percolator. When she returned, before she used the new pot, Mom threw out the unfamiliar stem and basket and kept only the pot and lid, continuing to make the coffee as she always had.

My siblings and I realized that our father was entitled to a variety of foods that were not offered to us children. Although the few hens we owned couldn't supply us with enough eggs to feed the whole family, in addition to Dad's bowl of hot oatmeal and two hot biscuits, he managed to eat two fried eggs every morning of the week.

Mom tried to please Dad in the way she prepared his food. She would melt about half an inch of pure lard in an iron skillet, heat it until it was bubbling hot, and then break two eggs, carefully dropping them into the hot grease. Since she considered a spatula to be a luxury item, she had become very proficient at flipping the hot fat over the top surface of the eggs with a spoon. Throughout the years, Mom never once burned herself while frying Dad's sunny-side-up eggs; however, she received several scathing lectures from Dad when she accidentally ruptured the soft-cooked yolks while transferring the eggs from the hot skillet to his plate.

Dad's lunches were packed inside a regular lunch pail, with the thermos of coffee placed in the dome of the lunch pail's lid. Unlike his children's lunches, Dad's sandwiches were made with store-bought, sliced bread that we always called "light bread." The light bread and lunch cakes were kept together in the kitchen cabinet, which was off limits to us children. We never touched any of Dad's food, no matter how hungry we were or how great the temptation.

Once Dad had eaten breakfast and had left for work with his lunch pail packed and his thermos filled with boiled coffee, Mom would add more water to the coffee grounds left from Dad's pot of coffee and boil the grounds once again for us children. Since coffee cost approximately fifty cents per pound, it was an economical warm drink for my siblings and me at breakfast. From the oldest to the youngest of us school-age children, my siblings and I would pour six to eight ounces of the weak coffee into our tin cans and then fill them the rest of the way with milk.

Besides the pan of biscuits that Mom had baked when she had prepared Dad's breakfast, she would cook about two and a half quarts of Mother's Regular Oats, which she always bought in three-pound boxes. By the time Mom had called my siblings and me for breakfast, the food was cold, requiring us to scoop the thickened oatmeal from the pot in chunks. My siblings and I would each cover the sweetened oats with fresh milk and then, with a big cold biscuit in one hand and our spoon in the other hand, cram the cold food into our mouth and wash it down with our can of warm coffee. We never expressed any displeasure about the cold food because the food had always been served the same way and would continue to be served the same way for as long as we lived at home.

Occasionally, after sugar was no longer rationed, our breakfast meals were alternated between oats and red Karo syrup that Mom would purchase in half-gallon buckets. My siblings and I would pour the syrup over a big hunk of homemade butter and mix it together with a spoon. We would then sop up this special treat with hunks of cold biscuits.

The month's supply of groceries was purchased the first Saturday of each month since Dad was paid once a month. Should all the flour have been used before the month was over, we children would have to sop our syrup with cornbread instead of biscuits. We disliked eating cornbread for breakfast, yet in these situations we either ate cornbread or got no bread at all.

Most of the bacon and sausage kept from the latest butchering for our use was reserved for my father's meals. On the mornings when my mother would fry some of the meat for Dad's breakfast, the mouth-watering aromas would awaken me out of a sound sleep; nevertheless, I, as well as the other children, would never ask for the special foods. Mom had explained to us children that, since Dad was the one working to make a living, he alone was entitled to certain foods and other things that were too expensive to buy for the rest of the family. This rule apparently made sense to my siblings and me because we never once questioned the practice.

Although our evening meals consisted mostly of pinto beans, fried potatoes, and cornbread, in early spring my mother and I looked forward to going into the fields to pick wild greens. A large sack of greens, which some people classified as mere weeds, would shrink when boiled, leaving barely enough to divide among our family members. When mixed correctly, the "weeds" became a very tasty treat. In our garden and fields, we had an abundance of blue violet (we used only the stems and leaves) and several plants the folks in our area called groundhog's lettuce, water-cress, bear's paw, and "medder leddus" (meadow lettuce). A good assortment of these greens enhanced with a few dandelion leaves, lamb's quarters, plantain, daisy, blue thistle, poke, a few blackberry-briar leaves, and a scant of elderberry sprigs could put a smile on Mom's face like nothing else could.

Mom and I would first wash the greens in several water baths and then boil our selected pickings in a large pot of water. When the greens were tender, we would remove them from the pot and squeeze out the excess water, chop them slightly, dump them into a skillet of sizzling fat drippings, add salt and pepper, and then fry them for a few minutes.

Knowing how to combine the proper amounts of the many varieties of plants was very important. A bitter taste in the greens was the result of mixing too many of the stronger-tasting varieties to the batch. A more serious problem developed when Mom added too many elderberry or dock leaves to the batch. On the few occasions when this occurred, the family was thankful Dad had built a "two-hole" outhouse.

In the spring we also picked what is known in our area as "dry land fish," a type of mushroom. This variety is shaped like a rounded-top Christmas tree, with a porous, light-brown, honeycomb body and smooth, whitish stems. After a rain, they would sometimes spring up overnight in shady, damp areas in the woods. When my family was fortunate enough to find several of the "fish," we would split them in half, soak them in saltwater for an hour or two, and then roll them in flour, sprinkle them with salt and pepper, and fry them in a small amount of lard.

During the months of July and August, we would gather what the folks in our area called "Braddies," another variety of mushroom. Mom insisted that we pick only these brown mushrooms that oozed milk when broken or punctured. She stressed to us that other varieties were poisonous and should be avoided. I would later learn, however, that folks in adjoining hollows picked only red mushrooms and avoided picking the brown ones.

After we had cleaned and washed the Braddies, Mom preferred to drain them and then fry them in plenty of pure lard until they were tender. I preferred to roll them in flour before frying them in hot grease until they were crispy. Even though the smell was worse than cooking a spoiled fish, a hearty helping of Mom's greasy Braddies, sopped up with one of her big, browned biscuits, would send anybody back for seconds.

While our garden was producing, we had fresh vegetables for the table. Just about the time we began to enjoy the change, the season would end, and we would have to return to eating beans and fried potatoes, with the occasional jar of canned vegetables.

Mom would "cold pack" the green beans and tomatoes we raised. After the beans had been strung, broken, and washed, she would pack the beans in clean glass canning jars, add two teaspoons of salt to a half-gallon jar of beans, and fill the jars with hot water. She would then apply jar rubbers and one-piece lids. The jars of beans were then placed in a washtub of water with rags pushed down between the jars to prevent the jars from breaking once the water had begun to boil. The tub of beans would be placed over an outside fire, which had been built between two stacks of rocks, and boiled for three hours. The tomatoes were cooked in an open kettle and then poured into sterilized glass jars and sealed. As a rule, most of our canned tomatoes would spoil and were then poured out.

Occasionally, our meals would be enhanced with wild game Dad or one of the boys had killed. Groundhog (woodchuck) was one of the special treats. After the animal was skinned and the head and tail removed and discarded, Mom would wash the meat and cut it into serving-size pieces. The meat would be parboiled in a pot of water with a small amount of baking soda to remove some of the strong wild flavor from the meat. After the meat had boiled for about fifteen minutes, it was drained and the water discarded. An ample amount of fresh water was added to the meat and the pot left to simmer on the wood-burner stove until the meat was tender. It was then removed from the pot; rolled in flour; sprinkled with salt, pepper, and ground sage; and then browned by frying it in a generous amount of lard.

Meat from one groundhog was not ample to feed our large family; therefore, we children were delighted when the hunters returned with two or more of the fat, tasty animals. Squirrel, wild rabbit, quail, and pheasant were also appreciated when these wild meats were in (and sometimes out) of season. The broth from these cooked meats would be reserved to make a delicious gravy, which could be sopped up with biscuits or eaten with crumbled cornbread.

Although some of the old timers in our area ate 'possum, Mom always swore that she would never cook a 'possum or raccoon. The old midwife who lived out the ridge beyond our property was fond of "'possum and sweet 'taters'." Her technique for preparing the rodent was to skin the animal; split the belly from the neck to the tail area; remove the eyes, intestines, feet, and tail; and then scrub the animal before boiling the carcass for approximately one hour. After she had removed the 'possum from the broth, she would add a generous amount of salt and sage to the meat, and then stuff the cooked body cavity with scrubbed sweet potatoes she had cut into halves. Next, she would place the stuffed meat in a pan and bake it uncovered in a medium-hot oven for a couple of hours, or until it was tender.

Mom once said to the old lady, "'At might sound kinda temptin', but I hain't persuaded ta eat one of 'em scavengers yit. 'Hey look too much like a big rat ta me." I agreed with my mother.

The women around our area, including my mother, didn't believe in following recipes while cooking or baking. My mother was offended should my father suggest that she measure the ingredients so that, when she lucked out and baked a good pan of bread, she would know the proper amount of each ingredient to use the next time she baked; especially since her breads never seemed to taste the same two days in a row. When Mom and the country women were asked how they had made a certain dish, they would proudly say, "Oh, I jist used a handful of this and pinch of that."

XXXV

A Matter of a Dime

Around 9:00 on a warm morning in late summer, Mom informed me that I would have to walk out to my aunt's house to borrow some kerosene for the lamp. Dad was at work, the boys were out working in the fields, and because Mom wasn't feeling well, she was staying inside for a change.

My younger siblings were turned loose every day without much parental supervision since there was very little danger lurking around their play area and also because the older siblings naturally took charge over the children younger than themselves. The baby at the time was usually the only child who required a little of Mom's attention.

Since "Sissy" was my favorite person in the whole world, I was pleased to have an excuse to visit with her; I was not at all thrilled, however, about having to borrow from family or friends since Mom seldom returned the borrowed goods. I had earlier overheard Grandma and Sissy discussing this problem, and although I was uncomfortable because of the reason for my mission, I could hardly wait for the short visit with my aunt. To reach her house, I had to leave the ridge road and travel out through the forest for at least a mile. Although her home, like our own, was merely a small, dilapidated shanty, to her and Uncle Clint the dwelling was their little mansion.

Sissy was three years younger than my mother and was unable to bear children. She and Uncle Clint had often remarked that they wished I could have been their little girl, and as I walked out the dusty road all alone and deep in thought, I wondered what Sissy would say if I were to tell her what my dad had been trying to do to me. I didn't know whether it would be the right thing to do since I had always been taught that only "bad people" speak about anything as "nasty" as sexual matters. Why, I felt dirty just thinking about the subject.

I was meditating on whether to bring up the subject, when I rounded a bend in the road about halfway to Aunt Sissy's house and was startled to see a battered red pickup truck parked near my path, with a strange man leaning against the fender. My heart began racing since I had never seen a vehicle parked on the remote road. Since there were no houses nor, in my opinion, anything else that might attract a person to the area, I looked cautiously and closely at the stranger and was shocked to see that he was holding a bottle of what I guessed was some type of alcohol. Stretched out on their sides on the ground near his feet were a couple of other men also holding bottles. My heart seemed to leap into my throat when I realized that all three of the men were looking straight at me. I hesitated, not knowing whether I should run toward my aunt's place or turn and run back toward home; nevertheless, although I felt I was in danger, I slowly and cautiously crept in the direction of Sissy's house. Walking on the well-trodden path would require me to pass within ten feet of the men, so I hovered instead between the edge of the road and the wood-line in an attempt to stay as far away from them as possible.

As I was passing directly in front of the man who was standing, he called out to me, "Come on over here ta me, loodle girl, an' I'll give ya a dime." I shivered when I heard his tone of voice. The seedy-looking character reached into his pocket and pulled out a coin, which he held up. I ignored the man's offer and began running as fast as I could toward Sissy's house. I had never been warned about a situation such as this, but I felt the same type of fear that I had experienced when my dad had tried to get me to do bad things with him.

I was not conscious of how hard and fast my bare feet were pounding on the baked clay earth; instead, I felt as though wings were attached to my feet, allowing me to sail through the air like a soaring eagle. Somewhere along the secluded roadway, realizing that the sunlight was no longer piercing through the heavy overhang of tree limbs, I looked back across my shoulder to make certain that no one was chasing me. Although I could see no human form behind me, I nevertheless sensed a presence hovering nearby. I slowed my pace and immediately envisioned the picture I'd seen on a calendar at Grandma's house, of a little boy and girl walking hand-in-hand across a rickety footbridge spanning a treacherous river. I remembered my grandmother saying that the angel hovering over the children's heads was their Guardian Angel. No longer afraid, I was convinced that God had sent my very own Guardian Angel, who had put the wings on my feet and swept me up and away from danger.

I soon found myself approaching Sissy's little rustic home. The rough boards used in building the house had never been painted and were now bleached from the sun and rain that had beaten down on them for years. Sissy met me at the door and gave me a big hug. As usual, she looked neat and well-groomed in a clean, pressed cotton dress that looked as though she had just stepped into it. The fragrance of fresh lilacs permeated the air around her. Her hair was neatly finger waved on the sides, with the bulk of the hair pulled back into a neat little bun, which she had pinned to the back of her head with hairpins. Unlike my pioneer mother, who at this time of her life didn't believe in removing any of the hair that God had placed on her body, Sissy always kept her legs clean shaven and her feet and toenails well-groomed. Her neatly trimmed fingernails with their snow-white tips further accentuated her graceful appearance.

Everything in and around the two-room house was always as immaculate as Sissy herself. The feather-tick bed with its frilly white bedspread filled one end of the living room. The living room and kitchen walls were covered with wallpaper patterned with blue and pink flowers on a white background. Long sheer lace curtains adorning the two living room windows brushed lightly against the pastel linoleum that covered the living room and kitchen floors.

Stiffly starched and ironed doilies, which Sissy had carefully embroidered, graced the few pieces of glistening mahogany furniture scattered around the small living room. All sorts of little figurines were arranged neatly on every piece of furniture.

As Sissy took my shoulder and whisked me through the cozy little house in the direction of the kitchen, I caught a whiff of the familiar aroma of freshly baked goodies. Sissy's happy smile assured me that I was in for a treat, as she seated me lovingly at the round wooden table and reached across to pull the glass-covered cake-saver to the edge of the table. I watched as she removed the cover and sliced me a hearty wedge of her special homemade cake. She did not frost her cakes with store-bought frosting nor icing made with powdered sugar; instead, she made a special, snow-white icing that was crisp on the outside and fluffy on the inside. She was not stingy with it either. She had heaped it onto the cake and then made pretty swirls across the top and sides. I thought it was no doubt the best cake in the whole wide world.

As I nibbled timidly at the delicious piece of cake, she pulled her chair close to mine and excitedly began telling me about Uncle Clinton's recent "conversion." I'd been in Sunday School and church for the past couple of years, so I knew that the term *converted* meant my uncle had become a Christian. I had always sensed that Sissy and Uncle Clint had a special marriage, and I now believed that their life would take on new meaning.

Time flew as we talked, and I realized that I hadn't said a word to Sissy about my dad. I could see how happy she was, and I was concerned that, should I talk to her about my father, it might somehow snatch away her joyful enthusiasm; besides, I was feeling embarrassed and ashamed just thinking about bringing up the subject.

Finally, Sissy brushed away my few crumbs and stepped outside onto her back porch to fill my jar with kerosene. After handing me the jar of lamp oil, she told me that I had better hurry on home so that I wouldn't get in trouble with my mom. I hesitated as Sissy nudged my shoulder with one hand, while holding the screen door open with her other hand.

I stepped outside and then turned and looked back at my aunt. Although I couldn't tell her about my dad, I felt compelled to tell her about the truck with the strange men loitering in the area. Quickly, I began blurting out the details, and as Sissy listened to my story, she quickly removed her starched white apron, turned around, and laid it just inside the door on the back of a chair. Stepping outside, she reached down and took my hand in hers. "I'mma gonna go out that fer with you to make shore at you're safe," Sissy said.

"I'm not afraid anymore. I can run really fast, an' they couldn' ketch me if 'ey tried," I said bravely.

Sissy insisted that she accompany me out to where I had seen the strangers. While we walked along the path on my way back home, Sissy continued to talk about her and Uncle Clint's happy life together. She told me that someday, I too would find a man who would make me happy. As she chatted on and on about my being happy someday with a good man, I wanted to say to her, "If only you knew! I don't want a man! The only man in my life scares me to death!"

Just before we approached the spot where the truck had been parked, Sissy whispered for me to be quiet and to stay behind her. She edged on closer, peeking out from behind the bushes and looking across to where the truck had been parked. I was beginning to think that Sissy was even more scared than I had been, when finally she moved out into the path and beckoned me to join her.

The truck was no longer where I had seen it earlier. Sissy pointed out that the tire tracks indicated that the men had headed back toward town. A smoldering campfire seemed to be the only thing the men had left behind; however, upon closer investigation we noticed several empty wine bottles and numerous cigarette butts strewn carelessly about. Sissy told me that the men were probably "fox chasers" who had spent the night in the area, drinking wine and listening to their dogs chase foxes. I accepted her explanation.

"You'll be okay goin' on home by yourself," Sissy said, as she hugged me and then turned to go back to her home.

"Bye, Sissy," I said as I looked down, my eye catching something glimmering in the dust.

"Bye, honey," Sissy said.

I reached down and picked up the bright, shiny coin and, holding it proudly between my fingers, excitedly yelled to Sissy, "Looky here, Sissy, what I found!"

Sissy turned, looked at the dime I was holding, and began clapping her hands together. "You got dat dime after all, didn' ye?" she exclaimed.

I began skipping down the road, holding the jar of kerosene against my bosom with one hand and my glittering dime in the other hand, feeling much lighter in spirit than I had felt when I had left home earlier.

Each year the school had been collecting money for the American Red Cross to donate to the March of Dimes. The money was being used to help find a cure for polio and tuberculosis. When the more fortunate students would contribute their money, usually dimes, they would receive a small red cross that the teacher would pin onto their clothing. I had for some time longed for a dime to give to the drive, and looking once again at the precious coin in my hand, I had no doubt of how I would spend it. I was ecstatic!

XXXVI

Terror in the Garden

Once again Mother Nature was tucking her summer babies in bed to protect them from the bitter cold winter that would soon be bringing frost to our area. Even the fall wildflowers that had replaced most of the summer flowers had seemingly begun to yawn and bow their heads lazily, signifying that they too were ready for a long, peaceful nap. The flowers and foliage had been performing in a magnificent manner, which was expected of them, and even now as they prepared to retire for the winter, they were leaving slowly in a splendid blaze of glory.

Every year around this same time, Mom would begin fretting as she prepared to outfit the family with new clothing to begin the new school year. None of us children were allowed to accompany our mother into town to make certain our shoes and clothing would be the correct size. Instead, Mom would measure our feet with pieces of twine and then size our shoes by buying them as long as the lengths of twine.

The new clothing would be charged to Dad's account at the small dry goods store. The store's management had always allowed my parents to make small monthly payments toward the debt. The account was rarely paid in full. By the time the bill was almost paid, it was once again time to outfit the family for the next school year.

There were no clothing vouchers for low-income families like ours, so Mom had no choice but to buy the cheapest clothing possible.

We children didn't fret over the clothing she chose; instead, we were thrilled that we could attend the first day of the school year wearing brand-new clothes like the rest of the class would be wearing.

Each of my brothers usually received two new pairs of blue jeans and two new shirts. The three oldest boys were also given new underwear, but because of the expense, the younger boys had to wear their pants without underwear until they too had reached puberty. Each child was outfitted with a new pair of shoes. In addition to my two new dresses, I received two pairs of socks and a few pieces of store-bought underwear.

We children realized that the new clothing would have to last us for the entire year, no matter how worn and frayed the articles might become. It never seemed to fail that toward the end of the nine months of school, our toes had crowded themselves through the already mended feet of the socks and soon were rubbing against the toes of our worn-out shoes. Since no one could see our bare toes inside the shoes, we thought nothing about wearing socks with holes in the toes; however, when our heels rubbed through our socks, Mom would mend the heel area until the stitches would no longer hold. Once this happened, I would try to hide the mending in the heels of the socks by pulling the front of the socks forward and tucking them under my toes.

Should it become necessary for our shoes to be repaired, our mother would take them on a Saturday morning to the old reliable shoemaker in town to have them patched or sewn so they would last us the rest of the school year. The shoemaker would polish and buff the shoes after he had repaired them and would have them waiting for Mom by the time she had finished buying the groceries. My siblings and I appreciated the shoeshines since Dad's shoe polish was reserved for his shoes alone.

Through all the lean, hard times, I can't remember even once when any of us children complained about the shoes or clothing we had no choice but to wear to school. I realized that although my siblings and I might not be the best-dressed students in the school, we could look around and see a few of our classmates who had even less than we had. Mom often said to us, "Young'uns, y'all don't haf'ta worry. Y'all might not have the best clothes in school, but at least thur clean an' patched good."

After supper one evening, shortly after school had started, my two older brothers went outside to feed the horse and pig. After I finished washing the dishes, I walked outside on my way to the privy. Passing by the garden, I noticed my brothers running through the garden on their way back to the house. Marvin had inadvertently stumbled upon a sponge ball that had been lost in the garden before the frost had killed all the vegetation. Woody ran to the far end of the garden and yelled to Marvin to throw him the ball.

On my way back to the house, I saw them passing the ball back and forth, when suddenly, holding the ball as if set to throw it in my direction, my oldest brother started yelling at me, "Run, er I'm gonna hit'cha with 'his wet ball!"

I did not run, however, because I knew that should I run, my brother would no doubt throw the ball at me to see whether he could hit a moving target. "If you run, 'hen I might miss ya. If you don't run, 'hen I know I'll hit'cha," he yelled.

Afraid that Woody would hit me with the wet ball, I stood as still as a statue, imagining that if I were to stand still, my big brother would allow me to pass by safely. However, should I run, I was sure he would do his best to knock my head off with the ball he had cocked and ready to throw.

How wrong I was! As I stood frozen in my tracks, he yelled at me, "I done tol'jee ta run, you loodle son-za-bitch!" Nervously, I stood my ground, staring in his direction and hoping he was only bluffing. Seemingly without blinking an eye, he reared back, took aim, and threw the ball with all the power he could muster. The ball came through the air with such speed that before I could change my mind and run it slammed into my thigh.

With my leg stinging and burning, I fell to the ground screaming, no doubt more from the anger boiling within me than from the pain caused by my thoughtless brother. At that moment, I found myself wishing that I were big enough to tear off his pitching arm so that I could use it to knock off his empty head.

Immediately, a large red welt appeared on the front of my thigh. I jumped up, screaming as though I had been shot. I quickly ran to the house and hobbled through the living room door, holding my hand over the welt and shouting through my tears, "Oh, my lag! Oh, my lag!"

Dad was sitting near the fireplace whittling on a piece of kindling wood. He looked up as I fell to the floor near his chair, still squeezing out every ounce of emotion possible.

"What'na Sam Hill happened?" Dad shouted quickly.

"Look at my lag! Woody hit me so hard 'at he jist 'bout tore my lag off," I lied convincingly.

"What'd he hit'cha with?" Dad angrily asked.

"With an old wet ball," I sobbed.

To my horror, Dad jumped up, leapt across the floor, and grabbed the .22 rifle off the wall, where it hung across two long nails driven into the wall. Quickly, he turned and jerked the dresser drawer open, angrily throwing the contents of the drawer onto the floor. Pulling out a box of ammunition, Dad went storming out the door as he rammed a live cartridge into the chamber of the rifle.

I followed closely behind my father, frantically screaming, "Daddy, please don't hurt Woody!" I was scared stiff but afraid that if I admitted I wasn't hurt as much as I had pretended to be, then Dad might turn around and shoot me.

Dad yelled, "Woodrow, you durdy loodle son-za-bitch, I'm gonna keel you!" My father didn't give Woody a chance to explain that he meant me no harm and was only playing.

Woody didn't break to run, nor did he say a word. Standing in the garden about fifty feet from where my dad was standing on the porch, and seemingly not moving a muscle, my oldest brother looked as though he were frozen in time. Marvin stood stiffly in his tracks on the other side of the garden, apparently in a state of shock.

I threw my hands over my eyes and began to pray silently as Dad threw the rifle to his shoulder. I was too scared to scream, realizing that only God could intervene at this point. As the sound of the shot reverberated in my ears, I stiffened in terror. With my legs no longer able to hold me upright, helplessly and hopelessly I crumpled slowly to the floor, feeling as though I needed to vomit. Afraid to open my eyes, I listened but was met only with an eerie silence.

"What have I done?" I asked myself, knowing that all this was my fault for having tattled to my dad.

Finally, I was able to breathe a sigh of relief when I heard my father shout angrily, "Nex' time ya might not be so lucky! You git y'ur ass inside right dis minute 'fore I do keel you."

I looked across the garden at Woody, who was still standing in the same spot and position in which he had been when Dad had walked onto the porch to confront him. A great sense of relief swept over me. I forced myself slowly onto my feet, wiped my eyes with the tail of my dress, and stood shaking as I watched my brothers moving swiftly toward the house.

Dad stormed past me and went back inside. I wanted to run to my brother's side to tell him that I was sorry I had tattled on him, but my body wouldn't respond to the desire of my heart. I held onto the porch support post as Woody walked past me and stepped inside the living room door. My heart ached for him as the look on his tear-stained face burned itself into my mind.

I looked into Marvin's eyes, when he too brushed past me, apparently as upset as I was over the senseless act. I immediately decided that from that moment forward I would allow my brothers to get away with murder before I would tattle to our father.

I was perfectly aware that Dad had begun protecting me in a way that seemed abnormal, so I blamed myself for everything that had happened. "I should've known better than to go crying to my father," I told myself. My only comfort was in knowing that there was no way I could have foreseen that my father would have reacted in such an aberrant and unbelievable manner. Considering that Dad was a sharpshooter with the rifle, that the rifle's sights were kept in perfect alignment, and that my brother was within firing range, I could conclude only that either my father had had no intention of shooting my brother or that God Himself had sent the bullet awry. To my knowledge, the episode was never mentioned to anyone while we children were growing up. The family no doubt chose to forget the horrifying act; however, it would be indelibly engraved in the innermost part of my memory.

XXXVII

Fighting Him Off

Another hot, dry summer had come and gone with our family having to make several trips down to "the bars" to do the laundry. School had been in session for over a month, and I was attending the sixth grade. I could hardly believe that in just one year I would be going down to the high school that my two oldest brothers were attending.

My twelfth birthday had come and gone like all the others had—without any recognition. I was not, nor were any of my siblings, given cakes or birthday parties on our birthdays; in fact, we were not even aware of the tradition.

I couldn't help but notice that my body had been changing over the past year. In addition to my height having increased, it was also evident that parts of my body were taking on a more mature look. From the unsolicited remarks from my father, I was concerned that he was taking particular interest in the changes. His new approach was to try to persuade me that it was my duty to honor his demands; however, I continued to strenuously resist his disgusting suggestions and actions.

One evening while my mother was at the barn milking the cow, I had once again been left alone in the kitchen washing the dishes. Before I could realize what was happening, Dad slithered into the kitchen and approached me quickly from behind, grabbing both my arms and pinning them tightly against my body. Turning me around forcefully, he shoved me back at arm's length and looked into my eyes.

I was panic stricken and immediately began screaming and kicking as I tried to free myself from his grasp.

My strong resistance seemed only to fuel his intentions. Second by second, I became even more frantic! I screamed loudly for my mother and brothers to help me; yet, no one came to my rescue. While I screamed and struggled, my father suddenly slung me to the floor and, holding me down with his knees and one hand, tried to peel off my underwear with his other hand. I felt helpless, yet I fought with all my strength, fully aware that I was no match for my father's strength; nevertheless, I intended to fight to the death before I would willingly give in to whatever he had in mind to do to me. The more I kicked and screamed, the harder he fought to restrain me. Somehow, I finally broke my right hand loose from his grip, and, while scratching him wherever I could feel flesh, I continued to fight with every ounce of strength within my body.

With my whole body trembling from fear, my teeth somehow made contact with the upper side of his right wrist. Quickly, I clamped down with all my might. As suddenly as my teeth had sunk into his flesh, he grabbed the nape of my neck with the fingers of his left hand and squeezed down unmercifully. To my dismay, I had no choice but to release the hold my teeth had on him. "You loodle son-za-bitch, I orta knock your head off'n y'ur shoulders," he yelled angrily as he released his hold on me and shoved me aside.

I pulled myself up onto my knees and then scurried to my feet. Without taking time to grab a jacket, I ran out the door and across the garden to the barnyard, where Mom had just finished milking the cow. She looked over at my tear-stained face and asked, "Now, what's wrong 'ith you?"

I had no doubt that she already knew what my complaint was going to be; however, I angrily and disgustedly cried out, "He was tryin' to do somethin' durdy to me, an' I hate 'is daggone guts!"

"Shame on you! You orta be 'shamed talkin' 'bout chur daddy like 'at," she said, shaking her head from side to side.

"Why, what do you 'spect me to do?" I cried.

"Git on back up 'ere whur you belong outta 'his col' air," Mom said.

"My God!" I cried. "You thank a cold's gonna hurt me worser than he's done hurt me?"

Struggling to regain my composure, I paced myself so that I could arrive back at the house alongside my mother. When we walked inside, my father was straddling a wooden chair with his back turned toward the heat from the open fire in the fireplace. His arms were folded atop the back of the chair with his head resting, face down, on his arms. "I wish he was dead," I said silently to myself. I felt guilty immediately over the troubling thought. Mom never said a word to my father about the incident, nor did Dad mention anything about how he had gotten the scratches and bite mark. I returned to the dishpan, my situation seeming completely hopeless.

XXXVIII

Wartime

In the country, the noon and evening meals were called dinner and supper. *Lunch* was the food a person carried with them when they expected to be away from home during the noon hour. Dad always expected his supper to be ready when he arrived home from work. He didn't tolerate excuses, no matter how bona fide they might have been. He never asked how Mom's day had gone, nor what she might have gone through in order to have his meal ready by the time he walked in the door.

Although my mother worked hard to have the food on the table on time, she seemed to take no pride in preparing the only meal of the day where we children sat at the table with Dad. Trying to feed a family the size of ours on Dad's meager wages apparently didn't leave her much choice on what to cook for the meals. Our evening meal consisted of pinto beans, fried potatoes, and cornbread—day after day.

With no source of refrigeration, a fresh pot of pinto beans, seasoned with a piece of pork skin or a chunk of pork fat, was cooked daily. We children recognized the fact that the added piece of pork was reserved for our father, and, thankfully, none of us acquired a taste for what we now know is unhealthy. It took approximately three hours to cook a pot of beans on the wood-burning stove; yet, regardless of how busy she might have been, Mom managed to accomplish the task—every day of the year. Even on the days we spent at the creek doing the laundry, a big pot of freshly cooked beans were always ready at supper time. Mom made certain there were no leftovers from the meals, being careful to cook just enough food to feed her ever-growing family.

None of our family members knew proper mealtime etiquette. Our mother tried to teach us what few manners she had acquired, and she expected us to practice those manners in the presence of others as well as in the midst of our own family. There was seldom any conversation among any of the family members seated around the table since we were taught that children should not speak during the meal. As a rule, the only time any of the family spoke was to ask for a dish to be passed.

Dad always sat at one end of the table, and, since Mom never sat at the table with the family, I sat opposite him at the other end of the six-foot-long table. Woody and Marvin would seat themselves at the front side of the table, with the smaller kids eventually filling the long wooden bench that lined the wall behind the table. As a rule, each of us recognized and respected the others' seating preference.

The tone of Dad's voice was always the same whenever and wherever he asked God's blessing on the food. He always repeated the same words each evening, and we knew how long the blessing would last before he'd even opened his mouth. Bowing his head, Dad would solemnly say:

"We thank ye, our Heavenly Father, fer 'hese an' all blessin's of life. Pardon us an' fergive our wrongs, an' Heaven save us fer Christ'iss sake. Hey-men."

After my sibling and I were grown, my brother Maynard said to me, "When I was loodle, I always thought 'at Daddy set in the same chair and ate from the same plate all the time 'cause he was readin' the blessin' outta his plate."

Although there was no conversation amongst us children and Dad, the mere fact that he sat at the table with us when we first moved onto the ridge was rewarding. It wasn't long, however, before mealtime with Dad became anything but enjoyable. He seemed to have regressed into the man he had been just before we'd left the hollow to move onto the ridge, often losing his temper over very minute matters. None of us knew what to expect when we went to the table. Sometimes, suppertime was peaceful, and sometimes Dad changed mealtime into "wartime."

I had picked up the unusual habit of twitching my nose and sometimes would absentmindedly wriggle my nose in Dad's presence. Since he had warned me repeatedly that he was going to "beat the daylights" out of me if I didn't break myself of the annoying habit, I had been trying desperately to do so.

One balmy summer evening, Dad, my siblings, and I had just seated ourselves around the table. I was seated in my usual place at the far end of the table, opposite my father. He had just asked the blessing on the meal. Seeing that nobody had bothered to pass the bread down my way, I looked across the table toward Woody, who was seated near the bread plate, and said, "Bread. Bread, please." Nobody responded. I tried again, with no luck. Finally, on the third attempt, I spoke a little louder and said, "Bread! Bread, please!"

Suddenly and without warning, I was struck across the bridge of my nose with a hard object I had glimpsed whirling through the air at my face. The unexpected and forceful blow brought tears to my eyes. Wiping the tears away, I looked down in my lap to see a chunk of Mom's flat, over-baked cornbread. I couldn't believe that such a horrible thing had taken place at the supper table. I had no idea who had thrown the bread, and since Dad would have responded if one of my brothers had been responsible for the dastardly act, I concluded that my father had thrown the "deadly weapon." Crying, I stood up to leave the table. "Git'chur ass back here'n eat'chur supper, young lady," Dad said.

I sat down at the table and tried to regain my composure; however, I couldn't hide my tears no matter how hard I tried. Dad sternly said, "Shet up'n eat! I tol' jue 'bout wigglin' 'at big nose of yern fer tha las' time!" I was tempted to run outside and not to stop until I was out of the state; instead, I sat at the table and pretended to eat my supper—minus the cornbread I had unfortunately requested just seconds earlier.

Finally, Dad finished eating and left the table. I jumped up as he entered the other room and quickly ran outside, sobbing until my nostrils were so stuffy that I could hardly breathe. I had realized that twitching my nose could be dangerous, especially while in throwing distance of my father.

For the next few weeks, Dad's act of cruelty turned out to be a twofold blessing for me. I was thankful that he had not approached me in an unseemly manner since the incident, and from that day forward I never again twitched my nose.

XXXIX

That Old-Time Religion

The garden vegetables had been gone for weeks, and the fields once again lay bare. No longer was there any indication that the landscape had, just a couple of months earlier, been overspread with wildflowers of all colors and descriptions. The mountains that had been ablaze with the Master's wonderful display of colors were now looking naked and gray, as though tired and drained after months of being ignored by the busy country folk. The wild animals and insects were no longer bustling about now that cold weather had sent them scampering for their dens and warmer climate. The red-breasted robins had migrated south and had been replaced by an assortment of little year-round birds searching busily for food.

I felt as though the cloak of death had blanketed the land, and a sadness deep inside me seemed to be gripping my soul. I had been thinking more and more about what my aunt had told me about Uncle Clint's conversion, and I often lay awake at night thinking about the desire within me to know God more personally.

After my uncle had been converted, he immediately began taking an active part in the church services. I could see that he was displaying a different attitude from that of Mr. White or my dad. I always listened when he prayed aloud in church and felt that he must have a direct line to God's abode. He had begun making an impression in my life that would soon influence me to want to become a Christian.

I had been concerned for some time, wondering whether or not I would go to Heaven should I die. I believed in my heart that there was a Heaven and a Hell, and I was certain that I did not want to spend eternity in the latter. Even at my young age, I believed that I had already been exposed to more hell here on earth than I cared to experience. I fully believed that God had His hand upon my life, and if anybody would be able to help me to climb out of the pit I felt myself sinking into, then truly it would be Him.

Our little church there on the ridge, Reamer Tabernacle, was beginning a series of revival meetings. Mom and Dad had sporadically taken my siblings and me to church before we had moved to the ridge, but they had never allowed us to attend Sunday School. Once we had moved to the ridge, however, although our parents refused to go with us, my brothers and I would walk to Sunday School every Sunday morning. I was looking forward to attending the revival services with our relatives and neighbors who would be coming in from the hills and hollows from all the settlements nearby.

The church property had been owned by the people who owned the house and property adjoining it (my birthplace). The owner had deeded an acre, more or less, on which the church was to be built. Should the property cease to be used for holding church services, the deed stipulated that the premises and land would revert to the original tract of land.

Upon obtaining the land, the interested families in the community had raised the money and then built the small building out of lumber bought directly from one of the sawmills in the area. The outside structure of the building was covered with rolls of siding that looked like red brick. The roof was covered with sheets of tin.

Ten or twelve wooden benches had been crudely built and then brought inside and lined up on either side of the one-room building. Several small wooden shelves had been built and attached alongside each wall to hold the kerosene lamps, the only source of lighting for the evening services.

Two pews on either side of the podium were arranged to accommodate the small "choir." Two mourner's benches had been constructed directly in front of the pulpit. There were three windows on each side of the room, with the bottom halves of the windows painted with gray paint to obscure the view through the window from both the outside and the inside.

A potbellied stove, fueled by coal, was placed in the middle of the one-room church, with the stove pipe extending through the ceiling and out the top of the tin roof. The stove was seldom used, since during the winter months the weather was too cold and the roads too muddy and rutted for people to travel.

Dad and a couple of other men from the church had agreed to paint the bottom halves of the plasterboard walls dark brown, agreeing that the top halves of the walls should remain white. After they had finished painting, however, Dad came home agitated and, in the presence of us children, stated to Mom that the paint job had been done shabbily, except for the sections he had painted.

I had taken special note of his statement, so a few days later my brothers and I decided to check out the men's work, since we were out looking for nuts in the woods near the unlocked church. It indeed appeared that on a few sections of the walls, thin coats of brown paint had been applied with up and down strokes, while heavier coats of paint elsewhere had been applied from side to side. The few panels that my father had apparently done were painted evenly, with no brush marks showing. I thought to myself as I looked at the walls, "No wonder Daddy was mad."

Dad had at one time said, "A job worth doin' is a job worth doin' right." The statement and the paint job had made an impression on me that I would never forget. Throughout the years I began to notice that a job done properly often received little attention, while a job done poorly attracted more attention.

Reamer Tabernacle was non-denominational. To my knowledge there was no constitution or by-laws; instead, everything was done with "mutual agreement" by the men of the church. The men would appear to be in agreement when decisions were made; however, on several occasions after we had left the church and returned home, Dad would voice his disapproval over the way business had been conducted or how new leaders had been chosen.

Should one of the men later change his mind over a previous agreement, he would avoid attending church for weeks at a time. Sooner or later, however, the disgruntled man would return to church, stand before the congregation, and declare that he had just been converted again. Upon hearing the good news, the rest of the flock would rejoice with the individual, and he was welcomed back with warm, hearty handshakes—no matter how often over the years the offenses had occurred.

The pastor was always a layman who had announced his call to preach. The church never paid the pastor a salary or contributed to his expenses in any way. He was usually one of the men from a neighboring community who worked either as a coal miner, as a carpenter, or in the logging business. The people did not believe in paying a man to be a full-time pastor. They felt that he should have a public job and work for a living in the same way they had to work.

The people did not believe in calling a pastor who had attended college. "We want somebody 'at won't preach over our heads," they often said. They considered a man who had gone to Bible school to be a self-made preacher who had gone to school to learn how to preach. The congregation believed that if a man was truly called of God, then when he stepped into the pulpit and opened his mouth, God would fill his mouth with what the people needed to hear. They also made it known that if the preacher couldn't preach fiery sermons without the aid of notes or outlines, in their opinion he wasn't much of a preacher.

None of the "members" believed in passing the collection plate during the services. I had never heard the word *tithing*, and doubt whether most of us could have defined its meaning. When the building needed to be repaired or Sunday School literature needed to be ordered, the money needed was solicited quietly from each of the church leaders.

At the time, I believed that the preacher was a sinless man; although, since I'd been taught that simply speaking about anything that pertained to sex was a sin, I wondered how the preacher and his wife had managed to have children. When I finally realized, from observing the animals, that a male and female had to mate in order to conceive any offspring, I decided that God apparently approves of copulation between a married couple—just as long as they keep it a secret between themselves and God.

When a question was asked pertaining to the Bible or church doctrine, the pastor, if he was present, or one of the leaders would say, "Well, 'his is what I thank about it." Instead of giving Scriptural references to show what God had to say about the matter, the speaker would elaborate on his own personal understanding of the subject. It was believed that the man in charge of the service was speaking with God's authority; therefore, no one would dare to question "God's man." Even when my father spoke in church on Sunday and then went on the warpath on Monday, I assumed his actions were normal and that all men acted in the same manner.

The attendance at Reamer Tabernacle averaged in the upper teens or twenties, occasionally climbing into the thirties. The people did not believe in placing their names on a church membership roll; thus, anyone who attended the church was considered a member as long as he/she had been "converted."

Most of the people, regardless of age, walked to church. Dad drove when road conditions permitted, but when he wasn't attending the church (Mom always stayed home with Dad), my siblings and I would walk to the church on our own. Mr. White sometimes rode his horse-drawn surrey for the three miles he had to travel from his home to the church.

While he was an active "member," Dad would sometimes lead the services during the morning worship hour, or hours. When my father declined to lead the services, Mr. White would resume the role. The rivalry between the two sometimes became a major problem for them and the congregation. Eventually, Dad would stay home when Mr. White was in charge, and Mr. White would stay home when Dad was scheduled to lead the services. Dad was convinced that he was the best song and service leader, and Mr. White apparently thought the same about himself. Sooner or later, Mr. White would come to our house to apologize to Dad, or Dad would offer his hand in repentance to Mr. White. It was no secret to the congregation that the two men were extremely jealous of each other's role in the small community church.

More problems were created when Uncle Clint began taking charge of some of the services after his conversion. Dad and Mr. White would meet on our front porch after church on Sundays to discuss what they thought were Uncle Clint's shortcomings. Neither man seemed to realize that the congregation was becoming discouraged and unfaithful while the leaders played their rivalry games.

When the weather permitted, our revivals, held in the months of April and October, sometimes lasted for two weeks. The pastor would usually bring the messages, or he would bring in a preacher from one of the other country churches nearby. For some unknown reason Reverend Foster, the only pastor I had known at the time, had recently resigned; therefore, my father asked one of his fellow school bus drivers, a preacher, to bring the messages in the October 1947 revival.

Dad did not attend the meetings since he had not attended church for weeks, after admitting that he was backslidden. Finally, however, after the service was underway on the last night, Dad walked inside the little church and seated himself quietly on the back row.

After the sermon was over and the evangelist had begun pleading with the unsaved to come to the altar to get converted, two or three young men from surrounding neighborhoods went forward and knelt at the altar. A few of the professing men and women immediately gathered around them and began praying. Sitting quietly in the pews, the remaining members would wait for someone to jump up from the altar to begin shouting that he had "got religion."

My heart felt very heavy because I knew that the week's meeting was coming to a close and I was still unsaved. Not only was I concerned that I would go to Hell should I die, I wanted to become a Christian so that I could show Jesus how much I loved Him. While I thought about the emptiness that had seemed to overwhelm me at times, my heart began beating much faster and harder than ever before. Tears began trickling down my face while something or someone seemed to be drawing me toward the altar; yet the uncertainty of knowing what to do or say had me glued to my seat.

Finally, Uncle Clint jumped up from where he'd been kneeling and began bellowing out, "Softly and tenderly Jesus is calling." With the words of the song echoing in my ears, the bonds of fear seemed to snap as I jumped up and hurried down the aisle to the altar. Falling on my knees, I momentarily forgot about my surroundings as I began to pray. I tried to think of all the things I had done in my young life that might have made God angry with me. "I'm sorry that I hit my sister, and I'm sorry I've said bad things about my daddy," I said to God. I waited for a few seconds, and, after experiencing no change in how I was feeling after confessing my horrible sins, I decided I needed to do more praying. "Jesus, I'm sorry for stealing the cigarettes and for lying about it," I said. "I promise that I will never smoke, steal, or lie again."

Momentarily, the evangelist moved over and put his hand on my shoulder and shouted loudly, "Hold on, little sister. Hold on!" He then moved away, and Uncle Clint knelt down beside me. He began to pray for me and to ask God to help me. I was also praying that God would tell me what I was supposed to do so that I could someday be in Heaven with Him.

Suddenly, Uncle Clint quit praying and shouted to me, "Turn loose, Betty! Jist turn loose!"

I wondered what I was supposed to turn loose, and what I was supposed to hold onto. "Jesus, I know that I want to be a Christian, and I'm sorry for anything I've done wrong," I whispered silently. "I don't know what else I'm supposed to say, so I'm just going to trust you to take me to Heaven with you when I die."

Immediately, something or someone seemed to assure me that I was now converted. I stood quickly to my feet, no doubt smiling from ear to ear. My first thought was to run to the back of the church to ask my daddy to come to the altar to get converted too; therefore, I ran to where he stood staring down at the floor, reached up, and threw my arms around my daddy's midsection. My fear of him never once crossed my mind as I began pleading softly for him to please "get converted." I knew that I wasn't asking my father to get saved for my sake; instead, I was sincerely concerned that my daddy would go to Hell. "Jesus, please save my daddy," I pleaded.

I soon realized that he seemed to be frozen to the floor, so I felt compelled to return to my seat. With the top of my head resting just below my father's rib cage, I realized that my hair had become entangled on one of his shirt buttons. Apparently feeling the tug from my head, he softly patted the top of my head and then quickly untangled my hair. Then, as I looked up at him and began returning to my seat, he tearfully walked out the door of the church.

After the service had closed and my family and I had walked outside, I looked over and saw my father leaning against our car, smoking a cigarette. The preacher, Mr. Young, walked up beside me and, holding onto my shoulder, steered me over to where my father was standing. Reaching over to shake my father's hand, Mr. Young said, "Romie, you have a purty little girl here, and you orta be proud of 'er."

"Yell, I know it," Dad replied.

Mom, Dad, and the smaller children loaded into the car and headed home. Woody, Marvin, Maynard, and I walked out the dark ridge together. Once we reached our home, none of my family said anything about my having become a Christian. I didn't know how they felt about my decision, but I was glad that I wouldn't have to lie awake at night worrying about whether I would go to Heaven or Hell.

For a few weeks after that most important event, my father did not approach me in any way. I was very thankful that he had changed. I felt sure that those nightmarish experiences I'd been subjected to had come to an end. I wondered, now that I was a Christian, whether Dad had stopped abusing me for fear that, should I backslide, God would hold him responsible. Whatever the reason, I thanked God, over and over.

Sunday School and church became a big part of my life after the revival. I tried to attend every service, although I can't say that I learned much about God or the Bible. The people were sincere enough, and I was anxious to learn, but no one seemed to have enough knowledge about the Bible to be able to teach anybody else. We each seemed to be trying to do what we thought in our own minds was right.

The Sunday School hour was scheduled to begin at 10 A.M. each Sunday. No matter who took charge of the services, they seldom began on time. The men would stand outside the door smoking their cigarettes and watching for any last-minute arrivers to appear from around the curves in the road. After deciding that nobody else was on their way, the men would flip their cigarette butts onto the ground and walk inside.

"Guess we might as well git started 'cause it don't look like nobody else is comin'," the leader would say drearily to the people.

Sunday School was attended mostly by children. Should any of the parents accompany their children, most of them would sit in the pews apart from the classes, waiting for the worship service to begin. I had heard my own parents say on numerous occasions, "I don't git nuthin' outta Sunday School. It's jist fer the young'uns."

I enjoyed Sunday School even though I can remember only one memory verse from all the years I attended the country church. We children were given little cards each Sunday with pictures of Bible characters or events on the front of the cards and brief stories on the backsides relating to the pictures. Once our teacher had read the story to the class, not once, to my recollection, did she explain how we children should apply the principles to our own lives. She would, however, admonish the class, saying, "You young'uns orta be good all week long, 'cause if ye ain't, den Jesus won't like ye, an' he'll let 'at ol' devil gitchee." She would then remind us to remember the following Bible verse: "Let your light so shine before men, that they may see your good works, and glorify your Father which is in heaven." Matthew 5:16 KJV

I had no concept that Bible events took place right here on this earth. I thought the events occurred in Bible times, to Bible people, in a world where only those people lived. When I was a teenager and learned the truth, I wondered whether my teacher had been aware that the Bible characters were men and women right here on earth.

Worship services would begin immediately after Sunday School had been dismissed, never beginning at the same time two Sundays in a row. It seemed that every ounce was squeezed out of the meetings every time we met. Each person present was expected to testify in every worship service, and for the lack of having something to say, some of the people would explain, in detail what their week had been like. Unfortunately, the devil often received more dues than did Christ.

At least once during every worship service, all the Christians were called up around the altar for prayer. When no room remained around the altar, the remaining men and women would fall onto their knees on the floor and in unison begin praying aloud. Should a Christian with no apparent excuse remain seated in the pews during prayer time, then he or she was considered to be backslidden.

When the last person praying had said, "Hey-men," the group would stand and begin filing toward their seats. One of the men would begin singing "Give Me That Old Time Religion," and, without prompting, the congregation would immediately join in. As the singing ceased, or sometimes in the midst of the song, one of the congregants would emotionally burst forth with a "burning testimony." At the end of the testimony, which sometimes lasted more than ten minutes, the song leader would begin singing a verse of another hymn. While the congregation joined in the singing, one by one each professing Christian would file by to shake the hand of the person who had just given his or her testimony. At the end of the first stanza of the song, another person would stand and testify, and the ritual was repeated. Sometimes, two or three people might be standing throughout the pews testifying at the same time. When this happened, the service was called "a popcorn service." If, however, there was a lull in the testimony meeting, the leader would ask, "Would there be another'n?" He would then wait for an indefinite period of time until every professing Christian in the meeting had spoken.

On occasion, one of the older women would say tearfully, "I've got a dear ol' mother over yonder 'at I'll see someday if I can jist hol' out faithful." These emotional testimonies were very heart wrenching for most of the congregation and would usually bring out our handkerchiefs. Indeed, the thermometer by which the worship service was gauged was how emotional the meeting had been, instead of on how many of the unsaved had been reached or on how penitent the congregation had been. The higher the excitement, along with the shouting and tears, the better the services were considered to have been. The louder the preacher shouted or the more he ran up and down the aisles, the more the congregation enjoyed the services. These emotions seemed to be stirred within us only during these meetings or at funerals.

Finally, after the leader had decided nothing else could be accomplished, he would say, "Well, if nobody hain't got nothin' else ta say, 'hen we might as well dismiss." It was common for the services to have lasted well into the afternoon. Once we had all gone outside and visited with each other for a few minutes, we would go our respective ways to our homes. It was common for one family to say to another family, "Why don't ch'all come home 'ith us fer dinner, an' see how poor folks lives?" When the invitation was unexpectedly accepted, the women always seemed to be prepared for last-minute guests. They had learned very early in their married lives to prepare tasty meals from practically nothing other than what they had gleaned from Mother Nature's cupboards.

What should have been an enjoyable church function often proved to be a disappointing experience for my brothers and me. Behind the church building and to the right of the men's and women's outhouses, a section of the forest had been cleared and the ground raked to make a place for the "All Day's Meetings with Dinner on the Ground." Boards had been nailed together and attached between some of the trees, forming tables to hold the assortment of home-raised and home-cooked food the ladies always brought for the feast.

Once the ladies had begun spreading their mouthwatering foods on the crudely built tables, my mother would draw us children aside to where she had spread our food in the trunk of our car or on the tailgate of our truck, depending on the vehicle Dad might have owned at the time. Having been warned by our mother ahead of time that we were not to expect or accept food from any of the ladies, my siblings and I would nibble at the food Mom had prepared while we silently coveted the tantalizing dishes spread abundantly on the tables for all who cared to partake of it.

Woody eventually broke Mom's rule after his curiosity had gotten the best of him, and he returned to our car nibbling on a piece of cake covered with purple icing. When Mom chided him for ignoring her command, Woody said, "I jist hadda have a piece of 'at purty cake."

I moved over close to him and asked, "Woody, what's 'at icin' taste like?"

"Hit tastes like grapes," he said. We later learned that the frosting had been made by adding grape Kool-Aid to powdered sugar.

Mom explained to me years later why she had forbidden us children to partake of the food. "I always was ashamed 'cause I didn' have nuthin' good ta take ta eat, an' I's afraid 'atta young'uns might not 'member thur manners when 'ey started goin' 'round'a tables gittin' food," she said.

During one of the droughts we experienced, I received my first lesson on the importance of faith and prayer. One Sunday before the church service had ended, a decision was made that the congregation would go home, eat lunch, and then return later in the afternoon to pray once again for rain.

It was about four o'clock when the people once again began gathering in the church yard for the prayer meeting. While we were standing around on the parched grass waiting for everyone to arrive, one of the men pointed toward my father's sister, Aunt Becky, who was walking down the dusty road toward the church with her closed umbrella in her hand. The man, laughing loudly, motioned toward the unclouded sky and called out to my aunt, "Hey Beck, what'chu doin' 'ith 'at umbrell' when 'hey hain't a cloud in'na sky?"

"Well-l-l, I figgered if we'z meetin' ta pray fer rain, 'hen I'za gonna come per-pared," she yelled back.

About thirty minutes later, once the prayer meeting was over, the congregation again met outside the church to bid each other farewell for another week. Suddenly, from out of nowhere, a dark cloud appeared, and as we all stood gazing toward the heavens in disbelief, an abundance of rain began pounding down upon every member present. "Why, glory be ta God!" Aunt Becky shouted, raising her umbrella over her head. "Hain't I glad I brung my umbrell' 'ith me?" The man who had earlier questioned my aunt's judgment shook his head in disbelief as we each, totally silent and thoroughly soaked, began walking toward our homes—no doubt wondering whose prayer amongst the group God had heard.

I can recall only once when our pastor was invited to take Sunday dinner at our house. Dad and Mom had extended the invitation the previous Sunday, and the pastor had immediately accepted. Early the next Sunday morning, Woody and Marvin chased down a couple of the white leghorn roosters that Dad had ordered from a catalog weeks earlier and we had raised from baby chicks—what we country folk called "doodies" or "biddies."

Holding each squawking rooster by the feet with one hand and stretching its neck across the chop-block with the other, Marvin seemingly held his breath while Woody swung the ax up over his head and brought it down with precision to chop off the head of the doomed bird. I shivered as each roosters was slaughtered, in fear that Woody would miss the bird's neck and chop off Marvin's hand.

Once Woody had carried the chickens to Mom, she immediately poured boiling water over the fryers and began plucking the feathers from their bodies. After the feathers had been removed, she then held a blazing piece of paper underneath each plucked fowl, searing the hairs from its body. She then washed the roosters and cut them into pieces, submerging the pieces in a pan of cold water to soak while we attended church.

When the church services had ended, our pastor drove behind our car out the dusty road to our humble dwelling. Once inside the house, Mom busied herself in the kitchen while my father entertained the pastor in the living room. We children had been taught that when anyone came to visit, we were to stay out of sight as much as possible; therefore, while the young children played outside, I stayed in the kitchen peeling potatoes while my mother attempted to start a fire in the cook stove.

Unfortunately, my mother had always used the term *son-za-bitch* as commonly as she used the word *hello*. She had on numerous occasions greeted folks whom she had not seen in recent weeks with her own term of endearment. "Why, howdy 'ere, you ol' son-za-bitch," she would say, smiling broadly.

Having struck several matches with no results in lighting the kindling wood, Mom stepped into the living room doorway and blurted loudly, "Bud, come in here an' see if you can git 'is here son-za-bitch'n far [fire] started."

Pastor Foster laughed softly and then cleared his throat as though he were trying to retract the laugh. Dad headed sheepishly for the kitchen as swiftly as possible. I, who over a period of time had realized that "son-of-a-bitch" should not be one of my mother's Sunday words, considered running out the door to hide in the chimney corner. Instead, without further conversation, Dad kindled the fire and then returned to the living room while Mom and I continued preparing the meal.

Within the hour the chicken was fried, the potatoes were cooked and mashed, gravy was made from the fried chicken drippings, and freshly cooked pinto beans were ready to serve. The cornbread, alongside the big dish of freshly churned butter, was set near the preacher's plate on the long, handmade table that I had covered with a white bed sheet, since Mom owned no tablecloths. Lastly, I fished several limp pickles out of one of the half-gallon jars that Mom had canned, placed them in a bowl, and set them at the end of the table.

Mom called out to Dad that dinner was ready, so he and the pastor quickly made their way to the table. Mom yelled for Woody and Marvin to wash their hands and to come eat with the men. She then placed a glass of buttermilk at the pastor's plate and a cup of hot coffee with milk beside Dad's plate. Before leaving the room, Mom then handed me a leafy branch from a sassafras bush and instructed me to keep the flies shooed off the food on the table.

After the men had bowed their heads and Dad had asked his usual blessing on the food, Pastor Foster began raving about the table of food as he picked up a piece of the chicken with his fingers and began eating. No napkins had been placed on the table; in fact, neither my mother nor I had heard of napkins at this time in our lives. I soon realized, however, that the men wouldn't have needed the napkins anyway. What food they hadn't licked off their fingers, they had wiped on the overhang of the "tablecloth."

After Dad, Pastor Foster, and my two brothers had eaten their fill, they stood and walked outside onto the porch. Dad immediately lit up a cigarette. I rounded up the younger children, and we joined Mom at the table. We divided the food left by the men, which of the fried chicken consisted only of backs, wings, and necks. Mom and I then washed the dishes, and after Dad and the preacher had visited about half an hour longer, the preacher thanked Mom for the meal and then left for his home, located in a little village on the other side of town.

Once the pastor was out of sight, Dad wasted no time in calling Mom over for the lecture that I knew was coming. In his own choice of words, he loudly warned my mother never to use the S.O.B. word in front of the pastor again. Mom knew better than to backtalk Dad. She did, however, whisper to me later that she had done nothing wrong. She continued to use the S.O.B. word for years to come but wisely refrained from speaking the expletive in the presence of our pastor.

Many decades later, I returned to the ridge where my nightmares had begun to find that the only thing that remained in the area was the house where I was born and the church where I was saved. Although the little church was now being used to store junk, in my mind, the old familiar hymns were still ringing from the rafters and each seat was filled with ordinary country folk worshipping the Lord in their own special way, while frowning upon those snake-handling and tongues-speaking churchgoers whom they called "Holy Rollers."

XL

A Scary Tactic

I was enlightened to the meaning of chloroform suddenly and in a very dreadful way. After trying unsuccessfully on several occasions to convince me that it was my duty to obey his wishes simply because he was the parent and I was the child, my father began to devise a plan that scared me even more than I had been scared before. After making suggestions that are too evil for me to repeat, he grabbed me and pushed back my head in an attempt to kiss me on the lips after I had walked near him to care for my baby brother.

"Let me loose!" I screamed hysterically.

"Hain't nobody gonna tell on ya," he disgustingly replied. "Don't chee know 'hat your poor ol' daddy's jis' tryin' ta give ye a loodle lovin'?"

I knew that he was trying to evoke my sympathy; however, I hoped that he was seeing the raging anger and deep disgust his actions were building up within me. I continued vehemently to fight and scream until, eventually, he grabbed my arms, pinned me against the wall, and, after striking me across the face, said in a low serious tone, "One of 'ese here days I'll git'chu. I'll cholor'form you, an' 'hen I'll git'chu, an' 'hey won't be nuthin' you can do."

Terror stricken and unable to move, I was startled when he suddenly slung me to the floor as though I were a rag doll. As he stomped into the kitchen, I managed to pull myself onto my feet in time to run out the door before he had returned to the living room.

More concerned about my father's statement than I was about my bruises, I wondered what he had meant when he'd promised that he would "chloroform" me. From the way my father had phrased what to me seemed to be a threat, I suspected that chloroform was something that would put me to sleep. "Why aren't you helping me, God?" I prayed tearfully as I huddled beside the house waiting for my mother to return.

When I was finally able to ask my mother the meaning of chloroform, she laughed and said, "Wha'chee askin' me such a dumb question fer?"

"'Cause Daddy tol' me he was gonna chlor'form me so he could do whatever he wanted to with me," I stated.

"Y'ain't got nothin' ta worry 'bout. He's jist talkin' ta hear his head roar," she said.

"Well, what is chlor'form, anyway?" I asked.

"Hit's sumthin' 'at puts ya ta sleep when ye breathe it," Mom said casually.

I walked away feeling very alone. Mom's lack of concern had given me no comfort, and I wished I could tell someone about the fear and anger I was fighting to control. I wondered what would happen to the family should I reveal the terrible secret hiding within our walls, but I was troubled that such a show of disrespect for my father would make me a very bad daughter. At least, I told myself, he had finally realized that in order to restrain me he would have to put me to sleep.

With all the fear, guilt, and uncertainty clouding my thoughts, I was feeling older than the young, innocent child I was at the time. I reminded myself that although my physical strength could not compare to my father's strength, I had proven to him and my family that I could defend myself by kicking, scratching, and screaming. In addition, I had also acquainted him with some very strong teeth that I hadn't hesitated to use against him. Yet, even as I tried to console myself with these sources of self-protection, my greatest assurance came from knowing that, although I hadn't seen His mighty hand at work during this particular incident, God was aware of the frightened little girl out there in the backwoods, who was as important to Him as any child on the face of the earth. I didn't know how He would get me through life without harm coming to me, but I knew that if He couldn't do it, then I was in big trouble. I wiped away my tears as I determined to make my ordeal a secret between this Almighty God and myself. I didn't know it at the time, but this commitment to share my grief with God would eventually be the major source responsible for helping me keep my sanity.

XLI

Brother Woody

Shortly after the ordeal with the rifle, my brother Woody began having bouts of depression and mood swings. He was a very masculine teenager and was already carrying out responsibilities that required as much from him as from most men. He plowed the fields with horse and plow and helped to do all the other work required of a man to run a small farm.

He had graduated from the childish games he'd previously played and in his spare time was now partaking in more adult activities. He enjoyed hunting wild game and was commended by my Uncle Clint and all the other men in the surrounding communities for his accuracy in shooting any type of firearm. While the other hunters were using shotguns to kill gray squirrels for meat for their tables, Woody would usually bring home a greater abundance of the game by shooting them with his .22-caliber rifle.

He liked target practicing with the rifle and was very knowledgeable about guns. When he was about sixteen years old, he traded one of his weapons for a .22 revolver handgun with a six-inch barrel. For no apparent reason, he began carrying the pistol with him while traveling the main roads up and down the hollows. When Mom became aware of what she perceived as a dangerous situation, she threatened to tell Dad about the pistol. Woody became very upset over her threat, but he refused to relinquish the weapon.

Grandma made a special trip to our house to inform Mom that she too had learned of the pistol and had spoken to Woody about the matter. As she and Mom talked, it seemed that Grandma had made no more progress than Mom in her attempt to persuade my brother to disarm himself. Grandma stated that when she had gently admonished Woody about his breaking the law, he had stormed out the door without responding to her warning.

While Grandma and Mom were wrestling with how to handle the sensitive situation, Woody, looking very sullen, walked into the room. Apparently aware that the women were discussing how to take the gun away from him, he became angry, and with tears welling up in his eyes said, "I'm gonna kill myself, an' maybe y'all'll be happy."

Grandma and Mom looked startled, and I was shocked and frightened because my big brother, who had always been strong and stable, had just walked out the door with tears running down his cheeks and the pistol sticking under his belt. I started to run after him, but Mom yelled for me to stay away from him. I too started to cry as I ran to the window to see in which direction my brother had gone.

"Marthy, jue thank he'll hurt hisself?" Grandma asked.

"No, he jist wants us ta feel sorry fer 'im," Mom said quickly, looking as worried as Grandma looked and as I was feeling. Mom explained to Grandma that she was afraid to tell Dad about the problem because she knew that Dad's solution would be to give Woody a hard beating with a hickory withe. "Bud'll beat'a far [fire] outta him," she said.

With her head bowed, Grandma walked out the door as she left to go home. Mom returned to her work. I slipped out of sight and began to pray. I was very concerned about Woody's attitude, especially since I felt that my brother's depression had been brought on by Dad shooting at him after he had hit me with the wet ball.

Later in the evening, just before Dad was expected home from work, Woody returned. He didn't converse with any of the family but very meekly walked over and put the pistol in the dresser drawer.

As time passed, Woody began picking fights with Marvin. Sometimes they would get into such bad fist fights and wrestling bouts that I sometimes thought they were trying to kill each other. My peacemaking efforts between them often made matters worse. They considered my concern and compassion as nothing more than interference.

For the next few weeks, I feared that each time Woody's feelings were hurt he might carry out his threat and take his own life. Although I wanted to help my brother, he continued to distance himself from me. His actions had added another worry to the heavy load I was already carrying.

Eventually, Woody's depression lessened when he and Marvin became more active in Sunday School and church. The fights between the brothers had almost stopped, and although he remained very sensitive, Woody was now handling disappointments and trouble much better than he had been earlier. Finally, both brothers went forward in one of the church services to receive Christ as their Savior. I could see immediately that they seemed to be trying very hard to set a Christ-like example.

One particular event happened shortly after Woody had made his profession of faith. The grocery store, where Mom shopped and Woody had begun working part-time, had run a special on canned sliced peaches. Surprisingly, Mom bought a case of the delicious fruit. The special purchase was the first time I could remember us having store-bought canned fruit.

Mom apparently knew that, given the opportunity, we children would eat all twenty-four cans of the golden sliced fruit during one sitting. In any event, she didn't give us the opportunity. She removed a couple cans of the fruit from the box and spooned out a small portion for each of us children. "If I don't ration 'ese here peaches, 'hen 'ey won't last no time," she said.

Woody loved home-canned peaches. In fact, he taught me to crumble a biscuit, or anything else we liked, into a bowl of peaches in order to make the food go further. While our siblings gobbled down their plates of peaches, Woody and I poured ours into bowls that Mom had been collecting in boxes of "Mother's Oats." "'Ese store-bought peaches are too purty to eat," Woody said, while he and I broke our biscuits into the bowl of peaches and then filled the bowl to the top with milk.

While savoring my first bite of the sweet, smooth peaches, I replied, "They hain't as purty as 'ey are good." I watched as my siblings devoured the last morsels of their peaches, tipped their plates to their lips, and drank the remaining juice. Woody and I nibbled slowly at our small portions, enjoying each spoonful. As far as I was concerned, the peaches Mom had canned throughout the years could not compare to the golden-yellow peaches in their sweet, heavy syrup.

The day after Mom had stored the remainder of the peaches in the cellar, Woody came inside the house and began confessing to Mom that his small ration of the delicious dessert had not satisfied his appetite. Reaching into his pants pocket, he pulled out the can opener he had taken from the kitchen and handed it to Mom. "If you'll go down over the hill from the cellar to 'at bunch'a tall weeds, you'll find a can of peaches," he said.

"'Ell, how'd 'ey git down over the hill?" Mom asked

"I stol'd 'em outta the cellar 'his mornin' an' hid 'em so I could eat 'em later," he said.

"Why didn't you go ahead'n eat 'em?" Mom asked.

"'Cause I started feelin' too guilty," he answered, with his head bowed.

Because I was still concerned about the threat my brother had recently made of ending his life, I was greatly relieved when Mom smiled and calmly said to him, "Uh huh, the Lord wouldn't let you do it, would he?"

Woody, shaking his head from side to side, slowly walked out the kitchen door. Knowing that Woody's craving for the can of fruit had tempted him to steal, and witnessing his penitence over the act, I was disappointed that Mom hadn't offered to reward his change of heart by giving him the can of peaches; instead, she sent one of my younger brothers to recover the canned fruit with the instructions for him to return it to the cellar.

The following Sunday, while my brothers and I walked out the ridge toward the church on our way to Sunday School, we were barely out of sight of the house when Woody and Marvin got into an argument. After exchanging a few heated words, they started pushing and shoving each other, until finally, they both ended up on their knees in the red-clay dust.

"Y'all are gonna be in big trouble when Mommy sees 'at dirt on 'em britches we jist warshed an' ironed," I said to them. Without acknowledging my warning, they recovered their composure, and we continued on our way, the dirt on the knees of their trousers being the only evidence of their squabble. We made it to Sunday School on time and returned home after the worship service with no further incidents.

A few days later when Grandma dropped in for a short visit, she mentioned to Mom that she had noticed dirt on the knees of my brothers' breeches when she had arrived at the church on Sunday. "I'm so glad 'em boys got religion," Grandma said to Mom. "When I seed 'eir durdy knees, I said'a Jim, 'Bless 'er loodle hearts. I bet 'hey've been down on 'eir knees prayin'.'" Although I didn't say a word, I felt like telling Grandma that the only person praying had been me. I had been praying that my two older brothers wouldn't kill each other before they got to church.

XLII

Fighting Despair

Once again I had been left alone inside the house with my father and the younger children while my older brothers did their evening chores and Mom milked the cow. I tried to ignore the gnawing feeling in my stomach as I tried to wash the dishes as quietly as possible—hoping that Dad would not notice that we were practically alone.

Just as I had feared, Dad soon entered the kitchen, walked over, and looked out the kitchen window. Watching him out of the corner of my eyes, I shivered when he turned as though leaving the room, only to lunge forward suddenly, grabbing me and pinning my arms to my side. Feeling his hot tobacco breath on the back of my neck and hearing his rapid breathing, I kicked, flounced, and screamed as I fought to pull away.

He pushed me to the floor and straddled my body backwards, holding my arms with his legs, and began pawing at my body. Looking to see that his hands were empty and assuring myself that he wasn't going to use chloroform on me, I finally wriggled my arms free. Quickly spinning around over my body, he reached for my throat. Somehow, I managed to sink my teeth into the back of his hand and bit down as hard as I could. While he threatened to kill me, I kept my teeth clenched as he struggled to pull his captive hand free. With my teeth locked onto the back of his hand, he suddenly struck me on the head with his free hand, and, to my horror, I felt a piece of his skin break off inside my mouth.

Realizing that I'd actually bitten a piece of the outer skin from the back of my father's hand, I quickly spat the sickening flesh onto the floor as he freed his hold on me and began cradling his injured hand in the palm of his other hand.

My heart was racing as I tried to scamper to my feet. Glancing toward him, I knew that my father's passion had shifted quickly to extreme anger, and I expected him to try to beat my brains out for what I'd just done to him. Before I was able to push myself off the floor, he grabbed me, but I quickly twisted free. As we both scrambled to our feet, he grabbed me once again and flung me against the wall as if I were a wild animal that had attacked him.

Just as I broke to run out of the room, he jerked a metal can of Prince Albert pipe tobacco from his shirt pocket and threw it at me, striking me in the right ribcage. Grabbing my side, I ran outside onto the porch crying and trembling from the terror of that moment and from the pain in my ribcage. Even more devastated than ever before, I stood on the porch for a few minutes, wondering what I should do.

Finally, realizing that my father had retreated to another room, I managed to pull myself together and return to the kitchen. I worked halfheartedly on the dishes as my mind spun in the thoughts of my dilemma. I was finding little solace in knowing I had won another battle in the ongoing war with my father, that he was in the other room licking the wound I had inflicted upon him, or that he was, no doubt, too angry with me to approach me anytime soon.

I looked up at Mom as she walked into the kitchen with the fresh pail of milk. I knew she had to have heard my loud screams for help, yet she merely glanced in my direction as she turned to strain the milk. Although I knew I couldn't say anything to her that she didn't already know, I deeply needed her to say something to me—good or bad. New waves of despair enveloped me as I again realized that it was futile for me to look to my mother for help; consequently, as I finished the job I was doing, I decided I would run away from home.

I stepped into the living room and picked up my baby brother, not once considering the absurdity of leaving home and taking the baby with me. I guess I believed that without me around, the baby would not get the care and love he needed, or perhaps I was finding some sort of comfort in having the baby with me. Anyhow, I was determined to leave that ridge, the house, my mother, and most of all--my abusive father.

Holding the baby astraddle on my left hip, seemingly in a trance, I began walking out the driveway to the dusty ridge road. A short time later, when I was passing by the cornfield, it dawned on me that I had no food for my fourteen-month-old brother, no diapers, no clothing for him or myself, no money, and no inkling of where I intended to go.

With darkness fast approaching, I stopped, looked back toward the house, and then trudged down into the cornfield, feeling confused, alone, and dejected. I sat little Romie Dale down on the ground between the corn rows and bowed down beside him. "God, I need help!" I cried out. Feeling empty and hopeless, I thought about the fact that I had recently become a Christian and about my desire to live a life that would please God. I wondered whether the reason God was seemingly ignoring my cries for help was because I had been thinking bad thoughts about my parents. Not knowing what else to say or do, I sat there on the ground and sobbed until it seemed the tears could no longer flow.

A long time passed as my baby brother and I sat in the darkening cornfield together. By now feeling all numb inside, I thought about how I had bitten my father's hand and how it had pleased me in knowing I had caused him physical pain. While I continued to sit there meditating, the darkness began to wrap me in a heavy shroud of hopelessness and fear. Slowly, I pulled my dress tail up and wiped at my eyes, nose, and face. I reached down and pulled my little brother out of the dirt and onto my lap, realizing there was no answer to why I was being left on my own to fight a war that was too big and too complicated for me to win.

Finally, believing that God was nowhere near, I began making my way through the shadowy night back to the hell-hole that I called home. In my troubled state of mind, I was beginning to feel more sorrow for my father and mother than for myself.

When I walked through the living room door, no one seemed to have noticed that I and the baby had been missing. Mom was sitting on one of the wooden chairs, patching a pair of denim jeans. The older boys were listening to "The Green Hornet" program on the battery radio, and my smaller siblings were playing on the floor. To my surprise, my father was reading the Bible. I thought to myself as I looked at my family, "Why can't things always be as normal as they appear to be at this moment?"

I sat the baby on the floor and picked up the Sears and Roebuck catalog that I'd been wanting to look at since it had come in the mail. As I opened the book, an unmistakable sense of warmth and calm began penetrating my body from the top of my head to the soles of my feet. The lump in my throat caused warm tears to trickle down my cheeks. I hesitated to move for fear that the calmness enveloping my body would disappear as suddenly as it had appeared. I returned the book to the top of the chest of drawers, and, quietly and slowly, I slipped into the bedroom and fell onto my bed. I realized that God had appeared on the scene to assure me that no matter how rough the battle may become, He would always be there with me.

I bowed my head once again, this time, however, to thank God for His watchful care over me and to ask Him to forgive me for doubting that He had been there all the time. "Thank you, God, for getting me through yet another day," I said.

XLIII

Pushing My Luck

Woody was seventeen years old and had been seeing one of the granddaughters of the old midwife who had delivered some of my younger siblings. He had asked a family friend, Bob, to drive his old car to our house to carry his girlfriend and him to a church that was holding a revival about seven miles from our home.

Bob's father had been killed in a freak accident while working for the WPA (Works Progress Administration). Bob and his older brother had dropped out of school to help support their mother, sister, and two younger brothers. The family had at one time lived near our home, and for months Bob had been showing interest in dating me now that I was past thirteen years old.

When Bob arrived, both he and my brother began asking my father to allow me to join the three of them as Bob's date. To my surprise, after much assurance from the boys that we would go straight to the church and then return home immediately afterwards, Dad reluctantly gave his permission for me to go along with Bob, Woody, and Mary.

The four of us drove straight to the church, sat through the services, and then returned immediately to our home, as promised. None of us had as much as a nickel in our pockets, and I would later learn that Bob had filled the car's tank with "drip gasoline" (unrefined, natural liquid gas) that he had siphoned into his gas tank from a nearby gas well.

Upon arriving home from church, Bob ushered me inside before leaving immediately to take Woody to deliver his girl farther out the ridge to her grandmother's house. I was anxious that my father would grill me about the time I had spent with Bob and was relieved when he neither said nor did anything other than to angrily order me to bed.

Since Woody had no source of transportation, and since Bob had apparently enjoyed the short evening we had all spent together, the two boys made tentative plans to attend another revival meeting later in the week. Once Woody had informed me of their plans, he and I decided that the best thing we could do was to forego asking for Dad's permission since he would no doubt refuse to allow me to leave the house again. "Just act like we thank it'll be okay'n maybe Daddy'll not say anythang to stop us," my big brother said wisely.

A couple of nights later, Woody walked his girlfriend to our house, and the three of us were waiting when Bob once again drove into our driveway. I was trembling from fear that my father would cause a scene in front of Bob and that Bob would leave and never come back to see our family again.

As I waited for my brother to take the lead, I slipped slowly toward the car, expecting at any moment to be jerked back into the house with Dad flailing away at my backside with his wide leather belt. Woody yelled back to Mom to inform her that we would be home as soon as the church service had ended. Holding my breath as I waited for some sort of reply from my father, my brother and I looked at each other in disbelief when we were met with no resistance.

"Get outta here 'fore Daddy changes his mind," Woody said to Bob. I didn't say a word. I couldn't believe how smoothly Woody's plan had worked. I wondered, however, what we would have to face when we returned after the date.

Once again we drove straight to the church and returned home immediately after the service was over. I had not left my brother's side, yet I couldn't shake the uneasy feeling I was experiencing since I believed I had done wrong in not asking for Dad's permission to leave the house with the others.

Dad was waiting for us at the front door. Woody stayed in the car, and Bob opened the car door and walked me to the edge of our front porch. As Dad grabbed me by the shoulder and shoved me across the porch and through the front door, the threesome drove away to return Woody's date to her grandmother's house, seemingly unconcerned over what was about to happen to me.

Once we were inside the living room, Dad slammed me against the wall and yelled, "Where y'all been at? I know you'n 'at no good feller of your'n parked somewhere by yourself." Without giving me any time to explain, he continued to accuse me of all sorts of immoral acts. I huddled in the corner, trembling from fear and sobbing softly.

Bob soon dropped Woody off at our front door and headed back to his mother's home. Woody shoved the door open and walked inside to be greeted by the bombardment of insults that my father was continuing to heap upon me. He stood and listened for a minute or two and then spoke in a manner I had never heard him use with our father. "Now Daddy, listen ta me," he said sternly. "Bethel was not outta my sight for a minute, an' even if she had'da been, if you're gonna trust her enough to let 'er go out with a guy, then you let 'er go, an' don't you meet 'er atta door accusin' her like 'his."

Dad stood looking at Woody in total silence. I couldn't believe he was allowing one of his offspring to talk to him in such a manner. I looked over at Woody, who was standing toe to toe with our dad. "If you're not gonna trust 'er, 'hen don't let 'er go again," he said. "It's just as simple as 'at."

Without uttering a word, my father stormed angrily out of the room and headed for his bedroom. I didn't know whether to thank Woody or to kick him in the shins. Although I appreciated his concern for the unjust tongue-lashing I had been subjected to, I wondered whether his remarks would cause my father to restrict me to the house for the rest of my life.

I wouldn't soon learn whether Dad would heed the advice he had received from my brother. The revival ended, and Bob returned to another state to find adequate employment. For the next year I looked forward to the few times each summer when Bob returned to see the family and me. I was allowed to leave our property with him only to attend church and only if I took one of my brothers along as a chaperon. Although church was important to me at the time, I'm afraid that I, and the rest of the young people I knew, attended the revivals only because the services were our only source of outside activities. Although we could have been untruthful and gone somewhere other than to church during the dates, the thought never once entered our minds.

I had always been taught that, to avoid being considered immoral, when a girl was dating a boy, she was not free to date anyone else. Usually, after a couple had begun to periodically see each other, the girl's parents and relatives assumed that a wedding date was imminent; therefore, I was not surprised when my family began teasing me about becoming Bob's young wife.

I had indeed already begun to dream of someday having a kind, loyal husband who would love and cherish me for the rest of my life, but I was certain that my present friend—who always smelled like drip gasoline—was not the mate whom God was preparing to be my husband. I was thankful for the taste of freedom I had enjoyed, yet I was wise enough to know that choosing a mate for life was not going to be a choice I would make lightly. Albeit I was keeping the matter to myself, I had decided to wait for God to bring me together with the special man I believed was being prepared for me.

XLIV

Mystery Meat

A new school bus driver had been hired at the beginning of the school year, and he and my father had begun "socializing" together. The man was younger than Dad and was known around the area as a womanizer. He was married and was the father of two small boys, but he had several girlfriends on the side. It was also common knowledge in the community that he was a heavy drinker. I had overheard Mom and Dad discussing the man's lifestyle and the bad influence he seemed to be having on my father, so I wasn't as surprised as Mom seemed to be when the two men began staying out late on Saturday nights.

On one of the occasions, after Dad and his friend had stayed out overnight, I was present when my mother tearfully asked my father, "Jist where in'na worl've you been all night?" Dad's only response was to clench his teeth, which caused his jaw muscles to move up and down.

As time passed, it was evident that Mom was very unhappy about the stressful situation Dad was causing. She was expecting again and had been spending a lot of time in tears. Once again I felt pity for my mother and wished I could make things better for her; unfortunately, it wasn't long before Mom and Dad's arguing and discontent began to mushroom.

Since they chose to "discuss" their differences in the presence of us children, I was stunned when Dad admitted freely that he had been staying out nights drinking with his friend Allen. "What about chur oath 'at chu vowed ta God 'at chu'd never take another drank fer as long as you live?" she asked.

Dad didn't attempt to refute her accusations when she told him that she also suspected he was being unfaithful to her; instead, he began boasting about the young women he had been seeing. When her sobbing intensified, I wondered how my mother could be so distressed and concerned about what might have been going on between Dad and some woman she didn't even know, when right in our own home she had been ignoring his regular attempts to molest his own daughter.

The thin thread of hope that was holding our family together seemed to be stretched to the breaking point. Although we children felt compassion for our mother, there seemed to be very little any of us could do to help her. We older children offered all the physical help and moral support we could; however, she either didn't notice the extra effort we were making, or she was too weary to care. Her depression and sad state of mind seemed of no concern to Dad. He no doubt realized that with ten children to care for—and baby number eleven on the way—she, like I, was trapped in the situation.

One night, Mom, my three oldest brothers, and I were sitting up waiting for Dad to come home from work. He was already about four hours overdue, so Mom had begun wondering aloud whether he was out running around again or had been involved in an accident. Since we had no telephone and lived miles from "civilization," the chances were slim that we would hear about it even if he had been involved in an accident.

About 9 p.m., we heard Dad's car pulling into the yard, and Woody ran over and peeked out the window. "There's another car behind Daddy," Woody said. Mom didn't utter a word but looked terror stricken as Dad walked into the living room and, without speaking, picked up his hunting rifle. When she asked him where he was going and what he intended to do with the rifle, Dad became belligerent. He dropped several rifle cartridges into his coat pocket and then angrily blurted out that he and Allen (whom I'd learned was the grandson of the old midwife who was rumored to be a witch) were going out the ridge to Allen's grandmother's property to spotlight rabbits.

When my mother reminded Dad that he was breaking the law by taking the rifle out hunting after dark, I became alarmed, knowing that my agitated father was standing in front of my despondent mother with a loaded weapon in his hands. "You orta come ta bed," she said to him.

"You mind y'ur own business an' you an' 'em young'uns git in'na bed," he yelled, storming out the door to join his buddy.

My heart ached when I looked at Mom and saw the anger and despair in her eyes. "I smelt sumthin' on your daddy's breath an' I know him an 'at man's been drankin' ag'in," Mom said to my siblings and me. "Hard'a tell what'll happen 'ith 'em drankin' an' goin' out dere 'ith 'em guns." Looking very forlorn, Mom extinguished the kerosene lamp and went toward her bedroom as my brothers and I scurried off to our own beds.

I was awakened sometime during the night when Dad opened the creaky living room door. Almost immediately, Mom entered the living room and asked, "What's in 'at coffee sack?"

"It's some fresh meat 'at Allen gim'me an' I wan'chu ta fry some of it fer my breakfast in'na mornin'," Dad replied. I drifted back to sleep while Mom and Dad were still talking about the mysterious meat.

Early the next morning I was awakened by the aroma of fried meat drifting into the room. The smell was absolutely out of this world. I sure hoped that, whatever Mom was frying, there would be enough of it left for us children to enjoy at breakfast time.

Dad left for work, and when Mom finally called for my brothers and me to get out of bed to get ready for school, I was the first to get to the kitchen. With my mouth watering, I hurriedly splashed my face with the water Dad had left in the washbasin. After swiping my face with the towel, I ran to the table, expecting to see the usual pot of cold, stiff oats that greeted us every morning. To my surprise, a big platter of brown biscuits filled with tempting slices of fried meat greeted me.

With my mother standing guard over the platter of meat-filled biscuits, I immediately found my spot at the table and reached to help myself to the special treat. Mom smacked at my hand as Marvin entered the room and said, "'At don't look like rabbit 'tween 'em biscuits."

"I don't keer what's 'tween 'em biscuits," I said. "I smelt it cookin' an' it smelt better'n anythang I've ever smelt."

"I hain't gonna 'splain but once, so jist chu wait fer 'em other kids," she warned.

While I waited for my siblings to join me around the table, I occupied myself by counting what appeared to be only enough for us children to have one biscuit each. Nothing I had smelled cooking before had whetted my appetite like whatever was between those oversized biscuits, which I feared was getting colder by the minute.

Finally, the table was surrounded by eight puzzled and hungry little children. Mom immediately began to explain in an apologetic manner why she had not cooked oats for our breakfast. I wanted to cry out, "Forget the oats! Just bring on that biscuit of meat!"

Mom explained that she had fried all of the meat at one time so it wouldn't spoil, and after she had given Dad his fill and had packed some in his lunch, there had been only one biscuit of meat left for each of us children. "Well, what is it?" Woody asked.

Mom looked very serious as she went on to explain, "Now young'uns, ya cain't tell nobody what I'm 'bout ta tell y'all. If anybody hears 'bout dis, y'ur daddy'll be put in jail fer huntin' by spotlight."

It seemed that Dad and his buddy Allen had indeed gone spotlighting the night before, and the meat we were now hungrily devouring was part of their kill. It was not rabbit, neither was it deer. The fact was, it was not wild game at all. It was meat from a hindquarter the men had cut from Allen's Herford calf, which they had accidentally shot and killed. My siblings and I, however, were unconcerned about anything other than the fact that we were rapidly consuming our very first sampling of fresh veal!

Mom explained that just a few weeks earlier Allen had bought the calf and put it out to pasture on his grandma's farm. While hunting illegally in the dark, Allen being "slightly" inebriated, had seen the eye of an animal in the spotlight. Having forgotten about his calf in the field, he aimed and fired, shooting the bedded-down calf directly between the eyes.

Dad had told Mom that once the animal had been shot, Allen had hurried over to its side and then yelled to Dad, "My God, Romie! We done went an' shot my calf plumb 'tween 'a eyes!"

"Then it's dead?" Dad had yelled to Allen.

"Deader'n a drownded rat," Allen replied.

Mom continued with the story. "At 'at point, 'ey figgered 'ey might as well dress it out so's it could be et," she said.

And eat we did, leaving not even a morsel of our scrumptious biscuit of fried meat. None of us children were aware of a meat called *veal*; in fact, neither my siblings nor I had ever eaten any kind of beef, except for the hamburger in Sissy's chili, which she had served me when I'd spent the night with her and Uncle Clint.

Mom swore us children to secrecy for fear that Dad's illegal hunting trip would land him in jail, and to my knowledge, he never again went spotlighting. I had a feeling that I wasn't the only one to thank God for Dad and Allen's mistake; however, I wondered what Mom had meant when she looked at the empty platter and said, "God shore does work in mysterious ways."

XLV

Laughter and Consequences

On a cold wintry morning in 1948, our family was awakened to find about four inches of snow on the ground. In our area, heavy snows were common. The schools were seldom closed because of the weather, so my brothers, sister, and I donned our coats and headgear to begin our long walk to school. None of us were fortunate enough to own gloves or mittens, and the boys had no boots to wear over their ankle-high shoes. Nina and I had been given ugly rubber galoshes with tops that came only slightly above our ankles. I would pull the boots off and hide them when we reached the railroad tracks, simply because when I had worn the boots to school, my peers had laughed and said I was wearing "old women's" overshoes.

I trudged along with the rest of the gang, shivering from the cold that was biting my bare hands, legs, and face. Despite the bitter temperature, the beauty of the undisturbed field of snow was breathtaking. Here and there, where the heavy snow had bent their branches almost to the ground, the small evergreens appeared to be bowing before God in thanks for their fluffy winter coats.

Woody led our little troop single file across the field to begin our descent over the hill. Only an occasional set of rabbit tracks had disturbed the fallen snow in front of us. The six of us children hurried on our way, knowing that stopping to investigate the tracks would make us late for school; besides, my feet already were feeling like two blocks of wood.

After walking over the snow-covered hills, through the icy creeks, across the slippery railroad ties, and down the ice-covered streets to our warm schools, I was glad I could warm myself by standing in front of the toasty air that blew from the furnace registers in the walls. Although our lack of proper clothing made the long walks painful, my siblings and I did not complain. We did our best to make the trips enjoyable and to move fast enough to create as much body heat as possible. By God's grace, we survived the freezing walks to school, sometimes being blessed with a few good laughs and able to salvage some very special memories.

This was my first year attending the high school, which included seventh through twelfth grades. By noon, I realized as I looked out the windows that at least two additional inches of snow had accumulated.

On our way home from school, my two older brothers and I made our way anxiously through the deep snow toward Grandma's house in anticipation of receiving our filled biscuits, especially since we hadn't eaten anything since breakfast. Shortly before reaching Grandma's weather-beaten house, we overtook our younger siblings straggling along on their way home from the elementary school.

Like children on Halloween Night expecting treats, the six of us walked onto our grandparents' porch and hovered outside until Grandma came out to hand us our filled biscuits, one by one. We each accepted a biscuit, thanked her, and then hungrily devoured the sourdough biscuit while we trudged through the heavy snow and up the hollow through Grandpa's pasture.

The legs on Woody's and Marvin's pants had become wet from breaking through the six or more inches of snow along the path, and clusters of ice and snow clung to the fabric. Since our school's dress code forbade females from wearing pants, my sister was whining from the cold that bit into her bare legs. I looked down and could see that her boots, like mine, were filled with wet snow that seemed to be intent on packing itself around our already icy feet.

By the time we reached the base of the hill, we were staying close to each other since the walk was becoming more laborious and treacherous. Walking underneath the heavy timber growth had become frustrating, as clumps of snow slid without warning off the drooping evergreen branches and fell in big splashes onto our heads, sometimes sliding quickly down inside our coat collars and onto our bare backs.

Finally, we arrived at the top of the hill and entered the edge of the open field near our house. The deep, undisturbed snow seemed to be inviting my siblings and me to stop and frolic as we admired the drifts that the winds had piled aimlessly across the field. Momentarily, Woody jumped to the side of the snow-covered path and lay down on his back. The remaining five of us children watched as he raised his arms above his head, and with one deliberate sweep, raked his fully extended arms down through the snow, bringing them to rest against the sides of his body. He then pulled himself carefully to his feet. With our eyes wide with astonishment, we each gawked as we recognized the unmistakable imprint of a "snow angel."

With our excitement building, we watched as Marvin jumped over beside Woody's imprint, fell backwards, and carefully repeated Woody's motions, before he, too, pulled himself onto his feet, leaving his own indentation alongside Woody's masterpiece. Throwing caution to the wind, I, Maynard, Arnold, and Nina, from the oldest to the youngest, made our impressions alongside Woody's and Marvin's unusual creations. We each then brushed the clinging snow from our clothing and stepped back to admire a complete row of snow angels.

After comparing the length of our own body impressions with the others, and deciding whose angel was more perfectly formed, we continued merrily on our way. We had no idea of the consequences we would suffer because of those few special moments we had spent playing in the beautiful snow.

Later in the evening when Dad got off work, the ridge road was impassable; however, with the aid of tire chains on the rear wheels to improve traction, he was able to drive his car up the hollow to Grandma's house. As he walked from there along the same route we children had taken earlier, he was evidently puzzled when he noticed the disturbance in the deep snow as he topped the hill near our house. Upon closer examination, however, he apparently counted the body imprints and realized that each of his school-age children had been frolicking in the snow. Unfortunately, our ill-tempered father was not impressed that his children had acquired angel's wings.

When he walked in through the living room door, he angrily called each of us children to his side and lined us up, side-by-side, from the oldest to the youngest. Shaking in our shoes, each of us looked at the other, no doubt baffled about what was about to happen. Recalling that Dad had warned us about hitting each other or anyone else with snowballs, I couldn't believe that anyone had told him we had indeed been throwing snowballs at each other, especially knowing that we had taken great care not to leave any evidence along the way. "Surely he's not objecting to us makin' our imprints in the snow," I whispered to Marvin.

Woody did not attempt to defend himself. He, as well as the rest of us, knew that to protest would only make matters worse. We each stood quietly, waiting for the hammer to fall, when suddenly, Dad jerked off his belt, grabbed Woody by the hand, and started whacking him across his back, legs, and rear-end with the belt. I noticed that Woody was almost as tall as Dad; nevertheless, he said not a word as Dad struck him four or five times with the belt before angrily pushing him aside. When he quickly walked away without shedding a tear or saying a word, I suspected from his expression that he had no intentions of taking any further whippings from our father.

Dad grabbed Marvin next and yanked him forward, whaling his backside with the heavy belt. Marvin, too, refrained from speaking or resisting. I shivered, knowing that I was next in line as Dad slung

Marvin to the side and then looked over at me. I tried to look as pitiful and forlorn as possible, hoping he wouldn't have the heart to use the belt on me. He hesitated, and for a moment, I felt a flicker of hope as the thought entered my mind that maybe he was thinking that if he whipped me, he might have a harder time convincing me to give in to his unwanted advances. I whimpered as he snorted something at me and then angrily grabbed my hand and started flogging me with the belt that had already been warmed up on my two brothers.

Dad was known for whaling away at us children until he had seen signs that he'd achieved proper results, and should he not see the evidence that he was expecting, he was careful not to turn us loose prematurely. We children had also learned not to scream too loudly. Dad was in control when he was holding the belt, so we younger children tried to adjust our cries accordingly to what we thought would bring an end to the beatings. After having taken a few whacks of the belt across my bare legs, I began bellowing like a dying calf.

After what seemed to be a hundred licks with the belt, Dad slung me out of his way as he reached for Maynard. After he had finished with Maynard and had given Arnold his share of the punishment, he stepped over to my seven-year-old sister Nina, while Maynard, Arnold, and I rubbed our welts and muffled our sobs.

Nina had been constantly sniffling from the time we had been called forward. My father approached her and, without saying a word, began running his overworked belt back through the loops of his baggy pants. Surprisingly, Nina's sobbing intensified, whether from fright or from sheer relief I didn't know. I presumed Dad thought that since Nina was the smallest and the youngest of our group, she would not have participated in the act had the rest of us not gone before her.

Although on the way home from school our backsides might have been freezing, it was obvious that Dad had warmed them up rapidly. When he went into the kitchen to wash his hands before supper, my brothers and I hovered around the coal-burning potbellied stove in the middle of the living room. With tears in my eyes, I looked over at Woody and proclaimed snidely, "It's all your fault! If you hadn'na started it, the rest of us wouldn'na thought of doin' it either."

"It's not my fault," Woody said. "Nex' time we jist hafta remember not to play in'na snow in full view of where Daddy's gonna be walkin'."

I smiled at Woody and dried my eyes. "Yell, after givin' five whuppins 'fore supper, maybe he'll be too tired ta fight with me this evenin'," I said.

The next morning my brothers, sister, and I decided to take the third route to school that was available to us. We walked out the ridge to where we were able to cut through the woods to Aunt Sissy's house. Once we had walked over the hill beyond her house, we came to the barbed wire fence that pastured Dad's sister's cow. Since there was no break in the fence, it was necessary for my siblings and me to climb through the fence between the strands of barbed wire. As Woody lifted one of the wires high enough for the younger children to crawl through without tearing their clothing on the barbs, Marvin and I stood back, waiting our turns.

Once I had cleared the fence and arrived on the other side, I turned and looked back at Marvin, who was making a garbled noise as if he had swallowed his tongue. I didn't know whether to laugh or cry when I realized that, with the temperature being below freezing, my older brother had stuck his wet tongue to the frosty fence, causing his tongue to stick fast to the ice-covered wire.

Hearing Marvin's grunts for help, Woody looked over to see the predicament his brother was in. Hurrying to his side, Woody gripped his fingers around the cold wire near Marvin's tongue in hopes that the wire would warm up enough to release its hold on our brother. I watched as Marvin's eyes rolled back in his head, and his garbled sounds began to increase. "Woody, you thank Marvin's tryin' ta tell you 'at he doesn't thank your plan is workin'?" I asked.

Woody turned and told Maynard to crawl back through and to run back to Sissy's house and tell her that we had an emergency down at the pasture fence. Maynard immediately began running for help as I again looked at Marvin and could see that part of the surface of his tongue was trying to pull away while he tried to free himself. "Marvin, wait for Sissy to help you!" I said. The picture of my older brother standing there in the cold with his tongue clinging fast to the icy fence was a sight I would not soon forget.

In what must have seemed like a lifetime to Marvin, Maynard returned with Sissy, who was holding a large box of kitchen matches in her hand. I wondered what she had in mind to do, and, as I looked over at Marvin, I noticed that his expression had changed from one of pain and anxiety to a look of sheer terror as he watched Sissy strike a match on the side of the box and then step toward him.

"What on earth made you do sich a stupid thang?" Sissy asked Marvin as she cupped her hand around the flame and held it close to the wire about six inches from Marvin's face.

"Ahhh, ah-own't-ow," was Marvin's reply, as the heat began to penetrate the wire. The rest of us stood watching with our own mouths agape.

Finally, the warmed wire released its hold on my poor brother's tongue as he looked at Sissy with tears in his eyes and his nose running like maple sap in the springtime. "I'z jist 'underin' what'd happen if I stuck my wet 'ongue ta 'at cold wire," he said.

"Guess you went'n found out 'a hard way," Sissy replied.

"Betcha I 'on't wry 'at ag'in," Marvin declared, his tongue still recovering from the cold.

The treacherous path over the hill was extremely steep—nothing more than a cow path that wound its way down through the brush and trees to the property at the back of Aunt Becky's house. Whenever there was a heavy snow on the ground, instead of walking the path off the steep hill, my brothers preferred traveling the cleared pipeline that ran parallel to the path all the way to the foot of the hill.

Sissy began walking up the hill to return to her house, and I held onto my younger siblings' belongings as we made our way to the pipeline clearing that ran straight over the hill. With Woody and Marvin in the lead, I watched as my younger siblings squatted down and began following their older brothers toward the bottom of the hill, using their arms and hands as ski poles. Periodically, they would slow to a halt and have to pull themselves back onto Woody and Marvin's trail to continue the slide downward. We felt relatively assured that, should we have a few spills, and we usually did, Dad would never become aware of our sliding abilities since he had no reason to travel over the steep mountainside.

Finally, holding onto our belongings, I squatted down and began sliding over the hill to the path going out of the hollow. After assuring themselves that the rest of the gang had landed on their feet with limbs intact, Woody and Marvin soon were out of sight as they hurried down the road ahead of my siblings and me. Although I, too, would be walking past the grade school and down to the high school, I paced myself alongside the younger children, watching closely that the only thing left behind in the freezing weather was the bits of Marvin's tongue that had stuck to the barbed wire fence.

With his tongue still smarting from the morning's run-in with the icy fence, Marvin found himself in more trouble after school—his pants being too muddy to wear again the next day. Since my brothers' wardrobes included only two pairs each of dungarees for the entire school year, it was necessary that, while they were wearing one pair of jeans, the other pair was in the laundry, waiting to be washed.

After Mom had threatened to beat Marvin to death now that both pairs of his jeans were soiled, she insisted he wear one of her dresses while she washed the pants by hand and then hung them to dry in the living room near the potbellied stove. Obediently donning Mom's long, ragged, baggy house dress, Marvin was visibly embarrassed as he walked out of the bedroom, and two of my brothers and I quickly added to his misery in teasing him mercilessly.

At dusk, when all the work had been done, and although we had been told to go to bed at the same time our parents had retired, we older children crept outside to play in the heavy snow; that is, with the exception of my improperly dressed brother, Marvin.

After Woody and Maynard had bravely built up a large bonfire in the snow-covered field beside our house, they quickly and efficiently began trampling down the snow to form a large circle, approximately fifteen feet in diameter. Woody then instructed us children how to trample "spokes" inside the big wheel to form his human-sized version of "Fox and Geese."

As Marvin watched from the living room window, his desire to participate in the fun soon weakened his better judgment. He quietly slipped out from behind the plastic drapes, and, holding up the long tail of the dress, he ran outside through the snow and jumped inside the circle to join in the fun.

Unfortunately, within thirty minutes Dad heard the commotion outside the house, crawled out of his bed, opened the door, and discovered that, instead of going to bed as he had ordered us children to do, we had gone outside, where we were enjoying playing in the deep snow. "You dumb idiots, git in 'is here house 'fore I come out dere'n beat chur asses off'n you!" he yelled from the front porch.

While Woody and Maynard hurriedly kicked clumps of snow onto the blazing fire, Arnold, Marvin, and I ran quickly toward the porch, with Marvin in front of me and the tail of his dress dragging limply through the snow. Shivering from the cold, Dad stood outside the living room door dressed only in his long underwear. When Arnold approached, Dad grabbed him by the nape of his neck and slung him in through the doorway.

When Marvin approached wearing Mom's rubber overshoes and her long dress, Dad jumped over near him and kicked his rear-end, yelling, "Don'chu ever let me ketch you doin' sumpin' so stupid ever ag'in!" While Dad was focusing his attention on Marvin, I quickly squeezed past him and ran into the frigid bedroom, where I threw my coat and shoes to the floor and jumped into bed.

Apparently too cold to wait for Woody and Maynard to finish extinguishing the fire, Dad returned to his bed just before they ran inside seconds later. With the five of us shivering safely in our cold beds, we no doubt realized how extremely lucky we were for having escaped the "whuppins" that we probably deserved but had miraculously escaped.

I would eventually realize that Dad seemed to resent hearing us children laughing and having a good time. Many times he had interrupted our laughter and fun, which he called "foolishness," by yelling out to us, "If you young'uns cain't fin' nuthin' ta do, 'hen I'll fin' somethin' ta keep ye busy." The guilt complex I experienced over the years when I occasionally found myself laughing and enjoying lighter moments in life, or from having idle hands during waking hours of the day, was difficult to overcome. It was early in mid-life before I was able to laugh aloud or participate in playful activities without feeling I had no right to do so. To this day, my hands are seldom idle, although it now is by choice that I have another project in mind before I finish one I may be working on at the time. Having received victory over that situation has served as another example of how God's grace has strengthened and sustained me throughout my entire life.

XLVI

Attending to Life

A new addition to our family had become a routine event; nevertheless, each birth was welcomed with a great deal of excitement, warmth, and pride. The newborn was treated special for a few weeks but would eventually be lost in the shuffle along with the rest of the siblings. It was the middle of winter, and although Mom could not afford to seek prenatal care from the doctor, her eleventh pregnancy had begun showing signs that she needed professional medical treatment. Like most problems or illnesses that occasionally affected our family, she believed the difficulty would pass, even though she was in her seventh month of pregnancy.

Mom had no choice but to rest in bed on the days when the bleeding intensified. I was sometimes kept home from school for days to take care of Mom and the small children and to assume her household responsibilities. I did not think about complaining about the situation since I felt that, being the oldest daughter, it was my duty. I was glad that at least Sissy came in once a day to clean Mom's bed and to change her clothing.

Carrying the baby to full-term was touch and go; nevertheless, when Mom finally went into labor, Dad opted to go for the neighborhood midwife, Mrs. Taylor. After a very short labor, the baby was born lifeless. I could hear the conversations drifting through my open bedroom doorway, where I had been instructed to stay during the birthing. I listened anxiously as the midwife tried frantically to "beat" life into my newborn baby brother. After a few failed attempts of starting his breathing by whacking away at his buttocks and the soles of his feet, she suddenly stuck her hand into a pitcher of drinking water that was sitting on a table beside Mom's bed. Grabbing a cupped palm full of the cold water, she sloshed it across the baby's face, and immediately I heard the welcome sounds of the baby's weak cries.

Mrs. Taylor then handed the newborn to my grandmother, who was assisting at the birth, before turning her attention to Mom. I did not know why my mother and baby brother had survived the difficult pregnancy and birthing; however, I chose to give the credit to God. I was thankful that they both were alive and well, although with his withered and wrinkled skin, my new baby brother undoubtedly could have won first prize in an "Ugly Baby Contest." Unlike Mom's previous babies, who had weighed in at birth between nine and eleven pounds, this little brother weighed barely five pounds. As I cuddled him and counted his fingers and toes, Mom whispered to me that I could choose his first name since she had already decided on his middle name.

"Why're you lettin' me name him?" I asked.

"'Cause you tuck sich good care'a me an'na family fer tha past two months," she said. I quickly obliged and named my darling little brother "Jerry." My new baby brother soon gained weight and eventually would grow to be one of the tallest and strongest boys of Mom's brood.

My parents insisted that I continue to stay home from school in order to maintain Mom's role while she stayed in bed the customary nine days after giving birth. Since I could not milk the cow, Woody took over the chore before leaving for school each morning.

The days passed quickly, and I successfully managed to carry the load that had been placed on my shoulders. After the ninth day, Mom was able to resume her role around the house, and I was able to return to school. I wondered whether baby number eleven would be our last or whether Mom and Dad would decide to try for an even dozen.

I was troubled as I thought about how my teacher and classmates would react when I returned to school, after having missed the previous two weeks. Just as soon as I entered the classroom, I was confronted with the fact that, while I had been absent, the seventh-grade classes had been competing in a perfect attendance contest. My peers were angry because, in their opinions, my absence had caused our class to lose any hopes of winning the contest.

Once I was seated, a few of my classmates walked over to my desk and continued harassing me. I became very sad and wished I hadn't been too shy to tell them that I was sorry for causing them to lose the award, and that I would have been in school every day had it been my decision instead of my parents' demand. Although I felt like crying throughout the day, I managed to keep my composure and to avoid allowing my classmates' rude remarks to interfere with my studies. It was too early to tell whether my absence from school would affect my grades, but for this day, the only thing I was concerned about was making it through the day without the boys having the satisfaction of seeing the tears that I had been fighting to suppress. I believed that, with time, my classmates would no longer torture me with their unkind words; after all, I knew in my heart that I had done what had been required of me at home, and I couldn't blame my peers for believing that I was responsible for their disappointment.

XLVII

Lurking Under the Cliff

My two older brothers, now that they had moved down to the high school, seldom walked to and from school with the younger children and me. Since I was making the decision on which route to travel to and from school, I most often took the path that passed by Grandma's house, since some of our cousins walked out of the hollow with us to school. Although we lived within two miles of each other, my school-age siblings and I seldom spent any time with our cousins, other than during these walks to and from school.

Two of these cousins were Uncle Hubert's children. Aunt Ruby, his wife, had begun bearing children around the same time that Mom had given birth to her sixth child. On a few occasions, when Mom went to town or to the state capitol on business, she chose to leave her baby with Aunt Ruby. Since Aunt Ruby at the time was producing milk for her own baby, she would nurse her baby on one of her breasts and then, after placing her child on the bed, pick up my baby brother and allow him to nurse from her other breast. Neither Mom nor Aunt Ruby had planned for their babies to be nursing during the same period; still, they took advantage of the convenient situation. Between the two women, they would give birth to twenty-four children over the next few years.

Although our two families were closely related, had a lot in common, and lived only a few miles apart, Mom eventually distanced herself and our family from her brother and his family. Though our family was no better off socially or financially than Uncle Hubert's family, Mom tried to persuade us children that we were of a higher class than our relatives. Despite all our negative teachings, however, a couple of my brothers and I chose not to sever our ties with our relatives, and to this day have a very close bond with the family.

Spring was in the air, and life was reviving everywhere around me. I was still escorting my elementary-age siblings to school each morning so they would not dally around and make themselves late for school. We had walked off the ridge and down the hollow and were making our way over the hill to the railroad tracks that ran alongside Elk River, when I turned and yelled back to my siblings, "Come on an' quit y'ur foolin' 'round back 'ere, or you'll make me late for school." When I turned and looked again at the path in front of me, I glanced through the trees to the other side of the river at something that looked out of place. I stepped to a spot where I could get a better view and gasped when I recognized a sight that I didn't want to believe. I looked back at my siblings carefully making their way down the steep incline and, satisfied that they were unaware of what I had observed, continued the walk until I had reached the railroad tracks, where I could see through the treeline more clearly. I glanced again across the river at the naked man who was standing beneath the overhang of a rock cliff about 200 feet from where I was walking. I could see plainly that he was watching my siblings and me as we made our way over the hill to the railroad tracks.

Feeling both ashamed and embarrassed for having taken a second look at the man and hoping he was unaware that I had indeed seen his stark-naked body standing against the backdrop of the riverbank, I pushed the children down the tracks toward the street that was lined on either side with houses. After ordering them that when school had recessed for the day, they should travel the motor vehicle road in order to bypass the railroad tracks and river, I rushed my siblings down the street to the front of their school, my heart racing from fear and uncertainty. I then loped down the street to the high school, arriving just in time to hear the first bell ringing.

No matter how hard I tried during the day, I couldn't get what I had seen out of my mind. I was afraid to mention the matter to any of my teachers since I had never heard of a situation such as this. I wondered whether the man would still be across the river when my siblings returned from school, and the thought upset me even more since I couldn't be sure they would remember to avoid the isolated area. All I could do was to pray and ask God to keep our little group safe.

On my home from school, I walked much faster in an effort to overtake my younger siblings in case they had walked the tracks. I hadn't seen my two older brothers and didn't know whether they were ahead of or behind me, so my heart pounded as I realized that I was going to be alone when I approached the area where the nude man had been standing earlier in the day.

At the base of the mountain where I was walking, the land for the railroad tracks had been carved out parallel to the Elk River. The tracks were approximately forty feet from the river's edge on the east side of the river. On the west side of the river, approximately fifty feet up the side of the mountain from the river's edge, a row of frame houses had been crowded between the river and the berm of the narrow highway that also ran parallel to the river and railroad tracks. The secluded cliff on the west side of the river, which the man had been standing beneath, was situated at the base of the hillside near the river's edge, hidden from the view of the houses.

Alone on the tracks and scared out of my wits, I approached the area where I had clearly observed the man earlier in the day. I wondered whether I should look across the river to see whether he was there, or pretend the whole thing had never happened. I shivered at the thought that he could have crossed over the river to hide somewhere in the bushes, waiting to ambush me.

With my eyes focused straight ahead, I left the railroad tracks and began hurrying up the side of the heavily wooded mountain. Assuring myself that I would feel more secure once I reached the motor vehicle road at the top of the hill, I wondered whether I would meet up with my siblings.

About halfway up the path, I reached the break in the trees that would allow me to see the other side of the river. To do this, I would need to stop and turn around, but in my young, confused mind, I was afraid that, should I do so, he might think I liked what I had seen on my way to school. Again, I felt a great sense of guilt sweep over me. I reminded myself that the evil man couldn't have been certain that I had seen him when we had passed by that morning. Unnerved, yet determined, I decided to find a way to sneak a peek without appearing to the man that I was deliberately looking in his direction. I took a few steps and then purposely dropped the book I was carrying, and, after taking another step forward, I slowly turned around and stooped over to retrieve the book. Before straightening my torso, I casually tipped my head downward, raised my eyebrows, and glanced toward the area where the man had been standing beneath the rock cliff. Seeing no one in the area, I scooped up the book and quickly turned and continued the climb up the narrow footpath that wriggled its way upward to the rock-based road, which split into three forks at the top of the hill.

Once I reached the main road, I looked anxiously up the rough thoroughfare on the right, which snaked its way up Birch Creek to where my grandparents lived. With my siblings nowhere in sight, I looked up Dry Ridge Road in the center to see whether the children could have taken the route that passed directly in front of my family's home. Still hearing or seeing none of my siblings, I began hurrying up the hollow toward Grandma's house. The left branch, Morris Creek Road, meandered alongside the hill above the river for a few miles and then wound its way through the valley that our home on the ridge overlooked, so I was certain that the children had avoided the left fork in the road.

As I dodged mud holes and ruts in the road, I wondered whether I should tell my younger sister and brothers why I had asked them to avoid walking the tracks. "They would probably tell Mom and Dad, and then my parents would think I had made up the whole story," I said aloud. I was becoming more and more concerned about what I had witnessed; nevertheless, I decided to remain quiet about what I had seen, and to wait and see whether it would happen again. I soon overtook my younger siblings, and together we hurried up the hollow toward home. Like the other secrets I was harboring, this was one more unsavory incident that had been shoved into my troubled young mind. I wondered how God was going to handle this one.

The next morning, as our little gang started down the hill to the railroad tracks, I found myself peeking through the trees even before I'd reached the clearing where I could see to the other side of the river. I had no desire to see the man again, but I wanted to know whether the threat was still there. I had no idea there were deviates in the world who sometimes could become violent, so I didn't realize the extent of the danger we could be facing.

With the rumble of the traffic on the highway just across the river in the background, we children, one by one, made our way toward the tracks. Without saying a word, I stepped to the side to allow my siblings to pass by me so that I could view the area thoroughly and be certain whether the man had returned to the riverbank. Suddenly, a shiver ran down my spine and I sucked in a deep breath as my eyes caught the man standing again under the rock cliff—naked as a newborn baby. Not wanting to alarm my sister and little brothers by bringing to their attention the creature lurking just across the shallow river, I again urged the children to move even faster. My mind was in a swirl as I pondered nervously what I should do about the situation. Should I tell Mom or Dad, after all? I feared that, should Mom believe me, she would think I had done something to cause the sick behavior of the man. Were I to tell my father, he might twist the facts to make it appear as though I were encouraging him to pursue his inappropriate actions toward me. Needless to say, I was very confused.

I surmised that, if the man had intended to physically harm any of the children or me, he would have already made an attempt. I even wondered whether there could be something wrong with me that caused all these vulgar experiences to happen in my presence. With no answers of my own, and afraid to ask an adult for help, I decided to lock the matter away in the back of my mind with all the other unpleasant problems for which I had no answers, and to trust God to take care of it. Throughout the coming weeks, I didn't know whether the man was continuing with his indecent exposure, since I had steadfastly refused to look toward the area.

It would be decades before I could bring myself to mention the troubling experience to my parents. While visiting in their home one day, I mentioned the unpleasant memory and inquired whether they had any knowledge of the "pedophile's" existence. With laughter in his voice, my father informed me that the man had been caught and arrested sometime during 1950, after a group of teenage girls had reported seeing a nude man lurking beneath a rock cliff in the same area I had seen him months earlier. Upon hearing for the first time about my encounter with the unseemly character, Mom asked, "Why 'in't chu tell us 'bout seein' the man back then?"

"Because I didn't think you would believe me," I said.

"Well, we heared later 'at two other girls you know see'd 'im when 'hey was walkin' on'na tracks to school," Dad said.

I then asked my parents whether they would have believed my story about the sightings of the man if I had told them at the time, and whether they would have done anything about the situation. My mother bowed her head in silence, and my father answered in the way I expected he would. "I don't know if'n I would've er not," he said. I bit my tongue and walked away in disgust, supposing that Dad's reply had answered both questions I had asked.

I later stopped and thanked my Heavenly Father for always having been there for me when it seemed I was alone in the world. I now have no doubt that without His help, I would never have made it through my teenage years. Thank you, Lord Jesus, for being my Savior and friend.

XLVIII

The Ol' Scarecrow

On a sunny afternoon near the end of the school year, I elected to forego Granny's biscuit for a walk alone out the ridge road. The isolated mountain was buzzing with birds, butterflies, bees, and little critters that flitted about in their own paradise of plenty. I walked along the car tracks, taking advantage of the beautiful nature and talking softly to the One who had made it all possible. With a prayer on my lips and a song in my heart, I skipped along the dusty road, refusing to allow the uncertainties in my young life to dampen my spirit.

I was carrying the proofs from my school pictures in a large envelope tucked beneath my arm, unaware that, within a mile and a half of home, I would come in contact with another questionable situation that would only add to the anxieties that had been popping up in my childhood.

The golden tassels of the stalks of corn glistened in the bright sunlight throughout the field that lay parallel to the dusty car tracks where I was walking. My eyes were transfixed on the wide brim of a straw hat, all but hidden about forty feet down over the hill in the cornfield. Thinking I was looking at a scarecrow, I was startled when the body beneath the hat began lazily bobbing up and down between the corn rows. I walked east on the road as the "scarecrow" moved west in my direction, and then I smiled when I recognized the faded bib overalls, the blue chambray long-sleeved shirt, and the red-and-black paisley bandanna tied around the shirt collar, standing out like a beacon against the stalks of corn.

Though I knew him, I didn't care to speak to the old farmer, so I pulled my arms tightly against my sides and tried to shrink my body in hopes that I could sneak past him. "What'cha got dere, purdy girl?" he called out as he moved through the cornfield to the edge of the road where I was walking.

"It's my pictures," I said shyly. He stopped and reached out for the envelope, which I removed from beneath my arm and handed to him.

"Le's see if'n you's as purdy in 'em pictures as you are in'na flesh," he said.

While I nervously waited for the return of the envelope, Mr. Luke removed the proofs and smiled as he studied one of the black-and-white photographs. "You purdy loodle thang, you're purtier 'an any movie star," he declared, stepping up from the corn row and into the road beside me.

I quickly stepped backwards as he reached out to touch me on the shoulder. "Now, honey, don't cha be 'fraid a me, I jist want a loodle ol' hug from such a purdy loodle girl," he said.

"Uh uh," I protested as I reached out to retrieve my pictures.

"You hain't 'fraid of your ol' neighbor Luke, are ye, purdy thang?" he called out to me as I grabbed my pictures from his hand and hurried out the road.

With the familiar, sickening tone of voice ringing in my ears, I began running as fast as I could down the deserted road, my heart pounding from fear that Mr. Luke was closing in behind me. When I reached the highest point on the road, I stopped and sighed a breath of relief when I looked back just in time to see the blue overalls and straw hat disappearing amongst the stalks of corn. I wondered, as I slowed my pace, whether my fear of the old gent had been warranted. I could not ask my parents about the neighbor, knowing that my father disliked the man already because he believed that Mr. Luke had, years earlier, flirted with my mother.

I hurried out the road toward my home, no longer noticing the wildflowers or bluebirds I had been admiring earlier. My happy thoughts had been replaced with the reality that not only was I having to fight at home, but now I was feeling threatened each time I walked to and from school. I wondered whether the whole world was like the area where I lived or whether I was just unfortunate enough to live in the midst of a bunch of "weirdos."

Over the next few days, I took a good look at myself and could see nothing in the manner in which I was conducting myself that would attract the behaviors to which I was being subjected. I wondered whether other girls were facing the unpleasant situations I always seemed to find myself experiencing or whether I alone was being exposed to these unfortunate encounters. I doubted I would ever know the answers.

Without realizing that I was doing exactly what God's Holy Word invited me to do, I gave yet another worry to the Lord. Throughout the coming years, I would find hope and solace in the Scriptural verse of 1 Peter 5:7, which prompted me to continue giving my cares to the Lord. "Casting all your care upon Him; for He careth for you."

XLIX

The Iron

My childhood had been snatched away like the white down of a dandelion swept into the air by the brisk ridge winds. At the age of thirteen, I had already proven myself a capable cook, housekeeper, and nursemaid for my siblings. I had successfully graduated the seventh grade near the top of my class and was looking forward to spending the summer months doing my share of work on the small farm.

Aunt Ruby was expecting her fifth child, and I had just learned that an agreement had been met between her and my mom for me to stay with her family when the baby was born. I expressed my concerns about taking on the responsibilities; nevertheless, Mom seemed confident that I was ready for my first job away from home.

Before the week was over, Uncle Hubert walked out to our house one morning and announced that the baby had arrived and that he was there to take me home with him. After hurriedly cramming a few articles of clothing into a large paper bag, I hugged my little sister and brothers and walked out the door with my uncle. "She's a woman now'n she'll make ye a good hired girl," Mom assured Uncle Hubert, as he and I walked out the driveway. Nervously, I wondered whether my work would indeed be satisfactory for my relatives.

Since Uncle Hubert didn't own an automobile, he had to leave his house each weekday morning at 5:30 so that he would arrive on time at his job as a carpenter's helper for a construction outfit that traveled around the county building houses. When he shook me awake and told me it was time to get up to prepare his breakfast and pack his lunch, I tried to work as quickly and quietly as possible in order not to awaken the rest of the family.

The hinges on the oven door of Aunt Ruby's dilapidated wood-burning stove were broken, and the door had to be propped shut with a shortened broom handle. Not knowing how to judge the baking temperature because the oven had no thermostat, and with the broken door allowing the heat to escape, I was nervous about the outcome of the big pan of biscuits I had just made and shoved in through the crippled oven door.

Once Uncle Hubert's lunch was packed and the pot of boiled sugar-syrup he had requested was of the right consistency to sop with the biscuits, I carefully removed the broom handle and dropped the oven door slightly in order to take a quick peek at the pan of biscuits browning inside the oven. To my delight, the long pan of biscuits had risen to the top of the pan. Holding on to the heavy cast-iron door with one padded hand and reaching inside the hot oven with the other hand, I grabbed the long pan of hot biscuits with a large dishtowel and began dragging it toward the front of the oven.

Upon noticing that the biscuits in the front of the pan looked underbaked, I tried to rotate the pan while also holding up the broken door. Suddenly, the heavy door slipped from my grasp, and one corner went crashing to the floor. In trying to retrieve the door, I lost my grip on the hot pan of biscuits, and they slid forward and dumped out of the pan onto the bare plank floor.

Uncle Hubert came running into the kitchen to see what had caused the commotion. I cringed and stepped backwards, anticipating his losing his temper at the sight of the pile of biscuits spread out on the floor. "My God!" he yelled. "Jue git burnt?"

Crying softly, I shook my head from side to side to let him know I had not been hurt. I was devastated. "What we gonna do?" I asked, as I began cleaning up the mess.

Uncle Hubert gently nudged my shoulder and told me to go back to bed, assuring me that he would have time to make himself a pan of what he called "batter bread." I didn't know what else I could do, so I went back to bed and cried for two hours. Not only was I concerned because my first pan of biscuits had been ruined, but also I was upset because I had noticed that my relatives' flour bin was almost empty.

At last the children were crawling out of their beds, and I could now make my second attempt at fixing breakfast for the family. I walked into the kitchen and over to the stove to see what Uncle Hubert had left of the pan of bread he'd baked for himself. The large pan was filled with a flat, wet, sticky goo, apparently the "batter bread" my uncle had baked. I picked up the pan and carried the sticky bread into the living room, where Aunt Ruby was lying in bed with her new baby boy. "Jue want me to dump 'is out an' make some more?" I asked shyly.

"No, I don't thank you orta throw 'at good bread out. The young'uns'll probably eat purt-near all of it soppin' their sugar-syrup," she said, smiling.

As I stood there with my head bowed, Aunt Ruby went on to say, "Hubert tol' me 'at I orta seen 'at big panna biscuits 'hat'chu made an' spilt. He said 'em was really good-lookin' biscuits." I knew she was trying to make me feel better, but she didn't realize that, deep in my heart, I was wondering whether maybe she wasn't questioning my readiness for this job I had taken on.

I returned to the kitchen with the pan of soggy batter and began warming the rest of the breakfast. I watched as the children, like hungry little pigs, gathered around the table and began gobbling up the tacky bread and hot syrup. I reached over to the pan, squeezed off a gob of the bread, and sopped it through my plate of syrup and fresh butter. To my surprise, Uncle Hubert's bread and my boiled syrup tasted pretty good!

I made it through the nine days with my aunt and uncle and all five children surviving the ordeal. I had tried to do everything as perfectly as I knew how. Both Uncle Hubert and Aunt Ruby had complimented me on the fine job they thought I had done. I was pleased because I also felt that I had prepared some pretty good meals after my first attempt had failed so pitifully.

At the end of the nine days, Uncle Hubert picked up my bag of clothing and left to escort me back to my home. I was almost in shock. I wasn't expecting my kind uncle to accompany me up the mountain. When we arrived at the front door of my family's home, Mom met us and immediately asked, "How'd she do?"

"She done gooder'n I even 'spected 'er da do," my uncle said, as he handed me a ten-dollar bill and thanked me for my help.

"You don't hafta pay me," I said as I reached out and took the money.

Before Uncle Hubert could reply, my mother looked at the money and then quickly asked, "Why, what's 'at in your hand?"

"Ten dollars," I said.

"What'cha gonna do with it?" she asked.

"What'cha want to know fer?" I replied teasingly.

Uncle Hubert interrupted our little conversation and bid us farewell as he turned to leave. Mom gave her regards and then returned her attention to me.

"I seen 'at arn [iron] 'hat Sissy got, an' I thought I'd order me one like it if I had da money," Mom said pitifully.

"We already have two arns, so why'd you need another one?" I asked.

"This uns got a loodle tank on it 'at you're s'posed ta fill up 'ith gas," Mom explained, with a twinkle in her eye. "Hit don't even hafta be hett up on'na stove."

I handed Mom my ten dollars before Uncle Hubert had walked out of sight. Although I was thirteen years old, I had never been inside a store to make a purchase. Being unaware of what I could have bought with my first earned income, I had nothing in mind to buy; in fact, I didn't feel as though I had a specific need for the money I had been paid.

Within the next day or two, Mom ordered the iron from the catalog, and later, when Dad brought it home from the post office, we children were as intrigued by the unusual apparatus as our parents were. Dad removed the iron from the cardboard box and then immediately shooed us children out of his way while he handed Mom the operating instructions, only to discover that what he called "white gas" (gasoline) was required to heat the iron. "I'll hafta git some gas tamarr 'fore we can check 'is here thang out," he said.

The following evening, after Dad had filled the small tank on the back of the iron with "white gasoline," he then pumped air into the lines with the built-in plunger located behind the tank. Once the gas had been turned on and lit, the blue flame from the gas fumes would rapidly heat the sole plate of the iron to the proper temperature for ironing cottons and dungarees.

"Shore beats 'em ol' flat arns 'at takes ferever to heat on the cookin' stove." Mom said, smiling broadly.

"Now, you an' I can finish a whole basket a' clothes in the time it took ta heat 'em flat irons," I said proudly, marveling at the new iron and wondering what else was on the market that my family didn't know about.

After I had gone to bed later in the evening, I lay awake thinking about how easy it had been for me to relinquish my ten dollars so that my mother could purchase the iron that she otherwise would never have been able to buy. I felt warm and satisfied about the decision, never once thinking about how on one day I could feel such tenderness and compassion for my mother and then, on the very next day, feel nothing but contempt for the way she continually ignored the way my father was physically and verbally abusing me.

As I reflect on this particular incident that God has seen fit to keep alive in my memory, I truly stand in awe at how He shielded me from the bitterness that could have festered in my life. Though wounded, my heart was kept soft, allowing Him to use these unpleasant circumstances to mold me into a vessel that can challenge and encourage others who have encountered their own assortment of hardships.

L

Confound the Confound Luck

Throughout the years our family had become accustomed to Dad's temper tantrums. For the past several months, however, he had added a new dimension to his wild outbursts—seemingly finding pleasure in threatening to take his own life.

After fussing and fuming for a while, he would grab the .22-caliber rifle off the wall and head out the door to the wood line. "I'mma gonna go out 'n 'em woods an' blow my brains out," he would yell for all the family to hear.

Mom's response was usually the same. "Bud, don't chu do 'his ag'in," she would plead while sobbing like a baby. Her pleas, unfortunately, seemed only to agitate him even more. When he walked to the door with the loaded rifle in his hand, Mom, my siblings, and I would watch as he entered the woods; then, we would listen nervously for the crack from his rifle, fearing that he might one day carry out the threat.

During these traumatic episodes, when we had heard no gunshot after we had listened for a few minutes, Mom would then station a couple of us children near the window to watch for Dad to return. "Now, young'uns, when he gets in'na house, don't anybody say nothin' to set 'im off ag'in," she would tearfully say.

One Saturday winter morning, in the midst of his continual threats, Dad abruptly announced that he was going into town, alone. "Now, Bud, why 'on't chu stay home 'ith your family?" Mom asked tearfully.

"I'mma goin' inta town an' see a Roy Rogers picture show, an' you might as well shet y'ur bawlin' up," Dad stated. "Fetch me my white shirt!"

"'At shirt hain't been arned, an' I hain't got no gas fer tha arn," Mom said emotionally.

"Ye never had'da worry 'bout gas 'fore ya got 'hat newfangled arn," he yelled. "I'd ruther be dead as ta hafta listen ta your blubberin'." He then grabbed up the rifle and began angrily searching for the cartridges. Stomping over to the dresser where the ammunition was supposed to be stored, he jerked open a drawer and began throwing clothing onto the floor, becoming more exasperated with each second that passed.

"Now, what'n a Sam Hill have you done 'ith my shells?" he barked.

"Now Bud, hain't no shells lef'. You done shot 'em all up," Mom insisted.

"Quit 'at lyin' an' fetch me 'em shells 'fore I beat chur brains out 'ith the butt a 'his here rifle!" Dad yelled.

I could see that Mom was afraid of what Dad would do to himself if he were to get his hands on the shells, but I suspected that she was becoming even more scared of what he might do to her should she refuse to tell him where she had hidden the ammunition. With her hands literally trembling, my sobbing mother slowly walked over and reached inside an earthenware pitcher and pulled out a handful of .22-caliber cartridges, stepped over to where Dad stood holding the rifle, and meekly dropped the cartridges into my raging father's opened hand. I watched as he immediately jammed one of the cartridges into the rifle's chamber and then angrily stormed out the door in the direction of the woods.

"He's on 'is way to kill 'isself for the fiftieth time," I said disgustedly.

Mom picked up one of the flat irons and stuck it in the hot coals of the fireplace to heat. She didn't own an ironing board, so she laid a blanket on the table and then placed the shirt on the blanket. Once the flat iron was hot, Mom removed it from the bed of hot coals, and, through her tears, wiped off the ashes before she slowly pulled the iron across the front of Dad's white shirt. I shivered when she shrieked in terror, "Oh my God Almighty! I done scorched Bud's only white shirt!"

I became as frantic as my mother when I looked out the window and saw my father slowly sneaking toward the house. "Here he comes!" I yelled to Mom.

Not knowing what else to do, Mom rolled up the shirt and stuck it in the dresser drawer out of sight. "Maybe he won't need it 'til I can git out 'hat scorch mark," she said. We then waited with bated breath while Dad walked in through the door, calmly hung the rifle back onto the living room wall, and, while acting as though nothing unusual had transpired, called out for Mom to fetch his shirt. I couldn't help but notice that he seemed confident that she had ironed the shirt for him while he was out in the woods "killing himself."

Mom obediently removed the stained shirt from the drawer and handed it to my father. Dad jerked the shirt out of Mom's hand and held it up to look at it. Seeing the wrinkles and scorched stain, he literally jumped over to the fireplace and threw the shirt into the flames. With fire in his eyes, he then turned around and looked at Mom. "Confound a confound luck! You cain't do nothin' right!" he yelled. "I wish ta God I'd went ahead an' kilt myself."

Mom continued with her chores, seemingly trying to ignore the barrage of insults that Dad was no doubt enjoying inflicting upon her. After Dad had exhausted his fury, he apparently realized that he had no choice but to settle down and stay home with his family; in fact, until he had made enough money to buy himself another white shirt, he stayed home for the next several Saturdays.

LI

Mom's Gas-Powered Washing Machine

The loud *clap-clap* noise from Mom's gasoline-powered Maytag washing machine was the only unusually loud sound, other than the roaring of the occasional prop airplanes flying overhead, that most folks regularly heard penetrating their quiet, country lives. During the few weeks in early summer when water was available, Mom would start the engine by stamping a foot pedal, sometimes repeatedly, located on the engine.

During wintertime, the washer was kept in the kitchen. On wash day, when the washing machine was in operation, its six-foot flexible metal exhaust hose with a round muffler at the end was run outside through the slightly ajar kitchen door, in order to expel the gasoline fumes and most of the noise to the outdoors.

Mom would begin the wash by heating a tub of water over a fire she had built on the ground near the front porch. The tub of water was balanced carefully on two piles of rocks that had been stacked high enough for the firewood to be placed between them and underneath the tub. Once the water in the tub was hot, it was then carried by the bucketful and poured into the washing machine.

After washing the first load, the clothes were wrung out through rubber rollers attached to the back of the washer's tub. The articles of wet clothing were guided with one hand carefully between and through the wringers, while the other hand turned the hand crank. Each article would fall into a tub of cold rinse water that had been filled from the rain barrels and set on a wooden stool that had been placed against the tub of the washing machine. The wash water and rinse water were used over and over until as many as six to seven giant loads of laundry had been done.

After the clothes had been run through the wringers from the rinse water, they were placed in a bushel basket and carried to the clothesline. The rinse water was then used to mop the floors. The water in which the clothes had been washed was drained from the washer's tub into a galvanized tub, and my brothers carried it outside and dumped it on the ground.

LII

On the Rocks

We rented our property from the land company that owned most of the sparsely settled and undeveloped land around the area. Generations of families had rented the same homesites and adjoining acreage for fifteen dollars or less a year. As the older generations died off, their offspring would continue renting the same piece of land, until around the year 1945, when the decision was made that additional residences could no longer be built on the land. The houses already occupying the land, however, could be enlarged and improved as seen fit by the leaseholder. Should a house be demolished, or should it rot to the ground, then the land included with that homesite would no longer be leased out.

When I was almost fifteen years old, my parents decided to leave the ridge on which we had lived for the past seven years. Dad had heard about a house being vacated about ten miles southeast of the ridge that the land company also owned. With the approval from the man handling the land company's rentals, Dad relinquished our present lease in exchange for the property that would also rent for fifteen dollars annually.

After work one evening, Dad drove up the hollow called Leatherwood to inspect the house before making the intended move over the upcoming weekend. When he returned home, he explained to our family what he had encountered once he had arrived at the front door of the supposedly vacated house. "When I got 'ere, I seen 'at somebody else'd done went'n started movin' inta 'hat house 'hat was s'posed ta been ourn," he said.

Dad explained that with no screen on the open front door, he was able to see inside the living room while standing outside. "'At big, fat, ugly woman of Thad Stanley's was settin' in'na cheer lookin' bug-eyed while two young men I figgered must'a been 'er brothers was standin' lookin' out at me," he said, grinning from ear to ear and shaking his head from side to side.

Dad explained that he had proceeded to ask the young man closest to the door, "What'chall doin' movin' in here without permission from Jarrett Lang?"

"Uh-uh-uh, people 'at u-u-use ta live here done t-t-told m-my sister uh-uh 'at she c-c-could have 'is h-h-house," the young man had stated.

"I done paid'a rent on 'is here place, an' I'll be 'spectin' 'is house ta be empty when I brang my first load'a stuff Saturday," Dad had said to the family.

Dad told Mom and us children that the young man who had answered the door had stuttered badly and appeared to be very nervous. "'Ere was a nice-lookin' young man standin' in 'ere lookin' out at me," Dad said. "I figger he was older'n 'at other feller. I told 'em, 'I'll be back here tamarr', an' y'all be outta here.'"

"What'chu gonna do if you git over 'ere'n they're still hol't up in 'at house?" Mom asked.

"Don't worry! They've prob'ly lef' the county by now," Dad boasted.

Leatherwood was on the opposite end of town from where our school was located. Dad had informed Mom that the area was more heavily populated and that the rock-based road that ran right by the front door of the property was maintained by the state. He also seemed pleased to announce that there was a country school in the community that included grades first through eighth.

From listening to the conversation between my father and mother, it sounded as though we would be entering into a new way of life. Dad's coworker had given him a description of the property. The house had three bedrooms, a living room, dining room, and kitchen. There was no running water but a well just a few feet from the house that Dad had been assured would never run dry. For the first time in our lives, our family would have a home wired with electricity. Even the rural mail route sounded too good to be true, since, up until now, a trip to the post office had been necessary to have our mail handed to us from across the counter.

The two-room country school just one mile up the road on Ed's Fork would be a blessing for my younger siblings but wouldn't be of help to me since I had just finished the eighth grade. Although none of us, except for Dad, had seen the property, the entire family seemed excited and anxious to make the move.

On the first Friday in August 1950, the evening before we were scheduled to move, Dad decided to check out the property to make sure the "trespassers" had indeed moved out. Since Woody had graduated from high school in May—with the honor of Salutatorian—and had left the state to begin work in Ohio, Dad informed Marvin and Maynard that he wanted them to accompany him to the place where we would soon be living. To my surprise, just before he pulled the car out of the driveway, he yelled to me and asked whether I wanted to ride with them to check out the property. I jumped for glee and ran to the door to tell Mom that I was going with my father and two brothers to see our new residence.

"You git'chur hine en' back here, young lady! Y'ain't got no business runnin' off'n leavin' me 'ith all 'is here work ta do," Mom yelled. Disheartened, I ran back outside to tell Dad that Mom wouldn't allow me to go.

"Git in'na car," Dad said. "Hain't gonna hurt nary thang you goin' 'ith us; 'sides, we hain't gonna be gone very long."

I hesitated for a few seconds, my conscience telling me it wasn't right for me to disobey Mom, especially considering how dangerous it was for me to be left alone with my father. I looked over at the car and saw Marvin sitting in the front seat and Maynard seated in the back. "They will both be with us the whole time, so I'll be safe," I told myself. I yelled back over my shoulder to my younger siblings, "Tell Mommy 'at Daddy said I could go. We won't be gone very long."

I jumped excitedly into the back seat with Maynard and settled down beside the window for the new adventure. I had no idea where I was going, yet I was thrilled to know that I would finally discover what was on the other side of the big mountain we had lived at the base of when we'd lived in the hollow above my grandparents' home.

The 1937 four-door black Pontiac sedan, which Dad had recently traded for, began bumping along over the ridge road as we began our ten-mile trip into a land foreign to our family. I noticed that Dad seemed to be in an especially jovial mood as he laughed and talked about the move.

When we entered the center of town in Clendenin and began bumping along down the cobblestone street, one of the first things I remembered, which was from the only two times I had accompanied Sissy or my mother to do their shopping, was the tantalizing odor hanging heavily in the air as we passed by the local pool hall. The distinct smell of what I had heard were the best hot dogs in the world filled the car with the tempting aroma, causing my mouth to begin watering.

The pool hall was known as the place where all the misfits and drunks congregated. Dad was known to frequent the place during the periods of his life when he was backslidden and out of church. I had overheard my dad and Mr. White talking about how the hotdogs were loaded with homemade chili, coleslaw, and chopped onions. I had never seen a hotdog, and I could only imagine what it would be like to sink my teeth into whatever was responsible for the most tempting aroma I'd smelled since the morning Mom had fried the fresh veal that Dad and his buddy had shot.

Downtown Clendenin

Dad whizzed through the center of the small town that, despite having no traffic lights, was in my mind a bustling little city holding all sorts of excitement. We approached the lower end of town, where I noticed a horse that someone had tied to a post, apparently put there for that reason. As we zoomed down the narrow paved road, I noticed that the rattles and squeaks in the car were not nearly as noticeable as they had been on the dirt road we had just left. I sat back in the seat and peered out the window, allowing the fresh air to blow in my face. I liked riding on the paved road. I could look behind and not see the trail of dust that followed us whenever we bounced along the ridge road. I gawked at every house along the way in hopes that I could get a glimpse of the lucky people who lived in those "fine mansions." Several of the houses were two stories high, and I was sure there was a millionaire living on each floor.

Neither my brothers nor I said a word as we sped along the paved road that none of us had seen before. Dad had become silent and seemed to be in deep thought, seemingly concentrating on the road as he stared straight ahead and puffed on the pipe that he sometimes smoked when running short on Camel cigarettes. I once again suppressed the uneasy feeling that had swept over me, determined not to allow my fear of my father to interfere with my enjoying this new adventure.

I gripped the armrest of the speeding car and looked down the side of the steep hill, taking note that the highway we were traveling was now running parallel with the railroad and Elk River below. The road was very crooked, with the heavily wooded hillside on our left blocking my view and a deep drop-off on our right making me very nervous. We had crossed the railroad tracks twice since we had been on the paved road, and I was aware that, should Dad lose control of the car, we would no doubt roll over the side of the mountain and come to rest on these same railroad tracks, which had many years earlier been laid between the highway and the river.

A row of painted houses spaced closely together had been built on the narrow strip of land running parallel to, and between, the river and the railroad tracks. A few of the houses had no tin or shingles on the roofs; however, both the outside of each house and its roof was covered with black sheets of roofing material called "tar paper." Stovepipes extending through some of the roofs were releasing slender whiffs of smoke into the air.

As I was busy gawking at everything in sight, my head suddenly hit the roof of the car when, without warning, Dad whipped the car to the left and onto an unpaved road that climbed sharply up a steep mountain. I sat back in the seat, bracing myself as I tried to look out the window while Dad accelerated rapidly up the rough road. Higher and higher we climbed until I could see nothing more than the treetops as I looked down over the mountain and across a deep ravine to the side of still another mountain.

Once we had reached the crest of the mountain, the road leveled out, so Dad slowed the car and maneuvered carefully around a very sharp left curve as we approached a settlement of houses on both sides of the road. To our left, white houses of different shapes and sizes were perched on the side of the mountain, which sloped gradually upward from the roadway and then became even steeper behind the row of houses. To our right, the sloping land had been raped of its trees and foliage in order to accommodate the mass of dwellings and outbuildings crowded haphazardly together.

After winding our way through the populated area, we began rolling down the other side of the mountain as quickly as we had sped up the first side. Dad slowed the car at the bottom of the hill as we approached a dilapidated wooden bridge with part of the flooring missing. I held my breath as I listened to the old bridge creaking and moaning in resentment of the weight of our big black Pontiac, looking no doubt like a hearse creeping by with her corpse aboard.

Up the winding road and alongside the creek-bed we continued, leaving massive dust clouds rising in the air behind us. Large laurel bushes with beautiful pink flowers stood out proudly amid the mass of undergrowth alongside the creek. Wildflowers at the edge of the road swayed in the breeze as the Pontiac picked up speed. Tall trees of many varieties covered the hillsides in what appeared to be one solid mass of forest. Here and there, where the contour of the land allowed, an occasional cottage sat sleepily near the dusty road. A slender trail of wood-smoke drifted lazily into the blue sky from the stovepipe protruding through each house's roof. "Supper is either ready or being prepared," I thought to myself.

Finally, we reached our destination. As Dad pulled off the main road and onto the driveway that stopped about fifty feet short of the house, he exclaimed, "Over 'ere she is!" Sitting across the creek from the roadway and nestled between two mountains was a run-down log house, looking nothing like what I had expected.

We drove down into the creek and crossed to the other side, where Dad stopped the car on a flat area just a few feet from a stream that ran across the bottom-land and emptied into the larger creek. I looked around quickly to see whether the strangers were anywhere near and was relieved to see that the house looked vacant. "Looks like 'em people tuck 'eir stuff'n hightailed it outta here," Dad boasted, as we each ventured ever-so-cautiously toward the front of the house.

The logs used to build the house had been hewn by hand and were flat on all four sides. I marveled at the thought of the size of the trees from which the enormous logs had been cut. Mud, instead of mortar, had been packed between the logs, each log interlocked with the next at all four corners of the house. Several missing sections of the mud-filling had left gaping holes between the big logs, exposing the backsides of the rough lumber that made up the inside walls.

There was no front porch, so I stepped up onto the two two-by-three-foot rectangular boulders that had been chiseled flat on all sides in the same manner as the logs, and placed, the first block slightly sunken into the earth, in front of the living room door to serve as steps. After I had entered the living room, the first thing to catch my attention was a light bulb hanging from the ceiling with a fly-speckled string dangling from its fixture. I watched curiously as Dad pulled down on the string once to turn on the light, and then pulled on it a second time to turn off the light. I stood mystified, never having seen an electric light operated by a dangling string. "We got 'lectric fer shore," Dad said.

I gazed at the design of the ragged wallpaper on the living room walls and the worn linoleum on the floors, realizing after a moment that both were identical to the wallpaper and floor covering at our house on the ridge. The living room had only a single window with no screen. After noting the three doors leading from the living room into the other rooms, I stepped to my left and looked into a small room that looked as though there was barely room enough for twin beds to fit inside. A cracked window graced the tiny room. The floor, made from six- to eight-inch-wide boards, was bare.

When I turned to begin exploring the other rooms, my father grabbed at me, muttering, "You can pick your bedroom 'fore anybody else does." I looked around and couldn't see my brothers anywhere, so I brushed past my father without commenting. Noticing that each bedroom had two open doorways with no doors, and afraid I could get trapped inside one of the rooms by my father, I ran through an entrance on one side of each room and then immediately exited the room into the next room. Little did I know that having no door for my bedroom would become a major problem for me.

I hurried out of the third bedroom and realized I must be in the room meant to be the dining room. I glanced around hurriedly and noticed that the room had three separate doorways—one exiting into the living room, another into a bedroom, and the third into a small kitchen, where I was quickly heading in search of my brothers.

I rapidly entered and exited the small kitchen and then found myself alone on a small deck. The deck's floorboards had rotted in places, leaving holes big enough to step through. I noticed four open boxes, filled with housewares, stacked on the plank banister on the backside of the deck. I realized that the intruding family had not removed all their belongings after all.

I looked around for my brothers and, seeing no one in sight, stepped near the edge of the porch so I could flee should the need arise. Looking around at the majestic mountains, the small parcel of bottom-land, and the inviting rustling brook nearby, I believed we would finally have more of an opportunity to see how the rest of the world functioned. The thought entered my mind that my hard-working and neglected mother would be pleased with the new property. I wondered how she would adapt to having the luxuries of electricity, plenty of water, and all the extra room for our ever-growing family, especially since baby number twelve was due any day. I couldn't wait to tell her all about the improvements she would soon be enjoying.

Curious, I looked back down the road about 500 yards at a house perched precariously on the side of a steep mountain. Having a neighbor living so close, especially a neighbor who wasn't our kin, would probably be awkward for a while. Just as I was wondering whether there would be anyone my age at the neighbor's house, I shivered as I noticed my father approaching. Looking very pleased, he stepped onto the deck and asked, "What'cha thank 'bout da house?"

Nervously, I smiled and told him I could hardly wait to get moved. I wondered whether he was truly interested in how I felt or was just trying to get close enough to trap me. My heart was palpitating, and I was prepared to jump off the deck and run should he move any closer, but before he had a chance to say or do anything further, my brothers appeared and began walking up the rotting wooden steps near where I was standing. I did not like having to avoid my father, but I knew, and I believe he must have known, that his own actions were responsible for my mistrust of him.

I was shocked when Dad looked over at Marvin and said, "I've borried [borrowed] a truck so's we can move tamarr, an' I want chu'n Maynard ta stay over here'n make shore nobody don't do nothin' ta 'his house." He told them he would return early the next morning with a load of our belongings and would then take one of them back with him to help with the moving.

Panic swept over me! "What have I gotten myself into now?" I asked myself. I wished I had listened to my mother and stayed home. I immediately realized that Dad had been scheming all along for us to be alone on the long drive back home. Even though I wanted to tell Mom about the house, I would have to try to get out of being in the car alone with my father. I suspected I already knew what his reply would be; nevertheless, I asked, "Daddy, can't I stay here 'ith Marvin an' Maynard tonight?"

"No! You know you cain't stay 'ith 'hese boys," he snapped. "Git in 'his car right 'his minute!"

Marvin apparently was feeling the same uneasiness I was, so he interjected and asked Dad for permission for either himself or Maynard to return home while the other stayed to "guard" the empty house. Naturally, Dad quickly rejected his idea. "All of you heared what I said," my cunning father said sternly. "Git in 'his car, Bethel!"

Obediently, I hurried over to get in the back seat. "You git up here in'na front seat 'ith me," Dad said. Knowing better than to defy him, I crawled onto the front seat and moved tightly against the passenger door, realizing that my well-being was in God's hands.

Dad started up the car and headed down the road for the ridge. My stomach felt queasy. Trembling from the unknown, I wondered whether I had indeed brought this situation on myself by ignoring my mother and insisting that I come along on the trip.

We had sped out of the hollow and through town before I realized I was not enjoying the ride like I had on the way to our new residence. I had hardly seen a thing, even though I had been staring out the window all the way. Dad had hardly spoken a word; still, I feared what lay ahead.

Once we were on the ridge road again, I realized we would be passing only two residences before arriving at our own house. If Dad had set a trap for me, then he would have to spring it soon. "Maybe he's so excited about moving that he'll drive straight home in order to help Mom ready everything for moving," I thought, reminding myself to trust God for my safety.

The big car labored up the steep hill until we reached a treacherous section of the road that was difficult to maneuver around without the underside of the car dragging across large, jagged rocks that protruded above the road's surface. People in the area referred to this section of the ridge road as "The Rocks." The area was isolated, with no one living within a mile or more in either direction. The road had been cut into the side of the mountain on the left side, leaving a four-foot, vertical earthen wall that graduated back into the looming mountain range. On the right side of the road, the terrain dropped suddenly into the hollow where my grandma lived.

My body stiffened when Dad slowed the car to a crawl and steered it to the very edge of the steep drop-off to my right. Realizing he was a careful driver and would never have driven this close to the edge of the road unless he had intended to, I became even more terrified.

I pulled myself even tighter against the door as my father abruptly brought the car to a dead stop, looked over at me, and began making suggestions like he had done so many times before. I looked at the door, knowing I had no way to escape from the car. "Oh, my Lord! I am trapped!" I frantically reminded God.

Breathing rapidly, my father reached for me as I clung to the door. "Hain't no way you kin git away from me 'his time," he boasted. "You might'uz well give me what b'longs ta me anyhow."

The very thought of my own father saying such repulsive things to me was almost more than I could stand. "You'll hafta kill me 'cause I ain't givin' in ta you," I said tearfully.

"Now you know 'hat you love your poor ol' daddy," he said.

"I don't love you! I hate you!" I screamed, every fiber in my body resisting his filthy suggestions. "If you lay a finger on me, 'hen God will strike you dead."

"You're the one 'at God'll strike dead fer sassin' your daddy," he said, laughing and still trying to grope my body.

I felt completely bewildered as I realized that nothing I could say or do would discourage my father's actions. I began sobbing hysterically when he reached over and grabbed me by the shoulder. With the car windows rolled down, I held onto the door with all my might. He jerked at me violently, forcing me to lose my grip on the door.

Shifting his body to the center of the car's long seat, he began groping for my underwear. I pushed myself even tighter onto the seat as I screamed in terror, "Help! Somebody help me!" I knew that we were too far from any houses for anybody to hear my cries for help, yet with all my strength I yelled again.

"You open your mouth ag'in ta yell an' I'll choke ye ta death!" he said angrily.

With him trying to push me down on the seat on my back, and with me resisting with every ounce of strength within my body, I screamed, "Kill me! Jist go ahead'n kill me! I'd be better off dead!"

Suddenly, the thought entered my mind that I had vowed to trust God to get me home without any harm coming to me, so I wondered where God was and why He wasn't helping me. "Oh, God! Please help me!" I cried out. Immediately, I was able to free myself enough to look out over the hood of the car, and, to my surprise, someone was walking down the road toward us. "Look!" I screamed. "There's a man comin' down the road!" I did not recognize the man, but there was no doubt that he was the biggest man I had ever seen.

Dad was still yanking at my underclothes, and I was still fighting. "There's somebody comin', an' if you don't turn me loose right this minute, I'm gonna tell 'im what you're tryin' to do to me!" I said in desperation.

Seemingly startled, my father quickly looked up, then with more haste than when he had first grabbed me, he released his hold on me. He scurried back beneath the steering wheel and rushed to start the car's engine. "When 'hat man gits closer, I'm gonna tell 'im why you stopped the car," I said angrily and tearfully, staring straight at my dad.

Squinting his eyes, pursing his lips, and with a trembling voice, he said, "You do an' I swear ta God I'll run 'is here car over 'is here hill an' kill us both." I realized that I was trapped again. I didn't know whether he would carry out the threat or not, but I felt that I had no choice but to stay silent. I didn't care if he did kill me, but Mom and the rest of the family needed him.

Looking again at the man, I was totally surprised when I recognized him to be one of the teenage boys who lived in the house just a mile ahead. He didn't look nearly as big as he had when I'd first seen him coming down the road. I wondered whether Dad had seen him when he'd looked to be seven feet tall. Trembling from exhaustion, I slid down in the seat and tried to hide, feeling ashamed and hopeless.

"Howdy, Chilton," I heard my father say nervously as the young man passed by.

As the young man returned Dad's greeting, my frustrated father pulled the Pontiac back into the car tracks as though nothing out of the ordinary had happened. I sat stooped forward, cowering against the passenger's door and holding my dress tail below my knees while I shivered in the August heat and whimpered softly. All I could think about was how close I'd come again to being raped by this man I called "Daddy."

While Dad continued driving back to our home in silence, my emotions ranged from fright to anger to disappointment. I was scared of my father, angry at myself for getting into this situation, and disappointed with God for not helping me. I no longer had the happy feeling I had experienced earlier when I'd seen the house. If Mom wanted to know what the house looked like, then she would have to ask Dad about it. At this moment, I despised the thought of the house, my mother, my father, and especially myself, who seemed unimportant to anyone—including God.

My father and I arrived home without further incident. My face was tear stained, my eyes and nostrils swollen from crying. Mom didn't bother to ask me about the house, why Marvin and Maynard had been left behind, or why I had been crying. I wondered whether she thought that, should she ask me any questions, I might tell her more than she wanted to hear.

Darkness soon moved in, and as I lay in bed surrounded by my sister and three little brothers, I attempted to pray. Still feeling disappointed because God was allowing my father to continue with his reprehensible actions toward me, and my mother to withhold the support and intervention I so desperately needed, I reminded God that I had committed myself into His hands—only to have Him fail me again. "What have I done to cause You to forsake me?" I asked Him silently. Once again, there seemed to be no answer. "I wish I had never been born," I said aloud.

Feeling both helpless and hopeless, I began thinking about the threat Dad had made to kill us both. I wondered what would happen to Mom and all the kids should Dad not be around to support them. Wrestling with my agony and finding no answers to any of my questions, I lay in silence in the dark room and cried myself to sleep.

Sometime during the night, I was awakened when one of the boys wet the bed, soaking my clothing. I made my way out of bed and felt my way over to the bed Marvin and Maynard had been sharing since Woody had left home to work in Cleveland, Ohio. I pushed the top sheet up under the wet place on my dress and then curled up all by myself. I wondered why I hadn't thought of sleeping in the empty bed when I'd retired earlier.

Unable to fall asleep, my thoughts shifted to my brothers. I wondered how they were faring in the empty house with not even a blanket to curl up on. I began to feel guilty for crawling into their bed. I also was feeling remorseful over my disappointment with God. Now that I was thinking more clearly than when I'd first gone to bed, I started praying again. I asked God to forgive me and to help me to learn how to really trust in Him. Almost immediately, I sensed the warm comforting feeling I had experienced on other occasions. I wondered how I could have missed it. God hadn't forsaken me—He had been there with me all along. I realized that He had timed it perfectly when He'd sent the neighbor boy on the walk down the ridge road.

It was all finally very clear in my mind. I started to cry again when I heard myself say, "He was right there keeping me safe all along." Feeling a new surge of hope, I listened to the wind that had suddenly begun whistling around the corner of the house. I imagined that God was riding upon the wind, so I curled up in His arms and went fast to sleep.

LIII

Electricity

The next morning, I jumped out of bed and ran into the kitchen. Breakfast was ready and spread out on the big table. "What's Marvin and Maynard gonna do for breakfast'?" I asked. Nobody answered my question, so I asked the question again in a louder voice.

"Tain't gonna hurt 'em boys ta miss breakfas'," Dad said grumpily. I felt sad being able to sit down at the breakfast table while my brothers were waking up on the bare floor with nothing in the house to eat; nevertheless, I swiped my biscuit through the lake of red Karo syrup and fresh churned butter that I'd just mixed together in my plate. Cramming the big hunk of bread and syrup into my mouth, I looked over at my father and then at my mother. Dad was busy breaking the crust off one of the over-sized biscuits to soak in his bowl of coffee. My mother was taking the dishes out of the cabinet and piling them inside one of the washtubs she had brought into the house. Both she and Dad seemed oblivious to my concerns.

I tried to eat the food on my plate, but the bread seemed to stick in my throat. I wondered what was going to happen to me. Was God really going to get me out of this mess I had been fighting for the past six years, or was I going to somehow die trying to protect myself from being violated by my father? I was startled when I realized what I had been thinking, and I wondered why my faith had wavered once again. I felt I had no choice but to push my concerns aside and to act as if my young life was normal.

Dad soon left to retrieve the truck he had borrowed to move our few possessions. Although she was hardly able to walk because of swelling in her legs and feet, Mom was busily packing clothing between dishes, jars of food, and other breakables. I was ashamed of myself for having had bad feelings about her the night before. Apparently, she could see no way to help me without hurting herself, so I decided she was doing what she thought was best.

When Dad arrived with the truck, he and I began loading the lighter pieces of furniture and items. I was almost fifteen years old and could lift almost as much as any male my age could lift. Once the truck was loaded, Arnold and Nina rode in the cab with Dad so they could stay at the log house while Marvin and Maynard accompanied Dad on his return trip to help load the heavier pieces of furniture.

Mom and I had been left behind with my four younger siblings to make ready the household goods for the second truckload. Mom was expecting baby number twelve later in the month, but she continued her pace even though she could hardly bend over. Dad hadn't given her much advance notice that the move was going to take place; still, he expected everything to be packed by the time he was ready to load it.

When Dad returned, Marvin and Maynard were riding on the back of the truck. They wasted no time in running to the kitchen table, where they each grabbed one of Mom's big, cold biscuits that I had spread with sugar and butter and laid aside for them. They didn't ask about my ride home with Dad the night before, and, again, I didn't volunteer any information.

The cattle rack on the bed of the three-quarter-ton truck made it possible to stack and haul the remaining goods needing to be moved. Marvin and Maynard jumped up on the back of the truck without asking for anything else to eat. Dad asked me whether I wanted to ride with him in the cab. "Is Mommy going now or later when you come back with the car?" I asked.

"What diff'rence 'zit make?" he asked.

Mom quickly spoke up and informed us that she didn't want to ride in the truck since it would be uncomfortable traveling over the rough roads. I sighed in relief and immediately told Dad that I would wait with Mom until he returned with the car. Mom no doubt knew that I was more concerned about my own welfare than I was about going for help, should she go into labor.

When Dad finally returned with the car, we drove away from the little farm, none of us turning to look back at the place we had called home for the past seven years. I, for one, was glad to be leaving the place and all the unpleasant experiences I'd had there. Little did I know that I would carry those memories for the remainder of my life, and, tragically, I had no idea that the place where we were moving would become even more of a nightmare.

I watched Mom's reaction once we had arrived at the new property and noticed that she'd looked over at the house stonily, without uttering a word. Before we crossed the shallow stream between the house and where our car was parked, I looked up to see two women and a young girl walking from the house in our direction. One of the ladies looked a little older than my mother and was wearing a pair of men's dress shoes. The younger woman and girl were carrying the boxes I had seen on the back porch the night before. Mom greeted the women as they hurried past, but the only comment from the women was when the older lady said to her married daughter, "They hain't gonna hur' chu." We later learned that the older lady lived in the house just 500 feet down the road from our place, and her daughter was our closest neighbor in the opposite direction.

While Mom and I continued walking toward the house, she remained silent, apparently feeling the same way I was. We knew that although the location may have changed, the circumstances would probably remain the same.

At the end of the day, my sister, three youngest brothers, and I lay in bed in the bedroom at the opposite end of the living room from where our parents' bedroom was located. There was no way I could have predicted the miseries that sleeping in this small room would eventually bring to me.

On Monday, an employee from Appalachian Power came to our house to read the meter. From the questions my mother was asking, he must have determined that she had never lived in a house equipped with electricity. After he had answered some of her questions, he escorted her into the kitchen, where he showed her the fuse box on the wall behind the kitchen door. Opening the control-box cover, he slowly explained the fuses and their functions. Noticing that one of the glass fuses had been unscrewed and was missing, Mom asked, as she moved her extended index finger toward the empty socket, "Why hain't 'hey anythang in 'is here hole?"

Grabbing Mom's hand and nudging her away from the box, the electrician replied excitedly, "Lady! You better be careful where you're stickin' your finger!" I shivered as he continued, "You can get yourself electrocuted that way!"

After the electrician had left, Mom turned her attention to the used refrigerator that Dad had delivered earlier during the morning. She wanted to know how to form ice in the ice trays. Having had some experience with electricity at a few overnight stays with one of my school teachers, I was able to explain to Mom that she need only put water in the trays and place them in the freezer compartment to freeze. I was intrigued to know that my mother, at the age of thirty-eight, had no inkling about how to use electrical appliances. I suspected we were in for some hair-raising experiences.

The used refrigerator looked very old and stood on legs about ten inches high; nevertheless, our family was finding it to be a welcome addition to our home. Later in the evening when Dad came home from work, he brought a whole pre-cooked ham to "store" inside the refrigerator. He explained that he had seen a picture in a magazine at the bus garage of a big ham stored inside a refrigerator. "Hit looked so good 'at I jist figgered I'd git one of 'em mouth-waterin' thangs to put in ourn," he said, grinning sheepishly.

It was two or three days before Mom could coax Dad to allow her to serve a few slices of the ham. Once the family had sampled the meat, which was our first time tasting store-bought ham, it was soon devoured, and never again did Dad bring home another ham to enhance the interior of our refrigerator.

Since our family couldn't afford to buy an electric washing machine, we had to continue using the gasoline-powered washer. At least we now had enough water so that Mom or I could do the laundry as often as needed. Although we had no running water and still had to carry our potable water from the well, I felt that life would be a lot easier than it had been on the ridge.

My mother and my preschool siblings were all amazed and intrigued by the bright light the naked light bulbs radiated throughout the rooms. "I wonder how in'na worl' we ever seed by usin' 'hem oil lamps," Mom mused aloud, to nobody in particular. The children were finding the fact that they could have light by merely pulling on a string to be an unusual and fascinating experience. On several occasions they had to be reprimanded for climbing onto chairs so they could flick the light on and off.

All our clothing had to be ironed since "drip-dry" clothing had not come into existence. A few days after we had moved up the long hollow, one of our neighbors came for a visit shortly after I had spread a blanket on the dining table and begun ironing the huge pile of freshly laundered clothes I had just carried in from the clothesline. I was using the gasoline-powered iron that Mom had bought with my first payday. After watching me refill the iron with gasoline, the neighbor lady kindly suggested that I go home with her and borrow her electric iron to finish the job.

Once I had returned with the iron, I discovered that the only outlet in the entire house, apart from the one behind the refrigerator, was located on the porcelain light fixture in the middle of the living room ceiling. Having no ironing board or table that I could readily move closer to the socket, I made myself a makeshift ironing board by placing two ladder-back chairs beneath the light socket. Turning the chairs back to back about four feet apart, I then laid a wood plank, five feet long and one foot wide, which I'd found inside one of the outbuildings, across the lower slats of the backs of the chairs. To prevent the chairs from tipping over, I piled a few heavy objects onto the chair bottoms. I then covered the plank with the folded blanket I had been using on the table. Mom seemed much more impressed with the electric iron than she was with my ironing board, so I wasn't surprised when she soon pushed me to the side and finished ironing the basket of clothing in record time.

When Dad arrived home from work, Mom petitioned him for her own electric iron. "I figgered 'at when you got 'is here 'lectric, you'd star'chur naggin'," he said impatiently. "I jist bought chu 'hat 'frigator an' now you're already wantin' a 'lectric arn." Mom continued to borrow Mrs. Belcher's iron until, weeks later, she was able to buy her own electric iron.

Now that we had moved closer to civilization, our groceries could, once each month, be delivered to our front yard. On his first trip to our house, the delivery man stopped and asked a man who lived at the mouth of the hollow for directions to our place. After following the directions he had received and having been assured that he indeed was at the Leshers' residence, the driver explained with amusement how he had found our place. "I was told to keep on goin' 'til I came to a place 'at looked like school'd just let out, an' then I'd know 'at I had the right family," he said. He laughed as he looked over at my siblings, who were running around whooping and yelling like little Indians, and said, "Them directions was purty ac'rut."

My little brothers soon found the creek that ran alongside our house to contain all sorts of adventure. They especially enjoyed wading in the water and peering under rocks for "crawldabbers" (crawfish). On several occasions, the youngest boys would come screaming to me with the crawfishes' claws locked onto their fingers. After I had removed the angry crawfishes from my little brothers' fingers, they would run right back to the creek for the unnerving incident to happen once again.

"Fix me a fishin' pole!" was the cry I heard, day after day. I, as their big sister, would bend straight pins into curved hooks and tie them with pieces of twine to the slender branches my little brothers had brought to me. Fishing for minnows in the shallow water holes would keep the active little boys occupied for hours. Splashing each other in the creek was much more enjoyable and a whole lot cleaner than playing in the red-clay mud or dust they had played in while living on the ridge. The Saturday night bath had become a thing of the past during summertime. As a matter of fact, I had never seen my little brothers looking so happy—and so clean.

LIV

The Owl and the Knight

I realized that I had been naive to think my father had come to his senses and would not subject me to his dreaded actions again now that we lived closer to society. To my horror, I soon learned that Dad had stooped to a new low. Although it had seemed for a couple of weeks that my concerns were over, I was still avoiding being alone with my father.

With no doors on any of the bedrooms, none of us could be assured of our privacy at night. I slept on the front edge of our bed, with my sister and three little brothers sleeping behind me. The head of my bed sat against the wall that divided the bedroom from the living room, and, besides the doorway between the living room and my bedroom, there was an additional doorway on the left side of the small room that led into my older brothers' bedroom.

A couple of weeks after we had moved to the area, I was awakened suddenly one night from a deep sleep. I lay there in my bed wondering what had roused me. No lights were left burning inside the house at night, and the outside light was always extinguished at bedtime. On this particular night, there was no moonlight, which sometimes illuminated our rooms. I listened, expecting to hear one of the children whimpering or begging for a drink of water. All I could hear, however, was the lonesome call of an owl coming from somewhere outside my bedroom window.

I lay there listening to the mournful sound of the owl, telling myself that the call of the bird was responsible for disturbing me. Since I could hear nothing other than the deep, even breathing of the little ones who lay sleeping beside me, I turned onto my side and tried to go back to sleep.

Suddenly, I again became alert when I heard the floorboards creaking directly on the other side of the wall that separated the living room and my bedroom. I knew that someone had to be slipping across the floor in the middle of night, and from the direction of the sound I doubted it was either of my older brothers, who were sleeping in the adjoining bedroom.

Cowering on the edge of my bed, I waited anxiously, hoping that the noise would either stop or that the intruder would make himself known. It didn't dawn on me that someone from outside the house could have entered through the unlocked door. I had never been concerned about an unknown person from the outside coming into the house at night, and up until this time in my young life, I hadn't worried about anyone from inside our house approaching my bed either. "It's got to be one of the family members up prowling around, and I pray to God that it's not the one I think it is," I thought to myself. Almost before I'd finished the thought, a chill ran down my spine as the creaking boards became silent very close to my bed.

I didn't want to believe what I knew was about to happen, but I recognized my father's familiar heavy breathing. Panic engulfed me when I felt him run his hand underneath the covers. There was no way he had come into the room with anything on his mind other than to see how far he could go before I would stop him. "Oh, my God, my God!" I cried out. "Get outta here, Daddy, and keep your hands off'n my body!" I began flailing my arms and legs and yelling loudly. I wanted Mom and the whole family to hear what was taking place. I thought that if my father knew that Mom and the rest of the family were aware of what he was attempting to do, he would be too ashamed and afraid to carry out his apparent plan. Anger and disgust filled my soul as I realized the implications of what he must have on his mind. I wondered how in the name of all decency my own father could think that I would lie there and allow him to do whatever he was intending to do. "When will this ever end?" I asked aloud.

Although I'd gotten no response from my cries for help, I felt him pull his hand from underneath the covers. I sighed with relief when I heard him stumble into the living room. With God's help, I'd always been able to defend myself against my father during the daylight hours, but I shivered at the realization that I would now have to be on guard against being assaulted after I'd gone to bed. Although he had swiftly left my bedside on his first nighttime visit, I felt certain that he would be back.

The nerves in my stomach were tied in knots as I lay there on my bed, wondering why none of the family had bothered to investigate why I had yelled. In my heart, however, I knew that, since they had each apparently become accustomed to my screams for help during the daylight hours, hearing my screams in the middle of the night was of no more concern to them. I listened for Mom to question Dad since he had apparently returned to their room, but the only noise I could hear was the sound of my own muffled sobbing.

The call of the owl had ceased, and I lay there in the dark room, sobbing and too afraid to go back to sleep. I couldn't understand why, if God had known that my father was going to take his abuse to this new low, He had allowed it to happen; however, I was thankful that I'd been kept safe, yet again.

The next morning, as soon as my siblings and I were allowed to get out of bed to eat our breakfast, the first thing I had to know was why Mom and my brothers had ignored my cries during the night. Dad had left earlier for work, and Mom had gotten up to fix his breakfast and pack his lunch. I doubted that she had confronted him about the matter at that time. She seemed to be avoiding me and failed to look up from what she was doing when I asked, "Didn't you hear me screamin' last night?"

"Yell, I heared you," she replied. "But jist what'd you thank I could do 'bout it?"

I slammed down the pot of coffee I was holding and ran from the room in tears. I wondered why I had even bothered to ask the question in the first place. As always, it was apparent that I wouldn't get any help from my family. Once again, I realized that the only thing I could do was to try to act as though my life was normal. I knew that I belonged to God and that I had been praying daily for Him to protect me from my father's abuse, so I determined in my heart that, somehow, my request would be granted.

Fishing had become a favorite pastime for my father. Since we'd moved, he had spent every Sunday at the river, presumably alone. Near the end of the first month at our new residence, Mom announced on Sunday morning that she was going fishing with Dad. Although the baby was overdue, Mom said to me, "Me'n Daddy're goin' fishin' by 'urselves. I need ta git outta the house fer a spell." It was the first time I could remember Mom going fishing, and I was surprised that Dad had asked her to go with him.

I looked at Mom walking to the car by Dad's side. I couldn't help but contemplate my mom's situation: she was nine months pregnant; her feet and legs were swollen to almost twice their normal size; at the age of thirty-eight she was the mother of eleven children; and her husband was always flirting with other women and, even worse, constantly trying to molest his own daughter. Still, she wanted to get away by being with the man responsible for most of her woes. I walked inside the house wondering aloud, "How can one person be so stupid?"

Later in the day, Woody drove into the yard with Mary, his girlfriend. Once they had walked inside our house and was surprised not to find Mom at home, Woody asked, "Dad didn't have to take Mommy to the hospital, did he?"

"No. If you can believe it, they went fishin'," I said, leaving him even more surprised.

"Well, I came to tell them that me an' Mary're gonna get married," he said.

I rounded up my siblings I was babysitting and began sauntering up the road with my big brother and his sweetheart. After walking about half a mile without seeing anyone or any houses, we began lazily winding our way back to the house. While Woody and I were seeing which of us could kick a golf-ball-sized stone the farthest without it leaving the roadway, he finally began explaining that he had quit his job in Ohio and would be joining the Air Force once he was married.

When we rounded the curve near our driveway, I was surprised to come face-to-face with my brother Marvin and a tall, handsome guy I'd never seen. Marvin stopped and introduced his new friend, Bill, to Woody and me. I stared at Bill, my heart skipping a beat when his eyes met mine. Without further conversation, he and Marvin continued walking up the road while the rest of us drifted toward our house. Apparently noticing the stars in my eyes, Woody asked me what I thought of Marvin's new friend. I laughed and said, "You want to know what I think about him? Well, I think he's the knight in shining armor I've been dreamin' about."

Woody laughed and, after giving me a little kick on the backside, said, "You sure do believe that, don't you, Sister?"

"Just you wait'n see," I answered. "I'll marry that guy someday." Everyone laughed except me. In my heart I already knew that I was dead serious. Something had stirred deep within my soul, and I knew at that moment that God was assuring me that Bill was going to be the mate He was preparing for me.

We hadn't been back to the house more than five minutes when Dad's car came speeding up the driveway. All of us watched as Dad ran over and opened Mom's door, took her by her hand, and began helping her toward the house.

"What's wrong 'ith Mommy?" I asked, watching her hobbling inside through the living room door.

"Git outta our way! She's 'bout ta have the baby!" Dad said frantically. I soon learned that the doctor had been called and that my unnerved father, since we had no telephone, would be leaving immediately to fetch one of Mom's lady friends who had volunteered to help with the delivery.

I started to sneak outside with my siblings when Dad ordered Woody to take them up the road until after the baby was born. "You git'chur rear-en' back in here'n' stay 'ith Marthy 'til 'at doctor gits here," Dad yelled to me.

I walked obediently back inside and headed for the corner of the house farthest away from Mom's bed. I yelled back to my mother, who was moaning with every breath, and said, "If you need me, you'll have to come'n get me!" I was almost fifteen years old and knew exactly nothing about childbirth.

Within twenty minutes, Dad returned with Mom's friend, and once she had discovered that I was in the house, she yelled to me, "Git a far [fire] starded'n git some wadder [water] on ta boil. 'Hen, you git me some clean towels er rags."

Frantically, I grabbed some towels and rags and threw them into the living room, where the delivery bed had been set up earlier. I hurried into the kitchen and loaded the stove with dry wood, since we were still using the wood-burning stove. Grabbing a nearby can of kerosene, I sloshed it over the wood, replaced the burner caps, and struck a match, setting it inside the opened fire-box door to light the sticks of firewood. Once the wood had kindled, I removed the front burner cap and placed a teakettle of water directly over the fire. The doctor arrived just as I ran for the back bedroom again.

With Mom's moans becoming louder, all I could think about was to get as far away from the situation as possible. Unnerved by the sounds, I looked at the window and wondered whether I could crawl outside without hanging myself. I soon realized, however, the futility of trying to escape what was a normal event that I too might experience someday. Not knowing from the sounds whether or not the birthing was proceeding normally, I forced myself, as my anxiety intensified, to stay in the bedroom to await the baby's arrival.

"Push! Push, Mrs. Lesher! Push!" I heard the doctor say. I wondered what he was telling my mother to push. Wringing my hands, which were wet with perspiration, I tried to muffle the disturbing sounds Mom was making as I quickly bowed my head in prayer and asked God to please take care of Mom and the baby, and to help the baby to be delivered quickly. After praying, I felt more at ease, so I moved closer to the living room, staying out of sight of Mom's bed. Finally, I was overjoyed to hear Mrs. Taylor (unrelated to the midwife) calling out to me to come and hold the newborn infant. "Is it all over?" I asked as I reached through the doorway into the living room to take the baby from Mrs. Taylor's arms.

"Yell, it's all over with," Mrs. Taylor said. "Your mom an' the baby're doin' good, an' your daddy went to bury the afterbirth."

"My goodness! You sure are a heavy little bugger," I said to the baby as I sat down in a chair and unwrapped the towel from around baby number twelve. "Thank you, God," I said, looking down at the plump little butterball that had weighed in at eleven pounds. I carefully checked all the newborn's body parts and discovered that I was holding another brother. Feeling exhausted, I wondered whether my baby brother's birth hadn't been harder on me than it had been on my mom.

Mrs. Taylor came into the room and took the baby from my arms. I watched as she washed his little body, pinned the tight belly-band around his abdomen, and dusted baby powder over his buttocks. Then she dressed him in a new, fresh-smelling kimono and pinned a cloth Birdseye diaper on him. She handed the baby to my mother and then watched as Mom wrapped him in a receiving blanket and, after kissing the top of his head, placed him under the sheet, close to her own body.

After the doctor was gone and Dad had left to take Mrs. Taylor back to her own home, Mom informed me that I would have to clean up the mess remaining from the birthing. "You'll hafta warsh 'em thangs fer me," Mom said to me as she pointed at a roll of bed linens.

I obediently picked up the soiled linens and walked outside, crossing over the brook in front of the building that housed our washing machine. Once I had carried water from the creek and filled the gasoline-powered washing machine, I unrolled the articles to be washed. "No way! No how!" I yelled, as I began running to the house. "I can't warsh 'em clothes," I yelled, as I ran into the room where Mom was lying in bed with the baby. "I'm gonna bury 'em!"

I must have looked as ill as I felt because Mom looked at me and asked, "What in'na worl'za matter 'ith you?"

"There's no way I can warsh 'em filthy bed clothes." I blurted out.

"Them thangs has ta be warshed," Mom said firmly. "If you'll warsh 'em fer me, when I git able ta go ta town, I'll buy you the purdiest dress I can fin'."

I knew that Mom probably had no intention of buying a dress for me. Her statement was merely a way of informing me that I was being required to wash the sheets and blankets, regardless of my sensitive gag reflex. "I'll try," I managed to whisper. "But I'm tellin' you right now, you better not ask me to do anything like this again," I wailed.

"You take keera me 'is las' time, an' when you git married and go ta have a baby, I'll come an' take good keera you, an' I'll do alla your work," she said.

I returned to the laundry and knelt on the floor, where I began asking God to give me the strength to finish the job I had been ordered to do. "I've been relying on You a lot lately, and here I am once again," I said aloud. I didn't know it at the time, but I was learning to trust God to help me through all kinds of trials and circumstances, no matter how significant or trivial they seemed.

After the bed linens had agitated for a while, I had to reach down inside the washer's tub and pull them out of the dirty water, where I guided them through the hand-cranked wringers into a tub of rinse water. After running the articles through the wringers for the last time, I carried them to the clothesline and hung them out to dry. I then returned to the house, where I immediately took over Mom's household chores for the next nine days. I hadn't learned a thing about birthing, but I had learned that, should I ever get married and have a baby, one thing was certain: I was determined to have the baby in the hospital where the staff could clean up the mess.

LV

No More School

August had sped by in our new world, and it was now time to get things ready for another school term. The two-room country school would certainly be an experience for the younger children. The larger room housed the children from the first through the fourth grades, while the fifth through the eighth grades occupied the smaller room. Students placed their coats in a small closet we called the Cloak Room.

Once most of the local students had made it through the eighth grade, there seemed, as far as their parents and the children were concerned, to be no further need of schooling. Rarely did any of the parents send their children into town to attend high school. If a student elected to go on to high school, he had to furnish his own transportation. The law at the time was this: if the student had to walk more than three miles to school because he or she had no means of transportation, then the student could not be required to attend school (at least, that was my parents' understanding). Most of the students were fifteen years old by the time they had finished the eighth grade and could no longer be legally required to attend school.

When Marvin, who was now a junior, inquired about transportation that would enable him to continue his education at the high school in town (now about five miles from our house), Dad explained that he could ride with him each morning at 5:30 when he drove to the school bus garage. "You'll hafta wait at'ta school fer classes ta start," he said. He also informed Marvin that he might be able to get a job at school doing janitorial work before and after school. Dad continued, "You can ride back home 'ith me in'na evenin' after I've made my runs." Marvin indeed was blessed with the job at the school, working as the janitor's helper.

Dad informed me that I would not be allowed to return to school. I would be fifteen in October and would have entered the ninth grade. I had known all along that I probably would have to drop out of school after I'd reached my sixteenth birthday, but I had counted on being able to finish the ninth grade. Dad and Mom agreed that I had received all the education I would be needing. "Don't take no edgycation ta pin dydees (diapers) on no baby," Dad said. As I pondered the situation, I assured myself that, although my classroom schooling might be over, I would have a lifetime to expand my knowledge.

My elementary-age siblings walked to the country school every morning and back home in the afternoons. They had no problem adjusting and made friends very easily, especially since all their classmates lived in the immediate area. Out of curiosity, I visited the school a few times and sat in the fifth-through-eighth-grade room. I was amazed at the conduct of the teacher and his students compared to that in the school in town where I had attended. After an hour of observing, I understood why there was a lack of respect for the country teacher, especially since the teacher seemingly had no respect for himself or for his students.

When one of the boys ignored the teacher's command, the teacher, his jaw loaded with a big wad of chewing tobacco, grabbed an eraser from the blackboard, drew back his arm, and threw the eraser, hitting the boy directly between the eyes. Another example that troubled me was when a young girl was called in front of the class to read a story. When she could not pronounce a word in the sentence she was reading, the teacher said to her, "Just call it 'dog' or 'cat,' and go on." She merely ignored the word and finished reading the story.

I left the school in the afternoon concerned that, once my brothers and sister had finished the eighth grade, they would not be equipped academically to advance to the high school in town. When I told my parents about the incidents I had observed, their only response was to laugh about the matter. "I always heared 'at 'hat teacher was like 'hat," Dad had said.

Mom had been to town several times since Larry's birth and had apparently forgotten the promise she had made to buy me a new dress. She had bought school clothes for all my siblings, but since I wasn't in school any longer, I didn't as much as receive a new pair of socks. I knew I'd never get the dress Mom had promised me, and I really had never expected her to buy the dress. It did concern me, however, that my mother could break a promise she had made, without a word of explanation or a sign of remorse.

On one of her trips to buy groceries, she brought home a portion of a stick of bologna and placed it in the refrigerator. Later in the day she cut the bologna into bite-sized chunks, fried the chunks, and then made brown gravy from the drippings and poured it over the bologna. The dish of bologna and gravy was very tasty, so the next time Mom started to town for groceries, I asked her to buy more bologna. After having asked on several occasions and receiving no response, I caught her just as she was walking out the door. Once again I asked, "Mommy, since you couldn' git me the dress you promised me, will you please bring me a few slices of b'loney?"

She scowled at me and said sarcastically, "I'll brang you some b'loney 'fore you have a baby borned with a ball a b'loney on its nose!"

Hurt and humiliated by her statement, I ran from the room in tears, wondering whether my mother was insinuating that I could be pregnant. After she and Dad were on their way to town, I couldn't get the thought out of my mind that she might have been inferring that my father had impregnated me. I was horrified at the thought and couldn't understand how my mother could be so heartless. She knew how hard I had always fought against my father's actions, and she had to know that I had "won" all the fights; furthermore, I had done everything possible to help make her life more comfortable. She knew I hadn't been with a boy since moving off the ridge. I had lost all interest in the guy who stole unrefined gasoline to fuel his car, after Marvin had introduced me to the young man whom I felt I would someday marry. "How can my mother be so cruel?" I cried out, as I looked up toward the heavens. "God, I've been trying to trust you. Can't You see that I need help?" I said aloud, half out of desperation and half out of anger.

When my parents returned with the groceries, I entered the kitchen to help store the food Mom had bought. When she removed a package wrapped in white butcher's paper and tossed it at me, I reached out and grabbed it as she said gruffly, "Git chu a slice of 'hat b'loney, but don't chu let 'em other kids see it."

I opened the refrigerator and tossed the bologna inside. "No, thank you," I said firmly. "I wouldn't eat it now if you tried to force it down my throat."

"Shet chur mouth talkin' ta me like 'at, young lady," she said. I walked out the back door, once again in tears.

I stood outside beneath a huge oak tree, feeling as though life had little meaning anymore. Not only was my father causing me much grief, but my mother was becoming more and more hostile toward me. I could not understand her actions. "Here I go again, Lord," I prayed. "I'm asking you to either make my life a little more bearable—or to just let me die."

After a considerable amount of time had passed, I dried my tears and walked back inside to help my mother with her chores. I was feeling sad for having sassed her, yet I could not bring myself to apologize. Once again, I didn't know what to do other than to act as though my life was normal; however, I wondered whether my life would ever be normal.

Before the day was over, I was once again accosted by my father; still, like all the many times before, I rigorously spurned his advances.

I had been attending the small church in the vicinity and had been contemplating telling the pastor about the abuse I was suffering at my father's hands. After having weighed the consequences of the good it would do for me to reveal my secret, I had decided it would be better for me to continue suffering than for our family to be subjected to the pain and humiliation that revealing the truth would cause. I knew that Mom had no way to support the family; furthermore, I loved my daddy, and I couldn't bear to see him arrested. I also had hope that maybe soon Dad would change. He had settled down a lot since we had moved and was no longer carousing with his friend.

Again I did the only thing that seemed to bring me any source of comfort. I looked up at the blue sky and cried out, "God, You know my secret, and You know I'm doing my best to trust You to get me out of this mess. Please, God, hurry up before this pain and suffering destroys my mind."

LVI

The Wonders of Television

My family heard about an invention that had recently become more readily available in our area and was already in some of the homes. It was hard to believe that a piece of furniture could bring moving pictures into a person's living room. Since my parents had always forbidden us children to attend the movies, and since Dad would never consider spending his hard-earned money on anything so expensive and unnecessary, I didn't think my family would ever own one of these black-and-white televisions. Why, we didn't even have a telephone.

When one of Dad's coworkers informed him how entertaining wrestling shows had become, it wasn't long before he started going to the friend's home to watch the programs. After viewing the wrestling matches on a few occasions, Dad would come home and excitedly tell our family about the wrestlers' performances. "I wish't 'at we could git one of 'em telly-visions so's we could see 'at 'rasslin'," he said.

Finally, after Dad had started taking Mom with him to the friend's home to watch the wrestling programs, they began to suspect after a few weeks that they were imposing on their friend's hospitality. After reluctantly limiting their visits to the coworker's home, my parents learned that a widow friend, who at one time had lived on the ridge, had married an elderly gentleman who lived in town and, coincidentally, owned a brand-new television set. I couldn't believe how social-minded my parents had become and how quickly they had renewed their friendship with Mrs. Palmer. Of course, while they were visiting with their friends, I was left at home to care for the house and the children.

A few weeks went by, and Dad's desire to own his own television set was becoming more and more evident. Mom, too, was hooked on the wrestling matches, so she readily agreed that Dad should invest in their own television set. I couldn't believe it. The man who had just weeks earlier griped about Mom's request for a new electric iron was now ready to go in debt for a new nineteen-inch black-and-white television set.

In order to get any reception, Dad and my brothers had to cut a right-of-way to the top of the hill behind our house, where they erected the antenna on a pole extending above the treetops. Once the quarter mile of antenna wire had been run down the side of the hill and inside the house and then hooked to the television set, the family members gathered around to see what had been, for the last several weeks, capturing much of our parents' time.

Dad tuned the set to the wrestling channel and settled down in his favorite chair, while Mom and a row of very excited little boys crowded onto the secondhand sofa we had acquired. The remaining siblings stretched out on their bellies across the floor. As I carried a chair from the dining room and placed it in the doorway, I looked at the crowded room, leaned over to Mom, and whispered, "We've got a bigger audience for this show than we had last Sunday in church."

The family immediately became very animated as soon as the match began; however, I was more amused by my parents' antics than I was with the wrestlers' moves. I had never seen Dad and Mom acting as though they were enjoying themselves. They were certainly taking the bouts seriously and were taking turns "killing the referees." Mom would frantically yell, "Ah shucks! Now you jist watch 'at Sonza-bitchin referee!"

"Kill'a bastard!" Dad would scream, as if he believed that his wrestler could hear his instructions.

I soon learned not to sit near my mother when one of her favorite tag teams was wrestling. Amid the excitement, she would grab the person closest her and pinch and thump him until it appeared she was part of the show herself. When Mom's hero was being thrown around the ring, or when his partner was being pinned while the referee pretended to be distracted by the wrestler on the opposing team, my mother's screams would drown out the voice of the sportscaster. I often wondered at the end of the bouts whether the boys sitting beside Mom weren't leaving the room with more bruises and battle scars than the wrestlers had received in the ring.

Only on Saturday mornings, while Mom and Dad went into town for groceries, my younger brothers and sister would be in charge of the television set, since Dad chose the programs while he was at home. *Howdy Doody, Superman,* and *The Mickey Mouse Club* were their favorites. No longer did the crawfish have to run for cover now that the children were inside huddled around this very intriguing talking box.

The Lesher family was being exposed to a way of life that none of us had realized existed. As time passed, I soon realized that I could learn a lot about the world by scanning the scenes of the programs the family was watching. I closely observed how the people dressed, walked, and even talked, and I studied the furniture in the homes and how it was arranged. I doubted that I would ever be able to dress as lavishly as the people on television, but I surmised that I might be able to learn a few social graces by observing the actions of those who knew about such things. I also studied how people acted in any given circumstance. I didn't intend to try to imitate the new class of people; I merely wanted to learn enough about how others lived and acted so I could properly function should I ever be fortunate enough to escape the confines of my small world. I knew that God was aware of how intrigued and excited I was about this new learning tool; therefore, I was trusting Him to help me to separate the good from the bad, and the correct from the incorrect.

A couple of my younger brothers enjoyed pretending to take on Superman's antics. One Saturday after the *Superman* program had concluded, the television was turned off and my little brothers went outside to play. I was sitting on the back porch changing the baby's diaper when an unforgettable incident took place. I had stretched my baby brother out on the floor and, after removing his cloth diaper, folded the soiled diaper over, and then placed it on the floor of the porch before I pinned on the clean diaper with two safety pins.

Arnold, my eleven-year-old brother, came running around the side of the house, holding his arms above his head and the palms of his hands pressed together as though he were gliding through the air. When he approached the porch, he quickly jumped up onto the porch, grabbed the soiled diaper, threw it back over his shoulders, and jumped back off the porch onto the ground. "Up, up, and away!" he yelled.

"No! No! No!" I screamed, as he jumped into the air as high as possible, landed on his feet, and disappeared around the side of the house with the diaper too wet and heavy to wave in the wind. Fortunately for my brother, the only thing to go "up, up, and away" had been the smelly contents of the diaper.

On his next trip around the house, I yelled for Arnold to take a better look at Superman's cape. He stopped, looked at the soiled diaper, and, with fire in his eyes, yelled at me, "Why'na shit didn' chu tell me 'at was a shitty dydee?" Obviously, he immediately discarded his cape and came crashing to earth in a hurry. I laughed so hard I almost fell off the porch.

Later in the day, when I recalled the episode and once again found myself smiling, I felt a wave of guilt sweep over me. I realized that the feeling of guilt wasn't from laughing at Arnold's attempt to turn himself into Superman; instead, I was feeling guilty because I was laughing.

LVII

A Way Out

The cold winter had proven our present house to be easier to heat than the house on the ridge had been. Since the potbellied stove heated the house using coal, the only wood needed was the wood the boys chopped for the wood burner in the kitchen. Being able to drive right up to our front door during winter was also a blessing. The family's workload had decreased tremendously since we no longer owned any farm animals other than our milk cow and since Dad had bought a gasoline-operated plow for the garden and the small field in which we planted potatoes and corn.

On one particular Saturday morning, Dad flew into another of his rages. After stomping angrily around the living room for no apparent reason, he finally approached me in a huff and yelled, "Hit's 'bout time 'his here freeloader gits off'n 'er dead ass an' finds a job!"

I was stunned. Dad's words had pierced through my heart like a hot knife cutting butter. Tears welled up in my eyes. I wanted to scream back at him that I was probably more anxious to get away from home than he was for me to leave and get work. At fifteen years old, I had intended to find work, but I had been told by a neighbor girl that since I had quit school, no one would hire me until I was eighteen. I was especially disturbed because I had always worked hard at home and had given my family no reason for grief. I watched tearfully as Dad stormed out of the room and left me alone to reflect on what he had just said to me.

Jobs around Clendenin were scarce. When most young men coming from the country reached employment age, they either joined the military, moved to another state, or stayed in the area working as unskilled laborers. Few women in and around our area worked outside the home; nevertheless, jobs for women were also scarce.

I had for some time hoped that I would eventually find work in town; however, I had no idea how I would get to and from a job should I find one. As I meditated on the problem, I realized that I was unskilled for any type of work, except for caring for children and doing housework. Although I was willing to take these kinds of jobs, I definitely wanted the challenge of doing something other than cleaning houses or waiting tables. With no contact with the "outside world," I had no idea to whom or where I could turn for help.

The following Saturday morning, my "ex-boyfriend" Bob came to our house for a visit. While I explained to him my need to find work, Bob informed me that a girl we both knew had recently been hired by the Ben Franklin 5 & 10¢ store in town. I was encouraged because, although the newly employed girl had graduated from high school, I knew I had made better grades than she had. "Well, if she can work at the store, then I can too," I said to Bob.

As Bob pulled out of our driveway to return to his mother's home, I was relieved to know that I was now free, should Bill become interested in me. Although Bob had seemed shocked to hear that I was not romantically interested in him, he vowed to forever remain friends with the family and me.

I assured myself that although I was only fifteen and had been forced to quit school, I would be hired and would learn quickly how to function in the world that was alien to my own way of life. I recognized the fact that I had a lot to learn, and as the nerves in my stomach tightened, I reminded myself to take one step at a time.

My small wardrobe consisted of two cotton housedresses and a pair of ugly brown shoes. Before I had left school, penny loafers had been popular at the time; however, the slip-on shoes that Mom had bought for me fit high on the top of my foot and resembled the wooden shoes I had seen pictured in a book about Holland.

On Monday, I started out early and walked the five miles to town, wearing my best dress and my brown shoes. At the age of fifteen, I had never had my hair cut. I had not chosen my hairdo; in fact, I desired hairstyles like all the other girls my age. My parents, however, had insisted that I braid my long hair into two braids, which I wrapped across the top of my head and pinned with bobby pins. All my life I had been warned by my father that should I ever cut my long hair, which hung below my waistline, he would kill me.

"Y'ain't never gonna bob your hair, 'cause if you do, I'll cut your head off," Dad had often said to me. I doubted that my father would literally kill me; nevertheless, should I defy him and cut my hair, I didn't want to find out how close he would come to it. The few times when Dad wasn't around and I had allowed my long, straight hair to hang loosely down my back, Mom would refer to me by the names of women in our area with loose morals. Although I was concerned that my old-fashioned appearance might hinder my chances for a job, to avoid her insult I braided my hair and pinned the braids across the top of my head.

Me at 17

When I walked nervously into the store, I could hardly remember my own name. I was pleasantly surprised, however, to find that the manager was a woman, so I felt a little more at ease while talking with her. After she had asked me a few questions, she handed me an application. The form was easy enough to understand, so I buzzed right through the questions, being careful to answer each as accurately as possible.

Miss Rohr, the manager, looked over the job application. Fortunately, I had acquired my social security card the previous year at the same time I had honored Marvin's request to send for his. Once the manager had checked the card, she asked whether I could begin working the beginning of the next week. I was surprised but thrilled. "Yes, ma'am," I answered quickly. "I'll be waiting at the door when you arrive." I was surprised that she hadn't asked whether I had my own transportation. I assumed she no doubt thought I would have made those arrangements before applying for the job. In fact, I had done just that; I had asked God to take care of the problem.

I must have been beaming when I walked out of the store. I couldn't wait to get home to tell Mom that I would be working forty-eight hours each week (no overtime law was in effect back then) and would be making, to the best of my knowledge, about fifteen dollars weekly.

Once I had walked back home, I found that Mom seemed nearly as excited as I was over the job. She asked how I planned to travel back and forth. She also stated that she didn't know how she would fare without my help around the house. I was stunned that she had finally recognized the fact that I had actually been relieving her of part of her workload.

"Nina is ten years old," I said. "Make her take up the slack."

Once Dad was home from work and I had informed him that I would be going to work on Monday, his temper flared. He was almost as upset as he had been when he'd called me a freeloader. "There's more 'sponsibilities in havin' a job 'en jist workin'," he said sullenly. I had no idea what he was trying to say to me; besides, I had thought he would be pleased that I had found a job. He shook his head and then walked into the kitchen to wash his hands before supper.

"I wish he would make up his mind," I whispered to Mom. I spent the rest of the week trying to find transportation to my new job. No matter which way I turned for help, I hit a dead end; nevertheless, I refused to accept defeat. I still had the weekend for my prayer to be answered, so on Sunday, my spirits soared when I saw Uncle Clint, Sissy, and Grandma arriving for a visit. Grandpa had passed away a few months before we had moved from the ridge, and Sissy and Uncle Clint had moved in with Grandma. Our families hadn't visited each other since we had moved.

Since it was almost noon, Mom quickly prepared a family-sized pan of cornbread and a large iron skillet filled with fried potatoes. The usual pot of pinto beans had been cooked earlier in the day. Utmost in her mind must have been the churn of fresh buttermilk she knew Uncle Clint would enjoy.

"Bethel, go ta the garden an' fetch some green onions an' ripe 'maydoes," Mom said to me.

Once Dad, Uncle Clint, Grandma, and my siblings had gathered around the table, my mother, Aunt Sissy, and I sat in the living room, waiting for our turn to eat. Uncle Clint offered the blessing and then helped himself to a big hunk of cornbread. He crumbled part of the bread into the bowl of buttermilk that Mom had placed beside his plate.

Mom smiled broadly as she listened to Uncle Clint raving about the meal. Although he was generally served the same type of food at his own home, he always delighted in praising Mom since he was aware that she rarely received a compliment.

"How ye gonna git ta work?" Sissy asked.

"I guess I'll hafta walk," I said.

"You cain't walk 'at fer ever'day," Grandma said.

Sissy immediately asked me whether I wanted to move in with her, Uncle Clint, and Grandma. She explained that I would have almost half as far to walk. I wanted to jump with glee, but I couldn't imagine Dad agreeing to my moving in with my relatives. I picked at my food while I thought about the offer Sissy had made.

Suspecting that Dad would forbid my moving out, I began to contrive a different approach. While Mom and Sissy finished their meal, I

Me hugging Aunt Sissy on Birch Creek.

slipped nervously into the bedroom and began secretly packing my few belongings into the dilapidated suitcase Woody had left behind. I then returned to the kitchen and washed the dishes while the adults visited with each other in the living room. Although I was trembling at the thought of what I was plotting to do, I continued to plan my getaway.

As I pondered the idea, I remembered something the neighbor girl had said to me when I revealed to her that I tried never to deliberately defy my parents. She had told me that I should do some of the things that I wanted to do, whether or not they allowed it. "They might kill you, but they ain't gonna eat you," she had said.

I didn't agree with her advice; however, I decided that when my relatives were ready to leave, I would walk out the door behind them, carrying the suitcase. I figured that if I tried to leave with my relatives, I might get away with it; otherwise, if I failed to try, I would never know how Dad might have reacted. I felt that it was about time for me to get something positive from all the abuse I had been suffering at the hands of my father. If necessary, I was ready to use a little blackmail to make the traumatic experiences work on my behalf.

The scene was set. My aunt, uncle, and grandma were bidding Mom farewell as they and my mother sauntered outside into the yard. I walked into the bedroom and picked up the piece of luggage that held my few belongings. Although I was trembling like a leaf in the wind, I nonchalantly started for the living room door. "I sure hope Sissy was serious when she asked me to stay with them," I thought to myself.

My stomach was churning as I anticipated Dad's reaction when he realized I was leaving; however, he was engrossed in a ballgame on television and did not speak when I walked past him. Holding my head high, I moved swiftly toward the doorway leading outside, when suddenly, Dad gruffly said, "Now, jist wher'd you think you're goin'?"

I stopped in my tracks and said, "I'm gonna stay with Sissy and Uncle Clint because I can walk out of the holler to work."

"Oh, no you hain't!" he stated firmly.

I quickly moved to the next step of my strategy. Calmly, I moved over beside my father and leaned over so only he could hear what I had to say. "Either you let me go or I'll tell them what you've been tryin' to do to me," I stated. I then stepped back, still holding the suitcase in my right hand.

My father jumped angrily to his feet. I held my breath, cringed, and closed my eyes, expecting to be knocked across the room; instead, he grabbed the piece of luggage out of my hand and threw it forcefully out the door and into the yard.

Slightly relieved, I walked calmly outside to retrieve my luggage. The force with which Dad had thrown the suitcase had broken the latch, allowing my clothing to fall out onto the ground in front of my relatives. With tears welling up in my eyes, I gathered my ragged clothing and returned it to the broken suitcase.

"C'mon an' 'et's go," Sissy said softly. Neither Mom nor the other adults uttered a word about what had just happened.

I was relieved when Dad remained inside the house. I was confident that he must have felt as though he had no choice but to allow me to go live with my relatives; he no doubt feared that I would otherwise expose the family's disturbing secret. I certainly didn't like what I had chosen to do, but I had decided to deal later with the fallout from what I'd done.

With Sissy and Uncle Clint in the front seat, I scooted onto the back seat beside Grandma, with my arm wrapped tightly around the broken suitcase. Peering through the glass in the door, tears began trickling down my cheeks as I watched Mom and my siblings standing in the yard watching us drive away. I wished, even at that moment, that I could have stayed home with my loved ones. In spite of all they had done to me, I still loved my father and mother dearly.

As Uncle Clint slowly maneuvered the car down the rocky road, I wondered what it would have been like if my father and I could have had a normal father-daughter relationship. I hoped that while I was gone he would think about what had driven me to this point. Silently, I whispered a prayer for the whole family as we drove out of sight.

It seemed that we had been driving for at least fifteen minutes before anyone broke the silence. Not only was I feeling fretful over what I'd just done to defy my father, but I was wondering whether Sissy and Uncle Clint really wanted me to live with them. Afraid they might tell me I could stay with them for only a few days, I remained silent.

While the old Dodge—with the bad shocks—bumped up and down over the potholes in the road, I pondered the fact that I would soon be entering into a world completely different from anything I had ever before experienced. I wondered what lay ahead for me, and what my father would do now that I was out of the house. "Oh, my God!" I unintentionally said aloud.

"What's a matter?" Sissy asked.

"Oh…never mind," I said. There was no way I could tell her that I'd just realized my little sister might soon be pulled into the cesspool that I was trying so hard to escape. I felt flushed from the unnerving thought, so I rolled down my window and allowed the cool air to blow across my face. I closed my eyes with the thought that God was sending the soothing wind to dry my tears and to comfort my soul.

LVIII

A Whole New World

Sissy, Uncle Clint, and my grandmother appeared to be enjoying my company as the days began to slip into weeks. I felt blessed to be living in their peaceful home. I still missed my family, but I had no intentions of returning to live at home. I was glad my job would keep me from thinking about the things that were wrong in my life. My heart's desire was to make my new family proud of me.

All of the girls working at the store were high school graduates, except for one other girl and myself. She was still in school but was employed full-time for the summer. She and I had attended classes together from the second through eighth grades. I was acquainted with the two Dewey sisters, who lived at the mouth of the hollow where I was now living and who were now my coworkers. With the exception of one girl (who was soon fired), the employees treated me with kindness.

After I had worked at the store for a few days, I began noticing that the other girls had been going out at lunch time and bringing back what they called "cheeseburgers and milkshakes." Having never heard of "burgers and shakes," I was anxious to try the tantalizing foods. I had never been inside a restaurant and had no idea how to place an order. Feeling embarrassed that my new friends might "discover" my ignorance, I avoided asking them for help.

By the time I had received my second payday, I had decided to meet the challenge and visit the restaurant. None of the girls had asked me to join them when they had gone to buy their lunches, so I was still uninformed about ordering a meal. I assured myself that at one time or another, the girls at the store had learned how to order the food; therefore, confident that I was as bright as any of my coworkers, I walked nervously across the street to the only family restaurant in town.

When I stepped through the door and looked shyly around the room, I realized that the six booths and three small tables were occupied. A line of people stood against the wall, waiting to be seated. Feeling that every eye in the room was focused on me, I almost panicked and ran back outside. I crossed my arms and held onto my elbows tightly, wondering what I was supposed to do in order to get some of the food that was saturating the restaurant's air with its tempting aroma.

A handmade sign hanging from the ceiling captured my attention: "Takeout Orders Here." I moved slowly to the line beneath the sign and continued to inhale the tantalizing smells wafting through the air. After several minutes into my lunch period, which was swiftly expiring as I was becoming a nervous wreck, a waitress wearing a hairnet and a white plastic apron trimmed with a red ruffle approached me and asked, "What can I gitchee?" I told her that I wanted a cheeseburger and a milkshake.

She asked curtly, "What kind a shake?"

Now, what was I to do? I didn't know there were different kinds of shakes. I timidly asked, "What do you mean?"

I must have looked confused as she sighed and then asked impatiently, "You want a chocolate, strawberry, er vaniller shake?"

"Chocolate, please," I answered nervously.

I watched as the waitress wrote my order on the small tab she was holding in her hand and then disappeared into another room, which I assumed was the kitchen. I could hardly wait for her to bring my food. "The worst is over," I told myself. Although I was still shaking in my "wooden shoes," I realized that not only had I discovered how to order a meal, I had also learned that the shakes came in more than one flavor.

I soon noticed that the waitress had returned and had begun taking another person's order. I was baffled. "What happened to my order?" I wondered. I stood there in the same spot trying to look around the room without turning my head. I was glad the room was packed because I figured that people would pay less attention to me.

Within the next couple of minutes, I was approached by an older waitress who asked me the same thing the first girl had asked. "I want a chocolate milkshake an' a cheeseburger," I said to the second waitress. She wrote my order on her tab and disappeared just like the first one had done. I thought to myself, "If they don't hurry up, my lunch period will be over, and I won't have anything to eat." I had no idea how long it would take to prepare the food. I assumed that all the waitress had to do was walk into the kitchen, stick the food into a bag, and hand it to me.

It wasn't long before the first waitress walked over and told me how much I owed, which was less than a dollar, and then handed me a brown paper bag. I removed the change from my pocket, paid for my food, and hurried back to the 5 & 10. Worried that I would have to eat my meal in the presence of some of the other employees, I was delighted to find the lunch room empty.

I hurriedly reached inside the bag and pulled out the wrapped cheeseburger. After removing the wax paper wrapping, I removed the top half of the bun and studied the contents of the burger. Slowly, I put the two halves of the bun back together and squeezed, trying to flatten it enough until I could bite into it. After taking a big bite and wallowing it around inside my mouth, I realized that I had never tasted anything as scrumptious. While slowly sipping the delicious shake, I reveled in the feeling of accomplishment. I was beginning to like this new world that was holding such interesting surprises.

Not until I was walking home from work did it dawn on me that I might have made a mistake by giving the second waitress my order.

I wondered what she had thought when she came back with the order and I was nowhere to be found. I was embarrassed and even more concerned. I wondered, if I were to return to the restaurant, whether the waitress would remember me and demand payment for the duplicate order I had placed the day before. The thought ruined what would have otherwise been a very pleasant experience.

I quickly learned the work pertaining to the hosiery and lingerie counter to which I had been assigned. I was permitted to sell merchandise anywhere in the very compact store, which seemed expansive at the time. The store had six small departments and a candy counter. Each department had a manually operated cash register, which only the clerk assigned to that department was allowed to operate.

Sales totaling one dollar or more were required to be added on paper by the sales clerk, and her math approved by the manager before the sale could be rung up on the register. Any money due to the customer was returned beginning with the lesser coins and counting upward from the amount of the sale until the sum equaled the total amount tendered.

I had been walking three miles to and from work six days a week and had begun wondering why God had not answered my prayer and supplied the transportation I had requested, not realizing at the time that I should have been thanking Him for providing me with the job and for giving me a home where I could be free of any type of abuse.

LIX

From Trouble to Hope

As the days began to ascend into weeks, I began anticipating being able to spend time with Bill, the tall, dark, and handsome stranger whom Marvin had introduced to me. Bill had turned eighteen in December and had immediately joined the U.S. Army. His mother had informed the young people at church that Bill would enjoy hearing from his friends in the community; consequently, he and I began corresponding. Within weeks, Bill's words on paper had begun to place a spark of hope in my heart that we would in the near future be able to spend some time together.

I missed my family very much, especially my siblings; still, I had been avoiding spending Sundays at home because I feared my father. One morning, after making his school bus runs, Dad appeared unexpectedly at my counter, leaned over, and ordered me to come home after work on Saturday night. He advised me that my brother Maynard would come to the store to walk up the hollow with me when I left work at eight o'clock. I was astounded, but before I could ask him to reconsider, he was on his way out of the store.

For the rest of the day, each time I thought about having to return to the awful situation I had been trying to escape, I felt a gnawing pain in my stomach. I worried that should I defy my father, he might come into the store and cause a scene that would cause me to lose my job. I realized that no one outside my immediate family was aware of the situation between my father and me, and that in and around town he had a good reputation. I believed in order to avoid revealing my problem, I had no choice but to honor his command.

On Saturday nights the walk down the highway and up the hollow to where my parents lived seemed endless. Up and down hills, over creeks and hollows, and around curve after curve Maynard and I trudged. Not once did anyone stop to give us a ride. I was thankful that I had a brother to walk with me who was braver than I was, especially on the nights when every wild animal in the forest seemed to be taunting us as we made our way up the dark, lonely hollow.

As a rule, Maynard and I tried to ignore the unnerving cries that pierced the dark nights; however, on a few occasions, our fears overpowered our common sense, and we literally ran as fast and as far as we could until I would drop to my knees from exhaustion. During these situations, Maynard would fill his pockets with stones in hopes that he could ward off any animals that we imagined were planning to ambush us.

On each trip I made home to spend Sundays with my family, I continued to feel threatened by my father. As Dad continued with his despicable acts, I always resisted strongly. I could not share the awful secret with anyone other than God, and on Monday mornings I usually returned to work in a state of depression. Even so, I always managed to conceal any sign of the dark cancer that had for years been eating away at the core of my existence. Through every setback, God had always proven that He would never forsake me and that He would protect me from what I feared most.

On one particular Saturday night, after having missed going to my parents' home the weekend before, I waited outside the store for my brother to walk home with me. My coworkers had left for their homes already, and with the foot traffic on the streets practically nonexistent, I almost panicked when it became evident that no one was coming to escort me up the long "wild animal–infested hollow."

The thought of walking alone up the hollow to where I lived with my aunt and uncle was even more frightening. I literally shivered when I thought of having to walk past the family cemetery that had been in the area since the early 1900s. I feared the corpses were waiting for a young, innocent girl like me to come along, so that they could prove to all the skeptics that they indeed were roaming the dark hollows and ridges after dark.

The minutes were ticking away, and the night was getting darker and darker. Frantically, I looked around for a familiar face who would either deliver me to my parents' or my relatives' doorstep. After waiting for at least thirty minutes with no sight of Maynard or anyone else, I spied a guy the same age as my oldest brother walking up the street in my direction. Since he was well known by my family and me, I assumed that, although his reputation was questionable, I could trust him to drive me to my parents' home.

He immediately agreed to drive me, so I walked to his old, dilapidated truck and got aboard. Having worked myself already into a highly agitated state of mind, I sat rigidly in the seat, wondering whether I had made a mistake by accepting the ride. Our conversation was casual for the first couple of miles as we traveled up the isolated, pitch-black hollow; however, Jed soon began with a line that my father had already tried to use with me. I was certain that Jed was already aware of my spotless reputation; nevertheless, I immediately reminded him that I was a Christian girl who had no intention of doing anything immoral.

He laughed at my statement and then asked me, "Jue thank I'd brang you up 'his here long, rough holler fer nuthin'?"

"I'll pay you for your gas," I said shakily.

"Ha! Ha! Hain't no gas I'm 'spectin'," he stated in a menacing voice. "You can either give me what I want, er else you can git outta 'his here truck an' walk up'pa holler!"

Unable to intelligently respond to his statement, I reached over in the middle of the seat and picked up a long, heavy flashlight, hoping Jed would realize that I was afraid of him—and even more scared of being put out of the truck. "God, I'm in trouble again," I prayed silently. I quickly realized that I'd probably have been better off subjecting myself to the wild animals and corpses rather than putting myself in the company of this slithering snake.

"I must be the dumbest person in 'his world," I said to Jed. He did not reply but laughed loudly.

As we continued up the lonely road, I clung to the door with one hand and held up the flashlight menacingly with the other. "If I were you, I'd be curful!" I warned. "You know 'at my dad or either one of my big brothers'll kill you if you harm me."

He evidently believed what I'd said because he began trying to convince me that he was only joking about the threat he'd just made. "I'z jist checkin' you out to see if you was 'hat kind a girl," he lied.

I sat clinging to the door, afraid to get out of the truck and afraid to go any farther with this guy. I was concerned that he might pull off the road anytime and force himself upon me. I had proven to myself that I could put up a good fight; however, I wondered whether I could stop a big, strong guy like Jed.

"God, where are You?" I prayed silently. "And why has my family left me to fend for myself?"

Finally, Jed pulled the car to the side of the road at my family's driveway. As I quickly opened the door, he flashed a mouthful of oversized teeth and asked, "Do I git a kiss fer gittin' you here safe?"

"Here's a dollar for your gas," I said, throwing the money in his lap and dropping the flashlight onto the seat while I scurried out of his vehicle.

He grabbed the money and threw it back at me. "Jist chu tell your daddy an' brothers 'at Jed brung you home safe," he said. I grabbed the dollar bill, slammed the door shut, and began running toward the house, thankful that this ordeal was over.

I ran across the footbridge and yard, jumped onto the large stone step, and practically fell through the opened door. Expecting one of my parents to immediately explain why I had been left alone in town on a Saturday night with nobody but the drunks, whores, and whoremongers roaming the streets, I snapped angrily, "Why'd nobody bother to meet me so they could walk me home?"

Dad looked up finally and asked, "Who was 'at dat brung you home?"

"I had to ask Jed Holt to brang me home," I answered, with the sound of total disbelief in my voice.

"Jed Holt?" Dad yelled. "Did dat no-good-fer-nothin' rascal try anythang on you?"

I felt like telling him that Jed had treated me just like he, my father, did; instead, I stated, "Now, do you thank he'd try anything on me, knowin' that he'd have to answer to you and my brothers?"

My question was met with total silence. I decided at that moment that unless someone was waiting to escort me home at closing time, then I'd not be going home on weekends. Dad could order me to come home all he wanted to, but I would not travel that road by myself, or with some undesirable I had been forced to pick up on the street.

It was common knowledge among the girls in town that a common practice for some of the high school young men was to take their dates out on a dark road and say, "Get out or put out!" It disturbed me that the guys would then brag about the results, with no concern of being held responsible for their own acts.

Some of us girls avoided getting ourselves into these situations. I realized that there were decent guys around town, but I had no desire to become involved with any of them. I had learned a valuable lesson when I trusted Jed to drive me home, and I would never again put myself in such a dangerous predicament. It seemed my nightly prayer had become a ritual when each night I kept hearing myself say: "God, You know that I don't have sense enough to take care of myself, and although I must keep you awfully busy, would you please protect me from all the harm that keeps threatening me?"

On the Sunday morning after the incident with Jed, I walked to the little country church with my sister and little brothers to attend Sunday School. Since the pastor, who lived in Charleston—about thirty miles from the church—did not feel that he could make the trip but once each Sunday, he held preaching services only on Sunday nights. Mom attended only the Sunday night services.

No evening service had been planned for this particular Sunday, however, so a group of the neighborhood teens decided to walk out of the hollow to a church we sometimes attended when our own church was silent. I had been escorted home from church a few times by a decent young man who lived in our neighborhood and was about three years my senior. With the permission of my parents, he and I joined the group as we began the two-mile trek to the church. Clay was very respectful of me, and although I had no romantic feelings for him, I had decided that I would be safe with him while I waited for the day when Bill and I could be together. I was still writing to Bill, and although I had never dated him, I still believed he would be the guy who would eventually win my heart.

I was expecting Bill to arrive home on furlough since he had just finished his basic training. Part of the reason I had asked Jed to deliver me to my parents' home the night before instead of driving me to Sissy's house was so that I could be in the area should Bill arrive at his folks' home on this particular weekend.

Our little group talked amongst ourselves as we strolled leisurely down the country road, and we were surprised when a taxicab approached. My heart pounded within my chest as the thought entered my mind that it would be Bill coming home on leave. When the cab pulled over to the side of the road, my heart seemed to shift into overdrive when the handsome soldier stepped out dressed in his khaki uniform.

Bill glanced over at me, then immediately began speaking with one of the girls who was his distant relative. My brain began working overtime as I wondered how I could get rid of Clay, who was also one of Bill's distant relatives. When Bill invited the group to join him at his house, I was thrilled. When Bill, the group, Clay, and I turned and began strolling up the road, I slowly began distancing myself from

Clay to pair myself with Bill's younger sister, hoping that somehow Clay would understand.

Once we had all arrived at Bill's home and had visited for a short while, each person began leaving for his or her own home, seemingly forgetting that we had been intent on attending church in the little village down on the paved highway. When Clay headed for the door, he turned, approached me, and solemnly asked whether I was ready to leave.

"No, Clay," I said, "I think I will stay here and visit with Sarah (Bill's sister) for a while."

I felt a little embarrassed and ashamed of myself as Clay reluctantly walked out the door without comment. Although I had rejected him in the presence of his friends, I told myself that it was important for me to be free just in case Bill was feeling the same attraction for me that I had felt for him since the first day I had seen him.

Bill had never dated anyone, and although I was feeling drawn to him, he seemed to be ignoring me; nevertheless, when his sister and two brothers agreed to walk with me to my parents' home, Bill decided to join us. I was elated! Deep within my soul, I somehow knew that God would eventually unite us to spend the rest of our lives together.

While on his three-week leave, Bill borrowed his brother's car on several occasions to pick me up after work and take me home. I was very discreet and careful not to allow Bill to know the deep attraction I was feeling for him. He had impressed me as a shy, masculine, intelligent, well-mannered, and very warm man. He was careful to treat me with respect and not once attempted to kiss me on the lips.

My family had liked Bill immediately, and, surprisingly, even my father treated him kindly. A glimmer of hope had been kindled within me, and I believed deep within my heart that someday, if only I could hold onto my sanity, that this shy, six-foot man would swoop me up and carry me away from all the pain and heartaches that for so many years played havoc with my soul.

Bill returned to camp and was soon shipped to Japan, eventually landing in the heat of battle in Korea. My heart was heavy once he was gone, but I lived each day with hopes that he would return safely. I prayed for him daily and read each of his letters with anticipation that someday we could be together, never to be parted again. Truly, I was in love.

LX

Strength for the Battle

When I informed my aunt and uncle about how I had been forced to ask Jed to take me home on the Saturday night three weeks earlier, they became very upset that no one had bothered to meet me after work. Uncle Clint told me that, henceforth, he and Sissy would pick me up on the nights I worked late. At least I knew I could count on my relatives.

A couple of weeks went by before I returned to visit my family. I had been hoping and praying that since Dad now knew I had a steady boyfriend, his actions would change toward me. On Sunday evening, when I once again found myself alone with the small children and my father while Mom was out in the pasture milking the cow, I tried to stay alert since milking time had long ago become a dangerous time for me.

As soon as I submerged my hands in the pan of water I had heated on the wood-burner stove, I heard Dad enter the dining room, apparently on his way to the kitchen. I didn't know what he had on his mind, but from past experiences, I figured he was up to one of his old tricks. Knowing that if I didn't act quickly he would have me cornered there in the small kitchen, I quickly withdrew my hands from the dishpan. Without taking time to grab a towel, I hurried out the kitchen door and onto the back porch—prepared to jump to the ground and run should the need arise.

Dad stepped behind the kitchen door and into the corner where the water bucket was located. I heard him remove the dipper and then hang it back on the nail. I listened for him to walk back across the floor, hoping he would leave the kitchen. Hearing nothing, I knew he had to be standing inside behind the door that opened onto the porch where I was standing. I decided that I could play the waiting game as long as he could, so I leaned against the outside wall and waited.

Finally, after a short period of silence, he stepped into the doorway. He looked around the side of the entrance and said to me, "Why'on't chu come on in here'n give y'ur ol' daddy a kiss? I shore do miss you when you're over 'ere 'ith Clint."

I was enraged! "I don't have a kiss for my daddy—now or ever!" I yelled. The tone of my voice should have left no question in his mind that I meant what I had said.

"Y'ain't got 'at feller of yourn to hol'jee now, so come'n give Daddy some lovin'," he said in his sick tone of voice.

I began to poke fun at my father, believing it would make him angry enough to cause him to hate the very sight of me. Unfortunately, it did not work. He continued standing there in the doorway, making sickening suggestions and trying to get me to approach him willingly. I put my hands over my ears and acted as if I couldn't hear a word he was saying.

I was startled when he jumped suddenly outside onto the porch and grabbed at me. Like a frightened deer, I leapt off the porch and out into the yard. With contempt in my voice, I said, "I've got all this open space out here, so go away so I can finish 'em dishes." He threatened again that one day he would chloroform me and then I would not be able to run from him. My stomach ached and my temper boiled because I knew that getting out of his reach was only a temporary delay to what I feared would be coming later.

"Leave me alone an' go up town an' get yourself one of 'em whores off'n the street," I yelled loudly enough for the neighbors down the road to hear. Shocked to hear my own words echoing in my ears, sobs of remorse and anger began wracking my body.

"Shet up'n git on back in 'ere an' finish 'em deeshes," he said, the sound of defeat in his voice. I watched as he walked down the steps, stomped around the side of the house, and started walking up the hollow beside our house. I returned to washing the dishes.

Mom returned with the usual pail of milk, strained part of it into a gallon jar, and placed the jar inside the refrigerator. She took the cover off the churn and strained the rest of the milk into the churn. I was confident that she had heard the commotion and was aware that Dad had been after me again. I was also certain that she was ignoring me.

Suddenly, I blurted out, "Why don't chu do something about the way Daddy does me?" Crying almost hysterically, I continued, "You know that every time I'm left alone 'ith him what he's gonna do, and still, you deliberately make me stay in this house just so I can warsh the daggone dishes!"

Mom seemed to be deaf to my frantic cry for help. She didn't even look up from what she was doing. Bewildered and angry, I yelled at her again. "Sometimes I think you want him to hurt me!"

"Bethel, 'ere hain't nothin' I can do! I've tol' jue 'at a hunnerd times," Mom said, her voice trembling. "He swears he'll chop off my head 'ith a ax if I tell anybody."

"He's got you scared, and you know it," I said brokenly. "I betcha a hundred dollars he's bluffin'."

"You want me ta take a chance an' find out if he's meanin' what he says?" she snapped at me.

I didn't answer her. I knew she had just put the responsibility on my shoulders—once again. I was hurt, confused, and getting angrier all the time. Somehow, somewhere, there had to be an answer to this mess. I just wished I knew how to find it. Neither I nor my mom went to the evening church services since my face was red and swollen from crying. I wanted to believe that the reason Mom stayed home was because she was afraid to leave me alone with my father.

Early on Monday morning, I got ready and rode out of the hollow with Dad and Marvin. I would be getting out of the car before Marvin was dropped off at school, so I had no qualms about riding with Dad. Once they had dropped me off in town, I walked up the stairs to where Miss Rohr lived in an apartment over a little snack bar. She welcomed me inside since she was aware that I would, on occasion, need to stay with her until the store opened. Finally, I felt I could relax until I had to return to visit my family again.

On my way to my relatives' home that evening, I decided that I would tell Sissy and Uncle Clint about my problems with my father. After supper, I joined them as they sat in the porch swing on their front porch, holding hands and swinging lazily back and forth. My grandmother had walked up the hollow to visit with Uncle Hubert, Aunt Ruby, and their family, as was her custom each evening. I sat down on the top step of the porch and leaned back against the support post. Fearing that I may change my mind, I hurriedly turned and faced my relatives. "I need to talk to y'all about something that's runnin' me crazy," I said, surprised that I had blurted out the words with such ease.

Neither Sissy nor my uncle seemed surprised as I began to unburden my soul. Without giving any of the horrible details, I began explaining how my father had been acting toward me for the past several years. "Don't come as no s'prize t'us," Sissy said, shaking her head from side to side. "He tried ta court me years ago 'fore I got married."

"He did?" I asked Sissy. "Tell me about it." I then listened as she recounted how my father had come to her bed one night when he and my mom were living with her and her parents.

"Him'n Marthy already had the two boys," she said. She went on to inform me that when she had heard him approaching her bed, she had immediately reached for the box of matches that she kept by her bedside to light the oil lamp. "He went'n scampered away like a skeer't rabbit when he heared me raddlin' (rattling) 'at box of matches," she said.

"Did you ever tell Mommy about it?" I asked.

"No, but I thank she knowed anyways," Sissy said. "Why, 'ere hain't none of the women in the family 'at feels safe to be alone 'ith him."

I was shocked! I had no idea that my relatives were aware of Dad's unacceptable behavior. "What can I do 'bout him bothering me almost ever' time he gets close to me?" I asked.

"You hafta decide 'at fer yourself," my uncle said sadly.

"You can have 'im put 'n jail an' leave your mommy 'ith all 'em kids ta feed, er you can keep on fightin' 'im off 'til you can git away from home fer good," Sissy stated.

I had been wrestling with these two options for years. I knew that should the authorities believe my story, which would no doubt result in my father's arrest, I could not be responsible for leaving my family without financial support, nor could I live with myself knowing I had left my little siblings without a father. I realized that Mom had learned a lot about society since she had moved from the ridge, but I doubted she would ever have enough confidence in her abilities to work outside the home. Besides, I pitied my dad no matter how he had treated me. I realized however, that it would have been simpler for me if I could have hated him.

After our talk, Sissy and Uncle Clint walked up the hollow behind the house to take the cow to the milk gap. I went inside the house feeling even more troubled than before. Unsure of what else to do, I walked over and picked up my little Bible that Woody had bought me a few years earlier. I realized that I had to make a decision on this problem. Could I allow this cancer that was eating away at me to continue, or must I take care of myself and let the pain fall upon my family? It was a decision I could make only with God's help. Bowing my head reverently, I prayed that God would help me to do the right thing.

I had never been told by anyone that I could find help by taking my problems to the Lord. Somehow, I had just realized over the years of torment and pain that my only hope was in the comfort God could give me. I knew very little about the Bible or how to have a close walk with the Lord. The sermons I had heard throughout the years had never been positive messages, so I didn't know how to search the Scriptures for comfort and the answers to my problems.

I opened my Bible and turned to the book of Mark, chapter four. As I slowly read verses thirty-five through forty-one, verse thirty-nine seemed to jump off the page and into my heart. The verse says, "And He arose, and rebuked the wind, and said unto the sea, 'Peace, be still.' And the wind ceased, and there was a great calm." I stopped and thought about the words, and when I looked back down at the pages of my Bible, I could hardly see the print through my tears. I meditated on the fact that Jesus had stilled a raging storm for His disciples, and as I read the verses over and over, a calmness seemed to be trying to replace the hopelessness I was feeling.

Slowly, I began realizing that Jesus was aware that I too was in the midst of a storm that seemed intent on carrying me out to sea. I looked down at verse forty, "Why are you so fearful? How is it that you have no faith?" As the words reverberated in my ears, I laid my Bible on the small table and walked outside, still meditating on the verses. I recalled all the times I had felt as though God had forsaken me. A Scripture verse that I hadn't realized I had committed to memory suddenly came to my mind, reminding me of one of God's promises. Hebrews 13:5 says, "...I will never leave thee nor forsake thee." My whole body was suddenly engulfed with a peace like I had not experienced since the night when I had trusted Jesus to save my soul. I wiped the tears from my face and smiled.

I didn't understand why God was allowing my life to be subjected to this ordeal, but here I was, once again being assured that He would always be there with me to protect me. I didn't know how many battles I would have to fight before it was over, but I believed that someday, victory would be mine. Although the circumstances might be slow in changing, I was assured that my Heavenly Father would deliver me—clean and non-violated. With renewed strength, I vowed to continue on, one day at a time.

LXI

Like a Butterfly

On a Monday morning after having spent an uneventful weekend with my relatives, a man dressed in a dark suit and tie and carrying a black briefcase walked into the store shortly after we had opened for business. He was directed immediately to the manager, who was normally found on the sales floor during business hours.

After he had spoken with the manager for a few minutes, I noticed that the stranger was walking around the departments, seemingly studying each clerk's face. From his demeanor, and from the troubled look on Miss Rohr's face, I surmised that the matter was of utmost importance. As I busied myself restocking the merchandise on my counter, I became aware that I was the only girl in the store whom he was totally ignoring. "Whatever the problem, it must have nothing to do with me," I thought.

Finally, after what seemed to be thirty minutes or more, the gentleman left the store. Miss Rohr called immediately for Elaine, my former classmate who was employed during the summer months. As the two of them approached my counter, the manager nervously requested that I join them.

We walked up the flight of stairs to the office, where Miss Rohr explained that the official from the courthouse in Charleston had informed her that he was investigating a complaint that a minor was working full-time hours at the store. He had verified the fact that Elaine was only fifteen years old and that she had not applied for a minor's work permit. Due to the infraction of the law, the store had been fined $20.00 on the spot, and Elaine was sent home until she could return with the proper document.

I was surprised, knowing that I too was only fifteen at the time. I had obtained no work permit to work full time; furthermore, I had no idea that the permit was required. I breathed a sigh of relief when Miss Rohr merely admonished me to remain silent about my age, since within four weeks I would be sixteen and would no longer need the work permit. "Thank you, God," I whispered. For the first time in my life, I was thankful for my old-fashioned clothing and hairdo.

Time soon came for me to take another step in my quest for independence. Having saved enough money to buy myself a new outfit, I made a visit to the store in town that sold the most expensive clothing. I was excited to be choosing the clothes that I wanted instead of having to accept the cheap housedresses that Mom had been compelled to buy. I was also thrilled that I could now replace my "wooden shoes"—the ugliest shoes in town.

The cool temperature of fall would soon be moving through the area, so I decided to select winter clothing. Immediately, my eyes fixed on a light blue pullover sweater and a blue plaid wool skirt. With my choice of pretty clothes hanging over her arm, the sales clerk directed me to the shoe department, where I took great pains in selecting a genuine pair of "penny loafers." When the sales clerk measured my foot to fit me with the shoes, she asked, seeming surprised, "Do you know that you're wearing shoes one size too big for you?" I smiled but did not disclose that I had been stuffing tissues in the toes of my shoes because they were too big for me.

After totaling the price of the purchases, I was even more thrilled to know that I had enough money left to replace my bobby socks with a pair of nylon stockings and my very first garter belt. I had never seen a garter belt before I had begun working in the lingerie department. When I discovered the unusual item on my counter, the manager had to explain its purpose. My mother and, as far as I had known, other ladies had always worn elastic garters rolled down over the tops of their nylon stockings to prevent the stockings from falling down around their ankles, as pantyhose had not yet arrived on the market.

The total sale tallied up to less than twenty dollars. I would have to work for weeks to replace what I'd spent, but I couldn't wait to go home to show my relatives the pretty outfit I'd chosen for myself. The first time I wore the new clothing, however, I was concerned that people would think I was trying to look and act like the city folk, whom I'd always been taught believed they were better than us country folk. Although I knew I had worked hard for the money I had spent on myself, I still felt guilty. I thought of Mom and my sister and brothers who needed new clothing, and I wished I could stretch my wages to outfit each of them in at least one nice outfit. Nevertheless, every time I went home, I tried to take some sort of food that I knew they had never tasted. On occasion, I would take Mom an article of clothing until, eventually, she began demanding more than I could afford to buy.

When she asked me to pay for her a full set of dentures, I couldn't bring myself to deny her request since the dentist had pulled her teeth four or five years earlier. After I received the dentist's bill on the account, I talked my two oldest brothers into helping me make the monthly payments. Marvin regularly paid his share, but Woody decided within weeks to stop paying because he and Mary were expecting their first child. Although I was left to pay the remaining charges, I was thankful that Mom finally had the teeth that she had needed for years.

LXII

A Penny Behind the Fuse

Winter had come and gone, and spring was a welcome relief from the snow, sleet, and mud I'd been trudging through as I traveled to and from work. Holiday shoppers had inundated the store for three weeks prior to Christmas Day. I had enjoyed the extra work I had been doing because it seemed to make the days pass faster. I was learning much about living in town but was still extremely shy and insecure. I still had not been inside a movie theater or attended a ball game, and there was no way I would eat a meal inside a restaurant.

I had spent Christmas Day with my parents and siblings and had been overjoyed to see my sister and little brothers' expressions when they opened the gifts I had bought with the few dollars I had been able to squeeze out of my meager wages.

I had accepted the fact that nothing I could do or say would affect the way Dad treated me; still, I was encouraged when during my last few visits he had practically ignored me. I certainly preferred being ignored over having to constantly fight against his behavior.

With spring now in the air, everywhere I looked God's hand was at work awakening life in the country and in the small town. I hadn't been to my parents' home for a few weeks, and since I was somewhat homesick to see my family, I decided during the day that I should go home for a visit. It seemed that God was using the spring weather to stir my heart and remind me that no matter how concerned I might feel about placing myself in harm's way, I could never completely shut my family out of my life.

After the store had closed, I walked outside to find my brother Maynard, as well as Aunt Sissy and Uncle Clint, waiting to escort me to one or the other of their homes. After apologizing to my relatives for their trip out of the hollow to give me a ride to their home, and with their blessings, I reluctantly chose to walk with my brother to my parents' home.

The long walk up the rocky road was very trying, so I was pleased to find that the family had already retired for the night when Maynard and I arrived home. On Sunday morning, after having spent a restless night because I could not allow myself to fall into a deep sleep, I walked into the kitchen to wash my face. When I bent over the enamel washbasin, I couldn't help but notice the strong stench coming from the water. I knew that Dad had brought drinking water and water for preparing the food from town, so I asked Mom about the foul odor coming from the pan of water.

"Yell, hit's 'at water outta the well, and it's been stankin' worser and worser the past few days," Mom stated, as she continued to knead a large batch of biscuit dough.

"Then make the kids carry water from the crick to warsh dishes and for warshing our hands," I said, as I stepped outside onto the porch and dumped the water onto the ground.

"Bud's gonna clean out da well after breakfas' an' see if 'ere's anythang rotten in it," Mom said.

After attending Sunday School with my sister and little brothers, we walked back home, where we quickly crowded around the work area to watch Marvin and Maynard hurriedly drawing the putrid water out of the well with a five-gallon bucket they had tied to the rope that ran through the pulley on the well curd.

Once Dad was satisfied that the water level had been lowered as much as possible, he ordered Maynard, who was about fourteen years old, to step inside the large bucket so he could be lowered down inside the well to finish bailing out the water.

Upon reaching the bottom of the well, Maynard stepped out of the large bucket and began dipping the rancid water from the well with a smaller bucket and pouring it into the five-gallon-bucket that was dangling inside the well from the rope.

Once the larger bucket was filled, Marvin pulled it up out of the well and emptied its smelly contents into the creek, barely thirty feet from the well. They repeated the process until all the water had been drawn from the well, and then Maynard began scooping up the muck at the bottom of the well, which he loaded into the five-gallon bucket. Numerous buckets of mud were pulled up out of the well and emptied, until Maynard finally yelled from inside the well, "I thank I found why the water's stankin'."

"Well, what'na Sam Hill is it?" Dad yelled back.

Maynard managed to reply, "I hain't shore what it is, but it's got feathers!"

"Maybe a bird fell into the well," I said.

"Aw bull!" Dad said. "Ain't no bird makin' 'at water stank like 'at."

Before Maynard had had time to identify the object, Mom walked out into the yard and said, "I heared what's goin' on out here, an' I betcha a nickel it's my ol' domanecker (dominique) hen 'at's been missin'."

"Take 'er up!" Maynard yelled.

Dad stepped over and pulled the heavy bucket up and out of the well. "Yep," he declared. "She hain't missin' no more."

Mom explained that days earlier she had noticed one of her best hens was missing. The chickens ran loose around the property and roosted at night in the trees behind the house, so it was assumed that an opossum or a fox had caught the hen. The mysteries of the missing chicken and the contaminated drinking water had at last been solved.

Dad lowered the empty bucket back to Maynard and yelled down to him to scrape the bottom of the well as clean as he possibly could.

Once he had declared that his job was done, Maynard climbed back into the empty bucket and was pulled to the surface.

Dad explained that the chicken had probably been chased by the dog, which happened sometimes when the chickens were trying to steal the dog's food, and that she might have attempted to escape by flying onto the enclosure built over the top of the well. Apparently, the lid on the well's covering had been left ajar, allowing the chicken to fall into the well, where she had promptly sunk to the bottom and drowned. Dad then warned all of us children to close the lid carefully after drawing water, insisting that the water would be clean once the well had filled again.

As far as I was concerned, the sight and odor of the decaying chicken were all the warning I needed. I had skipped breakfast already; moreover, I continued to fast for the next two days.

Later that night, I lay in bed thinking about the pleasure it had brought me over the past few months to be able to bring my siblings any type of food or mementos. Their sparkling eyes and smiling faces always gave me a lift and put a smile in my heart. I was always elated while watching them run across the yard to greet me when I returned home for a visit. I was pleased that I had paid them another visit.

I soon began thinking about the mail I had been receiving, almost daily, from Bill. From the tone of his letters mailed from Korea, I was more convinced than ever that someday God would bring us together as husband and wife. When my coworkers had begun dating the boys in and around town, I had strongly spurned any advances from the amorous young men. My reputation was important to me, and I was careful not to do anything that might cheapen me in the eyes of others; besides, I felt already that my heart belonged to Bill.

I had also become close friends with Bill's younger sister and enjoyed the time we were able to spend together each Sunday afternoon when I was in the area. Somehow, my friendship with her seemed to shorten the miles that separated Bill and me. I was trying very hard to enjoy life and not to allow the unfortunate circumstances surrounding my life to discourage me—or to send me into a state of depression.

Although my eyelids were getting heavier by the minute, I reminded myself that I could not fully relax since I felt the need to sleep with one eye open and with my hearing fine-tuned to detect and discern any suspicious sounds throughout the night. In my evening prayer, after asking God to keep Bill safe—since he was a gunner on a 105 Howitzer in combat in Korea—I stopped and thanked God that Dad had been distancing himself from me.

Later in the night, I was once again startled awake by the hooting of an owl coming from somewhere in the trees close by. With every muscle in my body tightening, I soon shivered from fear when I recognized the familiar sound near my bed that I had heard too many times before. Trying to convince myself that my imagination was deceiving me, and with the room in total darkness with no source of lighting within my reach, I lay tensely in the bed, with my sister and four younger brothers sleeping soundly behind me.

I wondered whether I should scream or jump out of bed and flee to another room. Before I could force myself to react, however, it was too late to decide. Feeling a slight tug on the blanket that I had pulled tightly around me, I frantically whispered, "Oh, God! Don't let it begin again." Then, holding the covers tightly around my body while I wriggled closer to my siblings, I finally managed to scream, "Get outta here, Daddy!"

"Shh, be still er you'll wake up'pa rest'a 'em," he whispered.

"What a dumb thing for him to say to me," I thought to myself. How could my own father possibly think that I would lie there quietly and allow him to violate me or my space? I hoped that if he knew Mom and the children were aware of what he was trying to do, then maybe he'd run out of the room and leave me alone; therefore, I screamed even louder. Before I could know what was happening, he quickly grabbed my face with one hand. I was horrified! The thought that he might have a cloth soaked in chloroform sent me thrashing about the bed as I fought to prevent him from holding onto my head. "Daddy, get outta here and leave me alone! Mommy, help me!" I screamed with every ounce of strength I could muster.

When my sister and little brothers woke and began screaming in fear, he grabbed my head and tried to muffle my screams. Absolutely panic stricken, I wondered why none of the other family members were responding to my screams for help, when finally, I heard Mom calling weakly to Dad from their bedroom at the opposite end of the living room. "Bud, my heart! Oh my God, my heart!" she muttered.

I yelled at Dad, "Mommy's havin' a heart attack! Can't you hear her?" He pushed my head hard against the mattress and then released his hold on me.

The house was still in total darkness, and I wondered why Mom hadn't turned on a light. I jumped up onto the side of the bed and groped for the string hanging from the light bulb in my room. Desperate, I yanked sharply on the string. To my dismay, the string snapped, preventing me from turning on the light.

Mom was still moaning, and there was no response from anyone else. Marvin and Maynard's bedroom was next door to mine, but I hadn't heard a sound coming from either of them. I jumped off the bed and tried to feel my way through the living room to where Mom was still moaning. My own welfare was no longer utmost in my mind; I was worried about my mother.

The light suddenly came on in the dining room, and Dad, wearing only his underwear, jumped through the doorway into the living room. He struck at me with his opened hand and whispered menacingly, "Git on back ta bed, you loodle bitch! It's all your fault."

I ran back to the bedroom, where my youngest siblings were huddled together in the bed we shared. I felt that if Mom died, it would be my fault. I suppressed my sobbing so I could hear what was going on in the bedroom where Dad had returned. I heard him tell Mom that he had gotten up to get a drink of water and had discovered that the electricity was off. He said that he had managed to locate the problem and was in the dining room when I'd started screaming.

The light in my parents' bedroom was turned off, and, after somebody crept into the dining room and turned off the light, the house was again in darkness. I lay trembling on the edge of my bed, no longer able to hear the call of the owl. Apparently, it had been scared away by the screams that my brothers had somehow slept through.

The next morning after Dad had left for work and the rest of the family had seated themselves around the breakfast table, Mom called me into the room and asked, "What was Bud doin' when you started hollerin'?"

"The same thing he's always tryin' to do!" I said angrily.

"He said he had ta put a penny 'hind the 'lectric fuse ta git the lights on," she said. "He said he didn' know what chu was hollerin' about."

"And I guess you b'lieve that big lie," I said, intent on making a strong statement instead of asking a question.

"Well, I did try'n turn on'na light when you hollered, an' it wouldn' come on," Mom said.

"I betcha anything he didn't put a penny behind'a fuse," I said.

I looked over at Marvin about the same time that he replied, "We'll just look an' see if he put a penny behind the fuse."

Marvin and Mom got up from the table, and we walked into the kitchen. Marvin stepped behind the door and opened the fuse box situated on the wall there in the corner. One by one, he removed and then replaced each of the four fuses. Just as we had suspected—there was no penny behind any of the fuses!

"Betcha anything Daddy removed a fuse before he came into my room," I said.

"Yell, an' then put it back when Mommy hollered," Marvin said.

"And your heart, Mommy, was that real?" I asked.

"Yes, it was. I was hurtin' 'roun' my heart real bad," she said pitifully.

"And somethin' else I'd like to know, Marvin. Where were you when I was hollerin' my head off?" I asked him angrily.

"I guess I was asleep," he replied quickly. "I swear to God I didn' hear you hollerin'."

"You couldn't 'ave slept through all that commotion!" I stated firmly.

"You don't b'lieve me? Then the next time you stay overnight, I'll be the one in your bed an' I'll grab his hand and pull 'im down in the bed with me an' really work 'im over," Marvin said. He seemed sincere, and I wanted to believe him, so I dropped the subject.

Mom and Marvin returned to the table to eat their red syrup and cold biscuits. I walked outside and cried like a baby. After a while, I had no choice but to pull myself together and push the unpleasant thoughts of yet another attack onto the sordid heap of memories that I had to keep hidden from the world.

Marvin had by this time acquired his own car, so he agreed to drive me out of the hollow to my job as he and Maynard left for the high school, where Maynard was also now attending. I would never have gotten into the car alone to ride out of the hollow with my father; besides, he was no doubt too furious with me to have allowed me to ride with him.

I wondered why God had allowed the torment to resume. I was also curious about Mom's heart pain. I wondered whether she had faked a heart attack in order to draw Dad away from me. I wanted to believe that she in fact had; yet, knowing that Mom had never lifted a finger to help me before, I could only hope that, if she had been faking the attack on my behalf, Dad would never learn about it.

In addition to all the other questions buzzing around in my mind, there was my brother's statement. Had he honestly slept through the ordeal? Or was he so scared of Dad that he just pretended to be asleep? After all, he had endured numerous beatings from Dad and had seen him out of control many times. The only thing I could be certain about was the fact that I had been spared again. Maybe God had touched my mother's heart, and she had mistaken it to be a heart attack? I doubted whether I would ever know the truth, but I praised God for sparing me once again.

LXIII

The Handprints

Woody and Mary had been blessed with a baby boy. Mary had returned to West Virginia and had moved into a little cottage near her folks while Woody was serving a tour at an Air Force Base in Alaska. Marvin was dating a girl who lived up one of the hollows that branched off the creek where our family lived. He would soon be graduating and was planning to find work in Ohio.

A few weeks had passed since the episode with my father that had brought on Mom's "heart attack." I had no immediate plans of returning to my folks' home; however, when a group of young people who attended the church near my family's home were giving a "going-away party" for Marvin, they invited me to attend. On Friday, Marvin came into the store and talked me into going to the party/cookout, after he had assured me that he would be spending the night at our family's house and would drive me to work on Saturday morning.

The cookout was a pleasant change from my mundane evenings and weekends with my relatives. I'd had no run-ins with my father, and it was now a typical Saturday morning at our house. I was helping Mom prepare breakfast when she asked me to make the biscuits. After mixing the batter, I began kneading the dough on a flour sack I had spread out on the dining table.

Mom was busy preparing the meal and was moving back and forth between the dining room and kitchen. Dad had been following her from room to room, fussing non-stop about something that seemed trivial to me. I had no idea what his problem was, but I'd listened to him lashing out at my mother since the time he'd gotten out of bed, about thirty minutes earlier.

Mom finally gave Dad a "wrong" answer, provoking him to grab her by the throat, back her into the corner near where I was working, and suddenly begin choking her violently. With my hands covered with flour and wet dough, I screamed for Marvin, who was in the bedroom adjacent to the dining room. He quickly ran into the room and looked over at Dad's hands clamped around Mom's throat. Stopping short of my parents, Marvin yelled, "Daddy, don't do that! Leave her alone!"

I panicked! Without thought of my own safety and not waiting for Marvin to react, I jumped over to try to free my mother from Dad's chokehold. Grabbing him by the shoulders, I pulled with every ounce of strength I could muster. Apparently realizing the urgency, Marvin jumped over to help me, and together we pulled our berserk father away from our mother, enabling her to stumble out of the room. Surprised at our own bravery, Marvin and I stood with our mouths agape while Dad went tearing across the room and out the door.

I smiled when I noticed the imprints of flour on the back of his shirt as he headed for the car, yelling back across his shoulder that he was going to run the car over a hill and kill himself.

I stepped into the kitchen, washed my hands, and returned to the biscuit dough. Mom came back into the room, holding her hand over the front of her throat and crying like a baby. "Whur'd he go?' she whimpered, her voice raspy.

"He said he was goin' to run the car over the hill an' kill himself," I answered.

"Now what have we done? Hard ta tell what 'e'll do to 'isself," she cried.

Looking over at her, I felt like choking her myself; instead, as I continued to knead the dough, I said, "He'll be back when he thinks breakfast is ready." Of course, I didn't know whether he would return safely, but at the moment, I really didn't care.

Marvin calmly walked over, looked at Mom, and said, "Mom, don't worry about the S.O.B. I promise, he will be back."

Holding true to his pattern, the bread was barely baked and out of the oven when I looked out the door to see a car approaching. "Daddy's back!" I yelled to anyone who was interested. The children ran into the bedroom and hid.

Dad walked in through the kitchen door with the white prints of my hands still on the shoulders of his dove-colored shirt. Although he was keeping his head bowed, he couldn't hide the embarrassed look on his face as he walked over to the washbasin and began washing his hands and face. After drying himself with the ragged towel, he calmly walked over and seated himself at the table. My sister and little brothers, realizing that Dad had calmed down, soon filled the bench behind the table. Dad looked toward the ends of the table at the empty chairs, hesitated, and then bowed his head and repeated the same blessing he'd been reciting for as long as I could remember. Watching from the kitchen, I wondered how I could love my father one minute and hate him so much the next. At the moment, I was feeling more hate than love.

Once he had finished eating his breakfast, he walked into the living room and, after picking up the Bible and wiping off the dust, began reading a few verses. He then replaced the Bible and stepped into the dining room, where Mom, Marvin, Maynard, and I were eating our breakfast. I shook my head in disgust when he began talking to Mom as though the whole, pitiful episode had never taken place. Looking and sounding amused, he explained how he had been flagged down by our neighbor Thad Stanley, who walked to town early every morning to manually sweep the streets. Dad had always enjoyed belittling the unfortunate but gentle man, so he made fun of anything the man had said to him.

Unable to resist the temptation, I walked over to where my father was sitting and asked, "Did Thad ask you whose handprints were on your shoulders?" Grating his teeth together and working his jaw muscles up and down, he jumped up and walked out of the room. I looked at Mom and said, "I wonder how he can be such a jackass one minute an' then act so normal the next." Mom didn't respond. Marvin and I drove away, wondering what would have happened if we had not been home.

LXIV

The Baptism

On a Sunday morning, weeks later, I awoke to the sound of birds singing and the bright sun rays bathing the room where I shared Grandma's featherbed. When I sat down at the breakfast table, my uncle broke the silence with the question, "Y'all like ta go ta a baptizin' I heared 'hey was havin' over'n Clay County 'his afternoon?"

I looked at Grandma and Sissy, hoping that Sissy would answer with her usual reply to such a question. "Yell, 'at'll be a good drive 'at'll git us outta 'his here holler," she said. "'Et's take our dinner an' have a picneck."

Since I knew the baptism would be held deep within the boondocks, after completing my share of the chores, I donned a straight-cut skirt and cotton blouse and then slipped on my penny loafers. After brushing and braiding my hair and crossing the braids across the top of my head, I pinned them in place with bobby pins. Clutching my wallet, which was bulging with pictures of family, friends, and Bill, I hurried outside, where I climbed inside Uncle Clint's old Desoto and seated myself on the back seat beside Grandma.

Uncle Clint placed our lunch in the trunk of the car and then began the thirty-minute bumpy drive to the area where the service was to take place. Carefully steering the car around mud holes, Uncle Clint glanced back across his shoulder at me and said, "Betty, you better be curful, or Ol' Andy Askew 'ill try an' take you home 'ith 'im."

"Yeah," Grandma said, pinching me on the leg. "Jist you 'member 'at Ol' Andy's 'bout two blubbers (bubbles) off'n plumb." I laughed and shrugged off the comment, never once believing that Andy would attend the baptism.

The four of us chatted jovially as we drove through town, continued up Elk River, and then turned onto a winding, narrow asphalt road that seemed to be going nowhere. I sat wondering whether my uncle would find the correct area, when, to my surprise, he abruptly left the pavement and pulled the car onto the wide shoulder near a huge oak tree. A small white church, accentuated by the heavily wooded mountain in the background, sat about thirty feet back from the road. Between the church and the road, eight or ten cars were parked, with a few elderly women shuffling among them, chatting with each other.

Grandma had grown up in the area, so a few of her relatives still resided in this section of the county. She exited the car and began moving leisurely among the women, greeting families she had not seen for years. One of the overweight younger ladies was explaining to my grandmother that whooping cough was rampant in the area. She pointed to a small gray sack attached to a string hanging around her child's neck and said, "His is a asseyfidditty (asafetida) bag 'at'll ward off whuppin' cough better'n ary other thang in'na worl'."

Granny nodded agreeably and said to me, "Bethel, you be shore'n hold your breath if you git close to anybody coughin'."

I smiled and said timidly, "Okay, Granny, I will." As far as I was concerned, I had already inhaled enough of the stench from the asafetida sack to cause me to be selective where and when to breathe.

I stepped to the side and watched the scattering of people making their way through the brush and around the side of the mountain. The older women, sporting a variety of pretty sun bonnets, pulled at their long cotton dresses as they crept through the underbrush, thigh-high weeds, and briars. I fell in step behind a man and his wife who were carrying their twin daughters and set my sights on a clearing where a group of onlookers were assembled.

Swatting at gnats and feeling briars grabbing at my clothing, I stopped short of the gathering and allowed my eyes to sweep over the canopy of tall, majestic timber that proudly reached toward the cloudless blue sky. Scattered here and there, young men and older gentlemen leaned against the trunks of trees or relaxed on rotting logs or large rocks. Some of the women and children had seated themselves in the sunny, grassy areas overlooking what I soon noticed was a shallow creek that had cut its way through the rugged forest, having carved out a pool of still clear water, creating what was a primitive but ideal site for performing the baptismal services.

I looked back at Granny, Sissy, and Uncle Clint inching their way toward the group of spectators. My eyes finally came to rest on a few folks who seemed to have the best viewing area, so I turned and started to approach the area, threading my way carefully through the thorns and vines. Terrified that a snake might be slinking in the tall weeds, I began passing cautiously in front of a decrepit old man who was sitting beside the narrow path that had been broken through the weeds. At the instant I stepped directly in front of the aged gentleman, my feet slipped, causing me to throw my arms into the air in an effort to recover my balance. To my surprise, I landed in a sitting position on the lap of the unkempt man, who was wearing a dingy white shirt and a disheveled gray suit. As I was attempting to push myself out of the old man's lap, my eyes widened when I looked up into the bearded but beaming face of "Ol' Andy Askew."

"Py Cod (By God), Ol' Andy knowed he'd git 'im a purty girl 'fore 'is here day 'uz over with!" Andy proclaimed loudly.

Embarrassed beyond explanation, I wanted to throw my hands over my eyes and run back to the car; instead, I heard myself laughing softly as I looked toward the other side of the hill at my relatives, who were clapping their hands and laughing hysterically. I managed to pull myself from Andy's clutches and then quickly began gathering the contents of my wallet, which had gone flying through the air, landing on the ground several feet away with pictures sailing in every direction. Just as I had reclaimed my possessions and straightened my clothing, I heard the familiar sound of the people bellowing out the old hymn "Shall We Gather at the River."

I looked down to the base of the hill and noticed the preacher wading out into the hole of water toward a tall stick that one of the men had fixed in the bottom of the pool of water, marking the appropriate depth for baptizing. He stopped beside the stick in the waist-deep water, tipped his head back, raised his arms toward heaven, and joined in the singing. The man who had placed the stick in the water began leading an obese woman toward the preacher. The woman's dress had been pinned between her legs to prevent the tail of the dress from floating to the top of the water once she had been submerged.

When the singing stopped, the preacher stood at the woman's side, with his left hand on her back and his right hand raised toward the sky. The other gentleman stood on the other side of the lady, with his right hand on her back and his left hand grasping her arms, which were folded across her breast. The minister began proclaiming loudly, "I now baptize you, my sister, in the name of the Fa-a-ther, the So-n-n, and the Holy Ghost."

The two men quickly lowered the lady beneath the water, and as they helped her to her feet, she pulled herself loose from the men's grip and began groping her way toward shore, clapping her hands together and shouting loudly, "'Ell glory! 'Ell glory ta God!"

At the water's edge, an older lady handed the dripping-wet woman a dry towel, and while embracing each other, they shouted and sobbed loudly. The crowd continued singing the chorus of the hymn: "Yes, we'll gather atta river. The beau-ti-ful, the beau-fi-ful river. Gather with the Saints atta ri-ver, 'at flows by the throng (throne) of God."

One by one, five more people were submerged in the chilly water. Then as the bystanders repeated the last verse and chorus of the song, the preacher, his assistant, and the men and women who had been baptized began slowly and carefully climbing the hill to where the crowd was waiting. Once they were all together, the crowd shook the new Christians' hands and embraced them heartily after the preacher had dismissed the group in prayer. Then, with an aura of excitement in the air, the crowd began to disperse and work our way back to our cars.

When the last car had driven away, Uncle Clint opened the trunk, and Sissy had handed me the luncheon cloth, which I spread on the ground in a grassy, shaded area. Sissy spread out the food onto the tablecloth, and after Uncle Clint had blessed the food, we ate our fill and then gathered our belongings and began driving across the hills and through the valleys in the opposite direction from which we had come, arriving back home at dusk.

My relatives' highlight of the day had been the sight of me sitting in the lap of Ol' Andy Askew. It would take a lifetime for me to live down that blunder.

LXV

The Kiss

When I returned to work on Monday, Miss Rohr invited me and one of the other salesgirls, Shirlene, to move in with her since her nephew no longer lived there. She explained that we would have full use of her apartment and that she would charge us only $5.00 each, weekly. I was overjoyed and, along with Shirlene, quickly accepted my boss's generous offer.

My relatives were happy for me that I would no longer have to walk in and out of the hollow each day. My grandmother had done housecleaning jobs for Miss Rohr's mother and had known both ladies for years; therefore, since she was aware of Miss Rohr's good reputation, she encouraged the move.

Once Shirlene and I had moved into the upstairs apartment, which was less than a block from the Ben Franklin 5 & 10¢ store where we worked, I could hardly believe that I could now be considered a "city slicker."

I had always been taught that it was sinful for a woman to cheapen herself by openly showing her husband or boyfriend affection in public or by appearing forward even behind closed doors. With this in mind, I knew I would have to be alert constantly in order not to reveal my true feelings to this man I loved.

For the next few evenings, once he'd picked me up after work, Bill would ask where I wanted to go for dinner. Being both shy and ignorant, I would tell him I didn't want anything to eat, although I was usually famished by the end of the day. He would then excuse himself, walk over to the little restaurant where I had bought my first cheeseburger and milkshake, and within minutes return with two scrumptious bacon, lettuce, and tomato sandwiches that literally caused my mouth to water once he'd pulled them out of the bag and offered one to me.

"No, thank you. I'm not hungry," I said each time, knowing I was not being truthful.

"You mind if I eat?" he would then ask.

"No, go ahead," I would reply

For the next two weeks, each time this happened, I sat silently by Bill's side, wishing I could muster enough self-esteem and courage to eat in his presence.

On Wednesday night, Bill picked me up at work, and we

My knight in shining armor.

joined three of his younger siblings, my eleven-year-old sister, and several neighborhood youth at Reamer Tabernacle, where we attended when our own church was having no services. After the service had been dismissed, Bill drove slowly up the road toward our parents' homes in order not to outdistance the group on foot. About a quarter-mile before arriving at his parents' home, Bill pulled the car to the shoulder of the road, turned off the engine, and pulled me close to his side while we waited for the group walking with his sister and brothers. With my sister looking on from the back seat, he tenderly turned my face toward his and then placed a long, warm kiss on my lips.

I was dumbfounded! "Listen!" Bill said softly. "I think I hear a horse running down the road."

With my eyes crossed and my head spinning, I managed to say, "I don't hear anything."

"Oh! That's my heart beating," Bill said amusingly.

I didn't laugh. I simply bowed my head and whispered silently, "Thank you, God, for bringing this wonderful, thoughtful, strong, handsome, and funny man into my life." Basking in the moment, I wished that time would stand still. Now, more than ever before, I had a reason to live! Somehow, I knew that my knight was at last holding me close to his heart. I was ecstatic!

On Sunday, Bill escorted me to the high school to attend Marvin's graduation. I was proud of my brother's achievement but even prouder to be seen with Bill. He continued to pick me up and return me at the doorway to my apartment each evening until he returned to his post three weeks later. Although he had known that I was alone in the apartment on several occasions, I was impressed when he refrained from asking me to invite him inside. I hoped he could sense that my heart belonged only to him; however, it was important to me that he know I was a virtuous young woman.

Bill received several weekend passes during the next six weeks. On several occasions, when he would come to my family's home to pick me up for a date, my eyes would be puffy and my face streaked with tears because I had been experiencing more of Dad's despicable behavior. Bill was careful not to delve into my private misery, although on a couple of occasions he asked me to share with him why I had been crying. I avoided sharing my burden with him because I feared that, should he learn my secret, I wouldn't know, when he asked me to marry him, whether it was because he loved me and wanted to spend the rest of his life with me or because he had felt compelled to marry me to give me an escape from my father's abuse. Right or wrong, I chose to remain silent.

LXVI

In the Huckleberry Patch

I was surprised when the manager assigned me, and me alone, the task of reading all the registers, counting and securing the money at the end of each day, balancing the books the next morning, and then making the daily deposits. I had also begun assisting the manager in the following ways: approving all sales over $1.00, answering the price-check bells from the other salesclerks, writing up employee purchases, decorating the display windows in the store front, checking in truck and rail freight, and pricing merchandise. I had memorized the prices of most of the merchandise on my own counter and throughout the store and was the only salesclerk authorized to ring up sales on registers other than my own. I soon was transferred to the hardware department, where I quickly learned the names and purposes of each piece of hardware.

I knew for certain that I was excelling at my first public job when I began receiving small raises, along with several compliments from the store's owner and manager because of the quality and quantity of work I was doing; however, I worked alongside the other employees and did not consider myself above any of them.

I enjoyed my work, never stopping to think where the job would or would not lead. I had no idea—until the owner informed me later on—that I was being prepared, at my young age, to eventually manage one of his Ben Franklin Variety stores in another town.

A coal-burning freight train ran through our small town daily, periodically delivering freight at the depot for the store. Since none of the employees owned a vehicle, the local merchants were accustomed to seeing a child's red wagon, stacked with crates of freight, being pulled across town by my coworker and me. On occasion, it was necessary for us to make three or four trips to and from the train depot. Although at times I was embarrassed to be seen delivering freight by the store's unusual mode of transportation, I reminded myself that early in life I had learned to handle situations even less glamorous.

While I became more secure and proficient in my work, I had become increasingly alert to customers picking up merchandise and leaving the store without paying. I had trouble believing that the people were actually "stealing" the goods. As a matter of fact, I refused to believe my eyes when a young man I was acquainted with stole an item off my counter. When we had lived on the ridge, the young man lived in the valley behind our house and had gone to the altar during a revival at our church. At the time, he had announced to the congregation that he had been "converted."

I had watched from across the aisle one Saturday morning when he entered the store and walked straight to the hardware counter, picked up a pair of pliers, and stuck them in his pocket. I did not mention the dishonest act to anyone, just in case my eyes had deceived me. The next Saturday morning, while I was squatting behind my counter retrieving merchandise from the under-stock to replenish the counter, I glanced between the countertop and the overhead shelving to see the same young man standing idly beside the counter. Unaware that I could see his hands, he quickly snatched a crescent wrench, lifted his shirt tail, and stuck the item in his waistband. I quickly stood to my feet and watched as he walked briskly outside onto the sidewalk. Feeling my hands shaking and my blood pressure rising, I immediately reported the theft to the store manager, who in turn alerted the clerks that the young man was a thief.

I was shocked and saddened to realize that a customer would actually take merchandise from the store without paying for it—especially a customer who claimed to be a Christian. The incident impressed upon me to begin observing customers acting suspiciously; consequently, during the time I worked at the store, I caught several adults and children shoplifting all sorts of merchandise. The manager allowed the juveniles to return the merchandise after warning them that if they were caught stealing again they would be prosecuted. Once I had caught adults shoplifting, the manager chose to have them observed closely on their next visit to the store. I soon suspected that if all the thieves stealing merchandise from our counters were arrested, the traffic in our store would be cut in half, and the city jail would be filled to capacity. On at least two occasions, I caught two of our own employees stealing money from their registers. Both of them were fired immediately.

I was thankful to have my first public job and didn't question the amount of my wages, because having never received money to spend before getting the job there at the store, I would have been satisfied with even less income. Evidently, I wasn't the only one who thought I was making all the money I needed. Mom and Dad soon requested that I contribute to their expenses even though I was not living at their home. When Aunt Sissy heard about the request, she was infuriated. "Hey orta be 'shamed of 'eirselves, 'spectin' money from you when you hain't even stayin' at home no more," she said angrily. I had never paid my aunt and uncle rent while I was staying in their home; furthermore, they made it clear that they did not expect and would not accept any money from me.

Although I loved my family and knew it was my duty to visit with them periodically, I often deliberately avoided going home. I was concerned that, should I openly defy my father, he would walk into the store and physically drag me to his car. Earlier in the week, Maynard had alerted me that Dad had threatened he would make me quit work and stay home if I failed to obey when he sent me word to return for a visit. After explaining to them the threat that had come from my father, Sissy and Uncle Clint agreed that, regardless of the sad fact that I might again be forced to fight for my own survival, I had no choice but to obey my father. I wondered at the time whether perhaps my relatives didn't fear Dad even more than I feared him.

On Saturday morning, I packed my newly purchased vanity case and carried it to work with me, anticipating my ride home with Marvin, who had quit his job in Ohio and was preparing to join the Air Force. During my lunch hour, I walked across the street and purchased some food items to take to my sister and little brothers. I enjoyed tremendously being able to take them a special treat each time I visited with them, so instead of thinking about the threat that my father posed, I meditated on the excitement my little brothers and sister must be feeling as they anticipated my visit.

It was late when my brother and I drove into the yard and were met immediately by four unkempt little boys squealing in delight. "What chee brang us?" they yelled in unison. It did not concern me that the little fellows probably were more excited about the treats they were expecting than they were at seeing their big sister.

"It's something to eat!" I replied excitedly. "Get on over to the house an' get your plates an' spoons ready."

I entered the house by the kitchen door, immediately found the can opener, and opened the tall can. After quickly dividing the food evenly among the children, I watched as they all began eagerly gobbling down the cold spaghetti. It did not matter to them that they had earlier finished a meal of the traditional pinto beans and fried potatoes. They slurped up the long, gooey strings of pasta in record time.

Thankfully, the night passed with nothing worse happening to me than lying awake half the night listening for the floorboards near my bed to creak. Shortly after breakfast, I noticed Dad bending over a pan of water, working up a thick lather throughout his hair. Knowing it was impossible to make that heap of suds with a bar of soap, I looked near the pan of water and spotted what remained of my small bottle of shampoo. Without saying a word to my dad, I quickly walked over, picked up the shampoo, and returned it to my bag, which I had thought would be safe on top of the sewing machine cabinet inside the bedroom where I had slept. Dad, Mom, nor my younger siblings had ever enjoyed the luxury of shampoo or deodorant. In fact, I had surmised they wouldn't even know what the toiletries were used for, so I had left my new bag unlocked.

Later in the morning, I stopped in my tracks when I stepped through the kitchen doorway and found my father nude from his waist up, rubbing his armpits with something. I glanced down and spied my small fifteen-cent jar of Veto deodorant sitting opened at the corner of the worktable. Sarcastically I exclaimed, "Furnish your own deodorant!"

Dad quickly grabbed the tiny jar and threw it across the room at me. I dodged just as it whizzed past my head and bounced off the wall. Without saying another word, I retrieved the jar and ran out of the room. I was infuriated that my father had rummaged through my overnight bag, helping himself to its contents. I immediately felt remorseful, however, because of the selfish way I had lashed out at my father.

Later in the day, Dad yelled at me, "You been cuttin' your hair, hain't chu?!"

I had indeed cut a couple inches off my hair and had been curling it like all the other girls my age were curling theirs. "Yes," I said. "I cut a little bit off'n the ends."

"You know what I tol' jue!" he screeched. "You cut any more off'n your hair, an' I'll kill you!" He whirled around and walked into the living room and turned the television channel to a ball game.

I was relieved. I decided that, since I had "escaped death" after having cut the two inches off my hair, I would shorten it another six inches. I disliked disobeying my father; nevertheless, I walked outside smiling because I had plans to have a modern hairdo the next time Bill was home on leave.

For some reason, I was given a Saturday off work in the middle of summer, and although Bill wouldn't be in the area, I was excited that Woody would be coming home for the weekend. I left my apartment early on Saturday morning and walked up the street so that I could hitch a ride home with my parents once they had come into town to buy their groceries.

Huckleberries on the surrounding hillsides were very scarce; nevertheless, with a lot of effort and perseverance each year, Mom was usually able to pick enough of the tiny berries to can a few pints. The wild berries grew on shrubs close to the ground. Mom had already scouted the woods and had found a few of the bushes near our home.

Shortly after we arrived home, Mom handed half-gallon buckets to two of my brothers and me, with instructions to go pick any of the ripe berries we could find. I realized it would be a backbreaking and tedious job to fill even one of the pails with the tiny berries, and although I wasn't looking forward to the chore, my two brothers and I obediently climbed the steep hill beside our house and began looking for enough berries to fill at least one of the pails.

To our dismay, when we finally discovered the patch of bushes that Mom had described, the ripened berries were almost nonexistent. I squatted among the scrawny shrubs and slowly and carefully began stripping the puny berries from the branches.

Recalling that, unlike the rattlesnake, the copperhead would never send a warning before striking its victim, I shivered at the thought of reaching for a berry only to have my hand bitten by a venomous snake. Looking around to ascertain that I was safe, I was surprised to discover that my brothers were nowhere in sight. Nervously assuring myself that they were nearby busily filling their pails with more huckleberries than I'd been able to pick from the scrawny bushes I had found, I stood peering through the trees, petrified from my fear of snakes but with no intention of leaving the area until my brothers had returned to lead the way.

As I stood listening for the sound of my brothers' voices, I was relieved to hear the snapping of twigs nearby. Moving cautiously around the side of a big patch of briars in order to get a better view of my surroundings, I gasped in disbelief when I realized that I was alone there in the isolated forest with none other than my father.

"How could this have happened? And where are my brothers?" I asked myself. I was trapped! Why had my uncaring brothers betrayed me? Not only had they left me alone there in the dense forest with all the wild animals and poisonous snakes, it was clear to me that they had left me prey to what I feared more than anything else in the world.

I stood shaking in my shoes, certain that my father wasn't slowly sneaking around the side of the hill to pick huckleberries. Quickly I began yelling for my brothers, only to realize that they were not hearing my frantic calls. I was desperate to flee, yet afraid to run deeper into the woods knowing that to do so would put me even farther from our house. Should I attempt to run in the direction of our house, I realized that I would have to pass closely beside my dad who was standing between a cliff on one side, and heavy brush with tall weeds and matted briars on the other side.

As Dad continued to move toward me, I wondered how he'd known just where to find me. I tried to convince myself that he had climbed the hill for no other reason than to help pick huckleberries; however, I feared that, somehow, he had found out that I had been left alone on the secluded hillside. When he stopped for a minute and reached down as though picking berries from one of the bushes I had just plucked of its precious fruit, my anxieties heightened and my stomach ached.

As soon as I started moving cautiously in what I hoped was the direction of our house, Dad immediately lost all interest in picking berries and moved quickly to block my path. "You know what? You an' me are up here in 'hese here woods all by 'urselves," he said.

I wanted to tell him that that disturbing fact was the reason I was scared out of my wits; instead, I said to him, "Oh no, we're not! Maynard an' Arnold are right around the hill from here."

"No, they hain't," he said.

Panic, frustration, and anger swelled up within me. I wondered what it was going to take to get my troubled father to realize that I had no intention of willingly submitting to his desires—now or ever. Without saying anything in reply to what he'd just said, I again yelled for my brothers. There was no answer.

Smiling in the same sickening way I had seen so often before, he said to me, "Ain't no needa you try'n ta git da boys ta help ye. They done wen' off'na hill ta the house."

Unable to accept the notion that my brothers had left me alone on that hillside, I once again yelled, "Maynard, where are you an' Arnold? Hurry up and come here! I need you!"

Dad tried to move closer, and I continued to back carefully away from him. "I come up here ta git me some lovin' in'na huckleberry patch," he said menacingly.

With him continuing to make filthy suggestions, I broke in and stated as seriously as possible, "Daddy, you know somethin'? I really think you're sick in the head!" It seemed logical that he had to be mentally disturbed to think that after all the encounters I had suffered because of him, that I would willingly yield to his lewd suggestions. I felt that two different men lived inside my father's body, and the one I was alone with at the moment was scaring me out of my wits.

Knowing I had to do something to shock him into reality, I decided impulsively that if I could say something harsh enough, maybe he would become sufficiently enraged to do me no more harm than knocking me down the steep cliff. It was my only chance. I couldn't run deeper into the woods, knowing he would only follow me.

With all the disdain I was feeling for him evident in my voice and countenance, I yelled, "If you need more'n mommy can give you, then why don't you go up town an' get one of 'em sluts off'n the streets?"

Hearing those awful words coming from my own lips made me feel like a cheap tramp myself.

With the sickening smile still on his face, I almost vomited when he replied, "You know I don't want 'em women. I wan' chu, an' you know 'at chu want me too."

Feeling ill, I spat on the ground and screamed, "Leave me alone! I hate your guts, and the sight of you makes me wanna puke!" Tears began running down my cheeks; still, his demeanor did not change. He attempted to move closer to me, but I moved closer to the edge of the cliff.

"I'll give ye 'his here fifty-cent piece if you'll give your ol' daddy some lovin'," he said cunningly, holding out the coin to me, adding insult to injury.

Becoming angrier and more frustrated, I yelled back, "You're sick in the head, Daddy!"

"I'll even take ye ta town this evenin' so you can spend it," he said, ignoring my strong language.

"If you had any sense, you'd quit trying to court your own blood an' kin," I cried out.

It seemed that no matter how I tried, I couldn't make him angry. Apparently realizing that he had me trapped between himself and the steep cliff, he suddenly lunged toward me. I sidestepped him and immediately began sprinting in what I hoped was the direction of the house. Unsure whether he had gone over the cliff or was moving in close behind me, I ran as fast as I could, dodging trees, jumping over rotten logs, and fighting my way through underbrush and briar patches. I had completely forgotten about the snakes I'd feared earlier. My love for Bill had given me a reason to live, and I was determined to arrive back at the house, fully intact and unspoiled.

Finally, bleeding from scratches and panting for air, I dashed across the creek and through the yard. I fell through the living room door and was infuriated to see Maynard and Arnold sitting calmly in the living room watching television. "Why'd y'all run off an' leave me by myself?" I asked them breathlessly.

"Didn' take no dummy ta see 'at 'hey wasn' no huckleberries on 'at hill," Maynard said, without looking up.

I stumbled into the kitchen to find Mom sitting calmly beside the opened back door with a towel spread across her lap, slowly churning the milk to make butter.

"You better make Daddy keep his dirty hands off'n me from now on, or I swear to God I'll turn 'im in to the law!" I bellowed frantically.

"Now, Bethel, you know you hain't gonna do that," Mom said. "What'd I do 'ithout Daddy, an' how'd I feed all 'em young'uns?"

I beat my fists against the wall and squalled. I knew she was right! And she knew it too! If I were to turn Dad in to the authorities, Mom and the kids would suffer more than he would. With tears streaming down my already-tear-streaked face, and feeling as though I needed to vomit, I ran out the door and up the path to the outhouse. There still was this one place where I could have a little privacy; however, I wondered how long it would be before he would deny me even this small privilege.

Sometime later, after a lot of prayer and meditation, I finally settled down and was no longer crying. Realizing I had no other choice, I walked back down to the house, and, along with the rest of the family, I continued pretending that nothing out of the ordinary had taken place.

Woody, his wife, and their little son arrived and stayed until early evening, when he announced that he would be leaving alone the next morning for the Air Force Base to await his upcoming discharge. Still feeling overwhelmed by my ordeal in the huckleberry patch, I realized I had hardly spoken a word to my big brother when he and his family began bidding their farewells before leaving for the home of his in-laws. "Will you drop me off at my apartment?" I asked quickly as I stepped into the bedroom and grabbed my belongings.

"Sure will, City Girl," Woody said with a chuckle.

My brother and I exchanged small talk as we drove out of the hollow and into town. Once back in the apartment, I tried to block the events of the day from my mind; however, I couldn't help but feel compassion for my family. I thought about the soft spot I had in my heart for my mother, even though she sometimes acted as though my life and well-being were of no concern to her. I also thought about the strong bond I had developed with my siblings over the years. Still, the way I had reacted when I caught my father using my shampoo and the measly jar of deodorant were haunting me. The hateful things I'd said to him in the huckleberry patch seemed to be causing me as much pain as my thoughts about his deplorable actions toward me.

On Sunday, as I sat alone in the apartment, my thoughts returned once again to the seemingly hopeless situation I was in. I was feeling as though I were caught in a trap and that the jaws of the trap were ripping me apart; still, as I recalled how I had talked to my father and the way I had lashed out at my mother and brothers, I feared that I was becoming bitter. Aware that the bitterness could eventually harm me more than it would hurt anyone else affected by it, I emotionally cried out, "Oh God, please, please help me to hold onto You and not to become a hateful, spiteful person."

LXVII

A Stake Through the Heart

Life had become more important since I'd begun anticipating a future with Bill. No one, not even Bill, knew that I'd fallen head over heels in love with him. I was too shy and afraid of seeming brash to reveal my true feelings to anyone. Bill was home on a three-day pass, and I had planned to spend as much time as possible with him.

When I got off work on Friday evening, Bill had borrowed his brother's car and was waiting to spend the evening with me while also visiting with his sister and her family. I knew I would be able to spend more time with Bill if he were to drop me off at my parents' home instead of my apartment, which he agreed to do after I had assured him that I would be able to find a way to work the next morning. Knowing that he was aware of my 9 p.m. curfew, I was surprised when he delivered me at my parents' home early. During our date I had noticed that Bill had seemed extremely cold and distant. Although I could sense something was wrong, I had been too timid to question his actions.

I knew that Dad couldn't know I had never mentioned to Bill how my own father had been torturing me for years, so once I was inside my folks' home, I wasn't concerned about spending the night, especially since Dad seemed to ignore me when he knew that Bill was home on leave. With the uncertainties weighing heavily on my mind,

I went to bed thinking about how unbearable life would be should I lose my darling's love.

On Saturday morning, after a restless night, I rode out of the hollow with Mom and Dad when they went to town to buy groceries, believing that Bill would pick me up after work. Bill and I had already made plans for me to spend the rest of the weekend at my folks' home so that he would be able to see me without having to borrow a car. Throughout the day, however, I worried about how distant he had been the evening before.

After work on Saturday evening, Maynard met me at the front of the store. He had heard that Bill had gone to Ohio to see another girl and knew I would need an escort home. I was absolutely heartbroken. I could not accept the fact that Bill could be this thoughtless. I wondered what had happened to change the way he'd felt about me. With my heart aching, all I could do was to trust that Maynard's information had been incorrect and that I would hear from Bill on Sunday.

I was glad that my family was in bed when Maynard and I arrived home. I didn't want to face them feeling so sad and dejected. Mom was expecting her thirteenth child any day, and I sure hoped she would not go into labor anytime soon. I was already dealing with more problems than I felt capable of handling.

On Sunday morning, Dad forbade me to go to Sunday School since Mom might go into labor and thus need me to stay with her while he went for the doctor (my family still had no telephone). I was disappointed because I knew that the only way I could hear anything about Bill would be from his sister, who would be at church. I was confident that she would tell me the truth; however, I had no choice other than to accept Dad's ruling to spend the day alone with my family.

Dad seemed intent on making me feel even more miserable than I was feeling already. "He's out 'ith some other girl, an' you orta know 'at he hain't never gonna be tied down ta you," he said.

"He will be here before the day ends," I replied.

"Y'ur a bigger idiot then I figgered if you thank he keers anythang abou' chu. He's jist out ta git what 'e's wantin'," Dad said, with a twinkle in his eye as if he were enjoying heaping even more pain upon me.

Knowing that my father would continue to badger me if I stayed in the room, I hurried into the kitchen, where I stood gazing down the road, in hopes that I would see Bill walking up the road toward our house.

Within moments I was surprised to see Bill's brother's car stop over at the main road. I was even more surprised when Bill stepped out of the car wearing his khaki uniform. Watching him walking toward the front of our house, I excitedly hurried through the house and to the door to greet my beloved Bill.

"I want you to go 'ith us up the road to the schoolhouse. I need to talk to you about somethin'," he said.

Reluctantly, Dad gave his permission, with the warning that I had better not go beyond a specified area. "You know 'at I might nee' jue any minute, an' I better not hafta go huntin' fer you neither," he said emphatically.

The neighborhood youth were holding a ball game and picnic on the school grounds, and I wondered whether Bill was planning to attend the function. I really didn't care where we were going just as long as we were together. Slowly, I walked by his side until we got to the car and joined his older brother, Denzil, and Denzil's wife, Larna.

On the drive up the road, Bill deliberately began trying to provoke me; still, I couldn't bring myself to say anything back to him. He confirmed that he had gone to Marietta, Ohio, to see a girl he had heard was interested in him. Receiving no reaction from me, he said to his brother and sister-in-law, "She's the biggest baby I've ever seen. There's hardly been a time that I've picked her up fer a date that she wasn't cryin'."

"You should be 'shamed a yourself talkin' 'bout her like you're doin'," Denzil replied.

My heart ached. I looked at Bill sitting there beside me, rigid and seemingly amused. I wished I could share with him the reason I was usually crying when he arrived at my parents' home. Even now, certain that he was planning to walk out of my life, I had no choice but to suffer in silence. I just hoped that someday I would be able to explain to this man whom I loved more than life itself why I'd been compelled to keep my awful secret from him.

At the picnic, Bill immediately walked over and joined the guys. I tried to act as though nothing was wrong while I visited with the girls. There was no doubt in my mind, however, that Bill was ignoring me and wanted me to know it. I fought very hard to hold back tears.

At least an hour had passed when Bill finally approached me. "Let's take a walk," he said coldly. "I've gotta talk to you." Although I knew the inevitable was about to happen, I walked meekly by his side like an innocent lamb being led to the slaughter.

When we were no longer in sight of the group at the picnic, Bill reached down and took my hand into his and guided me to a little grassy knoll just a few feet from the roadway. I wanted to run in the opposite direction because I knew that the end had come. He tipped my head back with his gentle touch and looked sadly into my eyes, seemingly sensing that I was not prepared for what was about to take place. I wanted to throw my arms around his neck and beg him not to say the things I feared were on the tip of his tongue; instead, I fell to my knees there in the grass, fighting desperately to keep my composure.

Quickly, as though he feared he would change his mind, Bill began babbling about what he had evidently been wanting to say to me since Friday evening when he'd picked me up at work. "You're the first girl I've ever dated, an' I gotta find out what my true feelin's are for you," he said softly. "I think I need to date other girls so I'll know whether or not I truly love you."

I could hold back the tears no longer. It was over in his mind. I knew I couldn't let him walk away from me without trying to tell him that he was making a mistake; however, the words would not form on my quivering lips. He seated himself in the cool, green grass beside me and touched my hand. I didn't look up at him. His tenderness was making it even more difficult for me to accept what he had just said to me.

Realizing with sadness that he was determined to walk out of my life, I had no choice but to allow him to go. I wanted very much to make him understand just how I felt about him, but another part of me wished I could tell him to go ahead and walk out of my life, that I didn't care; however, I felt no anger toward him. "Don't go, please. You don't know how important you are to me," I pleaded tearfully.

Before he could respond, a car came speeding up the dirt road with a cloud of dust trailing behind. I went limp when I recognized my dad's car. Dad screeched the car to a halt on the edge of the road where we were sitting and yelled angrily for me to come with him. After whirling the car around in the middle of the dirt road, he yelled forcefully at me again. I slowly pulled myself to my feet and began walking toward the car, trembling and weeping softly.

Once Dad had started speeding down the road, I looked back at Bill, who was still standing on the knoll looking in our direction. I wondered whether I would ever again see the man whom I believed God was intending me to marry. It was the deepest hurt I had ever experienced.

Dad showed neither concern nor mercy for me as he continuously made filthy accusations against Bill. While I sat weeping silently, I realized that his hateful words didn't seem to matter anymore. I remained silent when he finally dropped me off at our house and continued down the road to bring the doctor.

In what must have been record time, Dad returned with the family doctor and Mom's lady friend, who had married the man in town who owned the television. I was thankful to now be able to leave the room where Mom was moaning and groaning. As I retired to the back bedroom, I realized that the events transpiring in the living room, where Mom had taken her bed to give birth, had temporarily overshadowed my grief.

I could hear the doctor ordering Mom to push. I was too timid and scared to walk into the room where all the action was taking place; besides, I was sure that Mom would give me another chance to learn anything I needed to know about birthing. She was superstitious, so she surely wouldn't stop on number thirteen.

It felt close to thirty minutes after the doctor had arrived when I heard the cries of a newborn baby. In a very monotone voice, the same doctor who had delivered me almost seventeen years earlier said, "Mrs. Lesher, you've got another boy."

"Well, Doc, I was tryin' fer another girl, but I'mma gettin' too ol' ta keep on tryin'," Mom replied.

"This one's in fine shape and weighs in at ten pounds and nine ounces," Doctor Fleisher said.

A few minutes later, Mrs. Ross stepped from the living room into the dining room with the baby in her arms. "He's all ready fer you," she said, as I approached and she placed my new brother in my arms.

I looked down at the tiny little hands and small round face protruding out of the soft blanket Mrs. Rose had wrapped around him. I counted the ten fingers on his hands and then uncovered his little feet and counted his toes. I was pleased that my new brother seemed to be in perfect shape, but my heart was too heavy to feel any real excitement. I couldn't help but wonder whether Bill and I would ever be able to hold a baby of our own.

Mom had told me earlier before the doctor had arrived that if the baby was another boy, she planned to name him Michael. "You can give him his middle name," she had said.

I held him closely and kissed him on his little pink cheeks. "Welcome to the family, Michael William," I said.

Early the next morning, June 9, 1952, I was surprised when Bill suddenly appeared outside the opened, screenless window beside Mom's bed, leaned forward with his elbows resting on the window sill, looked in at Mom, and politely said, "Let me see that new baby, Marthy." While I stood in the background wondering what was going on in Bill's mind, Mom held baby Michael over to where Bill could get a good look at him. After he had exchanged a few pleasantries with Mom, Bill asked her whether it would be possible for me to go for a short walk with him.

From the tone of his voice, I knew already that my handsome soldier wasn't there to give me good news; even so, I held on to a thread of hope that he had changed his mind about walking out of my life. When Mom gave her approval, I felt that my body was almost too heavy to move; still, I forced myself to walk outside to once again hear the words that would finish driving in the stake that had from the previous day been piercing my already broken heart.

Bill stepped over beside me and, without saying a word, took my hand in his as we began walking toward the swinging footbridge spanning the creek that flowed between our house and the rock-base road. As we slowly edged our way down the road, Bill, seemingly unsure of how to say what he was intent on saying, began apologizing for coming back to make certain I had understood why he had decided to break off our courtship. With my tears already flowing freely, I couldn't believe what I was hearing and began to plead with him not to leave me.

With my face streaked with tears and my nose running embarrassingly, I wiped at my face with the palm of my hand. Bill held onto my other hand tightly, assuring me that he was sorry for causing me so much grief, at the same time leaving no doubt in my mind that he was severing all ties between us. Holding onto my hand tightly, he slowly turned around, and we began walking back up the road.

I was embarrassed that he was witnessing my weakness, but there was no way I could mask the pain I was suffering. He stopped, still holding my hand, and asked, "Will you give me a goodbye kiss?" I wanted to throw myself into his arms, never to let him go, but I couldn't prolong the agony. I knew that my entire face and my lips were wet from crying, and even while my heart was being ripped out of my body, I was too proud to allow Bill to kiss me under these conditions.

Slowly, he began backing away from me. I held on to him until, with our arms outstretched, only the tips of our middle fingers were making contact. As he turned and walked rapidly down the road, I managed to force myself over to our washhouse, where I fell to the floor and cried hysterically. Reaching up and feeling the chain around my neck that held Bill's military ring, I twisted the chain tightly until it cut into my flesh. I honestly wanted to die, but I knew I didn't have the nerve to take my own life. I tried to pray, but neither my heart nor my thoughts would cooperate.

I don't know how long I sat there alone. I was surprised when I saw my oldest brother drive over to the house and drop off his wife and son. Without getting out of the car, he then turned the car around and drove away. I remained in the washroom. I didn't want to return to the house, where I'd have to explain anything. "Oh God, why do I have to live?" I finally heard myself asking over and over.

Sometime later, with my body feeling practically numb, I slowly made my way down to the edge of the creek. I stooped down and cupped a handful of the cool water from the creek and splashed it onto my puffy face. I knew I had to force myself to return to the room where Mom would be resting in bed for the next nine days, with me missing work so that I could take care of her, baby Mike, and the rest of the family.

Mary, Woody's wife, was sitting near Mom's bed, explaining how Woody was looking for work in the area now that he was a civilian. The younger children were outside playing, so Mom asked curiously as I walked past her bed, "What did he wanna talk about?"

"He quit me," I muttered. "He quit me."

"Oh well, there's more fish in'na sea 'an one," Mom said coldly.

"Yell, you've got plenty time ta find somebody else," Mary said, giggling and shifting my little nephew from her left arm to her right arm.

"I don't want anybody else!" I managed to say sharply. I ran out the back door, where I huddled against the house and cried until the tears would no longer flow.

Later in the day, I walked up the hollow to a place where a huge sycamore tree had fallen across the cleared pipeline right-of-way. I sat alone on the log for what seemed like an hour or longer. My thoughts once again had turned to the Lord, and I finally realized that I was not alone after all. The One who had promised never to leave me was by my side and seemingly holding my hand. I rolled off the big log and dropped to my knees there on the ground. With a broken and contrite heart, I asked God to forgive me for temporarily losing faith in Him. I then asked Him to give me strength and direction for what remained of my young life.

Almost immediately, God assured me that He would never have allowed me to love Bill with the intensity with which I loved him unless Bill was going to eventually return my love. He also reminded me that somewhere in the scriptures (Psalm 27:14) I had read a verse saying, "Wait on the Lord: be of good courage and He shall strengthen thine heart: wait, I say, on the Lord."

Although I was only seventeen, I had realized for some time that I had been robbed of my childhood and that mentally I was more mature than other ladies twice my age. I had always believed strongly that God would send me a husband of character who would love me, cherish me, and protect me from the harm and evil I had been experiencing for most of my life. I knew deep within my heart that I had fallen in love with such a person, and at this painful moment in my life, I believed that God was simply asking me to allow Bill time to realize that he not only loved me but that he also wanted me to become his wife.

I stood to my feet and began walking toward the house with the assurance from God that when Bill was ready, he would be back. I also knew that no matter how long it might take, I would be waiting for my knight to return to me.

LXVIII

The Sympathy Game

Word had spread rapidly among the young people in the community that Bill and I had gone our separate ways, and within a couple of weeks I had already been approached by several young men in and around the area. I had no desire to date any of these guys, especially since their reputations had reached me before the guys themselves did.

I had returned to work and was still living in the apartment in town. As much as possible, I had been avoiding spending my weekends at home. Although I was still grieving over losing Bill's love, I tried to camouflage my feelings and to act as cheerful as humanly possible. Even during the weekends when I had learned that Bill would be home on pass, I avoided returning to the area.

Eventually, Dad once again began insisting that I spend more weekends at home. During the visits, I always attended our little country church, only to be badgered by some of the young men who were known to visit the church for no other reason than to try to pick up the local girls. One obstinate man in his mid-twenties was especially annoying, since he regularly insisted on escorting me from the church to my parents' home. Although I had repeatedly spurned the pest's unwanted approaches, he continued to annoy me. Finally out of desperation, while walking down the road toward my home with several of the neighborhood youth, I pushed him out of my face and deceived him into believing he could walk me home the next Sunday night—if only he would go away and leave me alone.

Once he had agreed and had turned around and was walking up the road in the opposite direction, I laughed and said to the rest of the group, "The guy is nuttier than I thought if he actually believes that I'm gonna keep that promise."

I not only worried all week about how to handle the problem I had created for myself, I also wondered why the undesirables were so persistent in trying to date me when the guy I loved wouldn't give me the time of day. Life sure was puzzling.

Dad hadn't been to church in years, and my mother still was attending only the Sunday night services. The very next weekend that I went home, in anticipation of attending the evening services, Mom had prepared the evening meal early. Since Dad no longer joined the family at the table, Mom had carried the washbasin into the living room so he could wash his hands before eating his meal, which Mom, as was her custom, also carried to him.

Just as the rest of the family had seated ourselves at the table, one of the children yelled to Mom that Uncle Clint, Aunt Sissy, and Grandma had just driven into the yard. Grabbing his plate and glass of water, Dad ran into the dining room and quickly seated himself at the table. Once my relatives were inside, Mom invited them to join Dad and my siblings around the table. After Uncle Clint and Grandma had washed their hands, they immediately seated themselves alongside Dad, as Mom, Sissy, and I proceeded to the living room to wait for our turn.

When the meal was over and Mom, Sissy, and I had eaten the leftovers, the children were all shooed outside while the adults seated themselves in the living room to chat. I immediately cleared the table and then placed a warm pan of water on it so I could wash the dishes while listening to the adults' conversation.

Since Uncle Clint had been raised in the same area where my family now lived, he knew most of the people. He was telling my folks that a man living in the area had been arrested for molesting his daughter. I stopped what I was doing and stepped into the doorway to see how my father would react to the news.

When my uncle finished with his story, my father, shaking his head from side to side in disgust, said, "'At durdy scoundrel orta be tarred an' feathered."

Uncle Clint, speaking sharply, said, "No, 'at'd be too good fer a man like 'at."

Mom quickly changed the subject and started telling Sissy and Uncle Clint about the wrestling matches on television. Shaking my own head in disbelief and disgust, I walked back into the dining room. I wondered how my father could criticize the man's behavior when he knew full well that he was guilty of trying to do the same thing to me. I wondered whether Uncle Clint and Sissy had been as dumbfounded as I'd been on hearing Dad's response to the matter. Once again, I wished I could understand how my father's mind really worked.

I was aware of the father and daughter whom Uncle Clint had spoken about, and I wondered how the authorities had learned about the situation. The man, his daughter, and his young son had come into the store on numerous occasions when the father was escorting his two children to school. Having myself been subjected to my dad's abnormal actions, I recognized what I perceived to be another case of sick behavior between a father and his daughter. The difference between their situation and mine was, in my judgment, the daughter seemed to be a willing participant. I based my opinion on the fact that she had never appeared to resist her father's questionable actions when they were in the store shopping for gifts for her, while her younger brother had quietly walked out of the store empty-handed. I was pleased to learn that the father had been arrested. I hoped that hearing the news about the man's arrest would cause my own father to become seriously concerned about his own actions.

My relatives had been gone about half an hour when Dad deliberately rubbed himself against me while I stood beside the bed, changing my baby brother's diaper. I couldn't resist taking the opportunity to remind him of what he had said earlier in the day. "A man like you orta be tarred and feathered!" I said firmly.

Dad pushed me down on the bed and then stormed into the dining room, where I heard him open, and then slam shut, the refrigerator door. He angrily yelled to Mom and asked, "What'na Sam Hill's happened to 'is bottom shelf in 'is here 'frigerator?"

"I set a pot a beans in 'ere on 'at glass shelf an' didn' know 'hey was hot 'nuff ta break da glass," Mom said, lying through her teeth. She knew perfectly well that one of the boys had accidentally broken the shelf while trying to adjust the shelves to accommodate larger containers.

"I orta kick your ass fer doin' sich a dumb thang!" Dad yelled. "You ain't got da sense 'at God give a hog!" Then, as if in total frustration, Dad grabbed the .22 rifle off the wall and started for the drawer where the bullets were supposed to be stored.

I walked into the room and stepped over close to my mother. "Oh no," I whispered to Mom, "He's back to killin' himself."

Unable to find the shells in the drawer, Dad sucked air through his teeth and then said in a very threatening manner, "Marthy, you better give me 'em shells 'fore I fine 'em myself an' 'en blow your head off!"

Dad sitting in doorway of our cabin on Leatherwood holding his rifle.

Mom stood whimpering, her arms folded across her chest and her fingers digging into her shoulders. I quickly muttered to Mom, "Give him the shells before he gits mad enough to bend the gun barrel over your head."

While Dad continued jerking clothing out of the dresser drawers, Mom looked at me with uncertainty and then whispered, "But what if he keels hisself?"

"He's bluffin' like he always does," I whispered.

Reluctantly, Mom stepped into the boys' bedroom and took the cartridges out of the pocket of a coat that was hanging against the wall. She then stepped over and handed the shells to Dad. He grabbed the ammunition out of her hand, jammed them into the rifle's chamber and magazine, and then stormed out of the room. I watched as he angrily stomped up the hollow behind our house.

Mom tearfully said, "Now Bethel, if he keels hisself, it'll be all my fault."

"You know somethin', Mommy, that's exactly why he kills himself so often," I said to her. "He doesn't care in the least what he puts us through. He's tryin' to make us feel sorry for him."

"My God, Bethel! What'd we do if he does shoot hisself?" Mom asked, sniffling.

"He hasn't done it in all 'ese years, so I doubt if he's gonna shoot himself 'his time," I answered.

Mom shuffled over and slumped onto the sofa, crying softly. I hoped that I had predicted accurately; however, I must admit that even I was apprehensive, but I wasn't about to let Mom know it.

A few minutes passed, and then we heard the unmistakable crack from the rifle. My heart and stomach seemed to change places in my body. I wondered whether my troubled father had really carried out his threat. I thought that, if he had, I—not my mother—would be at fault. I ran over to the door and, seeing Maynard walking up the path toward the house, frantically motioned for him to hurry.

"What's a matter?" Maynard asked, as he quickly arrived at the door.

"Daddy took the rifle up the holler threatenin' to kill himself ag'in," I replied.

"What's so differ'nt bout 'at?" Maynard muttered.

"Didn't you hear 'at rifle shot just now?" I asked.

"Yell, was that him?" Maynard asked in astonishment.

We knew that the numerous other times when Dad had gone to the woods to shoot himself, that he'd never once fired the rifle. "See if you can sneak up the holler an' see if he's okay," I said to my brother. "Be careful 'at he doesn't see you." It aggravated me to know that we might be playing into Dad's hands; even so, I couldn't ignore the situation, knowing that Dad could be lying up there in the hollow with a bullet in his skull. Maynard moved slowly, hiding in the bushes and behind rocks to prevent Dad from detecting his presence. After he had approached the spot where he had decided Dad had gone, I nervously stood and watched as he disappeared out of sight.

Mom walked over to the door and, with her hands clasped tightly together, asked me, "What's goin' on?"

"Maynard went to see," I answered. "He'll be back soon." She and I stood in the doorway and waited anxiously for Maynard to return.

Maynard soon appeared and looked at Mom with a blank stare. I held my breath and asked, "Well, what'd you see?"

Speaking in his slow southern drawl, he stated, "'At son-of-a-biscuit-eater had jist shot a big rock, an' is jist settin' up 'ere poutin'." My brother later informed me that he had lain on his belly and crawled to a point where he could get a good view of the area without Dad detecting his presence.

"Don't chu young'uns say nuthin' to him when he comes ta the house," Mom said.

It wasn't long before we looked outside and saw Dad walking past our house with a log about six feet long resting on his shoulder. His rifle was nowhere in sight. Puzzled, we watched as he crossed the creek, still carrying the log, and began climbing the steep hill on the other side of the main road.

About fifty feet up the hill, my father dropped the log, turned around, and headed back off the hill. He passed by our house again and continued walking up the hollow where he had gone earlier to kill himself. Moments later, he walked through the front door, hung the rifle on the nails he had driven into the bedroom wall months earlier, and turned around and picked up the big family Bible that had been handled very little since the morning he had threatened to run his car over the hill to kill himself. Without speaking a word, he walked over and sank down into his overstuffed chair, slowly opened the Bible, and began reading from the Old Testament.

Within minutes, Dad closed the Bible, walked across the room, and switched channels on the television set. Mom finally asked him about the log. "I fell an' hit my head on a rock, an' the nex' thang I knowed, I was tryin' ta clim' up 'at hill with 'at heavy log on my back," he said.

Watching from the dining room and being careful to stay out of his view, I felt like saying, "Liar, liar, pants on fire!" I wondered whether the family's attempt to ignore his threat would have any effect on him. At the same time, I suddenly felt a sense of compassion for my troubled father. I quickly walked outside, intent on not allowing him to detect my concern. Once again, I asked myself how I could have such deep contempt for my father one moment and then feel sincere compassion for him the next. I wondered whether I would ever find the answer to my question.

LXIX

The Ecstasy

I continued to work at the 5 & 10, and although Bill and I had not reconciled, I waited for the day when he would return to me. I had shared with Aunt Sissy how much I yearned for Bill to realize that he loved me, and she agreed with me that he would, sooner or later, return and ask me to marry him. She had shared with me the possibility that if Bill felt I was becoming interested in someone other than himself, he might feel the importance of making a decision more quickly. Believing her advice to be worth following, I had again halfheartedly begun dating the guy who had been escorting me to church the first time Bill had come home on furlough. I had always appreciated Clay and the respect he had for me. Excluding Bill, Clay was the only guy I could trust not to attempt to take advantage of me. Besides, he was aware that my heart belonged to Bill and that I would no doubt return to Bill's arms should I be given the chance. I had also discovered that having a steady boyfriend discouraged the undesirables from pestering me, since Clay had been my solution for escaping the date I had promised to Ray weeks earlier.

On that occasion, when I had attended church with the neighborhood youth on Sunday night, I had been concerned when I learned Ray was waiting for me outside the church. I had worried during the entire service how I would explain to him that I had not been serious when I had promised him he could walk me home after church.

As fate would have it, when the service had closed and I'd joined my group of friends as we walked toward our homes, Ray, the sot to whom I'd promised the date, approached me and grabbed me by the arm. I immediately started to resist, but he had become agitated and was insisting I keep my word. Suddenly, from out of the darkness, another guy had stepped up beside me and said sternly, "She's my date for tonight."

I was relieved when I recognized Clay, and most of all I was shocked but pleased how he had defended me from the scum who would not take "no" for an answer. Clay shoved Ray to the side and muttered something to him that I did not hear. He then hurried back to my side and took my hand in his, and together we walked the rest of the way to my folks' house.

Before he left me at my front door, Clay told me that his showing up at the right time had been planned ever since he had learned what a mistake I had made by promising Ray the date. He also told me he had warned Ray never to bother me again. I had no desire to be with Clay again, especially after I had dropped him to be with Bill; however, I did not discourage the concern he had demonstrated for me by rescuing me from Ray's clutches.

From that Sunday night forward, Clay had arranged to meet me after work every Saturday night to drive me to either my parents' or my relatives' home. Since he had no car of his own, his best friend would usually drive us to my relatives' home on Sunday nights after church; staying there meant I would not have to ride out of the hollow alone with my father on Monday mornings. To protect my privacy, I wouldn't return to my apartment because I didn't want Clay and his friend to learn the address where I sometimes stayed alone. The two guys had never asked me to explain why I always spent Sunday nights at Sissy's house; however, they were faithful to deliver me there safely every Sunday night.

In late fall, I was at work when I was astonished to see Bill walking across the sales floor in my direction. When he asked to speak with me, I pointed out that I was busy with a customer at the time and that he should come back a little later. He seemed to be agitated because I was unable to speak with him at that moment, so he blurted out, "I'm returnin' to the front lines of Korea when I git back to camp, and since I may not be comin' back alive, I want to be certain that you are not angry with me." He then turned and walked out of the store before I could respond.

I became extremely nervous and uncertain of what I should do next. I wondered what he had been attempting to say to me. For a moment, I wondered whether he hadn't been soliciting my pity. It certainly sounded similar to some of my dad's capers. I quickly dismissed the thought, preferring to believe he was merely finding a way to tell me he had finally realized that he indeed loved me.

Tears welled up in my eyes. I quickly rang up my customer's sale and then immediately retreated to the back stockroom to regain my composure. Miss Rohr and my closest friend, Louise, soon appeared at my side. Upon seeing my tears and listening as I brokenly recounted what Bill had said to me, Miss Rohr asked angrily, "What's he trying to do, rub salt into the wound he's inflicted upon you?" I wanted to jump to my knight's defense, but I bit my tongue and allowed Miss Rohr to continue. "Go upstairs to the washroom and splash cold water on your face, and then you and Louise walk down the street to the post office."

I did as she said, and when I walked back downstairs, my manager was again waiting for me. "If you see that heartbreaker on the street, you throw your head back and act as if you're the happiest girl on earth," she said. "Don't you give him the satisfaction of knowing that you're the least bit concerned about him."

Louise and I stepped out onto the sidewalk and began walking down the street. A few parking spaces away from the front of our store, Bill stood leaning against a parking meter. Reluctantly, I did as my manger had said. I held my head high and, without saying a word, smiled and continued walking past Bill as though he were a total stranger. Almost immediately, my smile faded when I suddenly realized that I might have just blown the only chance I would have to reconcile with this man who had stolen—and then broken—my heart. Nevertheless, no matter how much I was tempted, I refused to look back at him. At the moment, I trusted my manager's judgment more than I trusted my own.

When Louise and I walked back to the store, Bill was nowhere to be seen. The emptiness within my heart seemed overwhelming, and I knew that only Bill could fill the void. I fought back tears as the minutes seemed to turn into hours. Finally, after what seemed to be an eternity, I looked up to see Bill once again walking toward my department. I bit my lower lip and swallowed slowly and deliberately as our eyes momentarily met. I smiled at him, and my heart leapt for joy when he returned my smile. "We need to talk," he said in a trembling voice. "You have a date fer tonight?"

"Not to my knowledge," I said, knowing fully that Clay would soon be at the front of the store waiting for me to get off work. "Wait for me at the back door."

He tipped his head toward me slightly and then turned slowly and began walking away. He was more handsome and polite than any man I had ever met. Tears of joy filled my eyes. I felt sure that he was coming back to me. "Thank you, God," I whispered. "Maybe Sissy's advice is working."

The concern I had about an incident that had happened the day before, when Bill had seen me with Clay, vanished as swiftly as a snowball on a hot July day. Clay and I had been standing outside the church, watching the people gathering onto the church grounds for the evening services, when suddenly Bill had appeared, looking sharp and well-groomed in his khaki uniform.

My heart had ached when Clay reached down and took my hand about the same instant that Bill had looked toward us. I was surprised when Bill seemed to suddenly become angry and, at the same instant, began muttering a string of expletives. I had never heard a curse word pass through his lips. I wanted to run to him, to throw my arms around his neck, and to assure him that he and I belonged together; however, I knew, according to what my advisors had been telling me would be in my best interests, that I must keep my composure and pretend I was not even aware that he was near.

Now here I was again—scheming to drop Clay like I had done when Bill had come home on his first furlough. Knowing that Clay and I had made a date to attend a revival meeting in his neighborhood, I began scolding myself for planning to toss this kindhearted man aside again for Bill; nevertheless, I realized my heart was overruling my head. The opportunity to maybe get back with Bill was too important for me to dwell on the fact that I was jilting Clay.

I wouldn't be able to leave work for at least a couple more hours, and the anxiety was almost more than I could take. I did not know what Bill had on his mind to talk about, but I felt he would be asking me to wait for him until he could return from Korea. I knew what my answer was going to be if he did ask me, but again, I'd been instructed not to appear too eager. After all, Bill had walked away from me. I had been advised by "the experts" that I had to make him suffer a little for what he had put me through. Incidentally, the "experts" were the store manager, who was almost forty years old, and one of my coworkers, who was even older than Miss Rohr. It had never occurred to me that maybe the reason the two spinsters didn't have boyfriends or husbands themselves was possibly because they had treated their guys the same way they had been advising me to treat Bill.

The long couple of hours finally passed, and I walked out the back door to meet with Bill. I had asked him to meet me at the back of the store, deliberately omitting the fact that Clay would be waiting to meet me at the front of the store. I'd at least had the decency to ask Louise to inform Clay that I would be unable to meet him and that I would explain at a later time.

Once Bill had opened the car door and I had seated myself inside, he walked around and scooted himself under the steering wheel. He explained that he had borrowed his brother's car with intentions to take me somewhere quiet so that we could talk. We had driven only one city block from where I worked, however, when the car stalled and failed to start again. Bill managed to shove the car into a parking space, which we would soon learn was directly beneath a streetlight. We sat there in the car for the rest of the evening and late into the night. I had never stayed out later than 9 p.m., but on this night, time didn't seem to matter to either of us. Back in the arms of the man I loved, I could have been stranded on the moon and not have noticed.

Bill seemed to be as happy and relieved as I was to be a couple again. We talked for a while and then just sat and held onto each other, watching the night crowd as they passed by gawking at us. A policeman even peered through the car windows a few times but drove away when he realized that it was apparent this young soldier and his girl were doing nothing immoral. Sometime during the night, Bill walked me upstairs to my apartment, and once I had unlocked the door, he kissed me good night before leaving to find someone to help him start the car so that he could return to his brother's house.

Our evening together had been perfect. Bill had asked me to marry him upon his return from Korea, and I had happily accepted. There was no doubt in either of our minds that we belonged together. We vowed to remain faithful to each other as we joyfully anticipated becoming husband and wife. I had a few loose ends to take care of, but my hope was renewed and my faith strengthened. God had kept His promise to me. He had brought Bill back into my life, and I would forever be grateful.

On Sunday morning I awoke early, happily anticipating spending the day with Bill. I was elated when I heard his knock at my door. I had never invited him inside, and I was aware that we could spend the day alone inside the apartment; instead, I stepped into the hallway and closed the door behind me. Bill pulled me close to his chest, and, feeling his warm, strong arms around me, I looked into his eyes and knew that I was back where I belonged.

On our way down the stairs to the sidewalk, Bill said to me, "I couldn't borrow a car, so I walked out of the holler."

"That's okay," I replied. "We'll only have more time to spend together if we walk wherever we're goin'."

The sun was shining, and the warm, fall breeze seemed to be inviting us to walk into the country, where we could enjoy the splendor of God's handiwork. Although I was wearing a skirt, blouse, and saddle shoes—since I had always been taught that wearing trousers was a sin—Bill and I decided to spend the day hiking. We would begin the long trek by walking northeast four miles up Morris Creek Road and then Birch Creek, where we could stop and visit with Sissy, Uncle Clint, and Granny. After the visit, we would continue up the hollow to where my family had lived before moving onto the ridge. We planned to then walk over the gas pipeline right-of-way that crossed over the mountain, across the valley, up and over the next mountain, and then down the hollow to my folks' house on Leatherwood, where I planned to spend the night. Bill would then walk the 500 yards to his parents' home, totally unaware of the horror I could be facing when I stepped inside my family's home.

Mom's brother Hubert and his family were visiting with my aunt and uncle when we arrived. Both families were sprawled lazily on the cool, green grass beneath the row of pawpaw trees that separated the yard from the pasture. Bill and I dropped to our knees in the grass and sat down beside my relatives, chatting with the adults and playing with my little cousins. Sissy gave me a hug and congratulated Bill and me when we shared with the group that we had decided to marry as soon as Bill returned from Korea.

After visiting with my relatives for about thirty minutes, Bill and I bid our farewells and, walking hand in hand, began on our long journey. It was apparent that we could have been happier only if the coming year of separation hadn't been bearing heavily on our minds.

Once we had left the valley and begun the steep, dusty climb up the hand-mown pipeline right-of-way, I was particularly impressed that Bill was concerned I might become overly fatigued, knowing that we needed to finish the treacherous journey before dark since neither of us had brought along a flashlight. At the top of the mountain, we stopped and took in the breathtaking view of the valley below. An early frost had nipped the canopy of leaves, bringing out an assortment of colors that resembled a multi-colored patchwork quilt. Bill, knowing the area well, pointed out to me the lay of the land and where the hollow we were intent on reaching was located.

On and on we traveled, across the second valley and up the side of yet another mountain. With the exception of the right-of-way, the otherwise pristine mountain was heavily wooded and isolated from civilization. Bill and I watched as, here and there, small wild animals scurried into the underbrush, vacating what was rightfully their habitat. Absent from the scene were the white-tail deer, which today are prevalent throughout the region but at that time had not been introduced to the area.

Both Bill and I were perspiring and covered with dust from trudging through the loose dirt and sometimes muddy terrain. Inside my shoes, it felt as though mud puddles had formed from the mingling of the dirt that had worked its way down inside my shoes and the dampness from my sweating feet.

The sun had set by the time Bill informed me that once we reached the next valley in our view, we would be almost in sight of my family's home. Although I was hungry, tired, and filthy from head to toe, I silently wished the journey would never end, and that we could spend the rest of our lives hiding out in this peaceful bit of heaven that God was allowing us to survey—away from all the cares and uncertainties that lay ahead for both of us.

When we finally made our way off the mountain and alongside the creek to my family's front yard, darkness had already enveloped the land. There was no sign of life except for the light that radiated from the naked bulb protruding over the front entrance to the log house. Being careful not to alarm Bill about the danger I might be facing, and uncertain of how Dad might react to my disheveled appearance, I asked Bill not to accompany me inside. Having no inkling of what was about to transpire, he kissed me good night, and, after waiting until I had entered the house, the man I loved left to walk the short distance to his own family's home.

LXX

And the Agony

I had no doubt that my father believed Bill to be an outstanding young man who would be a loyal and supportive husband to me; however, I had felt for some time that my father disapproved of our courtship—for no other reason than his own jealousy. Knowing he was unaware that Bill and I had reconciled, I was concerned about how he would react when he learned of our reunion and future plans.

When I stepped into the living room, I was surprised to find Dad alone with the younger children. "Where's Mom and the other kids?" I quickly asked.

"They're up'ta church," Dad snapped. "What'na heck jue thank you're doin' comin' in here at this hour lookin' like you been laying out 'ith a man fer a week?"

"Bill an' I are back together, an' we walked over the pipeline from Sissy's house," I said to Dad nervously.

"You loodle tramp!" Dad yelled. "I guess you'n him had ta stop ever' half-mile, an' 'hat's how comes you're comin' in here after dark dirtier'n a hog."

As I listened to him ranting and roaring, accusing me of every lewd act imaginable, I couldn't believe how violent he was becoming. I was thankful that Bill had honored my request and gone home. There would have been no way he would have allowed this man to assault me with these unspeakable accusations—even considering that he was my father.

Already frightened beyond belief, I was afraid to say anything in my defense, knowing that my outraged father was completely out of control. Wiping at my tears, I wondered whether he were jealous for fear I had done something he couldn't get me to do with him. When I finally garnered enough courage to attempt to leave the room, I became even more terror stricken when he grabbed my arm and slammed me against the wall. Pulling myself loose from his grip, I finally yelled out to him, "Why are you sayin' all these bad things about us? We didn't do anything 'at we wouldn't do right here in front of you."

In what seemed like one long leap, he jumped into his bedroom and jerked the same .22 rifle off the wall that he had years earlier fired at Woody and on numerous occasions had used to "kill himself." Stomping back into the living room, he yelled, "I'll keel any girl a mine 'at acts like a daggone tramp!"

I shivered. "He's gonna kill me!" I thought to myself. I must have looked terrified because I was so scared that I felt faint. My little brothers ran from the room screaming, apparently horrified that their daddy was about to shoot their big sister, the only person in their lives who showed them any affection. I wanted to run to them and comfort them, but I knew better than to take one step with the cocked rifle pointed at my head. I stood rigidly, my legs feeling as though they were about to buckle beneath me.

"Git outta here 'fore I shoot chu right 'tween'a eyes!" he yelled. I instantly decided that whether he were going to shoot me, he would have to do it while I was facing him. I wanted him never to forget the look in my eyes. If I were to run instead, I imagined he would find it easier to shoot me in the back.

I gasped when, suddenly, this man I called "Daddy" jumped forward and, holding the rifle in one hand, forcefully grabbed the upper part of my arm with his other hand and flung me toward the open door. Before I could get my balance, he kicked my backside with his heavy shoe, sending me crashing, face down, outside onto the hard-baked ground.

"Don't chu ever let chur shadder [shadow] darken my doorstep ag'in, you loodle slut!" he yelled after me.

He didn't have to tell me to run. I scampered to my feet and ran as fast as I could, expecting any second to be hit in the back with a .22-rifle bullet. I was intent on getting over to the main road, where I could hide behind the bushes while deciding what to do. I knew that Bill was, by this time, safe inside his home, but there was no way I was going to ask for his help.

I crouched behind the bushes beside the dirt road. If I were to go to Bill, then he would have to know what had led up to tonight's horrifying situation. I feared that, should he learn what Dad had been trying to do to me throughout the years, either he or Dad would no doubt die at the hands of the other. Then, too, I couldn't let Bill know about my troubles at home. I was confident that he loved me with all his heart; nevertheless, I didn't want him to carry my burden to Korea, where he could do nothing more than worry about my safety. I decided I would rather die than jeopardize his safety. With a knot in my stomach and tears trickling down my cheeks, I prayed for an answer to my predicament. I had to get out of the hollow and back to the safety of my apartment.

"How could a day so perfect turn out like this?" I asked myself.

Finally, I heard the cars of the church members bumping along down the rock-napped road. I was relieved when the first car stopped just short of where I was hiding and Mom stepped from the car. Quickly, I ran over to the car and asked the pastor whether I could ride into town with him. He must have seen the pain and fear in my eyes because he wanted to know what was going on. Mom stepped over to where I was standing beside Preacher Thomas's car and wanted to know why I had been hiding in the bushes, crying and with my shoes and socks covered with dirt.

"Oh, it's Daddy again," I said. "He gotta gun after me and ran me off, 'at's all." I knew that Mom would believe what she wanted to believe, regardless of what I said.

After the preacher had assured my mother that he would deliver me safely to my apartment, I climbed in the car and cried all the way out of the hollow. The preacher did not ask me about the problem, and I didn't volunteer any information. I couldn't get the cries of my little brothers out of my mind. I wondered whether I'd ever be able to spend time with them again.

Bill did not learn what had transpired after he'd left me at my parents' door. After spending two heart-rending hours together the next evening, I sadly bid him farewell as he left for his twelve-month tour in Korea.

Upon hearing the news that Bill and I were engaged, Clay showed me the same respect he had always shown me. He accepted my apology for having walked out on him for the second time and assured me that he wished me nothing but happiness.

Within days of Bill's leaving for his overseas assignment, I was surprised when I went to the post office and received a small package he had mailed from Fort Lewis, Washington. My spirits were lifted when I opened the little box and found an engagement ring inside. As I proudly slipped the ring on my finger, for a moment it seemed I could sense Bill's presence. The sadness that his leaving for Korea had left within my heart seemed to lighten a bit each time I looked at the ring, especially knowing he had held it in his own hand before he had packaged it and mailed it to me.

As the lonely days began to add up into weeks, the estrangement from my family, along with my yearning for Bill, weighed heavily on my heart and mind. Since I was determined not to return to my parents' home without a sincere apology from my father, I had not seen my family for about eight weeks. Although I missed my siblings and felt compassion for my mother, I had no hope that anything would change within the near future.

Woody and his little family had rented a house near town, and he had found a promising job working for one of the leading oil subsidiaries in the state. On Thanksgiving Day I was alone in my apartment, since Miss Rohr and Shirlene were spending Thanksgiving Day with their folks. I was surprised when I heard my apartment doorbell ring and found Woody waiting at my door. "Bett, Daddy and the family wants you to come home for Thanksgivin' dinner," he said. "Mary is fixin' a big pot of spaghetti."

"There's no way I'll go back up there unless Daddy comes an' asks me himself," I said firmly.

"Mom told me why she thought you hadn't been home for weeks, so I drove Dad up here, and he's down in the car and sent me up here to ask you to come home for Thanksgivin'," Woody said. "He's probably kickin' himself for what he did, but you should know by now that he doesn't know how to tell anybody that he's sorry."

I knew that Woody's assessment was probably accurate; however, knowing that Dad would never change, I determined I would be better off staying out of his reach. "Woody, I can't go back to what I've had to live through," I said tearfully.

"Has he been tryin' to get you to do thangs you don't want to do?" Woody asked.

"I have to fight him almost every time I go home," I said.

"Next time he tries anythang, jist kick 'im in his jewel box," my big brother said unequivocally.

"What do you mean, 'his jewel box'?" I asked.

"Kick 'im in the nuts!" Woody exclaimed. "I'll guarantee you that'll get his attention." Woody stood in my room, pleading with me while we both wiped at our tears. He reminded me that although our father had done both of us wrong in many ways, he was, after all, our father. "We can't allow ourselves to hate him," he said to me.

"I don't think that I'm askin' too much to expect an apology from him," I said.

"I know that, but you've gotta come home today for the kids' sake," Woody pleaded. "Mom said they've been askin' 'bout you and Bill."

I smiled. "Yell, those little boys call Bill their hero," I said. "They think he's Superman because he lifted Dad's iron anvil with only one finger." Woody laughed.

"Woody, I just can't go down there an' act like everything's okay," I said. "It would help if he would seem remorseful."

"Don't forget he never did apologize to me," Woody said. "And remember, it was your fault 'at Daddy shot at me that time."

"You don't have to remind me about that," I said.

"Yell, but I almost let 'at drive me crazy before I was finally able to get over it," Woody explained.

After Woody had reminded me of how his incident with Dad and the .22 had almost sent him over the edge, I reluctantly grabbed a few essentials. If I decided to spend the night, I already had a change of clothing and an extra toothbrush at my family's home.

My oldest brother and I walked side by side down the steps and across the street to where Dad was slumped in the front seat of Woody's car. Woody helped me into the car, as Dad looked sheepishly up at me without uttering a word or acknowledging my presence otherwise. I had no problem in returning his silence and coldness.

Despite how appealing Thanksgiving dinner looked, I couldn't bring myself to enjoy the food or to converse with the adults. It was extremely difficult for me to be in my father's presence and remain quiet about his unacceptable actions. I was glad I'd agreed to spend time with my big brother Woody; however, the highlight of the day for me was when one of my little brothers had asked me when Bill would be back to play "Cowboys and Indians" with him and my other little brothers.

At day's end, Woody returned me to my apartment, and as I sat alone thinking of the day's events, I knew I could never forget how, years earlier, I had caused our father to shoot at my big brother with the same rifle he had recently used to threaten my life. I thought about all the problems our family had endured throughout the years, and I came to the conclusion that we were becoming skilled in hiding the truth from those with whom we came in contact. I wondered how much longer I, for one, could continue on this collision course.

LXXI

Making Matters Worse

Weeks passed and, despite knowing that I should stay away from Dad, especially when he had presented me with a good excuse, I found myself too often returning to a situation that I knew in my heart would never change. It had become particularly disturbing to me that he seemed to delight in trying to convince me that Bill would never return to marry me. Although I tried to ignore all the unpleasant thoughts hammering their way into my mind, I slowly recognized that I was becoming quiet and withdrawn.

Sometime later, after another bad experience with my father, I returned to work on Monday morning and was sitting in the office with the other employees, when Miss Rohr made a remark about me staring blankly into space. "If you don't get it together, you're gonna end up in the bug-house," she said sharply. I didn't recognize my boss's interest as concern for me but as interference into my personal life. I couldn't share with her what I had been thinking about at the time, nor why I had been staring into space. In my internal agitation, I immediately determined that she had said the wrong thing at the wrong time.

Looking her in the eye, I was shocked when I heard myself say angrily to her, "I'm sick of you meddlin' in my personal life. Get yourself someone else to do your share of the work!" Grabbing my purse, I bolted down the stairs, fuming. "I don't need this job or any of you!" I yelled tearfully back up the stairwell.

There was no response to my outburst. I stormed out of the building. Where I intended to go had not entered my mind; yet, like a programmed robot, I automatically began walking in the direction of my aunt's house, overwhelmed with what seemed to be more pain than I was capable of bearing. All alone and holding every muscle in my body tight to avoid sobbing hysterically, I felt that the whole world was against me. I wondered why the Lord had allowed me to be born in the first place.

My thoughts ran rampant as I reached the dirt road I had often walked before. With no one present to question my actions, I allowed myself to break forth with sobs that seemed to have no end. Before I realized what was happening, I had begun to question God's love for me, wondering aloud why He always seemed to forsake me when I needed Him the most. I tried to tell Him how I was feeling, but I had no words to describe my agony; besides, as far as I could tell, I had lost all contact with Him. A black shroud of despair seemed to wrap itself around me, as if trying to squeeze life itself from my body.

Time passed as I walked, crushed by my anguish, and I finally realized that I was extremely tired. If I were to stop to rest, I feared I would never get myself moving again. I continued to trudge along the rutted road and through the creek beds. "Where am I going, and what am I going to do?" I heard myself ask.

Reality had finally taken over: I was out of a job! There was no way I could give my kind aunt the news. Why, I didn't even know whether my aunt and uncle would allow me to move back in with them. I'd been living in the apartment for months, and all my belongings were still there in Miss Rohr's apartment. All I had with me were the items inside my purse. I wondered whether my aunt would understand why I had walked out and left my job, especially since employment in our small town was practically nonexistent. My stomach churned as the pressure mounted. "How can life be so cruel?" I asked myself.

In the depths of despair, my thoughts turned to Bill. I wondered whether he really did love me and wanted to marry me or whether he would change his mind before returning from Korea. "You can't even be sure he will return—alive," a voice seemed to say.

I stopped where the road crossed through the creek, taking a moment to splash some cold water on my face. Soon I'd be passing the house where Dad's sister lived, and then within a few hundred yards, I'd be arriving at Aunt Sissy's tidy home. There was no doubt in my mind that she would be shocked to see me coming to her house at this time of day.

While passing by Aunt Becky's house, the guy whom my cousin had been dating walked outside and yelled to me, "What'cha doin' comin' in from work at 'is here time a day?"

I was glad he wasn't close enough to see my eyes and nose, swollen and splotchy from all my crying. Trying desperately to sound as though I didn't have a care in the world, I answered, "I just quit!"

He yelled back, "Quit? Why?"

"'Cause I felt like it!" I snapped.

He laughed and muttered, "'At's a good 'nuff reason, I reckon."

Aunt Sissy's house would soon be in sight. I would never have thought I'd live to see the day when I'd have misgivings about going to see Sissy. "Wonder what she'll be doing this morning?" I thought. I was nervous, but there was nothing left to do but to barge in and hope she would understand.

I crept up to the door and peeked inside the big, almost-empty living room. Sissy had set up the ironing board in the middle of the room with a big basket of clothing nearby. Startled, she looked up at me and asked, "What'na worl's happened to you? Are you sick?"

I choked back tears and said, "Sissy, I quit my job."

She put down the iron and walked over to me, gently placing her hand on my shoulder as I sank down in Uncle Clint's big easy chair. "What on earth happened?" she asked.

I was embarrassed to tell her what had really happened. I said only that I'd walked out because I couldn't handle the pressure any longer. She seemed to sense that I didn't want to discuss the matter, so she told me not to worry, that everything would work out in due time. I looked into her kind eyes and asked, "Will I have to go back to live with Mommy an' Daddy now that I don't have a job?"

"Over my dead body," she replied brokenly.

I sat in the chair until I felt I could stand without support. I then walked over and took the gasoline iron from Sissy and continued ironing the clothing she had previously dampened and rolled inside a bed sheet. We continued talking, without Sissy prying into my inner thoughts. I was relaxed while alone with her but was dreading having to explain to Uncle Clint and Granny when they came home from work why I was there and not in town in my apartment. I had already realized that I had made a terrible mistake; however, I was too embarrassed to return and ask Miss Rohr whether she would forgive my actions and restore my job.

At the supper table I fully explained to my relatives, as best I could, the situation I had created for myself. They did not criticize my actions or delve into the matter any further. After supper, I helped with the dishes and then went to bed, feeling exhausted from worrying about the day's events. I realized tomorrow would be there before I was ready to face it, but I hoped things would look better after a good night's sleep.

The new day's dawning brought with it the same problems I'd taken to bed with me. I had slept soundly and felt that the good night's rest had been a blessing, but the gnawing pain in my stomach reminded me I couldn't get away from the fact that all my problems seemed to be closing in on me. I walked into the kitchen to find the table spread with Sissy's usual breakfast of biscuits, fried eggs, and plenty of freshly churned butter. Uncle Clint had already left for work, and Granny was getting ready to leave for her cleaning job in town. "I figgered 'at chu might as well sleep late since you'uz sleepin' so good," Sissy said in her usual jovial manner.

Sissy scurried about the room doing her chores while I nibbled at my breakfast. I had begun to wonder whether my aunt could have been wrong when she had told me months earlier that my stomach problems were nothing to worry about. "It's somethin' 'at runs in'na family," Sissy had said. I didn't know any family members, however, who had the same symptoms I was having. I had silently endured the pain for years, but the problem had recently escalated to the point that at times the pain was distressing. I was also having trouble keeping my food down.

When I noticed that Sissy had picked up the ten-quart pail she used when milking the cow, and had wet the rag for washing the cow's teats, I pushed back my chair and walked with her to the milk gap. Sissy delighted in caring for her Jersey cow, petting her tenderly each time she went near her. I was sure that Ol' Bessie received more affection from my aunt than a lot of the children in our area got from their parents. I noticed the strength in my aunt's small, white hands as she squeezed at the turgid teats that looked as though they were about to burst from the pressure of the rich, white milk that filled them and the cow's extended udder. Sissy was the only person I knew, other than my brother Woody, who could squeeze the cow's teats with enough force to cause the wide streams of milk to send white foam two inches above and over the sides of the bucket.

I watched as the well-groomed cow greedily slurped up the remaining bits of the dairy feed Sissy had poured into the wooden feed box that Uncle Clint had crafted. Giggling, I pointed out to Sissy how the cow was flicking her long, pink tongue up her nostrils to clear out the dry food she had apparently sucked up her nose. Both Sissy and the cow appeared not to have a care in the world. I wondered whether, someday, I would be as content as they seemed to be.

With the pail full and the foam slipping over its sides, the cow was turned out to pasture, and Sissy and I headed back toward the house. She seemed pleased to have me home with her. I was beginning to feel even more comfortable about confiding in her, confident that she would help me unravel the mess my life had become.

Sissy went out back to the little brook that ran alongside the cellar and removed a tall glass bottle of RC Cola, which she had placed in the cold water to keep cool, since she had no source of refrigeration. She popped the top off the bottle and poured half the drink into a glass, which she handed to me. "Et's set down an' enjoy 'is before we hafta go on the hill ta git in some stove wood," she said, seating herself in the weather-beaten porch swing and motioning for me to sit down beside her.

I immediately blurted out, "Sissy, what'm I gonna do?"

Looking puzzled, seemingly expecting me to continue talking, she asked, "Do? Do 'bout what?"

"Where'n the worl' can I find a job?" I asked.

"God'll take keera you an'll help you find a job," she said.

Before we could continue with our conversation, we noticed Sissy's brother's wife and their children crossing the creek on their way to visit with Sissy. We quickly gulped down the last swallow of RC, slipped the containers underneath an overturned basket, and jovially greeted our unexpected relatives.

Aunt Ruby had learned from Granny the night before that I had quit my job. She had come to tell me that her sister had mentioned an opening for a clerk in one of the oldest grocery stores in the area. I was aware that the lady working at the store at the time was planning to be married soon, but I had no desire to seek employment in the gloomy, run-down store; however, as I listened to my two favorite aunts discussing the job situation in our small town, I realized the unideal job would be better than having no job at all. I jumped up and ran inside to get ready to walk out of the hollow and see about the opening, confident that I would be hired.

I walked to the small, cluttered store, located in back of the store where I'd previously been employed, and entered through the opened door, two steps above the sidewalk. The store was centered along a row of attached buildings that had been built with their backsides constructed on block foundations that extended several feet above the banks of the Elk River.

I had been inside the store many times while working at the 5 & 10 and had become well acquainted with the seventy-year-old proprietor with bad eyesight. On those occasions, I couldn't help but notice the repulsive sight of the saliva oozing out from around the crooked stem of the oversized pipe that hung loosely from his lips.

When I announced to Mr. Oberly that I was there to apply for the job I'd learned was open, I explained that I had left the 5 & 10 for personal reasons. Grinning broadly, he reached to take the pipe out of his mouth. Wiping his mouth with the tail of the white butcher's apron he was wearing, he said, "If you can work for $13.00 a week, and work six days a week, then the job is yours."

Realizing I would have most of the responsibilities of the business resting on my shoulders, I wanted to ask for at least $15.00 a week; however, I feared that to do so might jeopardize my chances of getting the job. I had always heard that Mr. Oberly was as tight as the bark on a tree, so, fearing he might change his mind about hiring me, I quickly agreed on the salary. Just as quickly, as though he expected me to change my mind, he asked, "Can you come to work tomorrow?" I wasn't looking forward to working in the dirty, smelly store, but I agreed to begin the next morning. I was relieved to know that I would at least be working again, especially so soon.

I looked forward to the letters I received from Bill each day, so I walked down the street to the post office and was rewarded with another of his letters. With joyful anticipation, I stepped to the rear of the room and opened the letter. Encouraged from reading the warm, loving words from the guy I loved, and from knowing that I was once again employed, I was anxious to head back to my aunt's house, being in higher spirits than I had been when I'd left her earlier.

I walked up the steps to the apartment I had been sharing and shoved my few belongings inside my battered suitcase and the vanity case I'd bought. I carefully placed the door key on the pillow where I normally slept and walked out of the room.

As I walked alone in the same dusty tracks I'd made the day before, I reflected on Bill's words in the letter I'd just finished reading for the third time. I thought about our love for each other and was reminded of the love that God must surely have for me. I felt deeply remorseful for having questioned His love just the day before, so I somberly stopped and asked Him to forgive me once again and to help me be a stronger person than the weakling I feared I was becoming.

"Why do I have such a hard time trusting You?" I asked. Looking up at the white clouds swirling in the radiant blue sky, I realized that His hand was at work in my life, even at that moment. "Thank you, God, for giving me the job so quickly," I said.

Walking briskly—considering the load I was carrying—I approached the first creek crossing and jumped gingerly from rock to rock as I crossed the wide, shallow creek that traversed the road and wound its way down the long hollow. My mind was busily working. I wished I could undo the way I had left the store the day before and wondered whether maybe I hadn't been pitying myself by expecting too much out of other people. I realized that I needed to do a better job bearing my own burdens, without allowing others to detect my mental anguish. I decided to concentrate on the thought that if I could just hold on for a few more months, my loving Bill would return, and after we were married, I could tell him about everything that had been torturing my heart, soul, and mind for years. Surely he would know how to handle the situation.

For the moment, I needed to pretend that I was excited about the new job I would be undertaking the following day, although I detested the very thought of working in the crummy store six days a week, all alone with the stingy old gent.

I arrived back at Sissy's home just a couple of hours after I'd left, and walked up the steps and inside the house. Sissy was sewing herself a new dress out of a piece of fabric I'd bought her just the week before. She looked up from her treadle sewing machine when I entered the room.

"I got a job! I go to work in the mornin' an' work six days a week fer $13.00," I said.

"I'm glad fer you 'atchu got a job, but 'at man orta be 'shamed a hisself fer 'spectin' you ta work fer 'at measly amount a money," Sissy said.

My wages at the previous store had been raised to around $20.00 weekly, so I would be taking a significant loss in pay. Considering I had been paying Miss Rohr $5.00 a week to live at her apartment, and knowing my relatives would not expect me to pay them anything for staying at their home, I felt that with their and God's help, my needs would be met.

"Why didn' chu leave 'em clothes an' let Clint take you to git 'em?" Sissy asked.

"I didn't want to have to talk to Miss Rohr, so I went in the apartment when nobody was there," I said.

"Well, are you ready to go on the hill and drag in some stove wood?" Sissy asked.

"Just you lead the way," I said, feeling grateful to be loved by my relatives and, most of all, by God, whom I was still trying to learn to trust.

LXXII

Uncle O's Little Market

The store's 14' X 20' wooden floor creaked loudly as its pudgy owner shuffled from one side of the compact room to the other. Wooden shelves lined the two sides of the building from the floor to the ceiling. The two picture windows in the front end of the store faced the narrow alleyway running between the front of the market and the back of the 5 & 10.

On the inside of the market, a wide shelf fit snugly against each plate-glass window, with the front section sloping about six inches lower than the back of the thigh-high shelves. The shelves were covered with white oilcloth. Mr. Oberly had chosen to display the fresh vegetables and fruits on these shelves because he believed they were eye-catchers that would get the customers into the store. I soon learned, however, that the hot afternoon sun often dried out and wilted the produce before it could be sold, particularly since air conditioning wasn't available yet. Even though I doubted that the wilted, overpriced produce would attract much trade, being a new employee I refrained from offering advice on locating the produce to a cooler area.

Like all the stores in town, Mr. Oberly's store was not self-service. Canned goods were stacked haphazardly on shelves on one side of the room and to the rear of the small, smooth-worn wooden counter, and my boss and I collected one item at a time, upon our customers' requests. Some of the rusted cans looked as though they had come across the ocean on the *Mayflower*.

The meat-slicing machine and weighing scales were bolted onto the small counter alongside our work area. Both were in dire need of hot water and soap. On the opposite end of the counter near the ancient cash register, a metal ledger held the accounts of current customers and customers from years gone by. Leafing through the dusty accounts, I noticed that some of the unpaid bills had been on the ledger for such an extensive time that the paper they were written on had turned yellow. The edges of the aged sheets were frayed, making it difficult to determine the names and items on most of the bills. I was stunned to learn that most of the accounts were outstanding by as much as seven or eight years. Even more surprising was the fact that recent entries were included on some of these old delinquent accounts. When I asked Mr. Oberly about the puzzling debts, he said, "Well, some of those people came back in here and assured me that if I would allow them to start a new bill, they would make good on their overdue charges."

"Huh, it doesn't look as though they kept their word," I said, snickering.

"Nope, they stuck me with another'n on top of the first one," he said, grinning sheepishly.

I soon learned that the poor guy was so tenderhearted and gullible that he continued to fall for the same line, over and over. Some of the totals ran near $1,000.00, for groceries alone. After learning all this, I was too embarrassed to ask him for more pay, even though he seemed to trust and appreciate my work and judgment.

The candy and gum were displayed in a rectangular glass case that had two sliding rear wooden doors and was located on the opposite side of the store from the work space and cash register. The customers were not allowed behind the counters or the display cases. The wooden shelves behind the candy case had been built the width and length of the wall and were loaded with all the dried and boxed goods.

To the left of the candy case, a large refrigerated metal chest was used to cool the bottled soft drinks. The fresh, and sometimes not-so-fresh, meats and dairy products were displayed in a separate meat and dairy case near the center back of the store.

One of the stipulations at the time of my employment was that I would be expected to cook my boss's lunch on a two-burner hot plate located behind the store's displays. Near the burner, a six-inch tile drainpipe, open at both ends, had been run through the floor and strapped against the wall about waist high. A pot lid covered the inside opened end of the drain. Lifting the cover, I looked down inside the pipe and saw the ground several feet below. Mr. Oberly had informed me that I should pour the food scraps and dishwater through the tile pipe, where it would be deposited on the ground beneath the store.

Me standing in front of Uncle O's Store in Clendenin.

I later discovered that my employer was also using the drainpipe for a more urgent purpose. The nearest restroom was in the store next door, and I returned from the post office one day to discover my employer with his back toward the door and his upper torso stooped slightly over the pipe. To my surprise and disgust, I recognized quickly that he wasn't emptying the dishwater! I stepped quietly back outside onto the sidewalk, waited for a moment, and then re-entered noisily. My employer was never aware that I'd discovered he was using the pipe as his secret urinal. As naive as I was at the time, working for the old gentleman was proving to be quite an unusual experience.

As I familiarized myself with the goods in the store and what I thought I could do to improve the place, it was evident that I had quite a task ahead of me. I soon was no longer surprised when I was cleaning out a shelf to find a half-eaten dried-out or molded sandwich the former employee had laid aside and apparently forgotten. I was determined to tidy up the small market, and within my first week on the job, the customers had already begun complimenting me on the improvements I was making. The jobbers and salesmen who came by the store regularly to peddle their wares never failed to compliment me on the way I had improved the appearance of the little store.

Since the high school was located only a block north of our store, every Monday through Friday, a few minutes before noon, Mr. Oberly would tear off a large sheet of white butcher's paper from the dispenser beside the slicing machine and spread it out on the counter top. He would place two or three loaves of sliced bread on the paper, alongside a jar each of mustard and mayonnaise, which contained small wooden spatulas that he had carved specifically for the purpose of spreading the condiments onto the bread. He would then cut thick slices of bologna, spiced luncheon meat, and American cheese. My boss, who had somewhere along the way been dubbed "a miser," would then retreat to the corner near the large window where the produce was displayed and make himself comfortable in his wicker-bottom chair. Puffing on his crooked-stemmed pipe, he would watch for the daily ritual to begin.

Our regular customers had learned not to enter the store during this particular hour of the day. Regardless of what I might have been doing at the time, I would ready myself for the onslaught of students who I had learned would suddenly burst through the open door like a stampede of thirsty cattle racing toward a hole of clear, cold water.

Once the students had swarmed inside the small store and congregated around the sandwich makings, they each would make one sandwich and then reach down inside the drink case for a nickel soda. A student with extra money would also purchase either a nickel lunch cake or candy bar, while the majority of the students had only enough money to buy the ten-cent sandwich and the nickel drink. With their drinks and sandwiches in hand, the students, standing shoulder to shoulder in the middle of the store, would quickly begin gobbling down the food.

Since the owner had established no system other than the honor system for the students to pay for their meals, and considering that twenty to twenty-five students were jammed inside the small store at the same time, I did my utmost to determine what the students owed and whether they had paid for their meals. I did not have access to the register during this period, since I was stationed on the other side of the store behind the candy counter. When the boys and girls paid for their lunches, I would make change, during the few times any change was due, from a small paper tray that I kept on the shelf behind the counter.

When the lunch period was over and I had tallied the money, seldom did the amount paid for the lunches equal more than $3.50 total. It was clear to me that the store did not profit monetarily from the students. My boss explained, however, that from the time he'd gone into business back in 1912, he had provided a cheap lunch for the less fortunate people who cared to take advantage of his generosity.

Mr. Oberly once told me that when the one small restaurant in town had complained about his practice of serving lunches to the students, he stated simply that his business was legal since he neither prepared nor served the food to the youngsters. He pointed out the fact that he merely laid the food out where they could prepare the sandwiches and serve themselves and that, furthermore, he intended to continue the practice for as long as he was able to stay in business. I was satisfied that I had learned the reason these students, although they never acknowledged his kindness, chose to refer to the store's owner as "Uncle O."

Not all the giving was done by our store. Occasionally, our customers returned the kindness in the most peculiar ways. We sold pinto beans from a wooden barrel located underneath the work counter. When a customer ordered the dry beans, we would scoop up the beans, pour them into a properly sized paper bag, weigh them, roll down the top of the bag, and then wrap and tie a piece of twine around the bag of beans.

Mr. Oberly seldom tallied up at the end of each day, making bank deposits only when necessary. At closing time, the money was taken out of the cash register, and after my boss had placed five to ten dollars in his wallet, he would put the remaining bills and loose change inside a brown paper bag that he then buried in the barrel of beans. The next morning, upon opening the store, the money bag was retrieved and the money placed back inside the register drawer.

One day, one of our honest patrons came into the store and handed Mr. Oberly a cupped handful of coins. She told him that she would trade him the money for pinto beans weighing the same amount. She explained that, after returning home from buying her groceries, she had poured the beans into a bowl to wash them, only to discover that more coins than beans were in the bag. "Just in case you were testing my honesty, I want you to know that I have made a special trip to town in order to return the money," she said. After weighing the money, Mr. Oberly measured out the same weight in dried pinto beans and handed them to the puzzled lady.

When I decided to dig through the beans to retrieve any coins left inside, I found more than $10.00 in small change. Later, after I had removed the money from the barrel of beans, I noticed we weren't selling near the amount of beans that we had previously sold. Although my boss continued to use the bean barrel to hide his money, he did, however, keep a closer check on the condition of the paper bags. I marveled at how he would skimp in one area in order to be more generous in another. Truly, I was slowly beginning to enjoy working with the old gent.

One of our faithful customers, a middle-aged man raising three teenage daughters, came into the store at least twice weekly on his way home from work. He was a very quiet man who didn't have much to say to either Mr. Oberly or me. Knowing that Mr. Miles seemed to prefer being served by my boss, I seldom stepped up to take his order.

One evening at closing, as was his daily custom, Mr. Oberly was busy filling the small fruit basket, which he always hung across his arm, with groceries that he carried the city block that he walked to his home each evening. I stepped over to the counter and asked Mr. Miles, who had just entered the store, whether I could help him. He hesitated for a moment, and then, realizing that my boss was busy, began asking for the items on his grocery list.

I moved around the store picking up each item as he requested it. When I attempted to tally the list, the seemingly shy man appeared to be in need of merchandise that he was hesitating to ask for. I finally looked up at him and asked, "Will there be anything else, Mr. Miles?"

He walked over to the opposite side of the store and looked up at the shelf where the baking mixes, cereals, and other boxed goods were stacked. I walked over to where he was standing, as he said to me, in a barely audible voice, "I need a box of cake mix."

Our store carried only the Duncan Hines brand of cake mix, which came in three varieties: chocolate, white, and yellow. I looked at Mr. Miles and asked, "Which flavor did you want?"

Looking very flustered and embarrassed, Mr. Miles replied, "Flavor? I didn't know they came in flavors."

I quickly answered, "Oh yes! We have chocolate, white, and yellow."

For a moment Mr. Miles stared at me as though he thought I had lost my mind. Wondering why he was finding it difficult to choose which cake mix he preferred, I waited for a reply. Finally, the blushing customer pointed to the sanitary napkins located on the ledge above the cake mixes and said, "I asked you for a box of *Kotex*."

Blushing even more than my customer, I managed to say, "Gosh, I'm sorry, Mr. Miles. I think I'm more embarrassed than you are."

Mr. Oberly, now listening to our conversation, burst forth with laughter. "He was trying to be as quiet as possible, seeing as how he's already embarrassed to ask you for the Kotex, and you ask the poor man what flavor he wants." Each of us laughed while Mr. Miles's blushing face slowly returned to its natural shade and mine lit up like Rudolph's nose on Christmas Eve.

The episode seemed to break the ice between Mr. Miles and me. Thereafter, each time he came into the store, he always looked at me and asked, "What flavors did you sell today?" I always wondered whether Mr. Miles had gone home and informed his wife or daughters that he would refuse should they ever ask him again to purchase their personal needs. One thing was certain: he never again asked me for another box of Kotex.

As time passed, I began to notice that my elderly employer was becoming more and more senile and feeble. Constantly sucking on the pipe that he seemed to thoroughly enjoy, he would sit in the corner beside the vegetable bin on his worn straight-back wooden chair, gazing out the window at the people walking up and down the street.

His wife, Beulah, was a very grouchy woman who would make Cinderella's stepmother look like an angel. On rare occasions, she would come into the store from up the street where they lived to pick up a few groceries. The couple did not own a vehicle, so she always walked to and from the store. She never failed to snap sarcastically at me every time she came into the store; furthermore, she never once gave poor Mr. Oberly a kind word.

I had noticed that when my boss would see his wife approaching the store, he would quickly snatch his pipe from between his teeth and conceal it until after she had left.

When he finally shared with me that because of his increased drooling Beulah had forbidden him to smoke any longer, he asked me to warn him should I see her coming into the store when he was smoking his pipe. "If she ever catches me with my pipe in my mouth, she'll break my bald head," he said to me.

We were always busier than usual during the first three days of each month, when the country folk made their once-a-month trip into town to do their shopping. One day, after I had worked at the store for a few months, we were especially busy waiting on customers. As usual, Mr. Oberly was sucking on his pipe. To our surprise, the door suddenly burst open, and in walked Beulah.

My boss immediately and awkwardly jerked the pipe out of his mouth and jammed it into his pants pocket. As I continued with my work, I was concerned that the tobacco may have been burning when he had pushed the pipe into his pocket. Within minutes, I noticed he was squirming and shaking his leg as though a bee had crawled up his pant leg. Fortunately, Beulah finally left the store just as Mr. Oberly reached into his pocket and pulled out the pipe with the tobacco still burning.

"Are you okay?" I asked.

"Yell, except for my singed upper thigh," he said frowning.

"Does it hurt?" I asked.

"Sure, it hurts!" he said. "But not half as much as my head would hurt if Beulah'd caught me smoking that pipe."

Later in the day, the cooling system on our drink machine broke down, and after several futile attempts to solve the problem, Mr. Oberly finally gave his consent for me to call a repairman, who informed me that, unfortunately, he couldn't come to our store for at least three days. While waiting for the repairman, and knowing that ice had to be hauled in from Charleston, my boss poured cold water inside the chest around the bottled drinks. For the next three days I observed him on several occasions bending over the chest to check the temperature of the soft drinks. Sometime during the night on the third day, the motor kicked on unexpectedly, and after it had run all night, the bottled drinks had frozen in the six inches of water that Mr. Oberly had poured around them.

The next morning, upon arriving at the store, I immediately unplugged the machine to allow the ice to melt. When Mr. Oberly arrived, he began searching for his pipe, which he had apparently mislaid. Though we searched throughout the small store, neither of us could locate the pipe.

Finally, in late afternoon, when the repairman finally drove in from Charleston, he agreed to drain the water and clean the cooling chest since he had taken four days to service the motor.

As he began breaking up the ice chunks in order to remove the bottled drinks, he announced there was an unidentifiable object protruding from one of the large pieces of ice. Moving over to get a better view of the object, Mr. Oberly exclaimed excitedly, "Dad-burnit! That's my old pipe!" Apparently, while bending over the cooler to check the temperature of the colas, he had absent-mindedly dropped the pipe out of his mouth and into the cooling chest. Once the water had frozen, the pipe had been concealed inside the ice.

It was evident that my employer was more pleased over having found his pipe than he was about getting the refrigerated chest repaired. "I only had a little headache from a few disgruntled customers fussing about the warm drinks, but if Beulah had found my pipe in that drink case, she would've given me a lump on my head that I would be wearing on the day I die," he said, drooling like a baby cutting teeth.

A few days later, I was busy filling an unusually large order when Mrs. "Gag"—a rotund, unkempt woman who looked as though her dress, and her in it, needed to be soaked in a tub of lye water—waddled into the store. Her presence brought with it a stench that would no doubt linger long after she had left the store. My boss was busy warming the seat of his chair, which seemed to be his usual custom when I needed him most.

Mr. Oberly detested the very sight of the woman, yet he realized that her monthly trip into town meant a very substantial sale for our store that would be paid promptly on the first of the following month. Puffing on his pipe rapidly as though its strong odor would overcome the offensive odor Mrs. Gag was emitting, he slowly shuffled over to the counter to fill her order.

Once he had collected several items she had called out from memory, Mr. Oberly stooped over the counter and began scrawling the names of the items and their prices onto one of the carbon-copy pads we used to tally all groceries bought on credit.

A small boy had wandered into the store and had walked over to the candy counter, where he stood gazing through the glass case at the assortment of candies and packets of gum. Believing that the lad's mother would soon follow him into the store, I continued with the order I was filling. While Mr. Oberly, seemingly exasperated, fumbled with the list he was preparing, the impatient lad called out to my boss, "Mister, when you get fru wif 'at lady, I want a sucker."

Already disgusted, the aged proprietor quickly replied, "Dangit, boy! You can suck her now as far as I'm concerned!" Both the customer I was serving and I were flabbergasted! Without further comment, Mr. Oberly, giggling softly over what I would later learn was a slip of his tongue, walked over and handed the child the lollipop he had requested. Mrs. Gag didn't utter a word, nor did her expression change. She quickly retrieved her filthy, crumpled purse from the counter and began shuffling her oversized body out the door.

When the boy pulled out his penny to pay for the lollipop, my unpredictable employer said joyously, "Sonny, you keep your money. You deserve that free sucker." Then, he turned and looked at me as he stated, "I don't think we'll ever have to hold our nose again while we wait on Mrs. Gag." He was correct. She never entered our store again. The little boy walked happily away, licking his lollipop and no doubt wondering why he'd received it for free.

Eventually, I learned that most of Mr. Oberly's customers were people who had been loyal to him for years. While he sold groceries on "long-term credit," the three other markets, which also offered credit, were stricter. They insisted that their customers pay in a timely manner for what they had charged.

LXXIII

The Little Salesgirl...

I was busy pricing goods and stocking the store when the guy my cousin had been dating for months walked into the store. He had recently been caught stealing from one of the businesses in town and had been placed on probation. Bubba chatted with Mr. Oberly and me for several minutes; then, without making a purchase, he finally left the store. I suspected that he had come into the store for some purpose other than conversation; however, I continued with my work, unaware of how accurate my suspicions would soon prove to be.

I was behind the counter taking inventory of our candy supply, when within the hour my cousin Opa walked into the store. I looked up at her and asked, "May I help you, please?" I greeted every person who entered the store in the same manner, expecting no more than a polite reply.

Opa did not say a word but instead, without warning, reached across the candy case and slapped me very hard across the face. Instinctively, I hurdled over the three-foot soft drink cooling case at my right and landed on my feet beside my angry cousin.

Fortunately, there were no customers inside the store at the time. Opa immediately tore into me like a hungry lioness attacking her prey. Hearing the commotion from where he was seated on the other side of the store, my employer moved over to where he could get a clear view of what was happening. Almost immediately, he began yelling, "Get her, Bethel! Get her!"

I wanted to tell him that I was trying my best to get her. Once I realized that slapping and shoving her with all my might weren't getting the job done, I closed my fist tightly like I had seen my brothers do whenever they were fighting with each other, drew back my arm, and hit my berserk cousin in the mouth with all the force I could muster. Seeing a massive amount of blood running off her chin, I realized that the punch had damaged the inside of her mouth, and immediately also became aware of the pain shooting through my own finger and hand.

Trying desperately to defend myself from this maniac who seemed intent on destroying me, I gritted my teeth in pain as she grabbed my hair and slung me to the floor. At the moment I attempted to scamper to my feet, she landed on top of me, belly down, with all her weight. As we rolled around on the floor trying to exchange all the punches we could, somehow we got to our feet, punching and clawing at each other with all our might.

I was shocked and surprised at her strength and was still totally unaware of why she was trying to kill me. Realizing that I had injured her mouth, I decided to capitalize on the injury by copying what I'd seen the professional boxers do whenever Dad watched the fights on television. I closed my aching fist tightly, aimed for her mouth, and struck with all the force I could muster. When she failed to duck, I connected where I had aimed, causing blood to spurt out of her mouth and down the front of her black dress.

Hoping she would surrender, I asked whether she'd had enough. Her answer came when she charged at me, ramming her fist into my belly with great gusto. While trying to clinch onto her like a prize fighter would do, I lost my balance and fell to the floor, pulling her down with me. When I attempted to struggle to my feet, she yanked at my blouse, ripping off every button in the process. Becoming aware that I was in danger of losing the battle, I reached down and grabbed her by her shoulder-length hair and pulled hard. Panting and snarling like two dogs with rabies, we both clambered to our feet.

Seeing no break in the action, I locked my arms around her torso, only to have her lock her arms around my body and squeeze with tremendous pressure. I had no doubt whatsoever that her embrace wasn't prompted by her affection for me. Just as my bones began to crackle, I pulled loose from her and grabbed her by the shoulders, slinging her as hard as I could across the floor. As my "darling cousin" went whirling across the room, she crashed into a stack of boxes, each containing twenty-four cans of Carnation evaporated milk, the box on top partially opened. As the cans of milk went spinning in all directions, she lowered her head and once again came charging at me like a mad bull attacking a matador. I quickly stepped aside, taking particular notice of the fire in her eyes and the blood pouring from her mouth. Even at that crucial moment, I honestly felt a sense of compassion for her.

I glanced at my boss and noticed that he was cheering for me like a spectator at a prizefight. Flailing his arms, stomping the floor, and yelling as loudly as a seventy-year-old man could yell, I heard him shout, "Hit her, Bethel! Break her dad-blamed nose!"

I wanted to scream back at him, "What in God's name do you think I'm trying to do?"

Seemingly finding a new source of strength, she once again came charging at me; however, I again stepped aside at the moment she had thrust herself forward. I watched as she went sprawling onto the floor. I immediately jumped to straddle her, and, as I pulled my arm back to strike her again in the mouth, a great sense of pity swept over me. Once more, anxiously hoping that the answer would be in the affirmative, I asked, "Are you ready to quit?"

I was almost breathless by now, and she was fast becoming the same way. She turned her head and looked into my eyes as she said, "We'll finish 'is later." I didn't know what had started the fight, but I was glad it was over. At least, I hoped it was over.

I reached up and grabbed the edge of the counter, slowly pulling myself to a straight standing position. I was completely exhausted, and my right pinkie and adjoining finger were in extreme pain; however, there was no way I would reveal those facts to either my boss or Opa. Sizing up the situation, relief swept over me when I looked at Opa and could see that, even with all the bruises and breaks I was suffering, I appeared to be in much better condition than my pathetic cousin.

I looked over at my boss as Opa retreated from the store, still spouting out threats against me. Holding my blouse closed as I failed to locate the buttons, I informed my employer that I was going across the street to the variety store to buy myself a new one. "At least it's just your blouse. Opa's entire dress was bloody and half torn off her when you got through with her," he proclaimed proudly.

Still laughing and drooling, Mr. Oberly declared as I walked painfully out the door, "I guess you showed her!" Still clueless as to what had provoked the ruckus, I refrained from informing him that I had not found the surprise attack to be nearly as comical and entertaining as it had been to him.

Holding my blouse closed, I hurried across the street and sneaked in the back door to buy myself a blouse. All my former coworkers and Miss Rohr gathered around immediately to hear about the fight I had been forced into so unexpectedly. They, like my boss, found the details to be hilarious. It seemed that the fight was the most excitement we'd had in our little town for years.

One of the salesgirls warned me suddenly that I'd better get back over to the market since she had seen Opa's sister going inside the store looking for me. Opa's married sister was in her late thirties and had a reputation of her own, so I wasn't in any hurry to meet up with her, especially after what I'd just done to her baby sister.

I was still shaky from the fight when I walked back to the grocery store. I hoped that the older sister would tell me who or what had incited Opa to bring the fight to me. When I walked inside, however, my employer told me that Opa's sister had indeed come into the store to "finish me off." "I told her to get her rear-end out of this store before I called the police," he said. "She told me to tell you that they were going to meet you up the hollow on your way from work."

"I guess she was admitting it would take two of them to finish the fight," I said.

"She said that you'd better be ready to spend some time in the hospital for what you did to Opa."

I was baffled over what all this was about and who "they" could be. "Maybe if I walk down the street, I'll see somebody who can tell me what's going on," I said to my employer. I had never had any trouble with my cousins before, so I was totally mystified about the entire situation.

I went next door and asked my friend Louise to accompany me to look for my two angry cousins. Louise had just returned from the post office and had seen Opa and her sister coming out of the doctor's office. They had informed her that the laceration inside Opa's mouth had required five stitches. Freda, Opa's sister, had asked Louise to tell me that she was going to finish what Opa had started.

Louise also quoted Opa as saying, "I'mma gonna learn Bethel 'at she better thank twice 'fore she asks my boyfriend fer another date." The accusation added insult to injury as far as I was concerned. I wouldn't give Bubba Starcher the time of day! I had never had a desire to date him, although he had often shown interest in me. I was engaged to the man I loved and had been receiving one to two letters a day from him declaring his love for me.

"Why would I want ol' Bubba?" I asked Louise.

It was suddenly apparent to me that Bubba had gone home and made up the story to see how Opa would react. I was furious! Feeling as though I could take on the whole family if I had to, I reminded myself that fighting would not solve anything. I was now more concerned about the lie being spread than I was about the fight itself.

When Uncle Clint stopped by the store to buy cigarettes before going home from work, Mr. Oberly told him immediately about my grisly encounter with Opa, plus the fact that Freda had threatened to send me to the hospital. My uncle immediately insisted on waiting for me so that I could ride home with him, since he was concerned about Freda's threat. I stressed to the two men that if the family thought I was afraid to fight, the matter would never end. "I don't keer what chu thank. I ain't gonna let chu walk up that holler alone," Uncle Clint stated emphatically. I had not comprehended the seriousness of the "planned assassination" and felt that I had to go through with the meeting with my cousins. I wondered why my cousin had allowed a lie to cause all this trouble without at least giving me the opportunity to deny the ridiculous charges.

When my uncle and I arrived at the creek crossing, I really wasn't surprised when no one was in sight. Should Freda be on her way to the rendezvous, my uncle and I knew that we would meet her on the road, since she lived up the hollow a short distance below his and Sissy's home. I was relieved not be forced into another fight, especially since I was hoping I would be able to talk to Opa and resolve all the fallout caused from Bubba's lie.

I later sent Bubba the message that if he didn't tell Opa the truth, I would have no qualms about turning him in to his probation officer. The threat apparently worked, since I heard nothing further from him, Opa, or Freda. The fight had been the first and only fight I'd ever participated in—excluding the fights with my father and my siblings, of course. I didn't like the idea of hurting anyone physically. I tried to downplay the whole episode, but to Mr. Oberly and my friends at the Ben Franklin Store, it had been both comical and exciting.

Over the next few weeks, each time a salesman came into the store, my boss would immediately put his spin on the unfortunate encounter. I soon was branded with the embarrassing title "The Little Salesgirl Who Wields a Wicked Right."

I managed to laugh with those who found the altercation amusing, knowing I had fought only to defend myself from a raging, jealous girl who had come into the store intent on inflicting pain on someone.

The news about the fight soon vanished, and my life returned to "normal." Although Opa no doubt carried scars in her mouth for years, I was left with two crooked fingers that, to this day, remind me of the dreadful brawl that I almost lost. I also learned a lot about myself because of the fight. I realized that fighting was no way for a lady to resolve a conflict and that I had nothing but love and compassion inside my heart for others—including Opa and Freda. I also realized that I could forgive, although I was never asked for forgiveness. I praised God for the gift of love and for the spirit of forgiveness.

LXXIV

The Picture

Bill was on my mind almost constantly, and I prayed several times a day that he would soon be home. I reminded myself daily of his promise to me before he'd left for Korea—that he would come home to me, safe and sound. I planned to continue working until almost time for his return.

Dad seemed to have finally accepted the fact that Bill and I were planning to be married as soon as he returned. Even so, almost every time I saw my father after Bill left, he continued to try to shake my faith in Bill's faithfulness to me. He regularly told me that while I was waiting for my sweetheart to return, he was no doubt "messing around" with the girls around the base there in Korea. Although the accusations against the man I loved infuriated me, I tried to ignore Dad's remarks; nevertheless, at times I would tell my father that he should not judge anyone else by his own standards. "Just 'cause you cheat on Mommy is no sign that all men are the same way," I would snap.

I couldn't help but remember how, when our family was living on the ridge, Dad had come home late one evening from making his school bus runs. He had boasted to Mom, in the presence of my siblings and me, how he had allowed one of the high school seniors to remain on the bus until after he had delivered all the other students. He had proudly informed my mother that he had pulled the bus up a side road and had had sexual relations with the girl, whom he named.

He then had the nerve to show Mom a photo of the girl with her friend, stating that the one on the left side of the picture was the girl in question. Needless to say, Mom became even more depressed than she had been already. She eventually begged Dad to destroy the picture.

One evening, having had to walk up the hill behind Grandma's house to our house because the ridge road was impassable, Dad assured Mom that he had placed the picture on a rock down at the bars in Grandpa's pasture and had burned the picture with his cigarette lighter.

A few days later, Mr. White came by our house and stopped to ask for a drink of water. When Mom mentioned the episode about the burned picture, Mr. White told Mom that Dad had actually burned only half the picture—the side depicting his lover's friend.

"Wonder what he done 'ith 'at other girl's picture," Mom said.

"Look in'na back of his pocket watch," Mr. White said to Mom. "He tol' me 'at he tuck [took] the back off'n his watch an' put the picture inside."

After Mr. White continued on his way, Mom decided unexpectedly to "pay her parents a visit," which would require us to walk past the area. When we reached the area in question, there was indeed part of a charred picture lying on a rock beside the path. It was apparent that Dad had tried to burn only half the picture, just like Mr. White had said; however, the face of the innocent girl in the photo, only its edges charred, still stared up at Mom.

Mom's hurt and humiliation intensified. A couple of days passed before she sneaked out of bed one night and removed the back from Dad's pocket watch, confirming Mr. White's account. When she finally advised Dad that she knew about the picture hidden inside his watch, he pressured her to confess how she had learned about the secret. When she had to admit that Mr. White had told her a few days earlier, Dad, knowing that Mom had been in mourning for days, took out his watch, removed the picture, and handed it to her. "What'd you give Joe fer tellin' you 'bout it?" he asked. "Get outta here an' go burn that picture fer yourself, an' stop your daggone snottin'!"

Now here he was, years later, trying to convince me that Bill could not, and would not, remain loyal to me. He was also continuously humiliating me with his own indecent suggestions. I was thankful that Bill was totally unaware of what I was being subjected to back home.

After each of Dad's "invitations" for me to come home, I was always torn as to what I should do. Part of me wanted to refuse, knowing I would be subjected to the pain he always put me through; the other part of me wanted to be with my family, since I felt compassion and pity for them—and for my father. I didn't want the family nor anyone else to think I had turned my back on them. Although I had been exposed to a new way of life—earning my own money and wearing a new, shorter hairstyle and new clothing—and was slightly less ignorant than I had been before leaving home, I couldn't understand why Mom, for weeks, had been accusing me of thinking I was better than the rest of the family.

I was well aware that if anyone had reason to hate their parents, I did; nevertheless, I continued to feel remorseful for the many distasteful and hateful things I had said to them over the years. I also felt guilty, knowing that I still felt concern and compassion for my father and his troubled mind.

I had written to Bill every night and was careful not to mention the turmoil I was in. There would be time to talk after we were married, and then I'd never have to wonder whether he'd married me just to get me out of the deplorable situation I'd been in for so long. Besides, how could I talk to him about any of my mortifying experiences when I was too timid to eat a sandwich in his presence?

None of my relatives who had become aware of my problem with my father had since inquired of how things had been going between us; furthermore, I didn't mention the problems to them, since there seemed to be nothing that anyone was willing to do. I no longer approached Mom for any kind of help, knowing that she was fully aware of what was happening but had never tried to give me any support. I was, however, finding strength in the confidence that my God was aware of every tear I had shed over the agonizing ordeal. He had assured me that, someday, He would give me a way to escape; until then, I would, one day at a time, do my best to trust Him. I knew that Dad would have to answer for what he had done and that Mom and my relatives would have to answer for what they hadn't done. I was determined, with God's help, to survive the ordeal, having become a stronger person—with a sound mind and unviolated body.

LXXV

The Assault

It was the summer of 1953, and I would soon be eighteen years old. I had become more independent and less afraid to refuse when my father sent orders for me to pay the family a visit. I was still trying to stay within the bounds of showing my parents proper respect and allegiance. But I no longer jumped at their beckoning call, although my father continued to remind me that he was my boss and expected me to do whatever he said, whenever he said it.

Maynard came into the store on Saturday evening to inform me that Mom and Dad wanted me to come home after work to stay with the children so that they could drive to Fayette County to visit with Dad's brother, who was ill. Maynard agreed that he would walk me home once the store had closed, so I sent Sissy word that I would be going to my folks' house to spend the weekend, being careful to explain the reason why.

I got off work at 8 p.m., and Maynard and I walked up the long hollow, arriving home shortly after dusk. My siblings were excited to see me, and I was just as happy to see them again, having been away for weeks. I was surprised but pleased when even Mom and Dad said a few kind words to me before we all retired for the night.

I was able to get through the night with no unexpected awakening, so I was cheerful on Sunday morning and hopeful that I had experienced my last assault at Dad's hands, especially since he knew that Bill would be returning home before the end of the year to take me as his wife.

Mom and Dad got up early, ate their breakfast, and, after Mom had milked the cow, prepared to leave for the long drive to Dad's brother's place. Before leaving, my mother promised to be back in time to do the evening milking. Both parents seemed to be in unusually pleasant moods as they climbed into the car and headed down the road.

I got the smaller children ready, and we walked together to the little country church for Sunday School. After Sunday School, my sister and I received a request to sing the hymn "There Will Be Peace in the Valley." I tasted a bit of God's peace while singing the song, knowing that no matter what happened, my life was in His hands. Feeling especially close to the Lord, I could not perceive how quickly my state of mind would be shattered.

The afternoon passed quickly. I had cooked supper for the children and was preparing to wash the dishes when Mom and Dad returned. Mom hurried inside and immediately grabbed a pail to go milk the cow. My siblings, except for baby Mike, who was barely one year old, had gone outside to play. The aluminum dishpan filled with water was warming on the wood-burning cookstove in the kitchen. I had cleared the table and carried the dishes into the kitchen, where I stacked them on the small worktable. Dad was in the living room, but since Mom had decided to milk the cow near the house, I assumed I had nothing to worry about.

Just as I had submerged both hands in the soapy dishwater, Dad came into the room and, true to his pattern, moved toward the water bucket. Feeling the need to flee, I quickly jerked my hands out of the water and jumped toward the kitchen door, but I wasn't quick enough. I shivered as, within a split second, he jumped over, blocked my path, and encircled me with his arms. I tried to pry his hands loose, but my soapy hands were no match for his strength.

The nerves in my stomach tightened as he pulled me away from the door and somehow worked himself behind me, pulling me close to his body and giving me a wet kiss on the back of my neck. I couldn't believe how I could have been fooled into thinking that because Dad had been for a visit with his brother's family and had spent the day alone with Mom, he would not approach me with his usual line of vulgar suggestions.

I tried with all my strength to wriggle free, but he only gripped me tighter as he dragged me toward the living room, his footing steadied by his black work shoes, which reminded me of Bill's Army dress shoes. Although I was kicking and screaming, I knew I couldn't expect anyone to come to my rescue. I suddenly began hyperventilating when he grabbed the front of my blouse and yanked it partway over the top of my head—the front of the shirt now clinging to my face and upper back, my arms pinned helplessly behind my head, still inside the blouse.

The full-size bed in which Mike had been born was still set up in the living room. Dad threw me down onto my back on the bed. While I tried frantically to free my arms, he climbed on top of me, pinning the lower part of my body with his knees and the upper part of my body with his hands and arms.

I continued to scream with every ounce of my strength but to no avail. I was confident that the neighbors down the road must be hearing my screams, but I expected no help from them either. I was absolutely terrified! It seemed that Dad was stronger than ever before, and I didn't have the strength to free my seemingly helpless arms.

When he suddenly pushed my head tightly against the bed with one hand, I cried out, "God, please have mercy on me and save me from this hell!" Suddenly, I was able to jerk my arms down with enough force to free the shirt from over my head. Exhausted, I felt as though both my arms and legs had been nailed to the bed, and no matter how hard I tried, I couldn't pull them loose.

Finally realizing that my eyes were closed, I opened them and was horrified to see my father using one hand to fumble with the zipper of his trousers, while he continued straddling me and holding me down with his legs and other hand. I felt as if I were going to faint when I realized that, for the first time in ten years of abusing me, he had just exposed himself to me. "Mommy, please help me! Oh, my God! Please help me!" I continued to scream frantically.

My father had to momentarily release his hold on me while he yanked at my clothing. At that instant, I remembered Woody's advice. In one swift motion and with every ounce of strength left in me, I brought my knees up, causing him to lose his balance. Quickly, I raised my shoulders and jammed my closed fist into his groin, smashing the private parts of his body. Howling like a dog, he immediately rolled over on the bed, grabbed his private parts with both hands, and, while sucking air between his teeth, continued moaning as if he were drawing his last dying breath.

Finally, my mother stepped into the open doorway that led into the living room from outside. She stopped dead in her tracks as she looked at the predicament we were in. I was sobbing hysterically, feeling too weak to pull myself off the bed. Dad was curled up beside me in the fetal position, holding onto his exposed private parts while he moaned weakly.

Mom very calmly said, "Bud, you orta be 'shamed a yourself." Then, as though she had performed her duty, she very quickly turned and went back out the door. To my horror, my mother returned to milking the cow while I lay there on that bed with my "injured" father, who had been, and maybe still was, intent on raping his own daughter.

Feeling as though I were about to black out, and fighting to stay alert, I knew I had to get away before my father recovered. I could only imagine what he would do to me if he should realize I was unconscious.

Totally exhausted from the struggle and the sheer terror I was experiencing, I slowed my breathing, took a deep breath, and attempted to push myself off the bed, when suddenly he grabbed my shoulders and once again pinned me down on the bed. As he straddled my body, my eyes focused on his right hand that was now gripping an opened pocketknife with a four-inch blade. I watched as he raised the knife and pointed it toward my chest. I looked into his eyes and said, "Go ahead and kill me! Just please don't rape me."

With contempt rising in his voice, he looked down at me and said, "You loodle bitch, I orta cut chur heart out, but I hain't gonna durdy my knife on you."

Sobs wracked my body as my father slowly slid off the bed and walked out the door. Alone at last, I lay there wiping at the deluge of bitter tears running down the sides of my face and soaking into the bed covers.

Finally I was able to pull myself off the bed and onto my feet, battered, bruised, and mentally wrecked. I wondered why God had, once again, allowed this to happen. As though in a trance, I walked into the bedroom, and, as I gathered the few things I'd brought with me, I decided I would crawl out of the hollow rather than spend the night in that cursed house with my deviant father and cowardly mother. I felt that I would never again be able to look at either of them.

Darkness would soon be closing in, so utmost on my mind finding a way out of the hollow and into town. Weary and discouraged, I forced myself over to the door, my legs rebelling with each step. Mom had returned to the house and asked me where I thought I was going. "I'm goin' back to Sissy and Uncle Clint where I'll be safe," I managed to say.

Dad stepped into the room and, sneering at me, said, "Yell, you better git on back ta Clint. I always figgered you an' him was courtin' each other."

His accusation sickened me. I didn't give him the satisfaction of causing me to defend myself against his evil imagination; instead, I heard myself asking him, "What's wrong? You jealous?" Before he had a chance to respond, I walked out the door, my tears of anguish still trickling down my cheeks.

I walked weakly down to Bill's folks' house, where his older brother and family were just leaving for their own home. Denzil looked at me and asked, "Is somethin' wrong?"

"Nothin' I can't handle," I said. "Daddy's been quarreling at me, an' I just want to get away from him."

Without further ado, Bill's brother agreed to give me a ride. On our way out of the hollow, we passed my sister as she was walking up the road on her way home after spending the day with Marvin's in-laws. Chills ran down my spine as the thought struck me that she might be returning to what I had just left.

Denzil volunteered to drive me all the way to my relatives' home, but I declined. I didn't want him to take his car into the rough hollow; besides, I needed time to be alone, so I got out of his car and began walking up the street. He turned his car around and headed back down the road to his own home.

With nightfall imminent, I walked as swiftly as I could. When I reached the first creek crossing, I remembered that I hadn't prayed for Bill's safety since morning. I began trying to pray, but all I could think about was how God had allowed my father to fully expose himself to me for the first time in all the years he had been tormenting me. Sobs of grief once again caused me to gasp for breath. I stopped and sat down on a large boulder jutting from the creek bed.

My swirling thoughts returned to Bill. I knew he would protect me if only he were home and knew what I had been living through. Although I wasn't sure that God would hear me, I began to pray for Bill's safety, forgetting for a moment about my own. Despite being isolated in the hollow, which was becoming darker by the minute, and having no one around for at least half a mile in either direction, a calm peace began to settle over me. I recalled how God had assured me some time back that He would never allow my father to violate my body, and that He would someday bring Bill and me together as husband and wife. "Why, I'm not alone," I heard myself saying aloud. "God is, and was, with me all along." I slowly slid off the rock and continued on my way, sorry that I had again doubted the One who faithfully reassured me of His tender, watchful care.

When I finally arrived at my relatives' home, they were shocked to see me and to know that I'd walked up the hollow after dark, alone. I quickly explained to them what had happened without giving any of the gruesome details. "Somebody orta take 'at man out'n horse-whup him," Uncle Clint said angrily.

"His actions were worse than I had ever seen before, but thank God, I was spared once again," I said. I turned and sat down on Grandma's feather bed, once again tossing another traumatizing experience where I'd tossed all the others: onto the pile of bad memories that would prove impossible to forget, but which God had always somehow brought me through.

LXXVI

Shattered

October soon rolled around, and I had not spent the night at my folks' home since the close call I'd had with my dad. From what Bill was telling me in his letters, which were still arriving every day of the week, I knew he would soon be home—honorably discharged and anxious to marry me. I had just turned eighteen, and as I thought about the one and only birthday party I had received in my honor, I smiled and picked up the soft stuffed animal I was packing inside a box I called my "hope chest."

On my sixteenth birthday, while working at the 5 & 10, I had walked upstairs one evening after the store was closed to find my coworkers and my boss gathered around a large box wrapped in brightly colored paper and tied with a big, cheerful bow. I had never attended a birthday party, so I had no clue about what was happening, when suddenly, the group began singing "Happy Birthday to You." Stunned, I joined in with the singing, and only when they sang out in unison, "Happy birthday, dear Lesher," did I realize that the party was for me.

Excited beyond description, I unwrapped the gift to find a large stuffed leopard inside. I literally jumped with glee. No one had ever given me such an adorable gift. There could have been no doubt left in my friends' minds that I had been totally surprised and overwhelmed by their kindness and thoughtfulness.

Before packing my adorable, cuddly gift for my move to the apartment, I had decided to show it to Uncle Hubert, who had come for a visit at Sissy's house and was sitting in Uncle Clint's big easy chair. As I walked up behind my uncle and reached the stuffed leopard across his shoulder, I said, "Uncle Hu—" But before I could finish speaking his name, he turned slightly to look in my direction, glanced at the leopard, jumped up suddenly, and forcefully punched me in the nose with his fist.

Needless to say, I saw stars! Tears sprung to my eyes, and blood poured out of my nostrils. I immediately realized that my uncle, who was afraid of mice, had reacted from sheer fright. Concerned about how quickly my nose was increasing in size, he suddenly began apologizing to me. Trying my best to laugh, I assured him that I would more than likely feel fine once my head had ceased vibrating. After the bleeding had stopped and I had assured Uncle Hubert that I'd had no intention of frightening him, I continued packing the houseware articles my relatives had given me.

Now, within a few days I would be giving my notice that I would be leaving the grocery store to begin preparing for Bill's homecoming. No matter how I tried to avoid it, even with the excitement I was experiencing as I daydreamed about Bill, I found myself thinking about my little siblings and my mother.

I had decided that I would never stay overnight with my family again. I also had promised myself that before going there for a short visit during the daylight hours, I would secure for myself a ride out of the hollow so that I could return to Sissy's home at night. I felt certain my mother understood why I could no longer spend nights with them, and, having seen her in the store on a few occasions, she seemed to be relieved by my decision—even when Dad had insisted.

I hoped that Dad had realized that he'd better leave well enough alone; he hadn't spoken to me since the Sunday when he had threatened to cut my heart out. He knew that Bill would soon be home and that we intended to be married, so I hoped I had experienced his abuse for the last time.

Near the middle of November, I left the job in the grocery store after giving my notice. Mr. Oberly had told me that he had learned to love me as a daughter, respect me as a woman of character, and admire me for my loyalty to Bill despite his attempting to encourage me to date other guys.

As the days grew closer for Bill to arrive back in the states, I became more and more nervous and excited. I looked forward to the day when we could be married and have our own home. Knowing that Bill loved me just as much as I loved him was very comforting and assuring. I could hardly wait for the day when I'd be back in his arms.

Finally, on a cold, snowy Saturday morning in late November, I packed a few articles of clothing and then rode into town with Sissy and my uncle, who were planning to buy groceries. I was excited because I knew that Bill had been scheduled to arrive home during the night, and I hoped to meet him on his way up the slippery hollow to see me.

While my relatives were doing their shopping, I decided to visit with my former employer in hopes that Bill would come by the store, before traveling up the slippery hollow, to reunite with me. When I walked into the store, Mr. Oberly immediately informed me that Bill had just left the store after coming in to ask him if I was in town. He then told me that when he had told Bill I was probably at my relatives' home, Bill had replied that he had no intentions of driving up the rough, icy hollow to see me.

For a moment I felt as though life itself had been ripped out of my body. Fighting hard to avoid sobbing out loud, I turned, bolted out of the store, and hastened down the sidewalk, a flood of tears straining to flow freely down my cheeks. I had no idea where I should go or what I should do.

I turned the corner, still carrying my vanity case, and started down Main Street with no destination in mind. I thought to myself, "After

I've waited for a year anticipating becoming his wife, is this the way Bill intends to treat me?"

About halfway down the street, I met my oldest brother, Woody, and my mom walking up the sidewalk. Woody had driven Mom into town to buy her groceries. Both could see that I was hurting inside, and Woody immediately asked me why I looked so forlorn. Seeing my brother's concern, I repeated to him what Mr. Oberly had just told me. Woody took me by the arm and steered me toward his car, which he had parked nearby. "You sit and wait until Mom finishes her shopping, and then you can ride with us," he said.

My first instinct was to return to Uncle Clint's car and to stay with Sissy and him until I'd decided what I should do; however, I did as my oldest brother had suggested after he promised that he would return me to my relatives' home should the need arise.

I was surprised at how I was beginning to feel. Although I was devastated, there was anger boiling within me. I had never said anything to Bill out of anger, but I knew should he approach me at that particular moment, I would be unable to hide my disappointment. All the excitement and happy anticipation I'd felt earlier had vanished. I was heartbroken—feeling betrayed and abandoned by the man I loved more than life itself.

I hadn't been sitting in the car more than ten minutes when I looked out to see Mom walking toward the car with Bill by her side. Tall, dark, and handsome, Bill was dressed in his winter uniform, which sported another rocker on his sergeant's chevron. I wondered whether Mom had coaxed him to approach the car to talk with me. It seemed like something my mother was capable of doing.

Bill walked up to the car, reached over, and opened the door, and then looked at me as though he didn't know what to expect. I wondered what Mom had told him and whether she would be as surprised as I was in wanting Bill to see how angry and disappointed I was with him. Having waited a lifetime for this moment, I hadn't expected to be feeling so empty. I felt that if the roles had been reversed, I would have walked all night or all day, through all kinds of weather, for the opportunity to once again be with the one I was planning to marry.

It had not even occurred to me that Mr. Oberly could have misunderstood or was exaggerating what Bill had said to him.

The first thing I noticed when Bill bent over to speak to me was his neatly trimmed mustache. Having never seen him with a mustache and not knowing what to say, I looked at him and said coldly, "Dig that crazy mustache."

Bill looked very puzzled as he slid himself onto the seat beside me. Mom muttered something and then turned and went back down the street. Bill pulled my stiffened body into his arms and kissed me affectionately; however, feeling almost lifeless, I was unable to respond to his tenderness. I looked into his eyes, and he appeared to be as disappointed as I was feeling.

After a few awkward moments of small talk between the two of us, I felt almost relieved when Mom and Woody returned to the car. When Woody informed us that Mom had finished shopping and was ready for him to take her home, I announced to Bill that I would be going home with Woody and my mom. Bill told me that he had borrowed a car and would have to stay in town long enough to buy himself some civilian clothing. He didn't ask me to stay with him, and I didn't ask to stay; however, he wanted to know when and where he could see me again.

Reluctantly, I asked, expecting the worst, "When'd you want to see me?"

"I'll not be in town more than half an hour, then I'll be up to see you as soon as I'm finished here," he said.

I wasn't sure whether to trust him; nevertheless, I half-heartedly agreed to the meeting. One way or another, I had to know what lay in store for us as soon as possible—no matter how painful it might be.

I rode up the hollow with my brother and Mom and didn't think about the situation with my father. Sissy would think I was going to my parents' home, since she expected me to be with Bill.

I thought about how my dreams of a joyful reunion had been shattered. I still could not believe that I could be feeling so insensitive. I wondered why I wasn't crying. I'd experienced many different emotions in my lifetime—some good, many bad—and I could never remember feeling as numb and uncaring as I was feeling now. It really frightened me. I wondered, if things were to work out between Bill and me, whether I'd ever have the same feelings I'd had from the day I'd fallen deeply in love with him. I also wondered how my "knight in shining armor" could play with my heartstrings so carelessly.

I finally asked Mom how she'd met Bill in town. "He 'uz walkin' up a street an' seed me an' Woody, so he jist walked over an' ast if we knowed whur you was," she said. I was puzzled and didn't know whom or what to believe.

I'd been at my parents' house less than an hour when Bill knocked on the door. I didn't answer the door but stayed in the background. When he was satisfied that I was inside, he walked into the living room, stopped and spoke with my dad, who also gave him a "ho-hum" welcome, and finally located me amongst the nine children and three adults. He seemed to be waiting for a response from me; however, like an icy statue, I stood frozen in place. My heart seemed to be pleading with my body to move toward him, but my head would not release the brake.

Bill looked hurt and confused. I couldn't walk over to him, for fear that I would hear him confess that he had changed his mind and no longer wanted to marry me, so I didn't move. If he wanted the chance to talk to me alone, then he would need to convince me that I should accompany him to a room where we could have a few minutes of privacy.

After about five minutes of idle chatter with my little brothers, who were thrilled to see him again, Bill slowly moved over to me and took me in his arms. I could feel his strong arms tighten around me as he nuzzled my cheek with his clean-shaven face. He took me by the arm and steered me into the kitchen, where he turned my face toward him and kissed me on the lips. I felt a spark of life slowly returning to my body, but from deep within, I knew I needed some answers before I could open my arms to him.

After holding me and trying to talk to me for about ten minutes, Bill finally asked me, "What's happened that you're so cold toward me?"

I couldn't say a word. I wondered how he expected me to react after what he'd said to Mr. Oberly. Seeing the bewildered look on his face, I finally realized that he didn't have an inkling as to why I was upset. I bowed my head to avoid eye contact with him, while I softly repeated what Mr. Oberly had told me. Bill vehemently denied that he had said anything so ridiculous. He was shocked that I had become so cold and insensitive over the apparent misunderstanding. "If you remember, you told me that you'd try an' be at the store by ten a.m.," he said. "I was on my way to check again at the store for you before driving to your aunt's house, when I met up with your mom."

He apparently sensed that I was still skeptical, so he continued trying to assure me that the only thing that had brought him back to civilian life was the fact that I would not marry him while he was in the Army. "I want a find a job and a house as soon as possible, and then I want us to get married," he said. Even with his show of affection and promises, I still feared he would leave me again. I was sorry that his homecoming had not been as joyous as we both had anticipated; however, I needed time to understand why I had believed what Mr. Oberly had said without giving Bill a chance to explain.

I finally realized that from our very first date I had worshipped Bill and had been putting him ahead of God in my life. But each time I thought about the fact that it was God, rather than Bill, who should have preeminence in my life, then I was tormented with the fear I might lose Bill's love, if I were to put God first. When I found myself wondering whether I could fully trust Bill never to leave me again, I was also reminded that many times I had even mistrusted God, although He had always been by my side and had never failed to keep

His word. I wondered whether maybe God wasn't trying to tell me something. "Dear God, please help me to put You first, and to fully trust both You and Bill," I prayed.

Even though Bill found a job quickly, over the next two weeks we were able to spend our early evenings and weekends together, with me spending my nights either with my parents or with Sissy and Uncle Clint. As time passed, I became more assured than ever that Bill's love for me was no doubt equal to my love for him.

Having accepted the impending reality that Bill and I would be getting married, my father had stopped physically attacking me, although his verbal abuse continued. On the occasions when Bill picked me up at my parents' home and could see I had been crying, he no longer questioned me about my tear-stained face, since apparently, like the members of my family, he had grown accustomed to what seemed to be almost a regular occurrence.

LXXVII

Painfully Shy

I was ignorant of the tradition that the bride should have the honor of planning the wedding. When Bill brought up the subject of us getting married, I listened and was excited, but refrained from any discussion on the matter. Shy and naive, I thought it would be wrong for me to ask questions or to show too much interest. I believed that Bill was supposed to make all the decisions since he was the dominant man, and I felt that when he had everything ready, he would give me any information I might need.

I didn't know the significance of the traditional white bridal gown. When they had married, none of my relatives had worn a wedding gown or been married in a church, and they probably, like me, had never heard of anyone having a reception after the wedding. All my relatives' marriages had been performed either by a Justice of the Peace or with only the preacher and a witness present, absent of any ceremonies. I did not expect or desire that my own wedding be any different. I already felt I had done wrong when I'd secretly bought a navy-blue suit to wear on my wedding day, with money that Bill had sent me to help with my personal needs once I had quit work.

Bill had informed me that he planned to have an apartment ready before we exchanged vows. He hadn't asked for my help or opinion in finding the apartment, and here, too, I felt I had no right to question him. Although I was anxious and curious about any plans he was making, I feared that to question him about the plans would be presumptuous and improper of me. Besides, I didn't want Bill to think I was pressuring him.

Bill had bought a 1946 Mercury Sedan with some of the money he had managed to save, so on the first week of December 1953, on a cold, snowy morning, we slipped and slid out of the hollow to where he parked the car in the lower end of town. Four inches of snow lay on the ground, so I was wearing my winter coat and boots and, underneath the coat, a skirt and a long-sleeved, white blouse with tight-banded cuffs.

We exited the car and were walking up the street when Bill finally revealed where we were going. Holding onto my left hand, he said, "I guess you know we're goin' to the doctor's office to have our blood tests done today" (a requirement in WV before marriage). Although I felt panicked immediately, I refrained from saying a word. Even I knew that when blood was drawn for the test, the blood was sent to Charleston for the results, since there was no lab in our small town. Having never had blood drawn, I had a few days earlier asked my brother what to expect. Marvin had told me that he and his girlfriend had gone into the doctor's examining room together, and their blood had been drawn in each other's presence.

While thinking about the information my brother had shared with me, I became very unnerved. Since I was wearing the blouse with the tight armbands, I realized that, in order to expose my arm, I would need to remove my blouse, since the tight band wouldn't allow the sleeve to be pushed above my elbow. Even though the temperature was near zero degrees Fahrenheit, I had begun to perspire. Knowing I couldn't tell Bill I wasn't prepared for the test, I had to act quickly.

Promptly, I withdrew my left hand from Bill's right hand and shoved my hand up my right coat sleeve, hurriedly ripping the seam in the tight wristband without Bill knowing what I had just done. Feeling certain I would now be able to expose my "naked" arm without having to remove my blouse, I breathed a sigh of relief.

The doctor must have sensed my timidity when Bill and I entered the examining room. After exchanging a few pleasantries, he invited Bill to step into the adjoining room alone. I again breathed a sigh of relief as I sat waiting my turn, wondering what I should do if the doctor were to inform me he needed to draw blood from my left arm.

Moments later, Bill returned to the room, and Dr. Harper called out my name. Trying to hide my fears, I followed the doctor into the room, which smelled like what I would later learn was Lysol disinfectant. I quickly pushed up my ripped sleeve and exposed my arm, watching closely and curiously as the doctor pushed the needle into my arm and began drawing blood. "Your husband-to-be is a very nice guy," Dr. Harper said. "I believe you're getting a good man." I wasn't aware at the time that Bill and the doctor were related.

The doctor then escorted me back to Bill's side and congratulated Bill on his choosing me to be his wife. Bill and I left the office and walked along the snowy sidewalk to the car. I was relieved that the ordeal was over and that I hadn't fainted from embarrassment. I still didn't know our wedding date, but I didn't see any reason to ask questions. Bill seemed to have everything under control without any help from me.

About two weeks later, Bill was sent home from work because of bad weather. Mom had become accustomed to me running whenever Bill beckoned, and she no longer questioned us about where we were going or when she could expect Bill to bring me back. Once again, as Bill arrived and asked me to join him, although I was curious, I didn't ask about his plans for the day.

I was surprised and puzzled when Bill drove through town instead of stopping as I had expected. Without any conversation between us, we crossed the bridge that spanned the Elk River and began driving up the paved highway that ran alongside a small tributary that emptied into the river. After we had driven about three miles, Bill suddenly pulled off the highway into a residential area, stopping in front of a garage apartment. He turned off the ignition and then turned toward me and looked warmly into my eyes. "I found this apartment up here on my lunch hour the other day, an' I want you to look at it before I pay the rent," he said. I shivered with excitement.

We walked up the steps together, and I watched curiously as he opened the unlocked door to the living room. We stepped into the room, which I immediately noticed was in immaculate condition. The light oak floors glistened like glass. Wide-eyed and smiling from ear to ear, I held onto Bill's hand as we surveyed the kitchen, two large bedrooms, and a bathroom with an "honest to goodness" commode and bathtub.

Also smiling, and seemingly proud of himself, Bill looked at me and asked, "You like 'his?"

Thrilled, but too timid to acknowledge my excitement, I managed to softly say, "It's really nice."

Realizing that the apartment was unfurnished, I couldn't bring myself to ask what Bill's plans were for obtaining our furniture, especially knowing that if he was ready to pay rent on the apartment, our wedding date must be very close.

Hand in hand, we walked back down the steps and across the street, where Bill paid the landlord $55.00 for the first month's rent. "Our furniture will be delivered this evenin'," Bill told him.

"Furniture? What furniture?" I asked myself.

On the drive back to town, I realized more than ever that Bill was indeed, beyond a shadow of doubt, the person God had chosen to be my husband. I wondered whether I could ever be the wife he deserved.

When we arrived back in town, Bill informed me he had saved enough money to buy the furniture we would be needing. "Pick out whatever you want," he said, as we walked across the street to the furniture store. I had no idea how much money Bill was intending to spend, and again, I was too shy to ask.

While slowly walking around the small showroom together, I inconspicuously looked at the prices. Common sense told me I should select the necessities first, especially since I had no idea of the amount I could spend. Slowly, after asking for Bill's approval, I selected the cheapest of these pieces of furniture for the kitchen: a gas range, a wooden table with four chairs, and a utility cabinet in which to store our dishes, cooking utensils, and groceries, since the kitchen had no cabinets. Since it was the middle of winter, I knew I could manage for the time being without a refrigerator. Bill agreed that we should purchase an inexpensive sofa, one matching armchair, a coffee table, and two end tables. Our bedroom suite consisted of a double bed, a dresser, and chest of drawers. "Is that it?' Bill asked.

"Yeah, I guess," I said. "I can manage without a 'frigerator." I silently asked God to help Bill have enough money, as he turned calmly and asked the clerk for the final amount due.

When the clerk quoted the total of the sale, Bill stated that he didn't have quite enough money to pay for what we had selected. When the clerk made the adjustment after I had agreed to omit one of the end tables and the coffee table, Bill told her that he was still short a few dollars. "You two take a minute alone and decide what you want to do," the clerk said. Before I'd had time to decide what other alternatives we might have, Bill told me that he was reserving enough money to buy our groceries for a month. I reminded him that I could charge the food at the store where I'd worked and that we could pay Mr. Oberly on payday; so, after the clerk added in taxes and gave us the total amount due, we were able to make a deal.

When Bill asked what we could do about linens, I explained that I already had all our linens and dishes in the hope chest I'd been working to fill for the past year. Although our extra bedroom would go unfurnished, and I would need to manage without a refrigerator, we couldn't have been happier if we'd just bought a house full of the most expensive furniture in the store. After making arrangements to have the furniture delivered late in the day, Bill and I joyously walked back out to the car.

I looked up ahead just in time to see Uncle Clint approaching. Bill immediately asked my uncle to take me home with him so I could get my belongings ready to move. "We're gettin' married this evenin' at six o'clock," Bill said. His announcement surprised me since it was the first I had heard about the wedding date; however, by now I was becoming accustomed to surprises. Bill left immediately for Charleston to pick up our marriage license, since my mother had previously signed the parental consent form. Because I was eighteen years old, we had been told that Dad's signature was not necessary.

When Uncle Clint and I arrived and told Aunt Sissy the news, she was almost as surprised as I had been to know that by nightfall I would be married. In all the excitement over the surprise event, I would later realize that I had completely forgotten to invite my generous relatives to the private ceremony.

Bill had made the appointment with the preacher who formerly had pastored the little church our family had attended while living on the ridge. They had met while cutting timber for Mr. Oberly's brother, before Bill had joined the Army. As the day passed swiftly, I was becoming concerned, when Bill finally returned in late afternoon to pick me up from Sissy's home. He explained his tardiness, telling us that when he'd applied for the license, he'd been informed that since I was only eighteen, both my parents' signatures were required. He had driven back to town, gone quickly to the school bus garage and obtained my father's signature, and then completed another fifty-mile round-trip to and from Charleston with the signed document.

My soon-to-be husband loaded all my belongings into his car, which included the items in my hope chest. (I was unaware of the tradition of a bridal shower for the bride.) I thanked and then hugged my loved ones, overjoyed in knowing that I would soon be exchanging vows with the man whom I was confident God had prepared just for me. I couldn't have been happier!

Once we were back in town, Bill dropped me off at Mr. Oberly's store with instructions to buy enough groceries to last for a week.

Surprised once again, I managed to find enough courage to ask him what type of food he wanted me to buy. "Oh, buy some pork an' beans, peanut butter, and potatoes," he said. With an answer like that, I had no doubt that he was going to be easy to please. "Oh yes," he said, as I exited the car, "Be sure'n git flour so that you can make me some hot biscuits for breakfast."

Once I had made my selections, I wrote up the bill myself, assuring my ex-boss that we would pay the bill within two weeks. "Oh, well," he said, "I'm sure I won't lose any sleep over this charge account."

We drove quickly back to our new apartment. The furniture had been delivered and placed in the appropriate rooms. I looked around at everything and must have been beaming as Bill hugged me and said, "This is where we'll be spendin' the night—together." Shuddering, I felt my face begin to flush.

While Bill brought the groceries in from the car, I slipped into the bathroom to change into the suit I'd bought earlier. He was wearing blue jeans, a blue sports shirt, and his inspection combat boots with their "spit-and-polish" shine.

When I walked into the bedroom to don my nylon stockings, Bill walked into the room unannounced. He stared at me as I pulled one of the stockings over my ankle. Blushing, I asked him to please wait in the other room. When he smiled but didn't leave right away, I grabbed the other nylon and ran into the bathroom, where I locked the door until I was fully dressed.

When I walked out of the bathroom and entered the room where he "patiently" sat waiting, he said jokingly, "Just you wait. You won't hide from me much longer." Embarrassed and unnerved, I hastily blocked the thought from my mind.

Although we rushed to get to the preacher's house on time, we were still fifteen minutes late. Even so, Reverend Foster greeted us warmly at the door and invited us into his parlor. I was surprised when I noticed that the minister's wife and daughter were not present. I was under the impression that at least one witness was required when exchanging marriage vows. "Gee whiz," I thought to myself. "I hope this will be legal."

The preacher examined the marriage license that Bill had handed him, and then moved over near us with his opened Bible. He asked us to join hands, and Bill reached down and took my left hand with his right hand. Standing there in the quaint little parlor, with its linoleum-covered floor and plastic drapes hanging limply over the windows, I was overjoyed knowing I was about to be wed to my tall, dark, and handsome knight in shining armor. Reverend Foster asked us to repeat the appropriate vows; then, two and a half years after my first date with the man I believed God had chosen for me, Bill and I were finally joined together in Holy Matrimony.

The minister turned to Bill and told him, "You can now kiss your bride."

I was surprised when Bill replied, "I'll wait." I didn't know whether to laugh or to cry, but I was certainly relieved. I'd been feeling concerned about being kissed in front of the preacher. Apparently, Bill was feeling the same way.

The reverend showed us where to sign the marriage certificate and then reminded me that I had just signed my maiden name for the last time. He didn't have any idea how happy I was about that fact alone. I was not ashamed of my surname, but I was overjoyed to be married to Bill, and relieved that at last I had been freed from the hell in which I'd been living for the past ten years.

Reverend Foster bent over the small lampstand and signed the certificate. "Let me be the first one to wish you much luck an' happiness," he said, shaking hands with each of us.

"Thank you, sir," Bill said, reaching into his shirt pocket for a five-dollar bill and handing it to the smiling preacher.

When we reached our car and Bill opened my door, I slipped into the seat while whispering softly, "Thank you, God, for bringin' him back to me an' for keepin' me safe and sound for him."

I breathed a sigh of relief when Bill drove back to the highway and headed in the direction opposite the apartment he'd rented. I assumed we were going to collect our belongings from our parents' homes. Also, our parents needed to know that we wouldn't be spending the night at their homes. I snuggled closely to Bill as we drove up the winding road. Once we'd reached an isolated section on the side of the first hill we were crossing over, he stopped the car, turned, and kissed me with a long, tender kiss. Looking into my eyes, he said, "It's good to be married, don't you agree?"

I smiled contentedly and answered, "Yes, I agree." At least five minutes had passed since we'd left the pastor's home, and these were the first words exchanged between us. As we continued up the road, I felt toasty warm inside, although the heater in our Mercury was inoperative, and the temperature outside was hovering close to zero.

As I watched Bill carefully maneuvering around the icy turn on the side of the mountain, my thoughts suddenly shifted, and I pondered the fact that I would never again need to lie awake at night listening for the sounds of my father creeping into my room. I was confident my husband would protect me for as long as we both lived. Suddenly, realizing what I was thinking about, I pushed the thoughts of my father's sick behavior to the back of my mind. I didn't want to spoil the evening by thinking about the past. "I hope I can be a good wife, and I believe that God has given me a husband who'll make it easy for me," I thought to myself.

It was pitch black outside when Bill drove into his parents' driveway. When we stepped inside the room where his father sat listening to a program on the radio and his mother was crocheting a beautiful doily, he held my hand and announced, "At 1800 hours this evenin', Bethel and I got married."

His mother, avoiding looking up from her work, grumpily said, "Y'ain't dun it!" Bill told his mom that she could go down to the car and get our marriage certificate or that she could trust his word.

"I'm pickin' up my belongin's, and we'll be goin' to our own place to live," Bill stated. None of his family members welcomed me into the family nor exchanged further words with us during the few minutes that Bill was packing his belongings. As we walked out the door, no one acknowledged our departure.

Our next stop was to visit my folks and to announce to them that we were now married. I expected my family would believe us, since both Mom and Dad's signatures had been required on the application for the marriage license. When we walked inside where my family sat watching television, only my mother greeted us. Dad didn't seem to notice that we'd walked directly past him, since he was totally engrossed in the television program. Mom walked into the dining room with Bill and me, where I told her that we'd just been married. "I knowed you prob'ly was. I hope y'all 'll be happy," Mom said. She walked back into the living room, and I picked up my few belongings before Bill and I walked past Dad again on our way toward the door.

Mom nudged Dad and informed him that Bill and I had just been married. Dad slowly looked up at both of us and said, "Congratcheelations." Then, almost in the same breath, he asked, "Whur'bouts you gonna live?" I hadn't stopped to think that none of the family was aware of the house Bill had rented. When we told them about what we'd been doing all day long, Mom and Dad both seemed pleased. We bid them farewell and went back to our car.

I'd been a bundle of nerves the day Bill had asked Dad for my hand in marriage, just two weeks previously. Bill had invited Dad to go for a walk with him, and as I'd watched them walking up the road together, I wondered how Dad would react. Finally, after I'd paced the floor for fifteen or twenty minutes, I looked out to see them coming toward the house. Since they were still talking to each other, I knew that Dad must have given his blessings.

I had been trembling when Bill walked into the room, looking very relieved that he had the formality behind him. He later told me that Dad had not only given his blessing but had said, "I thank you'll make Bethel a good husban'.'" I was glad I hadn't told Bill about the problem I'd been having with Dad, so that my new husband could get off to a good start with my family. In spite of all I'd been through, I still longed for a "normal" father-daughter relationship.

It was about 9:00 p.m. when, as husband and wife, we arrived back at our own apartment. We walked inside and set our belongings in the empty room; then hand in hand, we walked into the kitchen. Bill took me in his arms and told me he was very proud I was finally his bride. Knowing he had probably had nothing to eat all day long, and needing an excuse to keep my new husband occupied in order to prolong our retiring for the night, I offered to fix him a sandwich. He asked that I make him a fried bologna sandwich while he showered, so I rummaged around in my pots and pans until I'd located an iron skillet. I was still trying to remove the sticky label glued to the bottom of the brand-new pan when Bill returned to the kitchen.

Just married.

Although we were now married, I was feeling guilty and embarrassed to be alone inside the house with Bill, and I believed he could sense my nervousness. Because of my excitement and nervousness throughout the day, I hadn't eaten since breakfast. Now, here I was—half starved and still too bashful to eat in front of my husband. When he offered me a bite of his warm sandwich, I smiled and said, "No, thank you. I'm not hungry."

Within minutes, Bill reminded me that he had to work the next day, and we needed to get ready for bed. Feeling uneasy about him seeing me in my nightgown and unable to stall any longer, I decided I would outsmart my new husband. I hurried into the bathroom, showered quickly, and donned my long-sleeved, floor-length flannel nightgown, with plans to sneak into bed while he was still in the kitchen.

In record time, I prepared for bed and then opened the bathroom door, hoping to sneak across the bedroom floor and get into bed without Bill seeing me. Thinking he was still alone in the kitchen, I quietly swung open the bathroom door, stepped into the bedroom, and was shocked to see my smiling husband lying in bed—looking straight at me. "Uh huh, I beat cha, didn't I?" he said teasingly. "Now, you have to turn off the light!"

The light switch was located across the room on the wall opposite the bathroom door. I backed up into the bathroom with my body hidden from his view, wondering how I could get across the room to turn off the light that he had deliberately left on. Realizing I had no alternative, I darted across the bedroom floor, switched off the light, and then, in one long leap, I literally jumped into our bed. As I hurriedly yanked the covers up to my chin, my husband laughed unmercifully.

Embarrassed beyond belief, I shivered when Bill took me into his arms and said softly to me, "I know 'at you're scared, so I'll give you until Saturday night to get used to crawlin' into bed with me, but if you come to bed wearin' this long flannel nightgown, I swear to God that I'll rip it off of you." From the sound of his voice, I knew that he meant what he had said. I realized that it was Tuesday night and that I'd need to overcome a lot of fears and apprehension in just four days.

Bill had no inkling about the anxieties boiling within me. I wished I could talk to him about my fears, but I could only trust God to make it possible for me to confide in my husband with the sordid details at an appropriate time. I lay silently in his arms, wondering whether I could ever be the wife he deserved. Neither of us had any way of knowing how our first ten years of married life would be affected by the secret that had been a part of my life for the past ten years.

Bill was tender and loving with me, and I was grateful that God had kept me safe and pure for my husband. Snuggled in his strong arms, I silently promised myself that someday soon, I would share my dark secret with him. One thing was certain, however: it wasn't going to be on my wedding night.

LXXVIII

Fifty-Two Pick Up

The next morning when Bill asked me to make biscuits and gravy for his breakfast, I was puzzled. Even though I was from the same part of the country that Bill was from, I had never known anyone to eat gravy poured over biscuits for breakfast. Mom had always called the brown gravy "poor man's gravy" and had never served it for breakfast. I thought to myself, "My people were some of the poorest folks around, but Bill's family must have been even poorer if they had to eat gravy for breakfast."

I rushed trying to get the biscuits into the oven while Bill showered and shaved. I didn't know why, but I became very uncomfortable when my husband walked into the kitchen just as I had begun kneading the wet dough. I hurriedly prepared the biscuits, placed the hot pan into the oven, and began frying a few pieces of frozen sausage that I'd stored in a bowl and set outside on a shelf. After moving the heated sausage onto a plate, I added about two tablespoons of flour to what appeared to be two tablespoons of drippings. After browning the flour and sausage drippings to a rich golden-brown, I added salt and pepper and a mixture of a half cup of Carnation condensed milk and a half cup of water. I then simmered the gravy, stirring it constantly, until it had thickened nicely.

Bill raved about the meal. I was pleased that he had enjoyed the food, but I wondered whether I would ever be able to eat in my husband's presence. Once he had left for work, I managed to eat a few bites of the first meal I had cooked in our own cozy home and was surprised that the gravy was indeed very tasty.

When Bill came home for lunch for the next few days, I was overjoyed to have the few minutes we spent together; however, because of my backwardness, I could eat only a few bites of lunch with him. By then, I had begun feeling weak because I still hadn't eaten a good meal, and my stomach hurt almost constantly. I tried not to let Bill know about the problem, however, since it was common knowledge that his mother was a hypochondriac. I certainly didn't want him to think the girl he had married was also one.

After Bill had left for work one morning, I decided to empty the items that remained in one of his Army satchels so that I could store them in the proper drawer. I was shocked when I pulled out a small box he had tucked away inside one of the pockets of the bag. My first thought when I looked down at the box was "Oh, my Lord! I've married a gambler!" I recognized the playing cards immediately, since I'd sold a few decks while working at the 5 & 10.

My family had always preached that cards were used only by bad men who gambled their wages away. "'Em thangs'r of the devil, an' 'hey'll send ya straight ta hell," Mom had said. Now here I stood, holding a deck of Bicycle playing cards I'd discovered in my husband's belongings. I honestly was scared that Bill had become addicted to gambling while in the Army. I didn't know how I was going to tell him that I had innocently stumbled upon his secret. I worried about the situation for the rest of the day.

Upon his arrival home from work, he sensed that something was wrong and immediately asked, "Why do you look so sad?"

I picked up the pack of cards and softly asked, "Honey, why are you carrying these gambling cards in your bag?"

Bill laughed and said, "You don't have to worry! I'm not a gambler." He then took the deck of cards from my hand and slipped them out of the box. Grinning cunningly, he asked, "You want me to show you how to play 'Fifty-two Pick-up'?"

Innocently, I answered, "I'd rather not play 'ith those things."

"Aw, come on, jist let me teach you this one game," he pleaded. "It's perfectly innocent an' will only take a minute."

"Go ahead and show me, I guess," I replied reluctantly.

He held the cards out in front of his face at arm's length, and at the instant he let them fall from his hand, he flipped them with his thumb, scattering the handful of cards across the living room floor. Gasping in disbelief, I asked timidly, "Why, what'd you do that for?"

Chuckling, he looked at me and then looked down at the cards. "There's fifty-two cards there. You can pick 'em up now."

Wide-eyed and with my mouth agape, I bent down silently to gather up the cards. Bill knelt down beside me to help retrieve the cards. "I betcha I don't fall for that one again," I mumbled softly. We looked at each other, and then as he broke forth with laughter, I smiled sheepishly.

After Bill had returned the playing cards to their pack, he handed them to me and said, "If you don't want 'em in our home, you can throw 'em out." Breathing a sigh of relief, I immediately walked over to the wastebasket and threw them in with the rest of the trash.

I could remember only two other times in my life when I had been this embarrassed. One of the times was when I was in the third grade. I had, on several occasions, been sent up to the blackboard to compete with the two highest achievers in our class, while our peers watched from their seats. Our teacher would call out three numbers, which the boys and I would immediately write on the blackboard. We would then turn our faces toward the teacher as she had instructed before the competition had begun. Each time she called out another group of three numbers, we would turn around and write them directly below the previous numbers, until, finally, she would call out, "Go!" We three students would quickly draw a line below the three columns of numbers and begin adding, in hopes of being the first to arrive at the correct sum.

For days I had been elated each time I had arrived at the correct answer before the two proud boys had finished summing up their final column of numbers. On this particular day, I had been the first to solve every problem; consequently, once the teacher told us to take our seats, after announcing to the class that I had won the competition, the boys hung their heads and muttered a few unpleasantries while we were leaving the blackboard. I smiled broadly and, with my head held high, arrogantly flipped past the boys as we hurried across the oaken floor.

Earlier in the morning, I had lost the rubber heel from one of my shoes, leaving the heads of several tacks exposed. Just as I passed behind the last row of students and turned the corner on my way to my seat, the tacks in my shoe caused my foot to slip, sending my small body crashing to the floor. I quickly jerked the tail of my dress back down over my behind and, with my face hot and my inflated ego crushed, shrugged off the boys' giggles as I continued walking inconspicuously to my desk. I hadn't felt so humiliated since the episode with the rooster.

Now here I stood, nine years later, once again blushing from embarrassment yet greatly relieved to know that I hadn't married a gambler after all.

LXXIX

Telling My Secret

Bill and I had been married only two weeks when he insisted that I see a doctor to determine the reason behind the increasing pain in my stomach and my decreasing weight. I finally agreed to see Doctor Harper, the local doctor who had drawn our blood weeks earlier.

After examining me and listening to my complaint, Dr. Harper advised us that he wanted me to go to Charleston to have my stomach fluoroscoped—the diagnostic method available to us in 1953. Bill made the appointment and took off work a couple of days later to drive me to Charleston. After returning home, since we had no telephone, we waited patiently for almost a week before receiving a card requesting we return to Dr. Harper's office.

Once we had entered the doctor's examining room, he informed us that the tests had revealed an active peptic ulcer located in the pylorus. Bill looked at Dr. Harper and said, "Okay, Doc, now what does that mean in our language?"

The doctor explained that the ulcer, which was shaped like a crater, had been gnawing at the muscle layers in my stomach—apparently for quite some time. I had been bothered for years with stomach problems and had suspected that my eating habits since I'd been married had aggravated the condition.

Dr. Harper prescribed medication, milk, and diet, stressing the fact that I should eat three nourishing meals a day. Smiling, the doctor said to Bill as he reached out to shake his hand, "She also needs to rest, so don't you be loving her too much."

Had I been aware that the emotional stress I'd been living under for the past ten years could have caused the crater in my stomach, I would have known that my recovery should have already been underway. I wondered, however, why the doctor had told Bill not to love me too much.

Married for 2 weeks.

My husband and I were very happy together, but I still hadn't been able to tell him about the situation from which he'd unknowingly rescued me. I lived in constant fear that I wasn't good enough for Bill and that he would leave me and return to the Army. He had never given me reason to doubt his commitment to me; nevertheless, I felt as though I didn't deserve my husband or his love. I didn't understand the reasons behind my fears and insecurities, and I was afraid to talk to him about my concerns.

Bill had been laid off because his boss was going out of business; consequently, we had no choice but to move to a small, cheaper house, located on an isolated farm. Shortly after we moved, our car had blown a head-gasket, and, having no money for repairs, we were left without transportation.

My dad had informed us that he had been told that a fourteen-year-old girl who had ridden his school bus at one time had shot and killed herself in the house where we had just moved. After learning about the suicide, and after discovering a dark stain on the floor of one of the rooms, I was terrified to be left alone in the isolated house. I would walk with Bill daily the three miles out of the hollow to catch the Greyhound bus, which we rode fourteen miles to Clendenin near where our parents lived. We would then walk five more miles to my parents' home, where I would spend the day with my mother and younger siblings while Bill worked all day helping the farmers in the area put up their hay. After paying our bus fare, he barely had enough money left to pay for our groceries (thankfully, credit cards were not around yet).

At the end of the day, once Bill had returned from the hay fields, we would return to our little home the same way we had traveled earlier the same morning. Bill never once suggested we stay with his parents, and I never considered staying with mine. Neither of us questioned the reason we preferred to return to our own "haunted" home, especially knowing that we'd have to make the same trip the very next morning.

Pondering the fact that I had been spending a lot of time at my parents' home, and fearing that my father might return home early from work someday before Bill had come in from the hay field, I began considering how to tell my husband about the problem I had endured with my father. I had finally begun to relax around Bill and was finding it easier to take my meals with him, so I decided I was ready to confide in him about the painful truth of my past.

After arriving home shortly before dark, I scavenged enough food to prepare our evening meal. Since we both were totally exhausted after we had eaten dinner and done the dishes, we retired for the night. After whispering my evening prayer, I curled up in Bill's arms and began brokenly spilling out all the penned-up secrets I had kept from him during the years we had known each other.

Once I had begun talking about the sordid ordeal, I was surprised at how easily the truth flowed from my quivering lips. Bill was surprised and shocked when he finally learned the reason I had often been crying when we had met for dates. After lying quietly beside me for a few minutes, he pulled me close to his chest and said tenderly, "I'm so sorry you didn' tell me in the beginnin'."

"I couldn't. I just couldn't," I sobbed.

"Honey, I do understand, and I want you to know that you'll never have to worry again," he said protectively. "I'll kill 'at son-of-a-bitch. I swear to God, I'll kill that bastard if he ever touches you again!"

"Just hold me," I pleaded between sobs. "We'll talk about that tomorrow." We wrapped our arms tightly around each other and cried ourselves to sleep.

When I awoke the next morning, I felt as though the world had been lifted off my shoulders. I knew that Bill would need answers, and I felt the time had come for me to give him those answers; therefore, I continued to enlighten my husband about the hell I'd lived through since childhood. Needless to say, my loving, gentle husband was not only shocked but was also very, very angry. He found my story to be even more painful when he learned that some of the worst episodes between my father and me had occurred while he and I were engaged, while I was waiting for him to return from Korea.

Neither Bill nor anyone else outside the family who knew my dad would have believed my father was capable of doing the things I'd just disclosed. I had avoided giving Bill some of the more sordid details, for fear that I'd cause him to hate my father. I had hoped that Bill and I could put the past behind us and that we would be able to develop a normal relationship with Dad. I was willing to give my father the chance to prove he'd never touch me again, now that I belonged to my husband. I also asked Bill, for my sake, to handle the problem in a way that would keep this hope alive. Should we ever be blessed with our own children, I secretly desired very much that they could come to know my parents as their grandparents.

Bill was anxious to confront my dad about the way he had treated me, so the next time we went for a visit with my family, Bill invited my father to join him for a walk up the road. He later told me that he had been wondering how to bring up the subject with my dad, when, suddenly, Dad asked him whether I had been a virgin when he married me. Bill said that he'd felt like killing him right there on the spot; however, with a lot of effort on his behalf, he said he had managed to control his outrage. "In the first place, I don't see where that's any of your business," he had said sternly to my father. "If the bastard she told me about would've had his way, then she definitely would not have been a virgin."

"What'd he say to that?" I asked.

"He kept his head down an' didn't say a word." Bill told me that he had also warned my father, saying, "I'll make you a promise right here and now. If any man ever lays a finger on my wife, or harms her in any way, then I will personally kill the bastard." Bill said that he had stressed his warning by saying, "Before he dies, he'll suffer a slow, painful death while I'm standing over him reminding him why he has to suffer before he's allowed to die." While Dad remained silent, Bill also told him that should we ever be blessed with a daughter, he expected her to also be treated with respect. Not only did Dad not respond to Bill's warning, but he also remained silent for the rest of the day, no doubt pondering the warning that Bill had so explicitly spelled out.

I was pleased with the way Bill had handled the situation. We both knew that Dad must have known he was the man Bill was referring to when he'd made his promise to protect me against "the bastard." I prayed that my father's evil actions were in the past and would never return to mar the happy and peaceful years that I believed lay ahead for Bill and me. I also believed we were totally committed to our marriage vows and that no matter what obstacles may lie ahead, my husband and I would face them—together.

LXXX

Secure

Bill and I had been married only eight months when we decided together that he would leave West Virginia and return to the U.S. Army. I had been unaware that I could accompany him on most of his assignments and that we would be able to live together in a home of our choice. So, after learning these facts and being assured that he would re-enter the service as an NCO (Noncommissioned Officer), his rank at the time of his discharge, we embarked on an entirely new way of life.

A soldier's pay back then amounted to little more than Bill's pay in the hay fields had been; yet, by God's grace and through His mercy, while being paid only once each month, we managed to survive without others knowing how much of the month remained beyond the end of our money. Our sometimes-overwhelming struggles seemed only to strengthen our love for each other and our bond in marriage.

I would soon learn—in this world that was foreign to the way of life in which I had been raised—just how often I would feel as though I were a mere toddler, stumbling and falling as I learned to walk among the throng of people who not only were already walking but were excelling in running marathons.

As I look back now on my younger days, I can see how, each time I slipped and fell, often amid the laughter of others, I rose quickly to my feet and, while shaking the dust from my trembling body, drank in a newly discovered portion of exciting information that enabled me to become a stronger and more enlightened person than I had been before. Almost daily, I would find myself soaking up knowledge like a giant dry sponge that had been thrown into a sea of troubled waters.

For the first ten years of our marriage, Bill proved his love for me over and over during the many flashbacks I endured because of my traumatic childhood experiences. A common occurrence, such as Bill walking up behind me and placing his arms around my shoulders, would periodically trigger the horrible memories. Once, I had innocently looked down and seen his Army dress shoes (similar to my father's shoes), and I immediately seized up and broke down with uncontrollable sobbing.

My concerned, patient, and loving husband seemed always to know how to handle any given situation. He never once failed to understand when I sometimes had to turn my back to him—this precious man whom I loved with all my heart. During those times, my faith never wavered in God's having chosen the right husband for me, since God alone could have known the strong character my husband would require in order to help me through those troublesome years.

Together, Bill and I raised three well-adjusted, dedicated, and "born-again Christian" children who blessed us even more with their own beautiful families. One of Bill and my greatest joys is in knowing that our children, their spouses, and our grandchildren are saved and active in their respective churches. We also rejoice to see them sharing their love for each other in the manner that Bill and I have demonstrated throughout our marriage of fifty years (1953–2003).

I received my G.E.D. (General Education Diploma)—the equivalent of a high school diploma—when I was fifty-five years old. Before receiving the certificate, I worked over the years in the States and overseas in several businesses and a bank, being advanced often and at times serving in an assistant manager or manager's position. I wanted to prove to myself and to my superiors and coworkers that I was capable of acquiring, and could successfully fulfill, the positions that my college-educated peers sometimes failed to obtain. I believe that my family, friends, and coworkers realized that my desire to achieve my goals brought me a healthy level of self-worth that was not viewed as inappropriate pride, since I always tried to balance that sense of satisfaction or feeling of accomplishment by applying instruction I received from spending time in God's Word and in prayer.

More than anything else in the world, I wanted to be a good witness for my Savior. I believed at the time, although I had never been shown from the Scriptures, that I was saved securely when I had accepted Jesus as my Savior shortly after my twelfth birthday. However, while we were visiting with Uncle Hubert's family during one of Bill's furloughs, I was telling my unsaved uncle about my faith and stated that I was sure I was going to Heaven when I die. Uncle Hubert looked at me skeptically and laughed. "Nobody can know 'at fer shore," he said. I was totally devastated and felt as though he had hit me in the face with a sledgehammer. I didn't respond. For the next several years I searched for a way to know for certain that my soul would go to Heaven, either when I die, or when Jesus returns to claim His church.

When Bill retired from the military in 1970, we moved into a comfortable home we had bought in Roane County, West Virginia, in a small community called Speed. Bill had rededicated his life to the Lord, so he and I had been asked to serve as youth leaders in the little Methodist Church near our home. Although our two teenagers and our twelve-year-old son had been "converted" by this time, we reluctantly agreed to the request, after explaining to the pastor that we felt incompetent to lead the group because of our lack of experience and our limited knowledge of the Bible.

Shortly after accepting the office, Bill and I asked the pastor whether he would teach a class explaining the appropriate scriptures to use when a Christian shares with an unsaved person what they must do to receive Christ as their Savior; in addition, we needed scripture references that would give assurance of salvation. Once again, I felt as though I had been struck across my face when the pastor looked at us and said, "I can't teach a class on those subjects.

That's something you have to grow into." We did our best with the class; however, when several of the youth claimed to have been "born again," we had no idea how to question or affirm their salvation experiences.

Shortly after that conversation with our pastor, I began seeking God's will for our lives, trusting that He would lead us to a church that would teach us fundamental truths of the Bible. Within the next couple of years, after our oldest son had enrolled in college and our daughter had joined the Armed Forces, Bill and I felt the need, due to my declining health, to put our home on the market and to move to Florida. Within the first week, our property sold, and we immediately purchased a new pickup truck and a thirty-two-foot travel trailer. Since school was in summer recess, my husband and I, along with our youngest son, Bill Jr., headed for sunny Florida with no particular area in mind in which to buy a home.

We traveled down the east coast of Florida until Bill was impressed to camp out in the town of Fort Pierce. Within days, we decided to stay in the small town. Bill found a job immediately, we bought a brand-new home, and our son enrolled in school.

A neighbor invited us to Bible Baptist Church, which we attended for nearly two years. Bill, Jr. was involved in the church youth group, and it was during this time he saw the truth of eternal security as shown to him in the Bible by his youth pastor, Chuck Arney, despite our ignorant warning to him not to accept that doctrine. However, no one from the church had ever sat down with us and shown us from scripture how we could know our salvation was secure. While still wrestling with the idea of eternal security, we decided to try another church in the area.

The evening after we attended Immanuel Baptist Church for the first time, the pastor, Dr. Fielder, and his wife Elizabeth visited with us in our home. We were surprised, yet delighted, when the first question Pastor Fielder asked us, after a few minutes of idle chatter, was this question, to which we had sought answers for the past several years: "If you should die today, do you know for sure that you would go to Heaven?"

Bill and I were excited when Pastor Fielder shared with us from Luke 3:3 and Romans 10:9–13 what a person must do in order to receive Christ as his or her Savior. Once we were assured from the Scriptures that we had repented and had followed God's plan for our salvation, we learned that God also assures us, in 1 John 5:13, that "we can know" that we have eternal life.

We were comforted in knowing that when we sin after we are saved, we can still be forgiven. 1 John 1:9 tells us, "If we confess our sins, He is faithful and just to forgive us our sins, and to cleanse us from all unrighteousness.".

Bill, our son, and I were reading our Bibles and attending church to learn more about God and His Word. I was finding that the more I read His Word, the more I loved Him, and the more I loved Him, the more time I spent reading His Word. With the assurance of my salvation, I now had that "peace of God which passeth all understanding" (Philippians 4:7) that I had spent years longing for.

LXXXI

As Time Passed

My father died in 1977, and the pain and suffering that riddled my life because of his actions are now gone also, leaving only the deep scars that will follow me to my own grave. Although Dad's abuse toward me actually ended when I married my precious husband, I was never able to have the father-daughter relationship I had coveted during my entire life. He approached me on numerous occasions, always in the presence of other adult family members, and attempted to place his arms around me. I've always wanted to believe that his attempt to show me affection had been innocent, but because the memories and scars of years gone by had been ingrained deeply within my being, my whole body would stiffen as those ugly memories rushed in, causing me to immediately reject his uninvited attention and to move quickly out of his reach.

Never once did my father attempt to explain or apologize for what he had done to me years earlier, and I could never bring myself to mention the subject to him. I suffered in silence as I watched our family meet with much tragedy and pain, no doubt with some retribution for the lives my father had injured or almost destroyed (I've since learned of other family members he abused).

He spent a few months in a mental hospital sometime around seven years after I married Bill, due to the trauma he suffered when my oldest brother, Woody, was accidentally killed in a hunting accident in Dad's presence. I want to believe that his memory was affected by several electrical shocks during his treatment, wiping from his mind memories that still remain vividly intact in my own mind. One positive aspect gained from his confinement was that his temper was brought under control, allowing him to spend the majority of his final years as a mellower and kinder man.

I tried year after year to develop a close relationship with my mother, only to have her turn and rend me in 1985. She spent the next eight years trying to destroy my Christian testimony with family and friends, to no avail. Thanks to my Heavenly Father, who carried me when I was too feeble to walk and taught me—through Psalms 27:10–14—to wait upon Him when my patience wore thin, Mom reconciled with me after I prayed with her shortly before she went into surgery to have a brain tumor, the size of a baseball, removed in 1993. She could never bring herself to apologize to me, even when I brought her to live in my home, where she died in 1998.

Mom and Dad shortly before his death in 1977.

Months before she died, I was able to ask her once again why she had left me to fend for myself during all those years that Dad had tried to molest me. "Bethel, I didn' have no choice," she said. "He swore he'd chop my head off if I ever manchuned [mentioned] anythang to anybody."

I forgave my mother many years ago for having neglected to protect me from my father's evil acts. I hold no bitterness in my heart against her nor anyone else, who could have, yet failed, to come to my rescue. I know that I alone am held responsible for my actions, just as other people are held responsible for theirs.

By God's grace, and with the strength I received from reading His Word and spending much time in prayer, I refused to allow the bitterness that was constantly rapping at my heart's door to set up camp inside a space I had long ago reserved for my loving Savior.

My extended family matured and conformed with the changing times, and they have come through those hard times with their heads held high; still, some of them recognize that their lives also carry scars from their childhood. Years ago, they moved out of the isolated part of the country where we were raised and now own their own homes, all but one of them presently living in the state of West Virginia. They have seemingly remembered the teachings of our father and have worked hard for what they have accomplished, refusing to rely on welfare as a means of support. My sister, Nina, matured into a hardworking, proper lady and has raised three sons and a daughter. I'm thankful that I have a close relationship with all of my siblings and their families. My brothers Woody, Arnold, and Larry, along with Aunt Sissy, Uncle Clint, and Grandma, have over the years been called home to be with the Lord. I miss them sorely.

Family gathering after Dad's funeral. Kneeling L-R: Mike, Maynard, Dee. 1st Row Standing: Nina, Mom, Me. Back Row: Arnold, Marvin, Jerry, Virgil, and Tom.

I recently returned to the small town near where I was raised and, while taking pictures, was shocked to see that it no longer resembles the busy little town I remembered. The shopping centers and malls in the city have claimed the majority of small-town "Mom and Pop" businesses, leaving empty storefronts displaying only cobwebs and cracked windowpanes. While walking through the quiet streets, I was amused at the size of the small town. I chuckled as I said to my husband, "I wonder how long it will be until the town's loyal residents"—whom I once thought were millionaires—"roll up the sidewalks and give our hometown its long-overdue funeral?"

LXXXII

Peace

Thirteen years have passed since I embarked on this silent journey into my past, after the call of an owl had stirred the torment that from childhood I had kept hidden behind the closed doors of my troubled mind. I have come to grips with the tragedy that was intent on destroying my mind, body, and soul. With God's help, I've opened the closed corridors that I had tried to seal long ago, and, with strength that only He can give, I've allowed myself to identify, dissect, and study the events that caused those ugly memories, no matter how painful the process has been.

It has been six decades since I straddled my father's back while he played "Horsey" with his children. I spent almost half of a century of those years unable to talk about what had started a long chain of events, never realizing that I'd been blaming myself for jumping onto the back of that funny "horse" while yelling, "Giddy-up, Horsey! Giddy-up!"

As I relived my childhood and young adult life, I've come to realize, with assurance from God and love from my immediate family, that I'm not to blame for the actions of my father. As an innocent child, I—and nearly everyone around me—sacrificed my well-being so that my large family could remain together. Reflecting on the past, present, and whatever future I have left, I'm convinced that the sacrifice was not in vain.

I stand amazed even to this day at the way God has held me in His hand from the moment He formed me in my mother's womb (Psalms 139:13–16). He has molded this once-naive, timid, ignorant little country girl into the strong, stable, and confident woman I am today, and although He has broken me many times as He continues to lovingly smooth out the flaws that mar this piece of clay, I rejoice in knowing that He is not finished with me yet.

Today, I rejoice because I have emerged into the light on the other end of the long, dark tunnel, a much freer and stronger person. I had from my early teens determined in my heart to make myself accountable for how I reacted to or handled the way my parents treated me. I tried my best not to allow my trials to form my character; instead, my heart's desire was that my trials would build within me a strong yet humble character. At last I am at peace with myself yet ever striving to become more than I am. While I continue with my studies, I have come to realize that I have indeed had a whole lifetime to gather knowledge independently and to seek wisdom from God.

I once believed that God would send me a knight in shining armor who would sweep me into his arms and carry me away from those days and nights of bitter tears. Today, after fifty years of marriage, as I look into the eyes of my husband, my heart still bursts with the love that began on that country road when I gazed into his eyes for the very first time. I praise God for allowing him to love me enough to see me through the first ten years of our marriage, while I struggled to overcome my fears. I am also grateful that God loves my sons and daughter and their spouses and children enough to have brought them to the place where they are living their lives loving and serving Him. (Both my husband and our oldest son are ordained ministers.) What a Savior!

In explaining in detail some of my father's actions toward me, I have endeavored to reveal what I'm confident is merely a sampling of what many children are experiencing today. I have traveled extensively and have been told by scores of people that I have touched many lives in my short walk here on earth. I've been surprised and am concerned over the vast number of people who are dealing, or have dealt, with this misery. I've spoken with girls and women from the ages of ten to eighty years old, coming from many different aspects of society, and regardless of their background or their present status in life, many of them are still harboring their own shameful secrets. I'm convinced that this problem is widespread throughout our country and undoubtedly is responsible for much suffering, physically and mentally, of those affected by these evil acts.

Bill and I in our golden years.

My heart's desire in writing about my young life, other than for my own therapy, is that my story will encourage others who are suffering or have suffered through this horrendous blight that is so prevalent in our country. Unlike when I was a child, there is help available today, so if you are among these, I urge you to seek wise, experienced Godly counsel for your situation. Also, be encouraged in the reality that if God could give me the victory, then He certainly can do the same for any of His children who will trust Him to do so.

In attempting to reveal from where I have come and to where God has brought me, I have made the account of my childhood memories as honest and unabridged as I was able. At times I have been very uncomfortable when using the language I chose as I tried to give readers a clear and truthful account of my childhood. I have been reminded, while returning to my childhood, that all my life help has come from my faith and trust in God, and I stand in awe at how He has protected me and cared for me throughout my lifetime.

I've been reminded of this scripture, which God shared with me when I was a teenager and feeling as though I had been abandoned on a storm-tossed sea: "And He arose, and rebuked the wind, and said unto the sea, 'Peace, be still.' And the wind ceased, and there was a great calm" (Mark 4:39). Thank you, Lord Jesus, for bringing me through the storm, and for surrounding me with the calmness that only you can give.

I try to live each day by applying Proverbs 3:5–6, which says, "Trust in the Lord with all thine heart and lean not unto thine own understanding. In all thy ways acknowledge Him, and He shall direct thy paths." Truly, I am blessed to know that even now, the best is yet to come, when I will be forever carried away in the arms of God.

THE END

www.ingramcontent.com/pod-product-compliance
Lightning Source LLC
Chambersburg PA
CBHW071226070526
44583CB00017B/2064